D0149587

N

SELLING THE FIVE RINGS

SELLING
THE
FIVE RINGS

*The International Olympic Committee
and the Rise of Olympic Commercialism*

Robert K. Barney

Stephen R. Wenn

Scott G. Martyn

The University of Utah Press

Salt Lake City

© 2002 by The University of Utah Press

07 06 05 04 03 02
5 4 3 2 1

LIBRARY OF CONGRESS CATALOGING-IN-PUBLICATION DATA

Barney, Robert Knight, 1932–
Selling the five rings: the International Olympic Committee
and the rise of Olympic Commercialism /
by Robert K. Barney, Stephen R. Wenn, and Scott G. Martyn.
p.   cm.
Includes bibliographical references and index.
ISBN 0-87480-713-1 (hard : alk. paper)
1. Olympics—Economic aspects. 2. Television and sports.
3. International Olympic Committee. I. Wenn, Stephen R., 1964–
II. Martyn, Scott G., 1966– III. Title.
GV721.5 .B32 2002
796.48—dc21
2001006781

To
Karel Wendl
inspirer and nourisher of Olympic historians worldwide
—honor to his name

CONTENTS

PREFACE

Early on the morning of 27 November 1998 Richard Pound stood in his thirty-ninth-floor Stikeman Elliott law office in the Canadian Imperial Bank of Commerce Tower in downtown Montréal, pondering his day's scheduled appointments. As an International Olympic Committee (IOC) member for more than twenty years, a former IOC first vice-president, and a long-standing member of its Executive Board, Pound has been a leading figure in the generation of television and corporate sponsor revenues for the coffers of the IOC and its constituent members: some 200 National Olympic Committees (NOCs), 35 International Olympic Sports Federations (ISFs), and Olympic Games Organizing Committees (OCOGs) of host cities.

Abruptly, Pound's fax machine began to buzz. He removed a one-sheet communication, viewed it for a few seconds, grimaced, and stared fixedly at the assembly of Olympic mementos adorning his office walls and bookcases. The fax message, sent from Salt Lake City, turned out to be one of the first disclosures of alleged improprieties during the city's lengthy and eventually successful quest for the right to host the 2002 Olympic Winter Games. The message was terse; it alleged that Salt Lake City bid committee officials had authorized payment of living expenses and college tuition at a university in Washington, D.C., for the daughter of the late René Essomba, IOC member in Cameroon. Had Essomba sought and been granted these payments in return for his vote for Salt Lake City's bid to secure Winter Olympic Games? "This does not bode well for the Olympic Movement," Pound reflected. In the months to follow the situation exploded with an intensity that few could have imagined. It rapidly became clear that the college scholarship issue was only the tip of a much larger pyramid of alleged indiscretion and corruption. Further allegations of improper conduct by bid committee officials, National Olympic Committee impresarios, and IOC members rapidly surfaced. They not only were pertinent to the Salt Lake City bid but also cast an ominous shadow on the general history of commercial and financial affairs in staging Olympic Games.

The pathway of bribery and corruption surrounding bidding for Olympic Games now lies strewn with the reputations of discharged IOC members, dismissed host city bid committee officials, discredited "go-between" agents, and embarrassed and compromised individuals and groups from one end of the Olympic Movement to the other. Many honest, dedicated, and hardworking Olympic officials the world over (most of them volunteers) were thunderstruck by the bribery and corruption disclosures emanating from Salt Lake City beginning in late November 1998.

Others—though sad—were not surprised, among them longtime Swiss IOC member and Executive Board official Marc Hodler. Shortly after the initial bombshell disclosure from Salt Lake City, Hodler announced publicly that inducements offered to IOC members by bidding cities for the purpose of engendering friendship and soliciting votes had accelerated steadily over the years. This was particularly the case after 1984, when Los Angeles employed a commercial formula of private sponsorship to pay for the Games, generating a profit of well over $200 million. For organizers of the Games of the post–Los Angeles era, the focus shifted dramatically from sports competition to business enterprise and the potential to earn huge profits. This change in part was stimulated by the necessity for Olympic Games Organizing Committees to underwrite expenses by securing financial resources from the private sector. Diminished financial investment in "the Olympic dream" by its traditional cost underwriters—municipal, state, and federal governments—dictated such an approach. Another factor in this frenzied fund-raising by successive Olympic Games hosts was the desire to "outdo" their predecessors in terms of glorious spectacle and grandiose new sport complexes. Prestige, historically the primary motivation for hosting Olympic Games, rapidly became secondary in the face of possible financial profit, gain in world economic markets, and leverage in global politics.

During the 1980s and 1990s IOC members witnessed a meteoric rise in the power of the Modern Olympic Movement to raise vast amounts of revenue from the sale of television rights worldwide and the marriage of the Olympic five-ring symbol to the products and marketing activities of various multinational corporate giants. For example, in the quadrennium closing the twentieth century (1997–2000) the IOC, on behalf of the Olympic Movement, reported an estimated gross income of close to 4 billion U.S. dollars. By the early 1990s only a few older IOC members could reflect back on times prior to 1980 when they all paid their own expenses to attend the annual sessions, when the administrative offices in the Château de Vidy had a staff of fewer than ten individuals, when world cities had to be solicited to host Olympic Games, when the IOC's annual budget was more often in the red than in the black—indeed, to a time when worthy Olympic dreams and initiatives were stymied by the lack of financial means to launch them.

By the last two decades of the twentieth century, however, leaders of the Olympic Movement, with some 100 years of history and tradition on which to capitalize, began to become far wiser in the ways of making money through linkages with business and technology. New wisdom rapidly translated into vast profits. Most IOC members were mightily impressed. Not all could resist the temptations that the prospect of so much money presented, however, as the sordid details disclosed in late 1998 and early 1999 attested.

If money, power, and influence drive Olympic affairs today, it seems an appropriate mission to examine how the Modern Olympic Movement arrived at this point in its history, with many of its constituent bodies resembling elaborate corporate business entities rather than simply sports organizations. That is precisely the mission we have undertaken. This book is a history of the International Olympic Committee's transformation from the instrument of peace and goodwill envisioned by its founder, Baron Pierre de Coubertin, to a transnational nongovernmental commercial giant of imposing power and influence in global sporting matters. Olympic Organizing Committees, International Sport Federations, and National Olympic Committees—foremost among them, the United States Olympic Committee—figure prominently in this history.

The Baron de Coubertin's original scheme for modern Olympic Games, presented at an international sports conference at the Sorbonne in Paris in June 1894, made few provisions for the financial underwriting of the grand project. Providence and the beneficence of host cities would somehow take care of financial costs. And this was indeed the case for three-quarters of the first century of modern Olympic history. National Olympic Committees begged and borrowed to send delegations of athletes to the Games. Host cities implored municipal, state, and national governments for contributions from public monies to help in hosting the Olympic festivals. IOC members and sports officials underwrote their own expenses to attend organizational meetings and the Games themselves. There were no great commercial endeavors tied to staging the Olympic Games. The modest commercial initiatives attempted from time to time were so minuscule that they went largely unnoticed. And they were usually designed not to help underwrite the cost of staging the Games but to provide information and consumer services for the spectators.

The advent of two phenomena, television and corporate sponsorship, transformed this picture of simple Olympic Games. Neither phenomenon was an overnight success story in Olympic financing, however. It would take years of confrontation and painful experience before payments from television networks for Olympic broadcast rights would make an appreciable dent in the financing of the Modern Olympic Movement. The first experiences of Olympic corporate sponsorship also demonstrated all too graphically the manner in which the commercial exercise should *not* be carried out.

Fundamentally, IOC-generated income for the needs of its Olympic organizations worldwide is derived from advertising. In very simplistic terms, global society has been highly successful in the production of goods and services, particularly in the last 150 years. Distribution of goods has been less successful. As we are told by the eminent Harvard economist John Kenneth Galbraith in his classic *The Affluent Society,* the exercise of distribution depends on the creation of a desire, perceived or real, for a product or service.[1] Advertising is the phenomenon that creates the need or desire for the fruits of production. It therefore becomes incumbent on production agents to bring goods and services to the attention of a prospective consumer public. This can best be done by an "advertising reach" that extends to a large audience. The larger the audience, the better the chances of a "need creation" and a consumer purchase. Advertising media include ads in magazines and newspapers, brochures, billboards, radio spots, and many others. Crucial to the Modern Olympic Movement is television advertising. Television networks could hardly exist if income could not be generated through advertising. Thus television networks seek huge audiences (Nielsen ratings) to attract product and service advertisers. Audiences, of course, are interested in entertainment and newsworthy events. The Olympic Games are both, so prospective advertising clients have a strong incentive to seek affiliation with a network's planned telecasts of Olympic festivals. The product advertised must also have an image that prompts the public to respond in the consumer marketplace. Enter the Modern Olympic Movement and its Olympic Games!

The attraction of the Olympic Games for the commercial sector is, of course, the opportunity to advertise products to a global audience unmatched in size by any other sport audience in the world. The five-ring symbol of the Olympics has few competitors as the most readily recognized brand logo in the world, inside and outside of sports. It is good business for advertisers in the global marketplace to link with the five-ring logo. If the image begins to falter, however, and the corporate sector loses interest, hard times could soon follow. The problem is compounded if television companies cannot sell advertising to business interests. Indeed, this was the greatest threat posed by the recent scandal sparked by revelations about Salt Lake City's successful bid for the 2002 Olympic Winter Games.

The five-ring Olympic symbol is the foremost image of the Olympic Movement and attracts advertisers. The IOC has realized that it must be zealously protected from unauthorized use to prevent its value and the corresponding generation of revenue from shrinking. We have attempted to document the role of protection of marks and symbols in the history of commercialism in the Modern Olympic Movement and the continuing challenges in this area. Ambush marketers (commercial entities that boldly employ Olympic symbols and marks without authority in their advertising or imply that there is a link between their product and the Olympic Movement) have existed since the days when the Olympic Games first reached global popularity and will continue to exist. Protection of brands thus becomes an even more critical key in future revenue generation and its connection with advertising. The stakes are getting higher and higher as the Olympic Games create larger and larger worldwide audiences. For instance, in late June 2000, just three months before the opening of the Sydney Games, the IOC "together with other members of the Olympic Family" jointly filed a civil suit in a U.S. federal court to shut down more than 1,800 unauthorized websites misusing official Olympic trademarks.[2] This is sobering to the IOC. Despite its initiatives on the question of protection, commencing mainly in the 1980s, it has directed much greater energies and resources toward producing and distributing wealth. The future may be marked by significantly increased protection initiatives.

The rise of the Modern Olympic Games from an idea in the mind of its late-nineteenth-century creators to an event celebrated in 2000 in Sydney, Australia, where the global viewing audience numbered some 3.7 billion people, is a saga featuring constant conflict between ideas and the people that drive them. The present global state of the Modern Olympic Movement and its Games is in part a testimony to the resolution of conflict—which, in effect, led inexorably to the current spectacle of commercialized television and corporate sponsorship. Another important element is the conflict among Olympic parties (IOC, NOCs, ISFs, OCOGs), each with its own agenda. We also examine the often troubled and sometimes tumultuous relationship between the IOC and its wealthiest and most powerful constituent NOC, the United States Olympic Committee (USOC).

This book reports history. As the reader might appreciate, when one starts to investigate the history of any nuclear unit (particularly the financial affairs of a family) there is certain to be caution, resistance, and, all too often, exclusion from the record. Nonetheless, we believe that our sources permit us to tell the tale truthfully and objectively. We take some degree of comfort in the words of Marc Bloch, celebrated French thinker and writer on the theory of history and the role of the historian:

> There are two ways of being impartial: that of the scholar and that of the judge. They have a common root in their honest submission to the truth. The scholar records—better still, he invites—the experience which may, perhaps, upset his most cherished theories. The good judge, whatever his secret heart's desire, questions witnesses with no other concern than to know the facts, whatever they may be. For both this is an obligation of conscience which is never questioned.[3]

We hope that we have been both scholars and judges in recording this history.

No serious history has yet been written that tackles the subject of the rise of the International Olympic Committee toward becoming a global commercial giant. Therefore, future works might expand on this history. Primary sources inform our investigation. We have depended in large measure on minutes of the IOC General Sessions, minutes of IOC Executive Boards, minutes and reports of various IOC subcommittees and commissions concerned with finance, reports of key marketing agencies, and the letters and memoranda of the scores of individuals whose action created this history. Thus, our investigation examines the subject "outward" from the perspective of the IOC rather than "inward" from the perspective of TV networks, corporate sponsors, and media. This history is not sponsored and endorsed by or written from the point of view of the IOC, however. We seek objectivity through a variety of sources, mainly in the form of written evidence on the roles played by various partners in the history of Olympic commercialism.

Where appropriate, we have also reviewed the work of serious scholars of the Modern Olympic Movement in order to lend further substantiation to our work. We have been fortunate in being allowed access to the private archives of several prominent individuals whose activities figure critically in this history. Obviously, we are indebted beyond measure to scores of individuals whose interest, experience, counsel, and just plain help aided us in our quest. To them we extend our grateful appreciation and lasting admiration. First on that list is Dr. Karel Wendl, to whom we dedicate this work. We first made Dr. Wendl's acquaintance in 1986 during an initial visit to the IOC archives in Lausanne. At that time the grand museum in Ouchy on the shores of Lac Léman, with its various archival departments, did not exist. In the 1980s the IOC archives were housed in the basement of the Château de Vidy headquarters. Few crossed the threshold of those premises to pursue research. A relaxed, informal atmosphere prevailed at the time, far different from the much more formal and complex current procedures. From the start we had absolutely no doubt that Dr. Wendl felt that archives were a primary record established and maintained in large measure as a repository of materials for investigation by serious scholars. On occasions when we requested documents that exceeded the allowed parameters Karel Wendl did his best—most often with success—to gain the needed review permissions. For over a decade from the time of our first visit we made repeated archival journeys to the mecca of Olympic research materials. Dr. Wendl and his staff, including those who came after his retirement in 1995, extended courtesies and gave knowledgeable and helpful advice. Their friendship and camaraderie provided a highlight of our long and arduous research. Most notable of such staff members were Michèle Veillard, Ruth Beck-Perrenoud, Patricia Eckert, Patrice Cholley, Antoinette Dufour, Claude Borgeaud, David Ollier de Marchand, Alexandra Leclef-Mandl, and Christine Fasel-Chapuis. We are grateful for the reception and counsel of Michael Payne, director of the IOC's Marketing Department, and for the insight of Howard Stupp, director of the Legal Department. We are also appreciative of the kind offices of José Sotelo, former director of the IOC Press Service, whose daily "in-house" publication *Olympic Press Review* helped to keep our fingers on the pulse of contemporary worldwide Olympic events pertinent to our investigation.

Parallel to Karel Wendl's assistance in critical importance to our work was the firsthand knowledge and no-nonsense insight of Richard Pound (identified at the outset of this preface). Pound, a scholar in his own right and an indefatigable servant of the Modern Olympic Movement since his training for and competition in the 1960 Rome Olympics, made his personal archives (gathered over a period of some twenty-five years) available for our examination. We are also grateful for the long-standing help and advice of Jim Worrall, IOC member in Canada from 1968 to 1994 and presently an honorary IOC member.

Scores of others contributed their expertise and knowledge to this book. Of enormous importance in our treatment of the IOC presidency of Avery Brundage was the vast repository of research material found in the Avery Brundage Collection. Use of this collection was facilitated by its original cataloger/indexer, the noted American archivist Maynard Brichford of the University of Illinois. To him we owe a formidable debt of gratitude. We are also grateful to Karl Lennartz of the Carl Diem Institute at the Deutsche Sporthochschule–Köln, John Lucas and Ron Smith at Penn State University, Norbert Müller at Johannes Gutenberg Universität–Mainz, John MacAloon at the University of Chicago, Wayne Wilson at the Amateur Athletic Foundation's Ziffren Library in Los Angeles, Garth Paton at the University of New Brunswick, Cindy Slater at the Library of the United States Olympic Committee in Colorado Springs, Bruce Kidd at the University of Toronto, Allen Guttmann at Amherst College, and Paul Wenn of London, Ontario. Our manuscript underwent several anonymous peer reviews. The reviewers' critiques proved to be critically important, and we offer our gratitude to each of them. Naturally, we are indebted to Jeff Grathwohl, director and senior editor of the University of Utah Press, and his staff for having confidence in the merit of our book. Grateful appreciation is extended to Kathy Lewis for her painstaking and comprehensive editing of the manuscript. Finally, as one might imagine, our research travels took us long distances from our homes in Ontario, on occasion for lengthy periods. This often necessitated sacrifices by our spouses. Our gratitude is extended to Ashleigh Barney, Martha Wenn, and Rebecca Martyn.

We would be remiss if we did not recognize the funding aid and support for two research visits to Lausanne awarded to Stephen Wenn by the Office of the Vice President–Academic and the Office of Graduate Studies and Research, Wilfrid Laurier University. Also, we acknowledge the support of the Social Science and Humanities Research Council of Canada (SSHRC) for two travel subsidies granted to Bob Barney, a decade apart, for research trips to Lausanne, Los Angeles, Chicago, Washington, and St. Louis. We extend grateful appreciation to the Social Science and Humanities Research Council of Canada on behalf of Scott Martyn for a three-year fellowship that in large measure supported his research activities related to this history. A six-month visiting "Olympic Fellow" invitation to Bob Barney by the University of Technology–Sydney was of immense help in contributing to the completion of our book. Finally, the value of our almost daily contact with the affairs of the International Centre for Olympic Studies at the University of Western Ontario probably can never be fully appreciated or assessed. The International Centre's mission, "to encourage, generate, and disseminate serious scholarship on the Modern Olympic Movement from a socio-cultural point of view," has stimulated hours of debate, discussion, and reflection on "matters Olympic." In collective fashion, these exercises have driven us toward the culmination of this work.

AN EPILOGUE AS PROLOGUE

Sydney 2000, "The Greatest Games Ever"

On the evening of 15 September 2000 the Games of the Twenty-seventh Olympiad opened in Sydney's mega–sports edifice, Stadium Australia. Two weeks and two days later the Games closed before an assembly of 112,000 spectators, a number roughly equal to that present at the opening ceremonies. Near the evening's end, before the final celebration including music, dancing, and brilliant fireworks, IOC president Juan Antonio Samaranch thanked the whole world,[1] bestowed some Olympic Orders on deserving Sydney officials, and watched as the Olympic flag was lowered and the great flame in the cauldron was borne aloft in the afterburner of an Australian Air Force F-111 fighter-bomber. Two days later Samaranch flew home to Europe. The city of Sydney began the process of returning to normal.

But Samaranch, with only nine months left in his presidency, had not quite terminated his Sydney experience. Scarcely two weeks later he returned to Australia to witness the opening of the Paralympic Games and to present the City of Sydney with the Olympic Cup, a distinguished IOC award. In front of 150 guests assembled at the city's Town Hall, including the lord mayor, Frank Sartor, Samaranch once again emphasized how well Sydney had carried off the grand project. "The winner is the Olympic city of Sydney," he proclaimed.[2]

Samaranch's obvious outward satisfaction was eclipsed by a sense of relief. Peering at him during the grand moment, more than one Olympic pundit may have reflected: "Sydney aside, the real winner here is the Modern Olympic Movement." Its image had been resurrected from the ashes of the disaster of Atlanta's commercial debacle in 1996 and the even more damaging fallout from the scandals that engulfed the IOC from late November 1998 to the spring of 1999. For many, Olympic luster and credibility were restored. So, too, was a goodly amount of Samaranch's much maligned personal image. The unhappy sagas had nearly faded from memory, superseded by an Australian Olympic Games production that future Organizing Committees will find it difficult to match. Despite ongoing concerns about the preparedness of Athens to host the 2004 Olympics, there was no doubt that everything had greatly improved in the Olympic world.[3]

The success story of the Sydney 2000 Olympic Games might normally be told as an epilogue; but we have placed it at the beginning of our history in order to demonstrate the extraordinary commercial consequences surrounding the organization and execution of the Olympic Games in contemporary times. In addition to being a showcase for athletic achievement as well as entertainment for billions of world viewers, the Olympic Games are also an unrivaled commercial forum. Before we embark on the history of the events that led to their current status, we offer a slice of the commercial portrait of the most recent Olympic festival, the Games of the Twenty-seventh Olympiad in Australia.

In September 1993 Sydney was awarded the right to host the "First Games of the New Millennium" by the slimmest of margins (two votes) over Beijing. The city—indeed the nation—undertook the bid for the 2000 Games before fully assessing its ability and commitment to mount what might and did become the largest, most complex, most expensive public event in Australian history. For most Australians, the Games provided the most exciting national event in their lifetime. They stimulated, galvanized, fascinated, and inspired. And if people the world over knew little about Australia before the great festival unfolded, most became enamored with the "Land Down Under" in a very short time.

Since its extraordinarily poor results at the Montréal Games in 1976 (a paltry three medals),[4] Australia had vowed to improve its stature in future Olympic Games. A steady influx of federal, state, and Australian Olympic Committee (AOC) dollars into elite sport opportunities translated into a commensurate rise in Australian Olympic fortunes over the next two decades. This commitment accelerated greatly after 1993 during the "run-up" years prior to hosting the 2000 Games. In fact, between 1996 and 2000 the AOC paid out a collective $18.2 million Australian in incentive rewards alone to all its Olympic athletes who had achieved "top four" status in the world rankings of their events.[5] Was this cost worth the benefit? Most Australians thought it was: Australia's achievement in the 2000 Games (fifty-eight medals, sixteen of them gold) roughly equaled the most conservative expectations embraced by the AOC before the Games began (sixty medals, twenty gold).

Drowned in the euphoria of the final medal count, however, was the concern expressed by the Federal Parliament's opposition leader, the

Labour Party's Kim Beazley. The huge sum directed toward producing the results, thundered the former Rhodes scholar, was ill-spent: "Australians have got fatter and more inactive in the past 20 years of increased funding to elite athletes."[6] His argument clearly made sense, but it was not new. Federal and provincial/state debate on the subject of elite vs. mass sports funding from public monies is timeworn in many of the world's industrialized countries. In general, funding for the elites has outstripped funding for the masses.

The glory of athletic performance was only one dimension of the Olympic production that Samaranch, on-site spectators, media, and television viewers worldwide generally proclaimed an unrivaled success. In 1993 the New South Wales (NSW) government assumed fundamental financial responsibility for the project. Throughout the preparation and execution it stood solidly behind that commitment, establishing an Olympic Ministry (Olympic Coordinating Authority [OCA]), appointing an Olympic minister (Michael Knight), and pledging public dollars toward meeting a deficit if one should occur. Generally effective coordination of the OCA, the National Government in Canberra, the AOC, the City of Sydney, and the Sydney Olympic Games Organizing Committee (SOCOG) produced what turned out to be an almost problem-free event. There were some difficulties, of course; but despite a considerable amount of pre-Olympic grumbling and some doomsday predictions, each was overcome.[7] Intense planning and preparation together with systematic execution—enhanced particularly by lower levels of supervision and volunteer management—carried the day handsomely.[8]

Sydney had done its homework, perhaps far better than any host city in the previous history of the Olympic event. It did not ignore the historical lessons to be learned from the 1996 Centennial Games in Atlanta. In the summer of 1996 over 100 Sydney Games officials convened in Atlanta to learn "what to do" and "what not to do" in putting on Olympic Games.[9] At the conclusion of the Sydney Games folks in Atlanta were asking themselves, "How did the Australians get it so right, when we got it so wrong?"

Beyond all other considerations, one 1996 lesson had to be heeded. The commercial tawdriness of the Atlanta Games must not be repeated. In Atlanta, the mercantile capital of the American South, municipal officials vied with the Atlanta Olympic Games Organizing Committee (ACOG) and the USOC to reap as much commercial benefit from the Games as possible. Each party pursued its own agenda with steadfast commitment and, for the most part, independently, without regard for or coordination with the "grand scheme." The result was an avalanche of Olympic commercialism in the form of municipally licensed, ACOG-authorized, and USOC-generated billboards, posters, booths, kiosks, tents, pavilions, roving street hawkers, and frenzied vendors, preying on residents and Olympic tourists like a horde of locusts. Ambush marketers were everywhere.[10] While the ACOG, USOC, and Atlanta municipality skirmished on the commercial battlefront, the IOC cringed. Hand-wringing was a constant exercise.

Sydney went to extremes to eliminate all this. Still, without viable support from the business/commerce sector, the Games simply would not have occurred in the illustrious manner they did. The NSW government passed an Olympic Arrangements Act, legislation that placed tight controls on what advertising might be permitted and where, including the extreme of prohibiting skywriting over Olympic Park. The municipal government banned vending licenses and controlled signage with a vengeance. The brand mark and product presence of the eleven International TOP (The Olympic Partners [Programme]) Sponsors, thirteen Domestic Millennium Olympic Partners, eighteen Sydney 2000 Supporters, and thirty-eight Sydney 2000 Providers could be seen in a variety of ways, from IBM's giant cruise ship docked at Sydney Harbor's Circular Quay, practically on the doorstep of the IOC's Regent Hotel headquarters, to colorful advertising banners adorning George Street and other "Olympic Routes." Nonetheless, the general commercial atmosphere was subdued. There was hardly a scent of the flea-market ambiance that made the Atlanta Games a byword for crass commercialism.[11]

FUNDING AUSTRALIA'S OLYMPIC GAMES: TRADITIONAL SOURCES

Traditionally, to finance its Olympic project a host city first draws upon known income factors, especially IOC-driven worldwide television rights fees and TOP sponsorship income monies. Beyond those two sources of revenue are monies raised by the host Organizing Committee from its own commercial sponsorship programs, the sale of tickets to Olympic events, and income from the licensing and subsequent sale of Olympic memorabilia.

Television rights fees, of course, are the largest commercial contribution in financing Olympic Games. And so it was in the case of Sydney. The IOC negotiated a sum of slightly more than $1.3 billion U.S. for total world rights for the Sydney Games,[12] the largest fees being paid by the National Broadcasting Company (NBC: $705 million) and the European Broadcasting Union (EBU: $350 million). To the Sydney organizers went 60% of the total, or $798 million. When converted to Australian dollars, gross television income amounted to more than $1.1 billion. In the final analysis, 3.7 of the world's 3.9 billion people in 220 countries who have access to television sets watched the Games. In Australia Channel 7's television production of the opening ceremonies was the most-watched program in the nation's television history (10.4 million viewers).[13] Next in importance in IOC-driven revenue is the TOP income. TOP-IV revenues directed to Sydney amounted to slightly more than $200 million U.S. (over $300 million Australian).[14]

Sydney built an impressive array of competition venues for its Olympic Games, particularly the Olympic Park complex, constructed at Homebush Bay, once a vast waste-disposal area for dangerous chemicals. Hordes of spectators flocked to the events in record numbers. On most occasions during the Games the venues were filled to capacity. Some 17,000 viewed each night of the finals in the swimming competitions; more than 110,000 spectators gathered for each finals session in track and field. In sum, almost 88% of the 7.6 million spectator tickets available for sale were sold, an all-time record, eclipsing the previous mark set in Atlanta by more than a million. Ticket sales channeled almost $551 million U.S. into Sydney's revenue pot, tripling SOCOG's original forecast.[15]

Although Australia's population is only 7% that of the United States, Sydney roughly equaled Atlanta in domestic Olympic revenue production results.[16] Sydney licensed approximately 3,000 different consumer products bearing official Olympic marks and symbols for sale in some 2,000 closely monitored outlets across Australia.[17] By the close of the Games approximately $550 million U.S. had been generated from Olympic royalties and product sales.[18] Yet another domestic revenue initiative was the commemorative Olympic coin program. Though some would deem it somewhat inconsequential in the final cost associated with putting on the Olympic Games, more than 5.5 million Olympic coins were sold from the start of the program in 1997 to the end of November 2000, more than double the figure sold for the Atlanta Games in 1996. Coin sales generated total revenue in excess of $12 million Australian for Sydney's Olympic treasury.[19]

AUSTRALIA OPEN FOR BUSINESS:
THE STAKES FOR COMMERCIAL ENTERPRISE

According to Michael Parker-Brown, spokesperson for the federal government's Australia Open for Business Program (Austrade), an initiative developed especially to take advantage of the Olympics, over $1 billion Australian in business for Australian firms was generated in the two weeks of the Games alone. The membership of the Business Club of Australia, formed in September 1998, grew at a rate of hundreds of new members per day during the Olympics, resulting in a total recruitment of over 15,000 new members from both Australia and overseas. Operating out of the Austrade venue at Pyrmont, 16,000 business executives from all over the world introduced themselves and their products, networked energetically, and even shook hands on deals worth some $400 million.[20]

For Glenn Kiddell, a small business manufacturer from the Sydney suburb of Camperdown, the chance to cultivate prospective European customers in a "one stop shopping" atmosphere could hardly be rivaled. "For us it was perfect . . . we believed we had a great product for export, and we were mingling down there with the big boys."[21] By early December Austrade's managing director, Charles Jamieson, reported to a West Sydney Industry Awards luncheon that, although the Games had already generated $700 million in export and investment business, "there was potential for further gains through marketing our Olympic 'knowledge' . . . but Sydney businesses need to stop thinking about the Olympic Games as a one-off event and start cashing in on the city's 'sexy' image . . . the current international vibe about Australia is very strong . . . the issue now is to translate those images and good feelings into export and investment dollars to ensure our firms continue to trade successfully in the global marketplace."[22] Clearly, it was not simply the athletes who competed at the Games. Business had its own Olympics.

New South Wales was also bent on gaining from the Olympic marketplace. Shortly after the conclusion of the great sports festival, NSW premier Bob Carr led a business delegation to China, seeking to "transform NSW's Olympic profile into investment." He was hoping for business: the sale of Australian expertise to Beijing, Shanghai, and Guangdon Province that would net "$26 billion in post-Olympic jobs."[23] On his first stop in Guangdon Province Carr signed two deals, one worth $3.5 million Australian for aid in private adult schooling; another for much higher stakes: subject to approval by the Chinese Ministry for Public Security, Australia was to provide police and security training in Guangzhou (Guangdon's largest city) and other parts of China of the type that enabled Australia to stage the Sydney festival without major incident.[24] In Quangzhou, too, the premier used the success of the Sydney Games to promote five Australian companies bidding for a share in the $4 billion construction of a new airport.[25] No sooner had Carr returned from China than he was off to the United States to promote New South Wales to American investors. "It is vital that we use the unprecedented success of the Games to win new investment and create jobs," he said.[26]

In presenting its Olympics to the world, Australia coveted huge dividends in one of the nation's most important industries: tourism. The number of tourists from abroad who appeared for the Games was disappointing. Australia's domestic Olympic pilgrims generated the huge attendance numbers. A popular international perception prevailed that the entire Olympic atmosphere in Sydney was underscored by inflated costs for travel, event tickets, and food and accommodation. Nevertheless, the Australian Tourist Commission (ATC), "in a bid to capitalize on the Games," launched a $45 million Australian advertising campaign to lure post-Olympic travelers from abroad (particularly tourists from Japan, Europe, and the United States) to spend their holidays "Down Under."[27]

This campaign reaped early dividends. Immediately after the closing of the Games in early October U.S., British, and German travel firms reported huge percentage increases in travel booked to Australia. A large British retail travel firm, for instance, noted a 62% increase in reservations for travel to Australia since the Olympics. "This has been the best October in the history of Bridge the World," stated managing director Jerry Bridge.[28] North American and domestic Australian retail travel firms uniformly reported better than 50% increases in tourist travel to Australia following the Games. But Australia's most lucrative tourism market is Japan. Agents reported increases in Japanese travelers to Australia up "11 to 13%," exceeding available aircraft seats. One frustrated industry source carped at Australia's international flight carrier, Qantas, for not increasing seat space and flight schedules at a time when "the Olympics have become the biggest single tourism influence in Japan."[29]

Hosting Olympic Games is almost certain to boost the tourism industry of the host country. After all, the worldwide television exposure is the type of advertising to prospective travelers that can hardly be equaled by brochures, flyers, and newspaper, radio, and television spot advertising. Some three months after the Olympics John Morse, managing director of the ATC, announced publicly that "the Games had raised the bar in all areas of tourism in Australia, from service levels in hotels and restaurants to the friendliness of the people . . . the Games helped clear up misconceptions about Australia."[30] An ecstatic federal tourism minister, Jackie Kelly, announced in early December that in the aftermath of the Olympics international visitors to Australia would double in the next decade, prompting an increase of domestic jobs in tourism from five hundred thousand to over a million. For the year 2010 Kelly predicted annual visitor spending of $30 billion Australian, compared to $12.8 billion for 1998, the most recent annual statistic for tourist spending.[31]

The world of art and culture, too, realized spin-off benefits from Sydney's production of its widely viewed "best ever" Olympic Games. The prestigious Sydney Dance Company, opening its season in New York's

Joyce Theater, was virtually sold out by late November on the eve of its first performance, a feat almost unheard of in the world of dance according to the company's artistic director, Graeme Murphy. "The Olympics were a wonderful boost for us," he said, "because we're about physical performance and so were the Games . . . our walk-up sales have been fabulous and I do think it has been a matter of Sydney being in front of the people's minds after the Olympics that brought us to capacity."[32]

Aside from Australian business firms and international corporate giants, others were intent on using the Games to market personal initiatives. Gold, silver, and bronze medal–winning athletes were both pursuing and being pursued for sponsorship endorsement contracts. Triple gold medal swimming star Ian Thorpe, dubbed Australia's "Thorpedo" by media and opponents alike, left for the United States right after the Games in an attempt to expand on the ten companies that already had endorsement packages with him.[33] Closely rivaling Thorpe in marketability was Cathy Freeman.[34] The engaging Aboriginal 400-meter gold medalist's track paraphernalia immediately became worth "thousands" on the Olympic memorabilia market; an autographed photo was worth $200.[35] But those figures paled in comparison to the projections of $5 to $10 million a year that some predicted her world fame would generate on the international market.[36] Unlike Thorpe and Freeman, who were well-marketed sports stars before the Games even began, Aussie pole-vaulter Tatiana Grigorieva, a Russian émigré from St. Petersburg, shot to fame by winning the silver medal. Blonde, statuesque, and attractive, Grigorieva immediately became a highly marketable product. "Show me the money" were among her first words uttered to her manager, Ric Carter, following her sensational performance.[37]

Sydney's domestic counterpart to the IOC's TOP initiative, the Millennium Partners Corporate Sponsorship Program, generated more than $315 million Australian in cash and millions more in Value-in-Kind (VIK) support. Further, the list of firms playing a secondary but necessary part in the production of the Games included eighteen Sydney 2000 Supporters, goods and service representatives like Nike and the Royal Australian Mint, and thirty-eight Providers, from Cadbury's confections to Sonic Healthcare. Two questions must be asked: what did commercial sponsors expect to receive in return for their investment in Sydney's Olympic extravaganza and was their investment sound from a business point of view? Three specific case examples help to answer these questions and are instructive in identifying the factors that draw the commercial sector to seek a link with the great Olympic event.

The case of Australian Mutual Provident (AMP) is one illustration.

AMP, the insurance and securities colossus of Australia, entered the Olympic sponsorship field for many of the same reasons that prompt most commercial entities to do likewise: (1) to generate new business, (2) to cultivate loyalty and retain existing customers (market protection), (3) to improve employee morale and productivity, and (4) to enhance brand awareness. AMP "signed on" to be the sole sponsor/organizer of the Olympic torch relay. To secure its Olympic sponsorship and execute the torch relay AMP spent more than $100 million.

The torch relay, an emotion-filled and people-oriented activity, was a fundamental factor in the eventual popular success of the Games. In fact it is sometimes referred to as "the people's event," evoking celebration and goodwill—exactly the qualities that AMP executives hoped would be associated with their company. The relay wound its way across each of the country's six states and two territories,[38] through 187 communities from the Indian Ocean coast of Western Australia to the nation's eastern Pacific Ocean shore, from Darwin in the far north to the island state of Tasmania, some 500 kilometers off the mainland's southern coast, finally arriving at the Olympic stadium in Sydney on the evening of 15 September.

When the Games were over, AMP claimed a 40% increase in several of its business areas and an increase in its number of clients from 230,000 to over 300,000. There were also less obvious benefits, such as the development and testing of improved marketing methods as well as experimenting with new customer relationships management programs. But in the end building goodwill between the company and its current and prospective clients remained the primary motivation. After it was all over, AMP glowed with satisfaction. Stated a company spokesperson: "We wanted to bring the excitement of the Olympics to as many Australians as we could, and it has all come together and we have done it. We wanted people to thank AMP for helping them to be part of the Games and they are. We have had hundreds of thank you letters—how do you put a dollar value on that?"[39]

The sponsorship example of Broken Hill Proprietary (BHP) is also instructive. BHP, a company wallowing in troubled financial circumstances before its decision to become a Games sponsor, is an Australian conglomerate with chief interests in steel manufacturing and mining. BHP's total sponsorship investment amounted to "tens of millions of dollars."[40] For its sponsorship BHP provided cash and more than 140,000 tons of steel for construction of Olympic venues and related infrastructure projects, from Sydney Airport renovation to building the Olympic flame cauldron. BHP's Cannington Mine also donated in excess of a ton of silver from which Olympic sculptures were created and sold at auction, generating $1.7 million Australian in revenue for the Sydney Olympic effort. According to

BHP's chief executive officer, Paul Anderson, his company made the decision to be a Millennium Sponsor two years before the Games. At that time, he said, BHP's Executive Board was faced with a hard decision: "The Games are just too big not to participate in . . . either we will [sponsor] and have the company in good shape, or be sorry we didn't participate and all be fired." They chose the former. Not to be part of such a proud event in the nation's history might well be considered to be "bad business."

Near the end of the Games Anderson reviewed the company's decision: "This is a wonderful outreach program for our customers . . . Every CEO of every steel company in the world is here and all our major customers—everyone we do business with . . . It's a great atmosphere to do business."[41] BHP's hopes for dividends accrued from its sponsorship were almost identical to those of AMP and most other commercial entities seeking a link to the Olympic Games—protection of existing market, expansion of business, promotion of brand awareness, and generation of employee pride and morale. By the end of the Games, BHP's Olympic sponsorship—together with strong crude oil prices, a flagging Australian dollar, and much improved steel sales—resulted in a 13% increase in revenue for 2000 ($5.2 billion Australian).[42]

One of the oldest, largest, and most prestigious wine-making businesses in Australia is Lindemans. Established in 1843 in the Hunter Valley, a two-hour drive north of Sydney, Lindemans is a division of Southcorp Wines Ltd., one of Australia's top fifty companies. Though Southcorp also manufactures and sells water heaters and packaging containers, the company's backbone economic endeavor is making wine, especially its flagship brands, Penfolds (its high-market item) and Lindemans (its mass-market product). Southcorp also has vineyard interests in France and California's Edna Valley. A mission to increase awareness of the Lindemans Bin 65 brand on the international wine market, particularly among consumers in the United States, Canada, and Great Britain, underscored Southcorp's decision to affiliate itself with the Sydney Olympics. The alcoholic nature of its product limited the company's involvement to membership in the "Olympic Providers" category rather than the higher-profile opportunities enjoyed (and dearly paid for) by dint of being classified as a Sydney 2000 Millennium Partner or a Sydney 2000 Supporter. In assessing the company's promotional efforts shortly before the opening of the Games, officials acknowledged that "[t]he Olympic brand is one of the most powerful brands in the world . . . [and] through leveraging this unique brand we have been able to deliver very strong promotional programmes."[43]

In attempting to realize its expectations Southcorp spent millions.[44] What were the returns on its investment? First, during the period of the

Games the company received unsolicited media attention (radio, newspaper, and television) in Australia, Canada, the United States, Germany, Switzerland, Norway, Scotland, and Thailand estimated to be worth $7 million Australian. Second, many of the one million visitors to Olympic Park each day visited or passed by the popular Lindemans Olympic Wine Bar, gaining an awareness of the firm's brand.[45] Finally, in more quantitative terms, during the run-up to the Games between January and August 2000 Lindemans' domestic volume sales increased 32%. Overseas volume sales increased by 75%, with especially strong showings in the United States and United Kingdom.[46] Indeed, Lindemans, whose overseas market is greater than its domestic market in volume sales, profited from the fact that wine exports from Australia in general soared astronomically in the wake of the Sydney Olympic experience. According to the Australian Bureau of Statistics, in October 2000 alone wine exports increased by 19% compared to the corresponding October of 1999: $165 million Australian in sales abroad. Aggressive marketing by Lindemans in the United Kingdom accounted for substantial percentages of the $165 million figure.[47] These performance barometers prompted Lindemans to confirm that its Olympic sponsorship served as "an excellent platform for the brand's future."[48]

There are certainly additional examples showing that money spent by business to sponsor the world's most widely followed sports event is well spent. The banking firm Westpac, a domestic Millennium Sponsor Partner, spent approximately $60 million Australian for its sponsorship rights and television advertising time. It eclipsed its predicted increase in business by $30 million.[49] Chief executive David Morgan commented on the value of his firm's Olympic sponsorship: although he noted that figuring these things "is more of an art than a science," he calculated the benefits from the bank's Olympic sponsorship as an investment "that achieved a return of $2 for every $1 spent."[50] VISA, a TOP-IV Olympic sponsor, reported a 15% increase in the international use of its credit card during the period of the Games.[51] Nike, one of eighteen Sydney 2000 Supporters, paid $5 million to garner its sponsorship and also provided the Australian Olympic team with its competition uniforms. It got more than its money's worth. "The whole point of being an event sponsor is to get visibility for your brand," said Martha Ivester, Nike's Olympic marketing director.[52] Nike was excluded from the precinct of Olympic Park except by way of seeing its Swoosh logo on competitors' running shoes and uniform gear. The giant sport shoe and apparel manufacturer made its play for brand identification by "wrapping" a twenty-story Sydney skyscraper in perforated film images of three Australian athletes who endorsed Nike shoes—Cathy Freeman and two other distinguished national sports personalities, tennis player Lleyton Hewitt and basketballer Lauren Jackson. The towering images peered down on the precinct of Darling Harbor, the second most important gathering place in Sydney (aside from Olympic Park itself) for Olympic events spectators and general celebrants of the Games.[53] Coca-Cola, Telstra, Adidas, Energy Australia, and others represented one success story after another in brand presentation awareness, existing market protection, and new market capture.

It was not all milk and honey for some of Sydney's business sectors. The original message from the SOCOG had been that all business ventures would benefit from the Games. The real estate market did not benefit; it "stopped altogether during the Games," announced John Hill, president of the Real Estate Institute of NSW.[54] The restaurant and "eating out" industry experienced a difficult month. A survey conducted by the NSW Chamber of Commerce completed in early December reported that more than 80% of Olympic visitors to the city stayed in the home of a family or friend, in a rented home, or in a hostel. Only 18% stayed in hotels or motels, which normally require one to eat out.[55] Many retailers hoping to cash in on an expected Olympic tourist boom were left disappointed. One of the biggest losers during the Olympics was the television network Channel 10. Competing for advertising revenue with Channel 7, the official Australian Olympic broadcasting network, and Kerry Packer's Channel 9, the nation's most-viewed network, Channel 10 recorded a dismal September, according to chief executive John McAlpine, losing some $10 million during the "Olympic month."[56]

Of deep concern to the IOC was the ire of one of its TOP-IV sponsors, United Parcel Service (UPS). TOP sponsors pay the equivalent of more than $50 million U.S. each quadrennium for affiliation with the Olympic Movement. In return sponsors are guaranteed exclusivity for their product service link to the five-ring symbol as well as protection from the encroachment on identification with the Olympic Movement by competitors. UPS, an international firm that had been active in Australia for nine years, wanted to use the Sydney Olympics to ensure its existing market and chip away at its competitors. A "zero hour" emergency and ensuing crisis to get Olympic event tickets delivered door-to-door to Australian households resulted in a UPS/SOCOG squabble over the added cost of the ticket distribution.

When the SOCOG engaged a local UPS rival to make some of the deliveries, an indignant UPS and IOC considered legal action against the SOCOG. Jim Kelly, CEO of UPS, let it be known that UPS's continued membership in TOP-V was problematic. "Any time you spend that amount of money (in the UPS case, $75 million) you want to evaluate if you're getting a good return on the investment . . . we'll make our decision after the Olympics," he said.[57] The IOC and organizers of the 2002 Winter Games and 2004 Summer Games in Salt Lake City and Athens, respectively, waited apprehensively. They had reason to be alarmed. Mere days before the UPS contract for TOP-IV expired (31 December 2000) the Atlanta-based company announced it would not renew for TOP-V, ending its $75 million global commitment to Olympic sponsorship for the next two festivals.[58] Olympic marketing officials scrambled to find a replacement.

THE BOTTOM LINE

Probably no one will ever know precisely how much the Sydney 2000 Games ended up costing. David Richmond, Michael Knight's top assistant in OCA, "guestimated" that the Sydney effort cost $7 billion Australian.[59] An "Interim Report" issued from Knight's office on 16 December 2000 stated that, after all revenues (commercial and otherwise) had been weighed against the best estimate of cost, the deficit incurred from the Games—in effect, the final bill to New South Wales taxpayers—was $1.7 billion.[60] But that deficit has to be put in context: the gross product (GP) of New South Wales is approximately $250 billion per year, and $1.7 billion is roughly 20% of the annual cost of road building and improvement in New South Wales. Also, Australia's first trade surplus in three years—in fact, the second highest ever recorded in the nation's history—occurred in September 2000.[61]

Were the Games worth the taxpayer liability? A majority of Sydneysiders and New South Wales citizens—indeed Australians in general—believe that the Games have already paid and will continue to pay significant dividends for Australia. For instance, a Melbourne market research company, Sweeney Sports, reported that seven out of every ten Australians thought the Olympics were good for the economy.[62] The factors that motivate a corporation to link its name and product to the Games exactly parallel the expectations of a city (abetted by a state and nation) in hosting an Olympic festival: global awareness, economic gain, citizen morale, and pride of identification.

The argument that the benefits of the Games more than warrant the expenditure of public monies appears to be sound.[63] Columnist Stephen Brunt of the *Globe and Mail* in Toronto, itself a city that vied for the right to host the Olympic Games in the summer of 2008, argued the case for tax-money support for public endeavors certain to be worthwhile to all citizens. Commenting on Sydney's Games, he wrote: "These were the Games of good spirits, the Games that, against all odds, worked nearly flawlessly . . . They were both an organizational masterwork and final proof that nothing smooths out the wrinkles better than vast quantities of public money well spent."[64]

In the final analysis the remarks of Premier Bob Carr provide us with a city's, a state's, and indeed a country's answer to the question: was public investment in the great festival worth it? "Without public funds there would be no festival," he stated. "One of the many lessons of the Olympics was that a great public festival—and that is essentially what the Olympics were—can unite and energize an entire community. What we are really doing during the Games is celebrating our achievements, character and history in a world where success is more than ever measured in terms of creativity and ideas. That is why the festival is needed, and why my Government supported it generously."[65]

Implied in Carr's remarks is the stimulus that prompts cities in every corner of the world to bid for the opportunity to host an Olympic festival. The competition to win the right to host the Winter and Summer Olympic Games is intense. Indeed, it is a struggle that dwarfs the most heated athletic competitions. Bidders spend millions of dollars to garner the IOC's blessing to stage the Games. The historical pathway leading to this contemporary world commercial phenomenon is detailed in the remainder of this book.

PART I

THE EVOLUTION OF OLYMPIC COMMERCIALISM

In the history of the Modern Olympic Games a half-century elapsed before the IOC awoke to the fact that it owned a product of considerable attractiveness to marketers of commercial enterprises. This attraction was closely correlated with a steady increase in global interest in the great quadrennial multisport festival. For the first four decades of modern Olympic history, expanding public interest in the Games was satisfied almost solely by mass communication's fundamental instrument—the newspaper. Radio joined newspaper coverage of the Games beginning in the late 1920s. Though "Olympic television" in its primeval form first appeared at the Garmisch-Partenkirchen Winter Olympic Games in 1936, it was not until the 1950s that the commercial romance between television and the Modern Olympic Movement really began.

The most critical financial factor underpinning the operation of all three communication devices—newspapers, radio, and television—is revenue gained from the sale of advertising. This is overwhelmingly the case with respect to American television. Elsewhere in the world, state-subsidized networks featured limited, if any, commercial advertisements in the early years of Olympic television. The greater the attention given to the Olympic Games by mass communication instruments, the greater the zeal of commerce to capitalize on that exposure. Producers of goods and services seek to advertise products in communication instruments reaching the widest possible consumer audience; the advertisement of goods and services in a newspaper with a circulation of 500,000, for instance, is likely to pay a bigger dividend in prospective consumer response than advertising in a newspaper whose circulation is 50,000. The same is true with respect to radio and television advertising.

But exposure is one thing; image is quite another. In fact image might be called "a growth industry." It is created and perpetuated over time. In order to be attractive to commercial initiatives, the Olympic Movement not only had to demonstrate that it offered wide exposure but also had to reflect an image accepted, indeed embraced, by public norms. When the noble qualities of the Modern Olympic Movement arose in the late nineteenth and early twentieth centuries, the founders were completely unaware of image implications, at least with regard to the consumer marketplace. Nevertheless, the images of peace, tolerance, goodwill, and noble amateur sport participation—all set in an atmosphere of high ceremony and ritual—eventually came to pay shockingly huge dividends.

Part I of this book describes and analyzes the evolution of the nexus between the forces of commercialism and the Olympic Games. The relationship between commerce and the Olympic Games in the 1980s and 1990s (discussed in part II) was preceded by an evolutionary stage of some eight decades. At the end of this period the Modern Olympic Movement, presided over by the International Olympic Committee, launched a series of commercial events that exploded its exposure to billions of people worldwide, astronomically increased its financial resources, and literally changed its image.

CHAPTER 1

ESTABLISHING A PROSPECTIVE GOLD MINE

The Early Years

As the Modern Olympic Movement begins the new millennium, there can be no doubt that the 100-year-old phenomenon faces a serious dilemma. On one hand, the Olympic Movement now has the resources to carry forward the spiritual ideals for which it has always stood. On the other hand, the very sources of wealth that permit the extension of its ideals to the world threaten to undermine the purity and nobility of its crusade. To understand the mission of the Olympic Movement, it is necessary to consider its formative history.

Traditional Olympic history says that the Modern Olympic Movement began with Pierre de Coubertin in the late nineteenth century. Well before Coubertin's time, however, festivals referred to as Olympic Games were organized in Europe and North America.[1] Though most were local or regional in nature, often with an ethnic orientation, their organizers were uniformly inspired by a literary knowledge of the important role of the Olympic Games in ancient Greek culture. Most notable among such early antecedents of the Modern Olympic Games were two initiatives inspired and sponsored by an English physician, William Penny Brookes, and a Greek merchant-philanthropist, Evangelis Zappas.[2] These two nineteenth-century individuals lent their passion and their resources to a rebirth of Olympic Games in a modern context. Each studied the classics and was inspired by the form and function of Olympic Games in ancient Greek society. Like many members of the small group of people in the nineteenth century who could call themselves "educated," Brookes and Zappas thrilled to the episodes of ancient sport grandeur noted in the works of the earliest translator-interpreters of the ancient documents. Homer's description of funeral games in the *Iliad* revealed glimpses of runners, boxers, wrestlers, discus and javelin throwers, and chariot teams vying for coveted prizes. In the ancient Olympic Games, an evolutionary extension of the funeral games, the worship of departed mortals was replaced by a celebration of the gods. During the first five centuries of Olympic history, victory laurel wreaths and civic idolatry were augmented by more tangible recompense—winning athletes were rewarded with cash from the public treasury, commemorative statues, social prestige, and adulation, like the world's leading athletes of our time.

But it was not tangible reward that inspired Brookes and Zappas. For Brookes, the positive health benefits and glorification of "body concepts" in ancient Greek society and their extension to his own nineteenth-century world were motivations enough. He first established his modern version of an ancient Greek sport festival in 1851 in the Shropshire village of Much Wenlock, where he lived. Beginning in this pastoral setting, Brookes's "Olympik Games" grew in stature across England, leading in time to the antecedents of an entity known today as the British Olympic Association. But Brookes dreamed of more than simply local Games or even all-England Olympics. Well before the idea ever germinated in Pierre de Coubertin's mind, Brookes envisioned modern international Olympic Games that would take place every four years in Greece. Brookes proposed Athens, rather than the ancient site of Olympia, then (and now) a sleepy, backcountry hamlet on the northwestern Peloponnese. When he attempted to convince Greek officials to reinstitute their nation's glorious Olympic legacy in a modern context, he was ignored. Brookes also tried the idea on a young Pierre de Coubertin, with whom he had struck up a correspondence as early as 1889.

Evangelis Zappas was not spurred by the possible positive health and fitness consequences for Greek youth. For him, recapturing the glorious Greek athletic legacy of antiquity was quite enough. In 1859 Zappas, a wealthy Greek grain merchant born in what is now Albania and at that time living in what is presently Romania, contributed funds to mount a national exhibition in Athens devoted to agriculture, industry, and an attempt to institute Olympic Games in modern Greek culture. The athletic affair, organized in Loudovikou Square, was a limited success. Brookes himself sent a cup to be awarded to the winner of the pentathlon. When Zappas died in 1865, he bequeathed much of his vast fortune to ensure that the legacy of the 1859 Modern Olympic festival would be continued. In 1870 a second Zappian Olympic festival took place in Athens, this time in a modest stadium constructed on the very site of ancient Athens's historic civic sport festival, the quadrennial Panathenaean Games.[3] The bill amounted to 200,000 drachmas, paid from the Zappas bequest. Subsequent Zappian Olympic Games were held in Athens in 1875 and 1889, each a failure in comparison to the first two episodes. Nevertheless, Zappas had ensured the reincarnation of an ancient Greek phenomenon called Olympic Games.

Pierre de Coubertin, though he scarcely admitted it, knew all about the Zappas-inspired initiatives as well as those of the English physician. Brookes carefully described Zappas's efforts in his correspondence with the baron. Coubertin even appeared at one rendition of Brookes's Much Wenlock Games. Despite what he perceived firsthand when visiting Brookes in England and what he learned of the Zappas initiatives from Brookes, Coubertin began to think of Modern Olympic Games as his own grand idea: Olympic Games for the celebration of youth, culture, and beauty, for the furtherance of health and fitness, for the promotion of peace, tolerance, and understanding—indeed, for the instillment of positive values. Unlike Brookes's Games, Coubertin's Games would be ambulatory, taking place in the great cities of the globe every four years. This scheme was perhaps the only difference from Brookes's earlier dream of a modern Olympic festival. But in time it was enough to galvanize the interest of supporters beyond the borders of England, France, and Greece.

ENTER PIERRE DE COUBERTIN

Coubertin, second son of a wealthy French aristocratic family, was born in 1863, just two years before Zappas's death. Several scholars have detailed how young Coubertin, appalled by the defeat of France in the Franco-Prussian Wars of the early 1870s, became disillusioned with two careers envisioned for him by his father, law and the military.[4] Instead he turned to the study of social philosophy, with a view toward helping to improve his nation's physical fiber through vigorous physical education in the school system. This passion was supported by travels in the late 1880s and early 1890s to England, the United States, and Canada, where he viewed models in which young men engaged in competitive sport and presumably grew in physical vitality as well as in resolve, discipline, courage, and a number of other positive values that sport is generally argued to cultivate. Coubertin's plan for altering what he felt to be "unphysical" French youth focused on the installation of physical education programs in the nation's public education system. Before his correspondence and subsequent personal meeting with William Penny Brookes, however, Coubertin had no thoughts about an international sport festival called the Olympic Games. He certainly knew about their legacy in the ancient context. Any person exposed to higher education in the nineteenth century could hardly have avoided knowing about them. But the first record of a modern Olympics in the consciousness of Pierre de Coubertin came in the form of his correspondence with Brookes.

In an effort to galvanize the physical education process in France, Coubertin dusted off a conference model he had encountered in 1889 in Boston, where he had presented a speech at what is now referred to as the Boston Normal Conference. He spoke last on the program and was the only speaker to extol the value of sports and games in the public school physical education curriculum. Back home in France he organized the Paris Physical Education Conference in 1892. At those proceedings he dropped the first hint that perhaps a world festival called the Olympic Games might be important to the greater question of physical education worldwide. The 1892 Paris conference on physical education produced little accord on the subject of exercise in the schools and absolutely no interest in anything called the Olympic Games. But Coubertin was persistent. In 1894 Coubertin organized a June conference at the Sorbonne, on the left bank of the Seine in Paris, for the express purpose of addressing a vexing issue facing international sport at the time: the definition of what constituted an amateur athlete. Buried in the less grand notations of the invitation documents was a reference to the question of renovating the Olympic Games in a modern context. When the delegates convened, most of them immediately became embroiled in the subject of amateurism, an issue that continued to defy all attempts at consensus for decades.[5] A small group headed by Coubertin discussed the Olympic issue and proposed to the general assembly that the concept of Olympic Games be approved and that the first such festival be celebrated in Athens two years hence, in the spring of 1896. Amid the euphoria of the conference-closing celebration and ritual, Coubertin's plan was approved. The Modern Olympic Games, at least in theoretical fashion, had been born.

ENTER THE GREEKS

Through intricate and still not completely understood circumstances, Athens was awarded the first Olympic Games. Support from the Greek royal family, the Olympic Committee's Greek representative, Dimitrios Vikelas, and pro-Games colleagues in Athens nullified opposition from government officials pleading poverty and the nation's lack of a record in mounting international meetings. Greeks worldwide rallied to the cause, donating much of the money necessary to underwrite the costs of the first Modern Olympics. By late March 1896 a donation of 920,000 drachmas ($177,560 U.S.) from George Averoff, a Greek living in Egypt, had translated into a glorious stadium for showcasing most of the athletic events. Before the Games opened, other Greek individuals and organizations contributed some 330,000 drachmas to the cause.[6] Revenue from event ticket sales, postal stamps, and commemorative medals completed the necessary financing for the Games.

On 25 March the Games opened.[7] By any standard the first modern Olympic Games were a glorious success. For the duration of the festival Athens was the gayest city on the continent, swathed in bunting, pennants, and festive appurtenances. The assembly of spectators and dignitaries at the opening ceremonies and athletic events, even by the most conservative counts, numbered over 60,000. As the week of athleticism unfolded, Greek, American, and German performers were usually the victors. Almost three hundred athletes from fifteen countries participated.[8] Fittingly, in the final athletics event, Olympic history's first marathon, Spiridon Loues, an unassuming Greek rural worker and former military conscript, triumphed. If basking in the glow of having mounted a superb international sports celebration was not enough, the triumph of one of their own gave Greeks an intense measure of national pride.

Of course, Coubertin was present for all this; but his role in the whole affair was largely inconsequential, which must have nettled his considerable pride. Near the end of the grand spectacle Greek officials, with the concurrence of sympathizers (including American athletes), stated categorically that the Olympic Games had returned to the home of their historical legacy and should remain there for all time, to be celebrated in Athens every four years. Faced with this alarming possibility, Coubertin reasserted the Olympic Committee's original Sorbonne agreement that the Games should be celebrated in various cities throughout the world.

In the end the baron brokered an agreement by which Greece would celebrate an interim Olympic sport festival every four years in the even numbered years between the quadrennial Olympic Games presided over by the International Olympic Committee (the IOC's Games would be celebrated in 1900, 1904, 1908, etc., while the Greek festivals would take place in 1898, 1902, 1906, etc.). Aside from 1906, when the Greeks did indeed organize an Interim Olympic Games even more illustrious than their initial effort in 1896, no further Greek festivals in this context took place. But the idea for interim sport festivals in the Olympic quadrennial scheme rose in other parts of the world. The Pan-American Games, Asian Games, Maccabean Games, and Commonwealth Games are only a few examples of such festivals.

GROWING PAINS

The Olympic Games of the Second and Third Olympiads, celebrated in Paris (France) and St. Louis (USA), respectively, have been described as failures and of little consequence in advancing the lofty ideals set forth by the founders of the Olympic Movement and promulgated so gloriously by the Greek organizers of the Games of the First Olympiad. In the case of Paris in 1900, World Exposition authorities controlled matters, shunting Coubertin aside from the arrangements. The "blue-ribbon" track and field events were carried out on the grassy expanses of the Croix-Catalan, a section of the Bois de Boulogne, the vast bucolic property of the Racing Club of France. Somewhat like the Greeks who had privately underwritten most of the costs for staging the 1896 Games, French private interests and exposition budget monies supplied the revenues to sponsor what passed for the 1900 Olympics. The word "Olympic" rarely appeared in associated advertising and reporting of the contests. "International contests," "world amateur championships," "Paris Exposition Athletic Events," and "French Games" were phrases found in both American and European press reports describing the second renewal of the Modern Olympic Games. Despite shortcomings, slightly more than twelve hundred athletes showed up for the competitions, held over a six-month period from July to November.[9] Twenty-eight nations were represented. Some of the events, unlike those in Athens four years earlier, featured world-class performers; most of the marks established were significantly better than those recorded in 1896.

After the 1904 Olympic Games were awarded to Chicago, a number of events conspired to prompt Coubertin arbitrarily to change the host city. Prospective fund-raising efforts among Chicago private and corporate sources failed miserably. In February 1903, little more than a year before the Games were scheduled to open, the baron bowed to hard realities and sent the Games packing to St. Louis.[10] Coubertin's decision also reflected assertive overtures by officials of the Louisiana Purchase Exposition, a macro-event scheduled for St. Louis in 1904. Immersed in the greater activities of the Exposition's Physical Culture Exhibit, the events of the 1904 Olympic Games took place between July and November.[11] The budget of the Physical Culture Exhibit, organized and presided over by America's czar of amateur sports, James Sullivan, funded the Games. Twelve nations were represented by almost seven hundred athletes. Only Germany, South Africa, Greece, and Canada mustered contingents of more than a half-dozen individuals. Coubertin did not attend; in fact, only two IOC members, Willibald Gebhardt of Germany and Francis Kémény of Hungary, were present.

Though Coubertin and IOC members lamented the fact that both the 1900 and 1904 Games had been "lost" in the proceedings of world expositions, they nevertheless belatedly awarded the 1908 Games to London, where they were celebrated as part of the Franco-British Exhibition. As much as IOC members may have looked askance at again associating the Games with a large exposition, sound reasons for doing so prevailed. Hosting an Olympic festival was an expensive proposition, and governments resisted providing taxpayer monies for support of a sports event. The IOC had no financial means to aid host cities in mounting the Olympic project. Thus local officials responsible for financing the Games turned quite naturally toward the cash cows represented by exhibition budgets. None of the first three Games generated much interest from business and manufacturing firms. Until the Games could demonstrate their wide national and international appeal, a relationship with the corporate and manufacturing world to help underwrite costs was not possible. When such wide popular appeal finally materialized, along with burgeoning technology, political change, economic realities, and "new thinking" within corporate boardrooms about producing and marketing products on a global level, multinational corporations became aggressive buyers of an association with the Olympic mystique. But this did not occur until decades into the future.

In the West London precinct of Shepherd's Bush an oval stadium seating 70,000 spectators was constructed adjacent to the Franco-British Pavilion. The stadium, which served as the central Olympic Games venue, featured two circular tracks, an outer track for cycling and another for track and field. An immense infield accommodated the field events as well as other sports. Also situated in the infield was a pool 100 meters long in which the swimming and diving events were carried out. It was not uncommon for spectators to view the simultaneous activities of runners, leapers, throwers, swimmers, divers, gymnasts, cyclists, and wrestlers. Indeed the athletic events often resembled a huge three-ring circus. Some two thousand athletes representing twenty-three nations took part.

Event organizers solicited advertising from commercial sponsors as a means of offsetting their costs. For instance, in the booklet describing the race procedures and listing entrants for the marathon, readers observed full-page advertisements for Schweppes Soda Water and Dry Ginger Ale, Vaughton's Medal and Badge Makers, and Wawkphar's Antiseptic Military Foot Powder.[12]

The London Games, however, were underscored by controversy. Hardly a day passed without tempers flaring, as American zeal to win confronted British organization and event officiating.[13] Through it all brash Jim Sullivan, administrative head of the American Olympic contingent, squared off against his British hosts.[14] It was not the type of Olympic atmosphere that Coubertin hoped for.

Stockholm hosted the Games of the Fifth Olympiad, which demonstrated that the Olympic Games stood on the threshold of becoming all that Pierre de Coubertin had envisioned for them when he first translated thought into action at the Sorbonne in 1894. Some 2,500 athletes from 28 nations participated in 102 events. A body of 260 foreign journalists and scores of Swedish reporters covered the proceedings. The Swedish hosts produced the first-ever full cinema coverage of the Games. The Games, held in a newly constructed red brick stadium, lasted eight days and cost the organizers approximately £23,000 sterling. Receipts from ticket sales amounted to £4,400. A special edition of the national Athletic Lottery provided the remainder of the funds needed to finance the project. Embedded in the great festival were examples of early Olympic commercialism that became commonplace in the future: purchases of "sole rights" to vend products in the Olympic precinct. Ten Swedish companies bought rights, including a photographic company, various firms selling Olympic memorabilia, and a manufacturer of weighing machines whose products were placed around the Olympic grounds for the use of patrons.[15] All in all, commercial endeavors provided an infinitesimal percentage of the money needed to pay for the Games.

FORGING A SYMBOL

In the euphoria produced by the successful staging of the Stockholm Olympic Games Coubertin announced a celebration to commemorate the twentieth anniversary of the Modern Olympic Movement to be held in Paris in June 1914 in the grand chamber of the Sorbonne, the historic birthplace of the Modern Olympic Games. But first there were matters to address. One of them, as it turned out, had immense consequences for Olympic financial health—the creation of a symbol or logo by which the Olympic Games might be identified. Coubertin accepted this task. He was familiar with a well-known model from which to draw inspiration, having served as president of the Union des Sociétés Françaises de Sports Athlétiques (USFSA), the powerful French umbrella sports-governing body. The USFSA adopted two simple interlocked circles as its logo in 1892, which signified the joining of the Union des Sociétés Françaises de Courses à Pied and the Comité Jules Simon. The simple two-ring symbol appeared on the jerseys of French athletes who competed internationally from 1896 until the 1920s, when the logo was replaced by the now well-known French National Olympic Committee symbol of a fighting cock. For Coubertin, the Olympic logo puzzle was logically simple. Borrowing from the earlier USFSA logo, he used interlocked rings as the basis for the new design. By the end of 1913 a five-ring symbol appeared on Coubertin's personal letterhead. Although he did not know it at the time, he had conceived a commercial gold mine.

The anniversary congress was no small affair. Coubertin found few sponsorship partners to help in financing the endeavor; he paid for most of it himself.[16] When French president Raymond Poincaré, IOC members, sports officials, thirty-two ambassadors from countries boasting National Olympic Committees, and almost two thousand guests and members of the world press arrived for the opening of the Congress in Paris on 13 June 1914, they were greeted in the hall by an impressive assembly of fifty Olympic flags, each one embossed with a cluster of five interlocked rings— blue, black, red, yellow, and green—set on a pure white background.[17] As the baron explained, the five rings represented the "five parts of the world won over to Olympism."[18] Coubertin stated that at least one of the five colors was found in the national flag of each nation that had taken part in the Olympic Games by 1912.

Within days of the conclusion of the great anniversary celebration the Archduke Franz Ferdinand was assassinated in Sarajevo, plunging a seething Europe into war. The Olympic Games scheduled for Berlin in 1916 were canceled. Germany, a serious Olympic participant, realized that regional and global political gain might be gleaned from international sporting prominence. The planning for the 1916 Games had been a state endeavor; the facilities, partially built by the outbreak of World War I, were designed to be superior to those of any Olympic Games yet celebrated.

During the war years Coubertin did his best to serve both his country and the Olympic Movement. Then in his early fifties, he volunteered to serve in the French military as a noncombatant. He maintained correspondence with IOC members, some of whom were wartime adversaries in the armies of the Allied Forces and Central Powers.[19] During this period the baron accepted an overture from the Swiss city of Lausanne to establish the IOC's headquarters there. In 1915 Coubertin moved the headquarters operation of the IOC to the picturesque Swiss city on the shores of Lac Léman. There he lived and worked in a stately mansion known as Mon Repos. For more than half a century the striking edifice near the City center pulsated with Olympic business.

POSTWAR RENOVATION

At the first IOC Session following the November 1918 armistice that signaled the end of World War I, the Games of the Seventh Olympiad were officially awarded to Antwerp, the great port city of Belgium.[20] The initial plan of Antwerp's civic leaders called for the Olympic Games to be an adjunct of a much larger commercial enterprise, a universal exposition. In the end, however, the nation's devastation from the war negated hopes of organizing a world fair. Stymied in their attempt to present such an extravaganza, Antwerp authorities refocused on organizing the Olympic Games. But visions of "what might have been" lingered, resulting in the creation of scores of exhibits and displays located around the periphery of the Olympic stadium—in effect, a miniature world fair.[21] Support for the Games and the surrounding pageantry of commercialism came from a federal grant of 1.5 million Belgian francs, a provincial subsidy of 200,000 francs, and a City of Antwerp donation of 800,000 francs. Having recently emerged from a debilitating war, the Belgian hosts organized and executed what appeared to be a highly successful renewal of the interrupted Modern Olympic Games. At the conclusion of the Games, however, a final accounting showed a deficit of some 625,000 francs. Aside from the unfortunate realities of the deficit, rumors surfaced of personal profit gained by volunteer members of the Organizing Committee.[22]

If Pierre de Coubertin ever harbored apprehensions concerning a link between the Olympic Games and the forces of business and opportunism, the commercial atmosphere of the Olympic precinct in Antwerp must have confirmed them. In his speech at the opening ceremonies the baron challenged the assembled crowd and sports leaders to "keep away the opportunities that are advanced [by profit-motivated people] whose only dream is to use someone else's muscles either to build upon his own political fortune or to make his own business prosper."[23] Coubertin's warning proved prophetic for the future development of the Olympic Games and their alignment with commercial forces.

Despite overtures from a dozen cities to host Olympic Games in the future (including a particularly strong and thorough bid from Los Angeles), Coubertin decreed that the 1924 Games, commemorating the thirtieth anniversary of the arrival of the Modern Olympic Movement, be celebrated in Paris and that Amsterdam should host the 1928 Games. The 1924 Olympic festival was Coubertin's last as president of the IOC. He retired the following year, succeeded by the aristocratic Belgian Count Henri Baillet-Latour.

The Paris Games, which opened on 5 July 1924, featured a formidable series of Olympic rituals developed over the years. Sixty thousand people gazed down on the great spectacle taking place on the field before them. By far the greatest number of Olympic nations (44) and athletes (3,092) in Olympic history to that time marched into the stadium. The United States sent the largest team; Haiti, the smallest. The Olympic flag was raised to the strains of "La Marseillaise." Guns roared, pigeons soared, as the oath was solemnly rendered. All this took place in the presence of a diminutive, stooped figure, Baron Pierre de Coubertin, father of the Modern Olympic Games. Two other phenomena at the Paris Games of 1924 had an impact on the manner in which the Olympic Games are organized. First, the French hosts envisioned an Olympic village to house all competitors. A modest complex was built, featuring small cottages not unlike the miniature rural cabins traditionally enjoyed by millions of past and present Europeans. Most athletes spurned history's first Olympic village, electing instead to seek accommodation in the hotels and hostels of downtown Paris. And, for the first time in Olympic history and the last, commercial advertisements appeared inside the stadium; Olympic athletes performed before the advertising imagery of Ovalmaltine, Cinzano, Dubonnet, and a host of other commercial products. Linking product advertising to activities in the Olympic stadium made sense to businesses, as evidenced by the 320-page guide to the Games published by the Organizing Committee, which featured ads on 256 different pages for products like Mercier Champagne, Spalding Sporting Goods, and Grand Marnier liquors.[24]

The challenge of financing the Paris Games, not surprisingly, was a major concern for the Organizing Committee. Under Coubertin's watchful eye a Propaganda Commission was established with a mandate to promote the Games at a national and international level. The commission made and distributed some 32,000 posters for display in France and abroad.[25] It also arranged for the distribution of 1.6 million luggage labels, 11 million vignettes in cigar and cigarette packages, 153 million Olympic stamps, 5,800 aerial photographs of Paris and the main stadium, and 84 million copies of an advertisement sent to French diplomatic posts for circulation in foreign countries. Commercial endeavors aimed at helping to finance the Games were growing.

In February 1924 a Winter Games festival was organized in the French alps at Chamonix. Eighteen nations sent athletes to compete in speed and figure skating, ice hockey, bobsleigh, nordic skiing (jumping and cross-country), and curling. Norwegian and Finnish athletes dominated the skiing events, although there was more parity among the competing nations in the skating events. After the fact, the Chamonix festival was sanctioned by the IOC as the First Olympic Winter Games. Plans were made to organize future Winter Olympic Games in February of the year in which the Summer Games were staged. If the Chamonix Games of 1924 were an organizational success, and perhaps even a political success, they were an economic disaster. They cost 3.5 million francs. Gate receipts totaled only 120,000 francs, of which 31,000 came from the ice hockey final between

Canada and the United States.[26] It remains unclear what action the Chamonix organizers took to resolve a final deficit of over 2 million francs.

Baillet-Latour's first Summer Olympic Games as president of the IOC were celebrated in Amsterdam in the summer of 1928. They opened on 28 July before some 40,000 spectators, the stadium's capacity. Frustrated patrons clamored vainly at the gates. It was a disappointing Olympics for the United States; the Americans were outshone by Finland, a nation whose population was forty times less than America's 120 million. To irk the Americans further, their neighbor Canada produced the bona-fide star of the Games. Barely graduated from high school, nineteen-year-old Percy Williams won both the 100- and 200-meter sprints. Lord David Burghley prevailed in the 400-meter hurdles. The Amsterdam Games exhibited one of Olympic history's notable experiments, women's competition in track and field athletics. Five events were arranged: high jump, discus, 100-meter sprint, 800-meter run, and a 4-by-100-meter sprint relay. The results, particularly in the 800 meters, sparked renewed debate on the issue of women in the Olympic Games. In general the IOC resisted including women, a stance originally influenced by Coubertin's Victorian values. Neither did Baillet-Latour espouse women's participation in the Olympic Games. But the relatively new International Amateur Athletics Federation (IAAF, founded in 1912) under the leadership of its president, Sweden's Sigfrid Edström, confronted the issue and led the way in convincing the IOC to include women's track and field competition in the 1928 Games on an experimental basis. The IAAF's action was strongly abetted by Alice Milliat and the Fédération Sportive Féminine Internationale (FSFI). In 1932 Olympic women's track and field gained permanent legitimacy.[27]

Although the Organizing Committee for the Amsterdam Games employed techniques for fund-raising like those of its Paris counterpart four years earlier, the IOC stipulated that the stadium grounds and buildings could never again be disfigured by signs and posters advertising business products. Despite this, "rights packages" were sold by the Amsterdam organizers to concessionaires, including a brewery that operated beer garden restaurants on grounds next to the Olympic stadium. The 1928 Games also experienced the beginning of one of the Olympic Movement's longest-standing corporate relationships, with Coca-Cola. The soft drink company, established in Atlanta in 1886, had expanded into international markets by the 1920s. Its first appearance at an Olympic Games occurred at Amsterdam, where hundreds of posters outside the stadium advertised its presence. Early in 1929 the company's publication *Red Barrel* proudly announced to its employees and shareholders that "Coca-Cola is now found within the bull fight arenas of sunny Spain and Mexico, at the Olympic

Games stadium below the dykes of Holland, atop the Eiffel Tower above 'Gay Paree,' on the holy pagoda in distant Burma, and beside the Coliseum of historic Rome."[28] Coca-Cola also supplied the American Olympic team's training tables at the squad's living quarters aboard the SS *Roosevelt*, anchored in Amsterdam's roadstead for the duration of the Games.

Intrusion into Olympic matters by business and corporate interests aroused concern within the IOC.[29] The dilemma was obvious: what effect would business commercialism have on the purity of Olympic values and philosophy? Still, revenue was needed to stage the Games. The IOC and OCOGs had no well-endowed treasuries to finance the work that had to be done in carrying out commitments. Olympic officials discussed and debated the question: who will pay? Even Coubertin, who devoted much of his own family fortune as well as his wife's to nurturing the Olympic Movement, occasionally strayed from his usual adversarial stance on commercial interests and the Olympic Games. For example, in attempting to relieve his personal costs associated with producing *Olympic Review* (the IOC's official bulletin), the baron solicited a full-page, inside-cover advertisement from a Parisian sporting goods firm for the January 1901 issue and a similarly placed advertisement from Bénédictine Brandy for the October 1902 publication.

IOC members were also increasingly concerned about growing encroachment on the use of the word "Olympic." As early as 1910 International Sports Federations (ISFs), of which there were only a few at the time, occasionally used the term "Olympic Games" to advertise their competitions. Coubertin sought to end such abuse, requesting that efforts be undertaken by IOC members to persuade the ISFs to avoid further use of the term in defining their competitions.[30] IOC members were requested to be vigilant for examples of misuse of the word "Olympic" in their respective countries. From time to time transgressions were noted. In 1921 a protest was raised over games in Spain being referred to as "Olympiade Catalan." It was consequently changed to "Jeux Catalans."[31] One year later General Charles Sherrill, an IOC member in the United States, requested that the IOC officially forbid the use of the words "Olympics" and "Olympiad" unless sanctioned by the IOC, NOCs, or OCOGs. Coubertin regretfully stated that this was legally impossible; the IOC could only "discourage" their use.[32] The baron was right. Despite IOC "discouragement," abuse of the words "Olympic" and "Olympiad" increased as various groups realized their value in promoting prestige and commercial return. At the 1926 session of the IOC held in Lisbon Baillet-Latour reported "a half dozen new cases" of abuse, including Olympic Games for Women, Student Olympic Games, and Workers' Olympic Games.[33] The offending organizations were warned; but the growing number of abuse incidents worldwide prompted the IOC to try to convince various governments and sports governing bodies that it, as the supreme authority of the Olympic Movement, owned a legitimate claim to the five Olympic rings, Olympic flag, Olympic motto, and the word "Olympic" or its derivatives.

The Games of the Tenth Olympiad celebrated in Los Angeles in 1932 presented a historic incident in the story of Olympic commercialism, which established a critical precedent in building the future financial health of the Modern Olympic Movement. As a result of the confrontation between the Helms Bakery of Los Angeles and the United States Olympic Association, the IOC established a platform to launch initiatives aimed at gathering revenues through marketing rights to Olympic activities. Further, such rights had to be protected. These two phenomena—protecting rights and selling rights—are the subject of the following history.

CHAPTER 2

AVERY BRUNDAGE AND THE GREAT BREAD WAR

An Olympian Precedent

In recent times the world has viewed the Modern Olympic Movement as a phenomenon permeated with the glitz of advertising and marketing. The Olympic Movement has grown to such a state of global awareness that commercial firms of practically every ilk seek a link to it. In the first half-century of Olympic history, when the Games were maturing in world recognition, that link came with little or no cost; but matters changed substantially following World War II. The Olympic Movement had two formidable qualities that made it marketable: a carefully projected *image* as a model of health and fitness for youth, fairness and altruism, and the epitome of excellence in performance; and *public awareness* that there is no sporting extravaganza of equal importance and global recognition (including soccer's World Cup).

As we have seen, manufacturers and purveyors of goods and services have long been interested in capitalizing on the glamour of the Olympic Games. One initiative sought linkage between the products marketed by business firms and the signs, logos, and words that identified the Olympic Movement—in effect, to become known as an official Olympic associate. In much the same vein was the quest to acquire the right to transmit the Olympic Games to listening and viewing audiences the world over. Such links in time produced financial treasure for the Modern Olympic Movement beyond the wildest imaginations of Pierre de Coubertin and his colleagues. Into the IOC and OCOG coffers flowed the fees charged for association with the Games.

As the value of the identifying marks of the Olympics rose in the commercial marketplace, the importance of protecting them from exploitation without authority increased. The most important precedent-setting episode in the history of protecting the Modern Olympic Movement's

most valuable assets—image and recognition—is the confrontation between Helms Bakeries of Los Angeles, California, and the IOC's representative in America, the United States Olympic Association (USOA). The
long struggle between the two adversaries and the case's eventual outcome
in the early 1950s established the parameters by which the financial future
of the Modern Olympic Movement was ensured.

LOS ANGELES, 1932

In 1932 some two thousand athletes representing thirty-nine nations
gathered to participate in the Games of the Tenth Olympiad in Los Angeles. On the afternoon of 30 July approximately 105,000 spectators crowded
into the Memorial Coliseum to view the opening ceremonies, the greatest
number ever to witness the inaugural of any Olympics in the first 100 years
of their history.[1] The economic depression gripping the world did not prevent a last-minute rush of ticket buyers from engulfing sales outlets in
downtown Los Angeles. President Herbert Hoover was absent, but Vice-
President Charles Curtis journeyed from Washington to substitute in declaring the Games officially open.[2]

Male athletes of all competing countries stayed in an Olympic Village
located in Baldwin Heights, a mere fifteen-minute bus ride from the
Olympic stadium.[3] To Los Angeles residents, the village was awe inspiring.[4]
It contained a reception area, recreation room, some 500 living cottages,
and intermittently dispersed bathroom facilities (called "comfort stations"), all arranged on more than 250 acres of beautiful rolling tract. Also
present in the vast village were forty team-designated dining buildings,
complete with kitchens, cooks, and menus compatible with various ethnic
tastes. Among items delivered to the Olympic Village kitchens each morning were 2,750 pounds of string beans, 1,800 pounds of fresh peas, 50 sacks
of potatoes, 450 gallons of ice cream, and hundreds of loaves of bread[5]—
and not just any bread: Helms Olympic Bread![6]

Helms Bakeries, a Los Angeles firm, was founded as a California corporation in 1931. Its owner, Paul H. Helms, a Kansan by birth, had formerly been president of two bakery businesses in New York City during the
1920s. Helms Bakeries, at 8800 Venice Boulevard, competed with a number of the city's other bakery establishments for shares of the greater Los
Angeles consumer market. Helms established himself as a leading citizen in
his new community, serving as director of the Los Angeles Community
Chest and the Los Angeles Civic Light Opera Association. He was a
Shriner, Rotarian, and thirty-second-degree Mason. His network of club
memberships, which left him well-connected with the city's business and

industry elite, included the California Club, the Los Angeles Country Club, and the Bel-Air Bay Club.[7] In the months leading up to the Los Angeles Games newspaper hype surrounding the Olympic celebration increased greatly. Paul Helms's attention was drawn to a newspaper sketch of the proposed Olympic Village. An idea evolved from his fascination with the village concept: athletes required meals, and bread was a staple commodity in most daily diets, irrespective of nationality. Helms's business connections and salesmanship convinced the Los Angeles Organizing Committee to grant him the bakery goods supply contract for the Olympic Village.

Providing bakery products to the Olympic Village was one thing; capitalizing on an affiliation with the Olympic Games in marketing products to the public at large was quite another. Realizing that competitors lurked in every corner of Los Angeles, Helms moved swiftly and with circumspection to register the identifying marks of the Olympic Movement in every state of the union: the five-ring insignia, the Olympic motto (*Citius, Altius, Fortius*), and the word "Olympic" and its derivations.[8] Only Washington objected, mainly because the word "Olympia" had several connotations in the state (in the form of geographical place names and manufactured products, Olympia Beer being the best known). Helms was also successful in registering the insignias and associated words in two U.S. territories, Hawaii and the Philippines. No prior registration of Olympic marks had ever been attempted, so no precedent existed for preventing such action. No laws or statutes were in place to deter Helms.[9] He saw to it that the registration information was announced in public notices published in Los Angeles newspapers and informed the Los Angeles Organizing Committee. No objections resulted.[10] After the registration was completed, Helms made up loaves of bread for nineteen different nations in distinctive wrappers adorned with each country's appropriate national colors and identifying Olympic marks and words. He received permission from the Organizing Committee to exhibit the loaves in a display case located at the entrance to the village.

Helms was not the only licensed supplier of products to the Village. Toilet articles, laundry supplies, beverages, and food products of every description were needed. In each supplier agreement with the Los Angeles Organizing Committee except Helms's there was an injunction clause against publicly advertising contracted products with the Olympic emblems included. Helms had the injunction clause removed from his contract, and Organizing Committee authorities duly signed the agreement.[11] Full-page advertisements of Helms's "official Olympic products" appeared in local Los Angeles newspapers.

Before, during, and after the Los Angeles Games Helms advertised Olympic Bread and other products (angel-food cake, rolls, doughnuts) in local newspapers. He was not alone in capitalizing on Olympic marks and logos in advertising business products. Scores of firms used newspapers to advertise their wares, many of them embellished with Olympic marks and slogans. For instance, the Broadway-Hollywood Store maintained an "Olympic Booth" on its street floor where consumers purchased neckties, handkerchiefs, and stationery embossed with the Olympic rings. Bullocks on Wilshire Boulevard regularly displayed the five rings in its newspaper advertising for women's apparel. And Nisley Shoes extolled the quality of its "Olympic Winners" product line.[12]

Helms's business thrived as the bakery's Olympic Bread cut a swath through its competitors. Rival bakers protested. Weber's Bakery, acting arbitrarily, attempted to obtain a contract to furnish bread to one of the competing nations.[13] Helms was prepared for just such an eventuality. He had directed his lawyers to secure bond and warrants of attachment in advance of possible circumstance demanding such a response. Knowledge of the rival baker's initiative sent him into action. He informed the Los Angeles Organizing Committee that if it interfered with his exclusive contract, or with his use of the legally registered Olympic emblems, he would sue for $1 million damages, citing breach of a contract duly signed by the committee. Facing this dilemma, the committee acquiesced; the competitor's request was rejected, and Helms was allowed to complete his contract under its original terms.[14]

On 14 August 1932, after witnessing two weeks of Olympic sports thrills that featured sixteen world and thirty-three Olympic record-breaking performances (including the swimming successes of the Japanese and the startling track and field victories of Mildrid "Babe" Didrikson, the most notable hero of the Games), some 100,000 spectators gathered in Memorial Coliseum for the closing ceremonies of the most successful Olympic Games held to that date. On the same day, continuing to capitalize on its association with the Olympic Games, Helms Bakeries ran a full-page advertisement in the *Los Angeles Sunday Times* extolling the qualities of Helms Olympic Bread.[15] Helms, understanding the fundamental principles behind effective advertising, had successfully established a sustained link between his company and the popularity of Olympic Games. He presented the following message of self-aggrandizing rationalization of his firm's selection and authority as the "official supplier of Olympic Bread":

Trained on the food of their homeland, athletes of the Xth Olympiad brought their own chefs along with their trainers and coaches. Forty separate kitchens and forty dining rooms made up the huge "training table" at Olympic Village. But to bake their bread . . . scores of different kinds . . . was another problem. Who was familiar with *Coburg* . . . or *Swarzrogge* . . . or "Bashed Bread"? Who could make *pain frais* to satisfy a French chef? Weeks before the Games, the master bakers at Helms baked these breads and many others for the Olympic authorities. They were tasted and tested by experts for the Committee. And because the bakers at Helms could best fulfil the exacting requirements of the Olympic Committee *in every way,* they were chosen to bake the bread of the Olympic Village . . . to bake whatever was required.[16]

Following its "official" association with the 1932 Los Angeles Olympics, Helms Bakeries continued to flourish, partly due to the popularity of its premier product, Helms Olympic Bread, marketed in packages bearing distinctive Olympic insignia. One Olympic figure who had experienced the quality of Helms Olympic Bread in the Los Angeles Village was Carl Diem, manager of the German Olympic team sent to the 1932 Games. Impressed, he requested that Helms supply the bread for the Olympic Village at the Berlin Games in 1936. Helms sent two of his most experienced bakers to Germany, along with bread recipes, to serve the bakery needs of Berlin's Olympic Village.

A GATHERING STORM: HELMS VS. THE USOA

In 1938 the sustained "Olympic advertising" activities of Helms came to the attention of Avery Brundage, president of the United States Olympic Association and recently elected (1936) IOC member. Brundage, perturbed that such an activity had been allowed to continue, reacted by forwarding a note of protest to William R. Schroeder, managing director of Helms's downtown office in Los Angeles, demanding that they cease and desist.[17]

By this time Brundage was one of the most important men in American sport. A self-made Chicago businessman in the heavy construction industry, he graduated from the University of Illinois in 1909 after a successful career in athletics, scholarship, and extracurricular activities. Brundage did not distinguish himself in competition (pentathlon and decathlon) in the 1912 Stockholm Olympics, a personal failure that haunted him for many years. He left an active amateur athletic career behind to become a sport administrator, highlighted by his election to the presidency of the powerful Amateur Athletic Union (AAU) of the United States and his appointment as chair of its subcommittee for Olympic affairs, the United States Olympic Committee. Brundage exhibited a few admirable qualities such as personal industry and complete commitment to the Modern Olympic Movement, but he is better known for exemplifying qualities of a less flattering nature. He was ultraconservative, righteous, confrontational, obstinate, dictatorial, and uncompromising—a man who had many acquaintances but few friends. There is little doubt that the acerbic Brundage grated on the more genteel Paul Helms.[18]

Los Angeles resident William May Garland, an IOC member, president of the Los Angeles Organizing Committee for the 1932 Games, and a personal friend of Helms, received a copy of Brundage's letter to Schroeder. In mid-October 1938 Garland wrote to Brundage, defending Helms as an "immeasurably fine American citizen." He asked Brundage to soften his demand: "It is always a joy to pass his [Helms's] business place for he has illuminated the shield of the I.O.C. on his building. In fact, in a nice dignified way, he keeps the thought of Olympism and the Olympic Games alive and before the people in a manner that surely is not objectionable." In closing Garland lamented that Brundage had not taken the initiative to meet with Helms: "I wish you could have come to Los Angeles, that I might have introduced you to Paul H. Helms, so that you could have become intimately acquainted with his friendliness to everything that the Olympic Games stand for. He is an immeasurably fine American citizen highly respected in his own community."[19]

Brundage was unmoved. Five days later he responded to Garland, firm in his conviction that Helms had sullied the Olympic Movement through his continued exploitation of a prior affiliation with the Games. "If manufacturers and dealers . . . use the name Olympic in their advertising," wrote Brundage, "they [the Olympic words and marks] will soon loose [*sic*] their meaning." He went further: "You cannot imagine how many attempts there are to capitalize on the Olympic Games and the difficulty we have in preventing promoters to use the Olympic Movement for their own personal gain . . . We have strict rules for athletes, and so far have had excellent cooperation from the public. [Another] serious violation at present is that of Mr. Culbertson who persists in operating a so-called Olympic Bridge Tournament despite the fact that the matter has been called to his attention several times."[20]

Helms, like Culbertson, ignored Brundage. For the moment, the issue died. It appeared that the USOA had little more than bluster in its arsenal of tactics for dealing with so-called infringers on the Olympic Movement. Besides, more pressing problems for all Americans were looming on the horizon. By the following year (1939) the first battles of World War II had been fought. America itself stood on the threshold of entering the war.

In the years following the 1932 Games Helms Bakeries expanded into billboard and radio advertising, continuing to capitalize on the five Olympic rings, motto, and words "Official Olympic Supplier." Helms himself became a well-known benefactor of amateur sport in Los Angeles and southern California, even establishing a foundation for nurturing amateur sport, the Helms Olympic Athletic Foundation. Knowing how Brundage would respond to Helms's use of the word "Olympic" in the name of his foundation, Garland approached the baking impresario and asked him to remove the word from the title. Obligingly, Helms complied.[21]

After World War II the USOA embarked on an energetic fund-raising campaign to send an Olympic team to the 1948 Games in London. Helms contributed $10,000. But Brundage's consternation was not diminished by this act of philanthropy. He remained convinced that Helms's commercial activity and persistent exploitation of Olympic symbols were desecrations of all Olympic traditions.

In late 1947 Paul Helms tendered a competitive bid to supply the American Olympic Team with bread during the team's residence in England at the London Games. At almost the same time he raised $50,000 among Los Angeles businessmen to aid in the expenses of the U.S. team. Helms received the bread supply contract with no restrictions as to advertising even though his method of capitalizing on Olympic insignia was public knowledge.[22] After the contract had been signed, the agreement came to Brundage's attention. The czar of American Olympic fortunes fumed, faced with a dilemma. On one hand, he castigated Helms for his continued misuse of Olympic symbols. On the other, he grudgingly recognized that Helms had been responsible for raising a great deal of money for the American Olympic Movement. True to form, Brundage downplayed the money and pressed his efforts to stop Helms's advertising. American Olympic colleagues compromised his efforts, including William May Garland, who considered Helms a fine booster of the Olympic Movement.

Raising the issue for discussion at a USOA meeting in New York City following the 1948 Summer Olympic Games, Brundage renewed his attack on Helms. In mid-December Brundage wrote John Jewett Garland, who had succeeded his father as an IOC member, arguing that Helms's advertising in the newspapers, on billboards, and over the radio featured untrue statements, violated all Olympic traditions, and was in very bad taste. "I have received many protests from the general public as well as from the Olympic family. As a matter of fact, some of Helms' competitors have suggested they might go further than a protest . . . Cannot something be done to stop this violation of Olympic principles, which has reached the proportions of an international scandal?"[23] Young Garland did nothing, however. Like his father, he admired Helms. Despite Brundage's assertion to Garland that he had received many letters of protest against Helms's "Olympic" advertising practices, there is no extant evidence of such letters in the Brundage Collection.

Brundage brought the issue to the attention of John Terry McGovern, a semiretired septuagenarian New York lawyer of note who was a member-at-large on the Executive Council of the USOA.[24] Following a meeting with Brundage on the Helms matter, McGovern reflected on the approach to take with Helms and then wrote to Brundage with his resolutions:

> Since our last meeting I drafted and redrafted until I thought I had a proper conciliatory form of approach to the attorneys for Helms . . . [USOA colleagues] think the lapse of time from 1931 to 1949 would ruin our chances. I realize their point but I am never convinced I am going to be licked when I know I have justice on my side. I am trying conciliation . . . Failing that course, I may decide it would be better to fight and take a beating, if necessary, than to have the people of the U.S. believe we consent to the outrage. At least a fight would show we did what we could.[25]

Adopting a velvet-fist approach, McGovern wrote to Helms's lawyers in Los Angeles. At the same time, an aroused Brundage contacted various American amateur sport and Olympic officials, voicing his displeasure with Helms's abuse of the Olympic words and symbols. His vocal indignation against Helms Bakeries soon came to the attention of Paul Helms himself.

THE HELMS CASE BOILS

In the midst of this controversy suddenly appeared Los Angeles's quest to be considered as a host for future Olympic Games, perhaps in 1952 or 1956. The chair of the committee charged with furthering this possibility was none other than the well-known, well-connected, philanthropic Paul H. Helms, impresario of Olympic Bread. In June 1949 a delegation of amateur athletic officials journeyed to California to hear firsthand of the Los Angeles plan. The delegation was composed of J. Lyman Bingham, assistant to the president of the AAU, and Kenneth "Tug" Wilson, vice-president of the USOA. The meeting took place at the California Club on Sunday afternoon, 19 June. John J. Garland and Bill Hunter and Wilbur Johns, athletic directors of the University of Southern California (USC) and University of California at Los Angeles (UCLA), respectively, also attended.

Most of the discussion focused on the Los Angeles plan to host forthcoming Olympic Games. Inevitably, though, the subject turned to Helms's perceived abuse of Olympic symbols in advertising his business products. In a letter to Brundage Bingham described the meeting's dialogue, noting that

> there was considerable bad feeling over the use Mr. Helms has made of the Olympic insignia. Mr. Helms . . . very graciously explained that it has been in use since the 1932 Olympic Games. He felt that had there been any objections they should have been presented directly to him years ago. He stated that he was familiar with Terry McGovern's correspondence with his attorneys and that he was well pleased with McGovern's attitude. He felt that the attorneys would work out something satisfactory . . . Incidentally, Mr. Helms voiced considerable displeasure at your having written on the subject to various individuals other than himself rather than taking the matter directly to him . . . Throughout the meeting the impression kept getting stronger with me that we should work with Mr. Helms on a friendly basis and take advantage of his willingness and the many opportunities he has to be of value to the Olympic Committee . . . I believe that at the earliest opportunity you should have a talk with Mr. Helms . . . I am sure you will like him and that he will like you. You both have a genuine interest in amateur sport and you cannot be too far apart in your thinking.[26]

Bingham's letter to Brundage contained another important message:

> Mr. Helms stated that he had been prevailed upon and was in a position to make use of the Olympic insignia on a national basis; that he was mad enough at one time to actually put some such plan into operation, but now he had definitely decided to continue his activities to Southern California and that he would definitely promise not to take advantage of his copyright in the other states. The weakness in the position of the Olympic Committee at the present time is that they accepted his $10,000 in 1948 with practically no strings attached being fully aware at the time of the manner in which he has capitalized upon the Olympic insignia ever since 1932.[27]

A copy of Bingham's letter reached McGovern's desk in early July. McGovern sought an amenable agreement between Helms and Brundage rather than have the matter degenerate into court proceedings. He felt that Helms was ready to compromise. Would Brundage? McGovern wrote to the USOA president with a gentle prompt: "Lyman [Bingham] believes he [Helms] will ultimately cease to use the circles, and other phrases that imply our official responsibility for his product, *if* he is continued to be approached in a friendly spirit. I agree with Lyman that it would be well for you to call on him and talk about the welfare of the Olympic movement."[28]

With pressure mounting against Helms, Brundage's tenacious character drove him toward a resolution of the prolonged stalemate. Clearly he thought that Helms's conciliatory manner had fooled Bingham and his colleagues. "I think Helms hypnotized you fellows," wrote Brundage. "He steals our insignia and builds up a fortune, then gives a few dollars to amateur sport and everyone thinks that he is an angel."[29] Brundage directed a brusque note to Helms's colleague W. R. Schroeder, abandoning the usual courtesies. "Dear Schroeder," he wrote, "The United States Olympic Association, of which I am president, has a long standing grievance against Mr. Helms because of his misappropriation and commercialization of Olympic insignia. The grievance has been growing more bitter throughout the years, and it is shared by the International Olympic Committee."[30]

Avery Brundage was not alone in his campaign against attempts to profit commercially from the Olympics; the IOC itself was taking modest steps to encourage protection of the Olympic words and symbols. The July 1949 issue of the *IOC Bulletin* contained a recommendation that all NOCs pay close attention to the dilemma. Further, the NOCs were asked to apply for juridical protection of the Olympic words and symbols in their respective countries.[31] In cases where Olympic words and symbols were being utilized for athletic events that in no way concerned the Olympic Movement or for "commercial purposes," the NOCs were asked to react energetically to stop the abuse.[32] The dilemma for NOCs throughout the world was characterized by the USOA situation. On several occasions over a period of twenty years prior to 1947 the Legislation Committee of the USOA had tried to gain a federal judgment in favor of allowing the USOA to issue federal income tax deduction receipts for contributions made to its program. The retort was always the same: the USOA is a sports organization, not an educational organization; therefore it does not qualify.[33] During the same twenty-year period the Legislation Committee had from time to time discussed taking the necessary steps to protect the USOA and the IOC and their interests regarding the Olympic name, motto, and emblems. No action was ever taken, however. As in the tax deduction matter, the USOA never devoted "the time or the expense necessary to do a professional job of protecting the Olympic name."[34]

Finally the Detroit Olympic Committee, spurred by the fact that it (like Los Angeles) envisioned bidding for the 1952 or 1956 Games, volunteered the services of a professional law firm (Cook, Beake, Miller, Wrock & Cross) to pursue the tax deduction issue. In December 1947 counselor Richard Cross reported that the USOA's quest had finally met with success. The USOA letterhead soon began to announce that contributions made to the organization were tax deductible. The precedent of gaining tax-exempt status had important overtones for resolving the Helms case.

The IOC had renewed the campaign against the ever-increasing misuse of the Olympic words and symbols. The November 1949 *IOC Bulletin* published a list of cases that had been reported. Among them, not surprisingly, was a familiar saga of commercialization—the Helms Bakery Company vs. the USOA: "In the United States of America there is a firm, manufacturing cakes, special breads and so on, and whose name we will not mention as we do not wish to make for it any additional propaganda! This firm has supplied the bread for the American athletes during the London Games. Since that time the firm considered itself entitled to put on all its packing and all its advertisements (which are far from being modest) the Olympic emblems. Our vice-president, Mr. Avery Brundage, has taken the matter up seriously."[35]

IOC president Sigfrid Edström wrote to John J. Garland in Los Angeles, asking him to lodge an official protest against Helms's use of the Olympic marks: "The Olympic circles and the Olympic motto may not be used for commercial purposes. It is against our Olympic Rules, and Los Angeles will never get the Olympic Games as long as this outrage continues."[36] A month later Garland responded to Edström, defending Helms and requesting an explanation regarding the use of the five-ring symbol in other nations for advertising purposes.[37] In fact, though, the IOC had absolutely no authority over use of the Olympic marks for advertising in the United States or any other country except Switzerland, where its headquarters was located. It had failed to register the Olympic marks as Helms himself had done in 1932.

The USOA finally realized that it must pursue legal registry of the Olympic symbols in order to head off future occurrences similar to the Helms case. To the rescue once again came the Detroit law firm, specifically Cross and his company's patent and trademark specialist, Arthur M. Smith, president of the Michigan Patent Law Association. Together Cross and Smith pursued trademark registration initiatives. Cross wrote McGovern in mid-September 1949, outlining a solid position for arguing the USOA's case in the face of Helms's prior use of the marks. "We definitely feel that the United States Olympic Association has the legal and moral right to protect all the intangible elements and properties that are attributes of its name and symbol and it would be remiss for the good of the movement if it were not vigilant and aggressive in enforcing those rights," opined Cross. "We feel that the Association cannot and should not conciliate with the California bakery that is so flagrantly commercializing the Olympic movement, short of demanding an immediate, unequivocal and final cessation of the use of the name, Olympic, when in conjunction with ring and/or motto and/or reference to official status as sponsored by the United States Olympic Association, or in any other manner calculated to mislead or misrepresent identity with the Olympic movement."[38]

BRUNDAGE VS. HELMS

The principal parties in the confrontation, Paul Helms and Avery Brundage, had never directly approached one another. Brundage, whose temper always seemed to rise when Helms's name came up, resisted getting involved personally but satisfied himself by firing broadsides at Helms from a distance and letting McGovern, Bingham, USOA-appointed lawyers, and other amateur sports officials carry on the confrontation. Helms, in turn, listened to envoys sent by Brundage, weighed the views of his lawyer, Charles McDowell, and in general maintained a low profile. The only meeting between the two protagonists occurred in January 1948 at the *Los Angeles Times* Sports Awards Dinner, where Brundage, seated next to Paul Helms at the head table, accepted the Sportsman of the Year Award. The two did not discuss Brundage's position on Helms's use of the Olympic symbols in his product advertising.[39] It was the sixty-year-old Helms who finally broke the stalemate, writing personally to the sixty-two-year-old Brundage in late September 1949. After reminding Brundage of "a most satisfactory conference at the California Club" (the Bingham meeting) and stating that he would meet with McGovern in New York the following month, Helms recounted some of his long history pertinent to Olympic matters in California. At the end of his letter Helms could not resist a remark on the commercialization issue. Referring to Brundage's letter of complaint sent a decade earlier to W. R. Schroeder, managing director of Helms Bakeries, Helms stated: "Our progress is no different today than in 1939—seven years after the 1932 Olympic Games in Los Angeles."[40]

It remained for McGovern, a man of patience and proven legal wisdom, to seek a meeting with Helms, whom he knew only by reputation. McGovern was well aware of the bristly character of Avery Brundage. It might be important to find out what the personal qualities of Paul Helms were. McGovern arranged a meeting with Helms for early October, when

Helms's business interests took him to New York. McGovern liked Helms from the start. The California baker was quiet, friendly, and unassuming, quite the opposite of Avery Brundage. Two meetings took place, each conducted in the cordial atmosphere of McGovern's office. Helms patiently related the history of his bakery's involvement in Olympic matters. Helms, knowing of Brundage's inference that he had "stolen" the symbol, informed McGovern that such statements were inflammatory and that his attorneys had advised him that he could proceed legally against Brundage.[41] He wanted an apology from Brundage, which the crusty USOA leader was not likely to extend. McGovern sent a report of the meeting to Brundage. Most important were its concluding statements: Helms agreed "in principle" to limit his advertising to the local community of Los Angeles and, more importantly, to redesign his advertising emblem to remove identification with the Olympic five-ring symbol and the Olympic motto.[42] Clearly, events now dictated that a meeting between the two antagonists take place.

In December 1949 (four days before Christmas) Brundage, accompanied by counselors Cross and Smith, met with Paul Helms and Paul Helms Jr. and their attorneys, G. E. McDowell and Albert J. Faries, at a luncheon arranged by the senior Helms at the posh California Club in downtown Los Angeles.[43] Against his doctor's advice, the senior Helms had risen from a sickbed to attend the meeting. Following discussions focusing mainly on trademark issues, an agreement was concluded. Upon their return to Detroit Cross and Smith prepared and sent Helms a typed draft of the proposed agreement approved "in principle" by all parties at the Los Angeles meeting.[44] The agreement between the United States Olympic Association and Helms Bakeries established that Helms would henceforth (1) recognize that pertinent to the United States and its territories the Olympic marks were property of the USOA, (2) provide no objection to the USOA seeking registration of the Olympic marks, and (3) discontinue use of Olympic marks in his firm's advertising. A concession by the USOA allowed Helms to retain the right to use the word "Olympic" in connection with his bakery products, except that the phrase "Official Olympic Bakers" had to be exorcised—"Official" went, "Olympic" remained. The first note of conciliation from Brundage was reflected in his short note to Helms following the meeting: "It was a pleasure to see you again last week, and I want to thank you for the enjoyable luncheon that you arranged at the California Club." He continued: "I am also gratified at the results of our conference. It will be a pleasure to report to the United States Olympic Association at its Quadrennial meeting next month that it can expect full cooperation from you. This will be most helpful in our campaign to protect the Olympic insignia."[45]

Although they had reached an agreement in principle, subsequent questions arose that delayed the "final" conclusion of the lengthy case.[46] A series of communications between USOA leaders and their lawyers and Helms and his legal counsel occupied the early months of 1950. Helms produced new advertising labels. The five-ring symbol, motto, and the word "official" in juxtaposition with "Olympic" had disappeared. Still, the USOA quibbled about Helms's advertising use of a red, white, and blue shield, commonly referred to as the "Olympic shield," in association with the word "Olympic." The shield was a distinctive USOA mark, having appeared on the jerseys of American Olympic athletes since the so-called interim Olympic Games in Athens in 1906. The shield also adorned the letterhead of USOA stationery. The shield logo had never been registered by the USOA as a trademark, however, whereas it had been included among the Olympic marks copyrighted by Helms in 1932.[47] A second contentious issue remained—the removal of the Olympic emblems from the facade of the main Helms office building in downtown Los Angeles, a costly renovation.[48] Through it all, Helms's legal counsel advised him to take a hard stand; he had already given up far more than they had advised. Brundage and his lawyers pushed for complete surrender.

January, February, and a good part of March came and went as nitpicking continued between the two parties. McGovern, the conciliator, was convinced that Helms would concede if only the testy Brundage would meet with the bakery owner in a manner other than his usual confrontation. Adopting a philosophical stance, McGovern attempted to prompt Brundage:

> I think it advisable for you to see Helms even if only as an evidence of friendly cooperation for the good of the games. No humans are perfect. Neither I, nor you, nor Helms, nor McDowell . . . Helms has been pretty sick. It would be nice if for that reason alone you greeted his return to health . . . I have repeatedly stated that neither side is entitled to a 100 per cent victory. We have not a clear and unblemished case; neither has Helms. What concerns me most is that lawyers may insist on proving how good lawyers they are, and forgetting that while we do not want to lose face and principle; neither do we want to lose good financial support when we need it . . . I'm always afraid of lawyers. I succeed because I deceive people into thinking I am a sincere friend of anyone who wants to settle things in a way that human frailties can be forgiven and forgotten, at the same time having them understand that when I get in a court battle I expect to win

it. So you see Helms can be a diplomat. Helms is not trying to dodge, but there are items which he wants to save.[49]

Despite McGovern's plea, Brundage's intransigent disposition combined with his busy schedule prevented a meeting with Helms.

THE HELMS CASE RESOLVED

Commencing early in 1950, USOA action focused on two initiatives. McGovern was in charge of both. The first, aimed at incorporating the United States Olympic Association by virtue of a federal act, he delegated to Cross and Smith. Success in that venture would secure trademark and copyright protection for both IOC and USOA marks inside the United States and its territories. The second initiative focused on consummating an agreement with Helms. McGovern himself assumed that responsibility.

The resolution of the Helms case occurred first. Brundage was not particularly disposed toward meeting with Helms; neither were Helms's lawyers keen to have the bakery magnate meet with Brundage. Past experiences had been fraught with uneasiness. Finally McGovern's resolve hardened. In mid-June he wrote Brundage: "I plan to leave for Los Angeles next week to settle the Helms case."[50] Shortly after his arrival in Los Angeles and following meetings with Helms and his counsel McGovern telegraphed Brundage at 1:42 A.M. on 27 June, announcing: "Case settled."[51] A second McGovern telegram was sent to Brundage some nine hours later: "He [Helms] asks no publicity of settlement."[52] Upon his return to New York a week later McGovern wrote to Brundage to report that Helms's lawyers had been smug, reinforced by exhibits in the form of Helms's contract with the 1948 Olympic authorities, which bolstered his legal position immensely.[53] Three months later, in early October 1950, McGovern wrote to Brundage revealing the evidence that in effect had made the final outcome of the case dependent on the goodwill of Helms himself:

I have never revealed (and do not intend to) the evidence Helms' lawyers had to mouse trap Cross and Smith. But they had it. Not way back; but in 1948. Notice in connection with the $10,000 contribution that Helms would use the insignia exactly as he had been; and he conditioned his contribution upon the privilege so to advertise *without any limitation whatsoever*. After the settlement his lawyers turned over to me copies of the documents. No wonder they were angry when Helms ordered them to surrender. During my 50 years of practice, in my safe are placed many writings which would embarrass clients and of which they have never been informed. So let it be with the Helms situation.[54]

McGovern also sent an illuminating report of his Los Angeles sojourn to officers and executive board members of the USOA:

Gentlemen: There will be no future devotion of two-thirds of our meeting discussion time to the Helms case. The Helms case is settled. I went to Los Angeles and Mr. Helms agreed with me there to place the integrity, ideals, and hope of the Olympic faith above commercial, legal and other individual considerations. Mr. Helms conducted himself, at our meeting with his counsel, in a spirit of generosity, cooperation, and quiet dignity. And this in the face of disapproval by his excellent and courteous counsel who were naturally chagrined to give up so much when they, with considerable justification from a legal standpoint, were confident of their position. Mr. Helms has agreed to eliminate the circles, the latin, the words "official Olympic bakers," and the word "Olympic" from the emblem and insignia. All that remains on the shield is "Helms Bread." The above elimination will be carried out on wrappers and trucks and more than 50 other varieties of advertising devices. This work will take much of Mr. Helms' time and a most substantial sum of his money. He also agreed that in any use of the word Olympic external to the shield, he would avoid the use of the word "official" or any other expression which might imply official or interested relation between him and the U.S.O.A. or U.S.O.C. He finally volunteered and signed an agreement to aid, if requested, the U.S.O.A. and U.S.O.C., through his able counsel and at his expense, to protect the integrity of my Washington registration of our Olympic shield, as it stands with the circles and other insignia. Even before I left California, Mr. Helms had begun black outs on signs and the first of the changed wrappers went out to customers. If you are bored you can put this down now. If your curiosity survives, you may read the annexed list of observations.[55]

McGovern had succeeded in tiptoeing through the minefields of strong egos, confrontational tactics, diverse philosophies, and prickly interpersonal relations. Plaudits were quick to come his way. Brundage's were the first: "My compliments to you again! You have accomplished even more than we expected. In view of the consistent success of the McGovern approach perhaps we ought to send you to see Stalin."[56] In reply McGovern wired Brundage some final counsel: "Decidedly advise you arrange see Helms. He admires your courage and honesty. He would like now to be your friend and work with you."[57]

Meanwhile attorneys Cross and Smith made headway in Washington on the USOA incorporation matter. By late February 1950 they had produced a preliminary draft. Arthur Smith wrote to McGovern on the next steps to be taken: "I have considered the tentative draft of the proposed Federal Charter and feel that this matter should be carried forward to a conclusion . . . I have noted a recent report of favorable action given on a bill to incorporate the Girl Scouts. Maybe the Girl Scouts have left Congress in the mood to pass necessary legislation for our proposed incorporation so it may well be that the present time is propitious for completing this work and presenting the proposed bill to Congress."[58]

Indeed, Congress was "in the mood" and on 21 September 1950 ratified an Act to Incorporate the United States Olympic Association. Among a litany of rights, duties, and responsibilities, the act gave the USOA sweeping jurisdiction on Olympic matters within the United States and its territories, including copyright/trademark ownership of its corporate seal (the Olympic shield), interlocking five-ring symbol, motto, and the words "Olympic" and "Olympiad." The act also stated that

> it shall be unlawful for any person within the jurisdiction of the United States to falsely or fraudulently hold himself out as or represent or pretend himself to be a member or an agent for the United States Olympic Association or its subordinate organizations for the purpose of soliciting, collecting, or receiving money or material; or for any person to wear or display the insignia thereof for the fraudulent purpose of inducing the belief that he is at such time a member of or an agent for the United States Olympic Association or its subordinate organizations. It shall be unlawful for any person, corporation, or association, other than the United States Olympic Association or its subordinate organizations and its duly authorized employees and agents for the purpose of trade, theatrical exhibition, athletic performance, and competition or as an advertisement to induce sale of any article whatsoever or attendance at any theatrical exhibition, athletic performance, and competition or for business or charitable purpose to use within the territory of the United States of America and its exterior possessions, the emblems of the United States Olympic Association.[59]

To Brundage's dismay, and despite the strong language of the act, Helms himself was protected from suit even if he persisted in using the Olympic symbols on his commercial products. The act concluded:

> That any person, corporation, or association that actually used, or whose assignor actually used, the said emblems, sign, insignia, or words for any lawful purpose prior to the effective date of this Act, shall not be deemed forbidden by this Act to continue the use thereof for the same purposes and for the same class or classes of goods to which said emblems, sign, insignia, or words have been used lawfully prior therefore.[60]

Although partially satisfied, Brundage remained discomfited by the fact that the act continued to provide license for Helms and the "scandalous" advertising of his bakery goods. Although Brundage and the USOA prevailed in the struggle to sever Helms Bakeries from its exploitation of Olympic marks, it was solely due to the fact that Helms personally had voluntarily agreed to relinquish everything, not because of a court order requiring him to do so.[61] Helms's legal position had in effect been secure. Even so, Brundage could not help but describe his victory as pyrrhic. "Helms has finally capitulated," he wrote to Fred Matthei of the Detroit Olympic Committee.[62]

It is obvious that Helms's right to capitalize commercially on the use of Olympic words and marks had been granted to him by the authority of an Olympic Games Organizing Committee (Los Angeles). The USOA had not been party to the agreement with Helms. But it is difficult to believe that USOA officials hovering over the 1932 Olympic Games could have remained entirely ignorant of the commercialization of Olympic symbols taking place in Los Angeles. In effect Helms's registration of Olympic marks (applied for in 1932 and officially granted in 1938) scooped the USOA, which realized too late that it should long ago have done what Helms did. Consequently the time, energy, and patience of Avery Brundage, leader of the Olympic Movement in the United States, were sorely tried in trying to resolve the issue. In the end it can be argued that Helms sacrificed his financial interests largely because he was a staunch patriot when it came to the nation's Olympic fortunes and wanted to help rather than hinder the process by which U.S. athletes competed at the Games. This ulterior motive led him to concede to USOA demands, even though the legal issues were decidedly in his favor. The USOA had learned a lesson, albeit a painful one: it must remain on guard where the subject of commercial exploitation of Olympic marks was concerned.

The Helms case, although establishing a landmark precedent, did not stem the tide of Olympic exploitation in the United States by the mid-twentieth century. The financial benefit derived from developing a link between a commercial product and the Olympic Games had become all too evident. In 1950, for instance, 148 industrial and mercantile establishments in Los Angeles alone assured the public through newspaper advertisements, telephone directory advertising pages, and even signs and facades on buildings that they provided "Olympic" goods, wares, and merchandise.[63]

Despite this, it was Brundage who sagely pointed out what the new act would mean for the future of the Modern Olympic Movement. In conveying his appreciation to Matthei and the Detroit Olympic Committee he proclaimed: "The International Olympic Committee as well as the United States Olympic Association can never thank you enough for your help in this great victory, which will serve as a precedence [*sic*] for Olympic Committees in all parts of the world in their effort to prevent commercialization of Olympic words and insignia."[64] On this point the future president of the IOC was correct: the precedent was indeed Olympian.

CHAPTER 3

SHOWDOWN IN MELBOURNE, 1956

Evolution of the Olympic Television Rights Concept

The rise of the mass media and their fascination with sport probably contributed more to the global popularity of the Modern Olympic Games than any other single factor. Captive audiences proved enticing to commercial interests seeking to promote products to consumers. Most business advertisements appear in newspapers and magazines or on radio and television. The print media have always displayed interest in the Olympic Games as a newsworthy event, dating back to the very first Games in Athens in 1896. Newspapers and periodicals also provided the first consumer advertising links to the Games, followed by radio and ultimately television. At the outset of the new millennium business is beginning to grapple with the ramifications of the next era of consumer advertising technology: cyberspace. It should not be forgotten that each medium of communication, from the newspaper to the Internet, is a competitor for the attention of the consumer. This reality places the IOC and its Olympic "products" in a favorable bargaining position.

Before commercial enterprise could exploit the Olympic audience market the IOC needed to develop the concept of television rights and policy governing their sale. This chapter addresses the IOC's first attempt to formulate policy concerning the sale of television rights and the procedure for distributing resulting revenue. The IOC's effort, spearheaded by Avery Brundage, occurred in the aftermath of a protracted squabble between organizers of the 1956 Melbourne Olympic Games and executives representing the world's television networks and cinema newsreel companies.

Prior to the Melbourne Games the fledgling nature of the television industry largely precluded the pursuit of revenue from the sale of Olympic television rights by Organizing Committees. Indeed, no policy governing their sale existed. Melbourne changed all that: officials there demanded payment from the television networks and cinema newsreel companies for the use of Olympic footage. They argued that prospective profit from an

Olympic film marketed at the conclusion of the Games would be compromised if the world's television audience and moviegoers witnessed extensive coverage from Melbourne, eschewing the notion of granting the networks free access to the footage. Television and cinema industry executives countered that newsreel companies owed nothing for access to the footage. They intended to use it merely for news programming. Besides, they lobbied, the news footage would be dated by the time of its delivery to their audiences (since satellite technology and the ability to transmit live event coverage vast distances did not emerge until the 1960s). Melbourne organizers and their counterpart negotiators working on behalf of U.S. and European television networks and cinema newsreel companies failed to settle their differences. Negotiations did not result in an agreement on the number of minutes of Olympic broadcast footage accessible to the networks and cinema newsreel companies on a daily basis without the need for financial compensation.

Avery Brundage lamented the failed negotiations and, with some prompting from IOC members Lords Killanin and Burghley, resolved to develop policy on Olympic television rights to be included in the *Olympic Charter*. The result of this decision was the reformulation of Rule 49 on publicity in 1958 to include directions to Organizing Committees on the sale of Olympic television rights. It proved an arduous challenge, not just in terms of crafting the policy but also in securing the compliance of the 1960 Squaw Valley and Rome Olympic Organizing Committees.

Even though Brundage's business background led him not to turn his back on this form of commercial revenue for the IOC and its partner organizations, he worried about its impact on the image of the Olympic Movement. To diminish his personal concerns on this point he ceded the right to negotiate television contracts to the Organizing Committees. This, he believed, shielded the IOC from disputes with the networks concerning money, which would inevitably draw the attention of the media. He retained the IOC's right to approve all contracts and distribute the money at its discretion, however. Together, these initiatives formed a recipe for conflict between the IOC and Organizing Committees.

RADIO BROADCASTING AND THE OLYMPICS

Radio predated television as a mass media instrument for raising global awareness of the Olympic Games. Hence the impact of radio broadcasting and associated advertising cannot be ignored in any commercial history of the Modern Olympic Movement.

When Frank Conrad, a Westinghouse engineer, pioneered public broadcasting by establishing the world's first radio station (KDKA in Pittsburgh, Pennsylvania) in November 1920, he set in motion a series of events that produced an explosion of similar initiatives. An entirely new industry was born and with it a zeal to exploit consumer markets through advertising. Scarcely two months after Conrad's epic KDKA initiative some thirty similar licenses were granted to operate radio stations in America. By May 1922 this figure had increased to 200; by early 1923, to 576. Following on the heels of Conrad's achievement, Horne's Department Store in Pittsburgh installed a demonstration radio receiver device, purchased newspaper advertising to publicize the phenomenon, and began selling wireless receivers. In 1922 alone, over 100,000 radio sets were sold in the United States.[1] An explosion of new radio stations and radio-set sales dominated consumer life in American entertainment culture in the 1920s and 1930s. The radio also reached the rest of the world in rapid fashion. For instance, the British Broadcasting Corporation (BBC) was established in 1922. On the other side of the world in Australia radio broadcasting began in 1923. The relationship between the development of the radio and sports programming was almost instantaneous. From the beginning of the history of radio, reporting on sporting events was a theme of great interest to both listeners and consumer advertisers. Professional boxing matches, major league baseball, and college football, in particular, spearheaded sports on American radio in the 1920s. Overseas, horse-racing, cricket, rugby, and even rowing matches were reported to a radio audience eager for the latest in sporting news.[2]

It is of some curiosity that radio produced only limited influence in advancing public interest in the Olympic Games. The technical improvements in radio equipment and transmissions occurred too slowly.[3] By the time radio technology permitted the transmission of live accounts of the Games, television technology was in its pioneering stages of development. The Paris Games of 1924 and the Amsterdam Games of 1928 received little notice from radio; only scattered news briefs were heard. In 1932 in Los Angeles the prospect of live radio coverage of Olympic events prompted fear in the Organizing Committee that ticket sales to events being aired by radio would be affected. Hollywood's film industry also opposed live radio broadcasts of the Los Angeles Games, fearing that its vigorous financial and material support of the Games would be undercut by the relatively new competing entertainment industry. Two days before the opening ceremony Los Angeles officials concluded an agreement with the National Broadcasting Company (NBC) and the Columbia Broadcasting System (CBS) that permitted the two organizations to provide limited Olympic coverage in the form of short late evening news summaries. Perhaps in part because of the limited radio attention to the Los Angeles Games, ticket sales soared, crowds flocked to the competition venues, and despite the Great Depression that gripped Los Angeles and the rest of the nation in the early 1930s the Games realized a profit for the organizers for the first time in Olympic history.[4]

Probably the most elaborate set of circumstances surrounding radio broadcast of an Olympic Games occurred in Berlin in 1936. Technicians in Berlin created an elaborate short-wave radio system that reached forty countries during the Games. German authorities estimated that some 3,000 reports, eyewitness accounts, and commentaries had been rendered by the end of the Games.[5] The Olympic Games were suspended from 1940 to 1948 due to World War II, but by the time of the first postwar Games in London in 1948 television was in the beginning stages of relegating radio to second place in public communications. It was television that exploited the visual quality of the Olympic Games, fostering their eventual status as the world's most viewed event.

THE BIRTH OF TELEVISION AND THE OLYMPIC GAMES

During the 1920s and 1930s scientists such as John Logie Baird, Philo Farnsworth, Vladimir Zworykin, August Karolus, and Denes von Mihály pursued the development of an alternative broadcast medium to radio. Their pioneering work in time revolutionized the communications field. Leadership provided by the Radio Corporation of America (RCA), BBC, and Nazi government officials also contributed to development of television technology, resulting in the telecast of Olympic events.[6] Germany's propaganda minister, Joseph Goebbels, took a keen interest in the medium. The calculating Goebbels, believing that television might serve as an effective propaganda tool for delivering the image and oratory of Adolf Hitler to the homes of thousands of German citizens, prodded the development of the world's first public television service in March 1935, an event largely motivated by Germany's desire to prevent the British and Americans from achieving the same goal.[7]

Delayed television coverage of the Garmisch-Partenkirchen Olympic Winter Games in February 1936 marked one of the service's earliest initiatives; this was the first televised coverage of the Olympics. The opening ceremonies of the Berlin Summer Olympic Games some six months later represented the first opportunity for televiewers to witness *live* coverage of an Olympic event.[8] The summary report of the Berlin Organizing Committee revealed that four competition sites, especially the Olympic stadium and the swimming facility, drew the interest of German television producers. Over a period of 138 telecast hours 175 events were covered.[9] Some 162,000 people watched events telecast live and delayed in television venues located in the immediate Berlin area in what might be best described as a closed-circuit television format. The result was less than spectacular. As a leading British newspaper reported the event, the pictures "resembled a very faint, highly under-exposed photographic film, and were so much worse than ordinary transmissions from a studio that many turned away in disappointment."[10]

During the planning stages for the 1940 Summer Olympics television matters also received attention from organizers. In 1935 Tokyo was named as host city for the 1940 Summer Olympic Games. By 1937 political turmoil in the Far East had escalated into full-scale war between Japan and China, prompting Tokyo to withdraw as Olympic host. In 1938 the privilege of hosting the 1940 Summer Games was given to Helsinki, Finland; the Winter Games, to Garmisch-Partenkirchen. In 1939 the Helsinki OCOG reported that "for the benefit of those who cannot secure seats in the Olympic stadium, television apparatus—with images about 6 ½ by 8 ½ feet—will be set up outside the stadium in four big tents accommodating 10,000 persons."[11] The Finns need not have worried about television plans. By the end of 1939 they themselves were at war with their Soviet neighbors. The Winter and Summer Games of 1940 and 1944 were canceled. World War II obliterated Olympic affairs until after the cessation of hostilities in 1945.[12]

In August 1945 Sigfrid Edström, acting IOC president in the wake of Henri Baillet-Latour's death in 1942, convened the Executive Board in London, its first meeting since May 1939. Reporting the results of the meeting in a circular letter dated 1 September 1945, he noted that in addition to himself only Lord Aberdare (England) and Brundage were able to attend.[13] Along with affirming Edström's recommendation that Brundage should be made second vice-president, the three-member meeting of the Executive Board unanimously agreed that the 1948 Olympic Games should take place.[14] A postal ballot of the membership confirmed a recommendation that London and St. Moritz serve as the respective sites of the 1948 Summer and Olympic Winter Games.[15]

On 3 September 1946 Edström and IOC members convened in Lausanne for the organization's first postwar session. Of the seventy-three members who belonged to the IOC after the close of the London Session in 1939, only fifty-one remained alive and only seventeen were able to make the journey to Lausanne. The first order of business was to elect a new

IOC president. A motion was put forth that Edström, who was not present, be acclaimed. With hardly any debate the session approved the motion and also confirmed Brundage as first vice-president.[16]

Returning to a sense of normalcy after seven years of moribund status, the IOC immediately addressed its principal task: the staging of the Olympic Games. The first postwar Winter Games were opened on 30 January 1948 by Swiss president Enrico Celio as a symbol of "a new world of peace and goodwill."[17] Some seven hundred athletes, male and female, from twenty countries took part in the St. Moritz Games. Except for the warmer-than-expected conditions, they were staged without financial or logistical difficulty. After all, Switzerland had experienced none of the destruction of the war suffered by its European neighbors. In fact it had profited immensely.

Hosting the Summer Olympic Games in a country with widespread shortages and a series of economic crises was quite another matter. The London OCOG, under the leadership of Lord David Burghley,[18] labored mightily to control the costs associated with the Games. The Olympic Village was eliminated; athletes were housed in schools, military camps, and private homes. The IOC allowed the organizers to cancel events for which fewer than six countries entered competitors. In an effort to generate money to finance the Summer Games, London negotiated the sale of various Olympic rights, including exclusive film rights to the J. Arthur Rank Corporation in exchange for a substantial donation.[19] The 1948 London Games marked the first time that a domestic television network (the BBC) agreed to pay an OCOG for broadcasting rights. The BBC negotiated to pay 1,000 guineas (about 3,000 U.S. dollars) for the right to provide live and delayed coverage of all Olympic events.[20] Even though the BBC signal reached as far as the Channel Islands almost 150 miles away, the broadcast focused on the approximately 80,000 television sets owned primarily by individuals in the vicinity of London. The scope of the project paled in comparison to the Berlin initiative in 1936 in terms of total telecast hours (a mere 64) but average audiences numbered 500,000.[21] At the London Games the IOC Session convened to consider several changes to the *Olympic Charter.* One addition had important ramifications for Olympic commercialism in the future. The new *Charter* declared the IOC the exclusive owner of the five-ring Olympic symbol and the motto *Citius, Altius, Fortius.*

At the annual IOC Session held in 1947 in Stockholm the 1952 Summer Games were awarded to Helsinki, the Winter Games to Oslo.[22] Norway, though it had suffered occupation by German military forces during World War II, was spared from most of the gross destruction inflicted on greater Europe. The Oslo Games occurred without much fanfare. Helsinki's challenge was greater. The city, still suffering the ill effects of the prolonged and savage war, was neither willing nor able to stage opulent Games. The Helsinki Games, described as the "poor man's Olympics," were marked by improvisation.[23] A sales department was established to sell various rights to do on-site business at the Games. Further rights were awarded to eighteen companies from eleven countries for donating "value-in-kind" products ranging from food for athletes to flowers for medal winners.[24] Among the companies involved were Coca-Cola (of France) and Nestlé and Omega (both of Switzerland). Despite the financial restrictions the Helsinki Games were praised for their "exemplary precision" and above all for the "great hospitality of the Finnish people."[25]

The Helsinki IOC Session will be remembered for a number of debates, but none more important in shaping the Modern Olympic Movement than the election of a new president. Edström was almost eighty-two years of age. Assisted by a cane whenever he was on his feet, he was adamant about stepping down as president. There were several potential candidates as his successor, including Avery Brundage. Though the Executive Board recommended Brundage, a number of IOC members were hesitant about an American serving as president, particularly one who even then demonstrated a gruff and intransigent persona. They proposed England's Lord Burghley. In the secret balloting process that followed, Brundage finally emerged the winner.[26] Brundage, noted for his fanatical devotion to Olympic ideals and zealous protection of amateurism, led the IOC through the next twenty years.

EARLY IOC DISCUSSIONS OF TELEVISION REVENUE

During the summer months of 1955 Michael Morris (the Lord Killanin), IOC member in Ireland, broached the subject of commercial television revenue to Avery Brundage.[27] Only two months had passed since Bunny Ahearne, an official with the International Ice Hockey Federation, had raised the issue at a meeting of the IOC Executive Board in Paris.[28] The Executive Board took no action, but it seems clear that Ahearne was interested in positioning the ISFs to share in the distribution of any future Olympic television revenue. Claims to television revenue embroiled Brundage in many a lengthy debate in the 1960s. Lord Killanin, a "working peer" with experience in journalism, business, and film-making, viewed the television medium as a lucrative source of funds for amateur sport.[29] In time television revenue served a pivotal role in IOC budgets established during his term as president (1972–80). The growing dependence on television money during the latter years of Brundage's term and through-out Killanin's term forced the IOC to seek alternative revenue sources. In 1955, however, Brundage, too, envisioned the emerging sport television market as a useful tool for Olympic administrators.

It is unthinkable that Killanin's approach or Ahearne's brief mention of the subject in Paris prompted Brundage's initial consideration of televi-sion as a source of funds for the IOC. Brundage monitored the growth of the sport television market in the United States in the post–World War II years. As early as 1940 he was well aware of the notice that live sports tele-casts had been accorded in the United States. In May 1939 RCA produced a telecast of a Columbia–Princeton University baseball game. Even though a *New York Times* writer judged the telecast less than a critical success when he compared the players' appearance on the television screen to "little white flies," coverage of basketball, hockey, football, and tennis soon fol-lowed; sport in general gained a solid foothold as a component of televi-sion programming.[30] Following the war U.S. television executives recog-nized sport as an important element of programming that served to spur the sale of television sets, a crucial element of the industry's attempt to es-tablish itself as a home entertainment medium.[31] Advertisers, too, increas-ingly viewed sport programming as a meaningful promotional link to con-sumers.

During the postwar era U.S. businesses purchased television rights to specific sport events in exchange for exclusive advertising privileges. The value of television rights to sports programming soared. Between 1947 and 1950 the fees paid for television rights to the World Series, for instance, in-creased tenfold. By the end of the 1940s Major League Baseball reaped the benefits of an $800,000 contract. In 1950 Major League Baseball peddled five-year rights to the World Series (1951 to 1956) for $6 million.[32] Notre Dame University received $100,000 in exchange for television rights to its home football schedule in 1949. The following year the University of Penn-sylvania, a school with less national prominence, sold the rights to its home football schedule for $75,000.[33] As president of the United States Olympic Committee during the early era of sport television rights Brundage also at-tempted to draw upon this source of funds.

All NOCs must engage in fund-raising. Each committee is responsible for logistical arrangements pertaining to its team's participation in an Olympic festival. Transportation, accommodation, and clothing costs ne-cessitate significant lobbying in corporate, government, and public sectors. As president of the USOC and vice-president of the International Olympic Committee (1948–52) Brundage considered television a viable source of revenue for the USOC. Prior to the 1948 London Summer Games he unsuccessfully attempted to negotiate a contract for the sale of television rights to the U.S. Olympic Track and Field Trials. Disappointed, he nevertheless remained keen on future prospects. He supported an Olympic Telethon hosted by Bing Crosby and Bob Hope to raise funds for the 1952 U.S. Summer Olympics Team. Brundage also offered to negotiate a U.S. television contract for the 1952 Helsinki Organizing Committee in exchange for a share of the proceeds payable to the USOC. Though a contract never did materialize,[34] any attempt on Brundage's part to avoid dealing with Killanin's 1955 suggestion on television would have been surprising in this context.

Acting upon Killanin's advice, Brundage directed a circular letter to members of the IOC Executive Board: Armand Massard (France), David Lord Burghley (Great Britain), Prince Axel of Denmark, S. E. Mohammed Taher Pacha (Egypt), Miguel A. Moenck (Cuba), and Count Paolo Thaon de Revel (Italy). Referring to the "huge potential value of television rights," Brundage informed Executive Board members that additional revenue could assist the IOC in its efforts to promote Olympic ideals and provide for the long overdue and desperately needed expansion of the headquarters staff in Lausanne.[35]

Yet Brundage fretted about the impact that a relationship with the television industry might have on the IOC's image as an organization that purposefully had distanced itself from commercialism. What would the Baron Pierre de Coubertin, founder of the IOC and staunch opponent of commercialism, have thought about the sale of commercial television rights? Brundage, who shared this idealized view of the Olympic Movement, certainly gave some thought to whether the acceptance of television revenue compromised Coubertin's beliefs. "I'm not sure that we should ever get into business," mused Brundage, "but on the other hand certainly we should not give millions of dollars away."[36] His internal conflict on this matter was not resolved until nearly the end of his presidency.

David Lord Burghley, a former Olympian (1928 and 1932) and a member of the IOC Executive Board, pledged his support for an initiative designed to improve the financial status of the cash-strapped IOC. "I quite agree with your [Brundage's] comments on television," noted Burghley. "This would seem to be a splendid source of revenue to tap for the IOC and its work."[37] Killanin, too, was gratified that his idea had drawn Brundage's attention toward formulating policy in this area. "What is important," concluded Killanin, "is that this source of high revenue should be diverted to the future of amateur sport, and not to the pockets of commercial enterprises."[38]

While Brundage seemed willing to accept television revenue as a source of future income for the IOC, his decision to remain aloof from the protracted negotiations surrounding Melbourne television rights reflected his lingering concern over the potential damage to the Olympic Movement's pristine image if the IOC became entangled in disputes involving commercial organizations. Brundage's biographer Allen Guttmann has noted that "Brundage was not entranced by the sugarplum dream of television revenue."[39] But perhaps some qualification of this assertion is advisable. Brundage's experience with television negotiations in the United States in the years immediately preceding his election to the office of IOC president in 1952, together with his openness to Killanin's approach, indicated that he greatly valued television's revenue potential for the Olympic Movement. For Brundage, cash for the Olympic Movement and his convictions about Olympic tradition and ideals presented a paradigm of conflict.

RULE 49 AND EARLY SIGNS OF OLYMPIC TELEVISION POLICY AS A SOURCE OF CONFLICT

Six months after the conclusion of the 1956 Olympic Games Lewis Luxton, deputy chairman of the Melbourne Organizing Committee, reflected: "A great deal could be written of the negotiations between the Organizing Committee in Melbourne and the proprietors of television networks and cinema newsreel companies. To write such a history would probably not be profitable, because at the end of writing one would have to come to the conclusion that the whole operation was handled extremely badly by both sides of the argument."[40] Luxton's contemporary assessment understandably lacked insight into future events and television's massive influence on the Olympic Movement from both a promotional and revenue standpoint. Studying the circumstances that led to a breakdown of negotiations and a virtual television and newsreel blackout of the 1956 Summer Olympics is critical to understanding how and why the IOC became involved with television matters.

Because of the rapidly developing status of the Olympic Games, the problem-filled discussion of the television and cinema newsreel industries' right of access to Olympic events as arms of the world's media placed officials representing these groups and members of the Melbourne Organizing Committee on opposite sides of the negotiating table. International television networks, specifically major American and European companies, eschewed extensive telecast operations because of the time required to transport footage from Australia to Europe and the United States and the inherent "staleness" of the delayed coverage. The opportunity to provide accounts of Olympic developments on their morning, midday, and evening newscasts intrigued news departments affiliated with the television networks, however. Cinema newsreel networks also sought to enhance their motion picture previews with Olympic reports. Pleading budgetary restrictions, executives in the television news industry lobbied Melbourne Organizing Committee officials for royalty-free access to nine minutes of Olympic film each day. Melbourne organizers believed that this concession threatened the commercial viability of the Olympic film to be sold for profit in the months following the festival. Negotiators failed to bridge the gap to bring about an agreement.

The failed efforts of Australian organizers and television network executives to conclude an agreement on the role of television in Melbourne is a starting point for dealing with the IOC's relationship with the television industry. Olympic drama first appeared on television in 1936, and a select number of Organizing Committees in the ensuing years received a token amount of money in exchange for permitting television and/or cinema newsreel companies to cover Olympic events. It was the unsuccessful Melbourne negotiations, however, that heralded the establishment of the concept of Olympic television rights.

Avery Brundage, the IOC's president, resisted interfering in the negotiation process. But he was determined to prevent a recurrence of the problems encountered by Melbourne organizers. Brundage launched a thorough investigation of the television industry that resulted in the expansion of the IOC's rule on publicity (Rule 49). In 1958 his efforts resulted in the establishment of the IOC's first official policy governing the sale of Olympic television rights. Consequently all television and cinema news agencies were granted access to nine minutes of royalty-free daily coverage; but television networks seeking exclusive rights to more extensive coverage would have to pay for this enhanced level of programming.

The Melbourne negotiations, Avery Brundage's ensuing investigation of the television industry, and the recrafting of Rule 49 revealed Brundage's internal conflict concerning television revenue. He harbored severe reservations about exposing the Olympics to the taint of commercialism. Brundage also believed, prophetically as it turned out, that available monies accruing from the sale of television rights would promote conflict among Olympic officials. As an astute businessman committed to the propagation of Olympic ideals, however, he believed the television medium might provide two potential benefits: revenue and publicity.[41] In order to protect the IOC from direct contact with commercial agencies while at the same time providing the Olympic Movement with access to television money, Rule 49 enunciated two principles: (1) that future OCOGs would negotiate television rights deals and (2) that the IOC would rule on how the money would be distributed. American and Italian organizers of the 1960 Winter and Summer Olympic festivals in Squaw Valley and Rome, respectively, resisted the implementation of this policy in what would be the first of numerous skirmishes between the IOC and OCOGs concerning Olympic television policy.

As a result of his decision to devise a policy for future negotiations to avoid the difficulties experienced by Melbourne's negotiators and at the same time welcome television revenue Brundage embarked on a veritable odyssey replete with conflict, administrative challenges, and frustrations. Throughout his IOC presidency (1952–72) he struggled with problems caused by the Olympic Movement's need for money, his philosophical misgivings about commercialism, and the internecine arguments that television money provoked among the IOC, OCOGs, NOCs, and ISFs.

THE MELBOURNE NEGOTIATIONS

The Organizing Committees for the 1956 Winter and Summer Olympic festivals adopted radically different methods of approaching their relationships with the television industry. Technological advances in television broadcasting allowed live transmission of the opening ceremonies of the Cortina Winter Games to eight European countries. Executives of Radio Audizoni Italia (RAI) and members of the Winter Olympic Games Organizing Committee invested substantial funds into the construction of facilities that would permit extensive international coverage through live telecasts and newsreel footage. Although Cortina organizers demanded no compensation from foreign networks for the right to cover the Games, television and newsreel networks from several countries contributed to the fund for film processing and construction of the necessary transmission facilities and studio equipment.[42]

The Melbourne Organizing Committee, under the leadership of Wilfrid S. Kent-Hughes, pursued remuneration for the right to televise the summer Olympic competitions. This clashed with the position of foreign television and newsreel network executives who championed the right of their companies to enjoy open access to the Olympics as a news event, access traditionally extended to the print media. Despite being confronted by an agitated Australian media community that aggressively lobbied him to grant television and newsreel footage free of charge in order to publicize the country, Kent-Hughes and his colleagues on the Melbourne Organizing Committee were resolute. Even pressure from Australian government authorities to concede to network demands failed to shake their resolve.[43]

Free access, they maintained, endangered the economic viability of the committee's official Olympic film targeted for commercial distribution following the festival.[44] Peter Whitchurch, the filmmaker in charge of the Olympic project, later informed Brundage: "If the newsreels had been allowed their requested 9 minutes per day for 15 days, their total output would have been 2 hours and 15 minutes." The commercial film prepared for distribution to theater audiences, he reported, was of a shorter duration.[45] The search for a compromise solution agreeable to both parties proved fruitless. This issue, concluded a rather wistful Lewis Luxton, was the "rock upon which the ship foundered."[46]

Following Melbourne's initial consideration of the television and film issues in 1954, U.S. television networks decided against undertaking any large-scale reproduction of the 1956 Summer Olympics. Kent-Hughes and Luxton pursued other channels in order to offset some of the Organizing Committee's expenses. In 1955 Luxton negotiated a tentative contract with Associated Re-Diffusion, a London-based company, for exclusive film rights to the Melbourne Olympics. While U.S. television networks declined to mount a major production of the Games or entertain the thought of a series of short films because of the logistical problems imposed by the three-day flight time between Melbourne and New York, they asserted that no single company should possess exclusive film rights.[47] They advanced their right to cover the Games free of charge as a news event, which would not be possible if the Organizing Committee failed to distinguish newsfilm from the rights granted to Associated Re-Diffusion or opted to charge a fee for news footage. Foreign news agencies shared this view. Executives within the newsfilm industry rallied together to retain this privilege, which they viewed as sacrosanct.[48]

In the wake of Luxton's bombshell, administrative officers from the Australian Broadcasting Commission, BBC, Fox-Movietone News, Cinesound Review Newsreel, the National Broadcasting Company, and United Press considered their options. Collectively, representatives forwarded a bluntly worded document to the Melbourne Organizing Committee asserting their right of access to news coverage of the festival without payment.[49] Subsequent meetings in the United States and Great Britain yielded similar stances.[50] The newsfilm industry, claimed its representatives, sought nothing more than the rights accorded to print journalists and still photographers. "I think that you will agree that the whole world would be aghast if the right of newspapers and other older news media to cover the games were ever to be put on the auction bloc," Roger Tatarian of United Press Association wrote Brundage, "yet this is apparently being contemplated in the case of television coverage of the Melbourne Games . . .

despite the fact that television is only another arm of the press." Since the IOC upheld the right of the print journalism industry to free access, "it would certainly be a contradiction in that principle," concluded Tatarian, "for another branch of the press to be denied the same privilege, just because it is a newer branch."[51]

Henry Lawrenson of Australian Movietone News and Ken Hall of Cinesound Review Newsreel reiterated this message when they reminded Kent-Hughes in April 1956 that the newsfilm industry would not retreat from its firmly established position. "We trust that you and the members of the Committee will understand very clearly," wrote Lawrenson and Hall, "that a matter of definite principle is at stake—i.e. no payment for news coverage of anything . . ."[52] Using reason rather than rhetoric, they pointed out that newsfilm companies and news departments affiliated with television networks lacked funds for this unplanned budgetary expense since such organizations finalized their budgets at least twelve months in advance. Their limited news coverage offered no possibility for financial profit. Shane Cahill asserts that the U.S. networks adopted their stand as a result of ongoing discussions concerning the possible emergence of Pay-TV. In short, the networks took a rearguard, protectionist stance in claiming free access to the Olympic Games.[53] Making little headway with Kent-Hughes and the Melbourne Organizing Committee, negotiators representing the newsfilm companies pressed forward in their attempt to draw Brundage into the discussions.

William McAndrew, NBC news director, informed Brundage that the perceived wealth of television networks complicated the negotiation process. The perception that the networks were awash with money was "a most unfortunate and untrue canard," wrote McAndrew.[54] While it was true that large salaries were paid to stars such as Milton Berle, Bob Hope, and Mary Martin, news departments did not possess large budgetary resources. Moreover, the sizable contracts consummated for the privilege of telecasting World Series games or major boxing events were based on the concept of live exclusivity, a factor not present in any contemplated news coverage of the Melbourne Games. To consider the market value of delayed and limited news coverage of the Olympic Games somehow comparable to the value of a live telecast of the Rose Bowl or some other major sport event, stated McAndrew, demonstrated a misunderstanding of the sport television milieu.

Brundage considered McAndrew's position and responded with a number of cogent questions. Though not inclined to interfere in the ongoing squabble and the affairs of Melbourne, he sought a solution to the problem in advance of the 1960 Winter and Summer Games scheduled for

Squaw Valley and Rome, respectively. Informing McAndrew that Melbourne required significant funds in order to stage the festival successfully, he pledged his support for the OCOG's demand for financial contribution from the television networks. At what point, Brundage asked McAndrew, did news coverage become entertainment? Second, what assurances were given Melbourne officials that news organizations would refrain from editing their coverage into some form of commercial package to rival the Olympic film?[55]

McAndrew, sensing an opportunity to advance his side's negotiating position, indicated that a reasonable time limit on daily news coverage could be established. He argued that a show qualified as an entertainment package if it had been specifically scheduled for the purpose of displaying Olympic updates. Since any coverage of the Melbourne Games was intended for normally scheduled newscasts and standard previews shown in cinemas prior to the feature-length motion pictures, one can understand McAndrew's stance; he did not consider the networks' proposed coverage as a form of entertainment requiring financial remuneration. Any attempt to package their coverage into a commercial context, offered McAndrew, would require the authorization of the IOC.[56]

In April 1956 executives from the BBC, Australian Movietone News, and Cinesound Review Newsreel, who had been entrusted by the U.S. networks to carry out negotiations on their behalf, offered a proposal to Melbourne that officials accepted in principle. They requested three minutes of royalty-free footage per day. The Melbourne OCOG sought to delay final negotiations, however, until all arrangements pertaining to production of the Olympic film had been finalized. This delay proved unfortunate. When Paul Talbot, the Melbourne Organizing Committee's chief negotiator on broadcast matters, reopened discussions in July, the promising proposal offered three months earlier unraveled. Access to three minutes of newsfilm satisfied cinema newsreel companies, but television news departments held out for nine minutes of film that could be distributed equally across their morning, midday, and evening telecasts. Kent-Hughes did not favor granting this degree of access to the television networks, but Talbot appeared somewhat more conciliatory, although he noted that an agreement hinged upon Melbourne gaining assurance that profits to be derived from the sale of the Olympic film remained secure. As it turned out, such guarantees were not forthcoming. Melbourne officials learned that the demands of the television networks threatened prospects for revenue from the lucrative U.S. market.[57]

A worldwide advertising campaign launched by newsreel companies publicizing upcoming coverage of the 1956 Melbourne Olympics revealed a misplaced optimism that Melbourne negotiators would withdraw their opposition to the television networks' position and their insistence on editorial control in the face of continued pressure and the loss of an opportunity to publicize Australia.[58] J. P. Meroz, general director of the Société Suisse de Radio Diffusion, complained loudly that the Melbourne organizers had reneged on an agreement for access to nine minutes of newsfilm per day.[59] George Griffith Jr. of Hoyts Theatres Ltd. (Melbourne) bitterly criticized Kent-Hughes's desire for editorial control of Olympic news clips, thereby preventing international companies from tailoring footage to the interests of their national audiences.[60] Melbourne OCOG officials held fast to their original offer of three minutes of newsfilm, asserting that any further compromise would set a dangerous precedent prejudicial to the financial interests of future OCOGs.[61] The Games passed with virtually no international television coverage.

In Australia three channels in Melbourne provided live telecasts of the Games. Daily coverage was permitted only from sold-out venues. Heavy ticket sales, however, allowed for thorough telecasting of the track and field events. Sydneysiders viewed delayed coverage. Television stations owned by the Australian Broadcasting Commission had only recently initiated operations. In the United States a small number of independent television stations carried six 30-minute "packaged" programs produced by Paul Talbot's company, Fremantle Overseas Radio. Though Melbourne received only a nominal fee for the U.S. programming, petrol conglomerate Ampol paid the committee £1,000 (Australian) for the privilege of linking its advertising to the Olympic Games.[62] Lewis Luxton believed that the restricted coverage reflected poorly upon both the Organizing Committee and the television and newsreel negotiators.[63] The fallout from this failed process prompted *New York Times* columnist Jack Gould to observe that "the Olympic Games as an institution, Australia as a nation and television as a medium of the free world all have suffered as a result of the consequences of the extensive blackout."[64]

While the sense of regret penetrated deep within the television and cinema newsreel industries, executives accepted little blame for the bitter impasse in negotiations. If the organizers had granted the television news industry the same rights provided to still photographers and print journalists, namely free access, stated George Griffith Jr., the problems would have been avoided.[65] Angered by the IOC's unwillingness to support the interests of the television news industry during the Melbourne debate, a number of U.S. executives—including Harry Robert, sports editor of Tele-News, Frank Donghi of CBS, and Leonard Allen of NBC—ventured that "some soul searching is in order for the [International] Olympic Committee and this seems to be a good time for it." They viewed the IOC's rigid enforcement of amateur rules that prevented athletes from deriving income from their athletic skills as hypocritical in light of its tacit approval of the actions of Melbourne officials who sought to "put these skills to work for great financial gain for their own tills."[66] This stinging criticism pointed directly at an element of Brundage's unease—commercial involvement with the Olympic Movement.

BRUNDAGE STUDIES THE SPORT TELEVISION MARKETPLACE

To Avery Brundage's credit, he recognized the need to become more conversant with the operations of the television industry before attempting to structure appropriate television policy. In the months following the Melbourne Games he continued the information-gathering and consultation process that he had pledged to undertake at the 1956 IOC General Session in Cortina.[67] At the Cortina Session IOC members engaged in a lengthy discussion of the financial potential of television. Count Paolo Thaon de Revel of Italy did not see television as a threat to anticipated ticket sales for the Cortina Winter Games but did foresee many Italians staying home to watch extended television coverage of events four years hence when the Summer Games would be staged in Rome. Revel pledged a share of the profits from the sale of television rights for the Rome Olympics to the IOC and the ISFs.[68] Prince Axel of Denmark suggested that the IOC adopt a friendly attitude with television executives because the Olympics as a television spectacle held financial promise for both the IOC and the television networks. "We must . . . explain to them our difficulties and our everlasting lack of funds required to achieve the vast and heavy tasks assigned to us," observed Prince Axel, who pushed forward Revel's claim regarding the potential impact of televised coverage on Olympic ticket sales. Television was a viable source of revenue for the IOC, continued Axel, but televised Olympic drama would benefit the television industry by stirring "world-wide interest [that would] bring them a great number of new subscribers and publicity contracts."[69] In other words, money would flow to both parties if they formed a partnership arrangement.

Axel's vision prefigured by forty years the thinking of Richard Pound and NBC president of sports Dick Ebersol, who made headlines in 1995 with the consummation of two separate U.S. television rights agreement packages for the 2000/2002 and 2004/2006/2008 Games. Indeed, there was money to be made by both sides through a partnership approach.

The crux of the matter remained: to establish a policy that distinguished between "Olympic television rights"—the rights purchased by a network granting the buyer the exclusive privilege of televising extended coverage of an Olympic festival—and the extent of access afforded for news purposes to television and cinema newsreel companies. Brundage tackled this task in the wake of the Melbourne Olympics. Rather than trying to impose his thoughts on the industry, he considered proposals from the European Broadcasting Union (EBU) while arranging at the same time to meet with a number of representatives of U.S. commercial television networks.[70] His efforts reflected the counsel provided by Prince Axel in Cortina. Brundage began to work toward a consensus with television executives.

BRUNDAGE REVISES RULE 49

In 1958 Brundage's carefully planned, deliberate consultation process (initiated in 1956 and continued in 1957) resulted in the modification of the *Olympic Charter*'s Rule 49 on publicity. The fundamental principle of the revised statute was the distinction between news coverage and live television rights. The legislation specified that OCOGs were responsible for concluding arrangements for live television rights to the Games. All resulting contracts remained subject to IOC approval. The IOC retained authority regarding the distribution of the money accrued from the sale of Olympic television rights.[71] These stipulations reflected Brundage's desire to protect the IOC from potential commercial disputes involving sponsors or negotiators representing the television networks.

The anticipated financial bonanza from the sale of live television rights to Olympic Games staged in the United States also figured prominently in discussions. Marcello Garroni, secretary of the Rome Organizing Committee, suggested that the network covering the festival in the host nation should receive gratis television rights in exchange for costs associated with production facilities.[72] Although Brundage was willing to grant such an arrangement to the Italian television network (RAI) for the 1960 Summer Games, he refused to extend any degree of permanence to this provision. The IOC, he said, would not sacrifice the revenues as a result of this proposed stipulation when the Games were staged in the United States.[73] David Cecil, the Marquess of Exeter (formerly Lord Burghley, hereafter called Exeter), speculated that the domestic television rights for an Olympic festival staged in the United States might exceed $2 million.[74]

On other matters, however, Brundage compromised. He and IOC chancellor Otto Mayer, a key correspondent with European television officials during this consultative process, favored the establishment of a six-minute daily time limit for news agencies (no payment required).[75] The newsfilm industry lobbied aggressively for a nine-minute limit, the same position steadfastly maintained during the aborted Melbourne negotiations. U.S. networks, confirmed Harry Robert, wanted to provide news coverage of the Games three times per day: "to try to cover a subject as varied and exciting as the Olympics in less than three minutes would be harrowing to an editor."[76] The nine-minute limit appeared in the 1958 *Olympic Charter.*

Avery Brundage adopted a cautious approach to the IOC's involvement with television. Through the revision of Rule 49 he attempted to chart a course that would allow the IOC (1) to benefit from television, a medium that he believed "could be a great source of profit for the IOC,"[77] (2) to maintain control over the distribution of television money, and (3) to protect the IOC from what Coubertin termed the travails of the "[descent] into the slough of commercialism."[78] Organizing Committees, not the IOC, would be exposed to image problems stemming from disputes arising during negotiations since they had been granted the right to negotiate the contracts—subject, of course, to IOC approval. Naturally, this plan hinged on a solid working relationship between OCOGs and the IOC. Brundage coveted the money because he envisioned the good that could be done in Lausanne by a financially solvent IOC; at the same time, however, he sought to avoid the commercial implications of embracing television revenue. His position represented a philosophical tightrope fraught with problems.

Brundage's efforts at brokering a meaningful compromise for television and cinema news agencies and the IOC proved successful; but officials representing the 1960 Olympic Winter and Summer Organizing Committees dissented. Having been awarded the right to host the 1960 Olympic Games (in 1955) before any policy regarding television existed, the Squaw Valley and Rome Organizing Committees argued vehemently that the IOC could not impose Rule 49 retroactively. They wanted to distribute the television money rather than cede this privilege to the IOC in accordance with the revised statute.[79] The Pandora's Box of revenue from television was open, and new arguments between the IOC and OCOGs overshadowed resolution of the early conflict between the IOC and the television industry.

THE SQUAW VALLEY GAMES

When Avery Brundage returned to the United States in the aftermath of the IOC's Fifty-first General Session in Paris in June 1955, he wrestled for an answer to a burning question: How did Squaw Valley, an underdeveloped winter resort community in the northern reaches of California that he likened to a "picnic ground," emerge as the host city for the Eighth Winter Olympic Games, scheduled for 1960? Some IOC members possibly interpreted his silence concerning the bid as an attempt to provide the appearance of neutrality. Perhaps Squaw Valley's 32–20 vote win over Innsbruck could be attributed to some members' desire "to please the President," he mused. The rivalry between European winter resort communities, concluded Brundage, assisted the efforts of Alexander Cushing, who mounted a "superb high pressure salesmanship campaign" on behalf of Squaw Valley.[80] Brundage also speculated that Detroit's failed effort to secure the right to host the 1960 Summer Olympics elicited a sympathy vote for Squaw Valley. Perhaps the exemplary work of the organizers of the 1932 Los Angeles Olympics, he conceded, might have fostered the belief that Americans possessed the organizational talents required to stage a successful festival. Nonetheless, these answers did not alleviate his doubts about the wisdom of the IOC's decision to place the Games in Squaw Valley.

The construction of an Olympic Winter Games complex in Squaw Valley represented an enormous undertaking, one Brundage believed the community was ill-equipped to manage. "Even if you get the men and the money required," he told Cushing, "it is not going to be a simple matter to provide the facilities and organize the Games properly in four years' time."[81] He questioned Cushing's ability to lay the groundwork for a successful operation. Brundage confided to Kenneth "Tug" Wilson, president of the United States Olympic Association, that Squaw Valley's failure to meet the challenge promised a "blackeye for the whole country, and I as President of the International Olympic Committee will be especially blamed because I am an American."[82] While facilities and an appropriate atmosphere posed two hurdles for Squaw Valley organizers to clear, Brundage also believed that inadequate road access threatened to strand spectators at the site in the event of a winter storm. His nagging doubts, which he eventually made public, irritated Alexander Cushing.

Cushing remained confident that Squaw Valley could establish the infrastructure required to host the 1960 Winter Olympic Games.[83] He had been able to extract $1 million from the State of California in order to launch the project. Brundage considered this sum wholly inadequate and surmised that Squaw Valley required an additional $4 million.[84] His repeated expressions of concern to local and national media about the Squaw Valley project tried Cushing's patience. "For every expert you can produce who says Squaw Valley is not capable of holding a proper Winter Olympics," protested Cushing, "I can produce ten who will tell you it can." "Of the latter," he continued, "I can produce a substantial number who will tell you that the site is without equal in the world."[85] Brundage remained skeptical. Even California governor Goodwin J. Knight's expression of confidence to Brundage in January 1956 that the state legislature would approve his request for an additional appropriation of $4 million for Squaw Valley did little to assuage him.[86] Brundage, who had previously concluded that Squaw Valley officials "would be much better to give up the Games until they are ready to handle them in a first class manner," linked the appropriateness of Squaw Valley's status as the host community to the receipt of the promised $4 million by the end of March.[87] Support for Squaw Valley remained strong, and the State of California approved the second appropriation. State legislators had committed a total of $7,990,000 to the Squaw Valley Organizing Committee by mid-1957.[88]

The terms of the various appropriation bills provided a source of concern for Brundage, however, because Squaw Valley pledged monies accruing from gate receipts, concessions, and the sale of television rights to the state treasury.[89] He received no satisfaction in his attempt to overturn this pledge. Brundage believed that any profit should be forwarded to the USOC to further the work of the organization.[90] The correspondence of Brundage, Otto Mayer, and Squaw Valley organizers with respect to the appropriation bills—and hence the question as to which organizational body controlled the revenues created by the sale of Olympic television rights—provides an early indication of how television policy could have an impact upon IOC/OCOG relations.

Without firmly entrenched policy concerning television negotiations and the distribution of television money, however, Brundage's task was difficult. Soon after the Paris Session in June 1955 he launched what turned out to be an unsuccessful attempt to establish the IOC's authority over the distribution of Squaw Valley television money. Writing to IOC Executive Board members in August, Brundage reemphasized that the IOC had deferred consideration of television policy until 1956 and had "made no reservation of [television] rights for the Games of Rome and Squaw Valley," even though "perhaps we should have done so." "It may be that even now it is not too late," he reflected.[91] In order to finalize preliminary budgeting by September 1955, Cushing sought confirmation that television revenue accrued to the Organizing Committee.[92] Brundage seized the opportunity. He informed Cushing that the IOC, OCOGs, and ISFs shared interest in the revenue potential of television. In a statement that mirrored an element of the yet-to-be-finalized Rule 49, Brundage told Cushing that "negotiations for the sale of television rights will be handled by the Organizing Committee, but the disposition of the proceeds will be determined by the IOC."[93] Cushing ignored the latter element of this decree. Otto Mayer directed a similar message to the Rome Organizing Committee.[94] Armed with wisdom gained from discussions with television executives in meetings held before and after the 1956 Melbourne Olympics in an attempt to establish a modified Rule 49, Brundage and Mayer revisited this issue with Squaw Valley organizers in 1957.

Mayer informed Alan E. Bartholemy, executive director of the Squaw Valley Organizing Committee, that Brundage had engaged in discussions with U.S. television executives and reached an agreement that newsreel coverage should be granted free of charge to the networks but that access to the event for the purpose of entertainment programming required payment. The entertainment rights, stated Mayer, belonged to the IOC. He also advised Bartholemy to initiate discussions with the U.S. networks.[95]

This renewed correspondence startled Squaw Valley. In the wake of Alexander Cushing's resignation, prompted by allegations of a conflict of interest, Goodwin Knight revamped the Squaw Valley Organizing Committee. Bartholemy and Prentis C. Hale, Cushing's replacement as president, headed the organization.[96] Though Brundage's concerns about the organizational talents of those heading the operation eased, he remained adamant that Bartholemy and Hale defer to his wishes with respect to television money. Bartholemy expressed bewilderment at the contents of Mayer's letter, since he could locate no paragraph detailing the IOC's ownership of television rights in any available IOC publications. Even *IOC Bulletin* 58, published in May 1957, Bartholemy observed, revealed that the IOC deferred any policy decision on television until its General Session scheduled for Sofia in September. Having promised the money from the sale of television rights to the California state treasury as a condition for receiving financial assistance through various appropriations, Bartholemy protested the IOC's intent to impose its will on the Squaw Valley Organizing Committee in retroactive fashion.[97] Brundage remained resolute in his belief that the IOC needed to secure control of Olympic television revenue. This observation is supported by a review of his attempts to invoke revisionist history in his response to Bartholemy's missive.

In direct contradiction to the contents of his letter to members of the IOC Executive Board written in early August 1955, in which he stated that the IOC *had not* reserved the television rights for Squaw Valley and Rome, Brundage informed Bartholemy that the Executive Board, indeed the IOC, *had* reserved the television rights revenues from the 1960 Olympic festivals. Squaw Valley had been selected as host city for the 1960 Olympic Winter Games during the Paris Session, noted Brundage, and Cushing's contingent had been advised of this decision, pending the move to establish a formal policy governing television. Later in the same letter he contradicted himself yet again. Cushing's confusion upon being notified of the IOC's intention to establish new policy, Brundage said, was easily explained. With respect to the question of ownership of television rights money, IOC officials had informed Cushing in Paris that "the IOC had made no decision on this point."[98] In September 1955 Brundage had clearly stated in a letter to Cushing that the IOC retained control of the television revenue accruing from contracts negotiated by the Organizing Committee. This point had been repeated to Squaw Valley organizers orally and in writing, noted Brundage.

There is no evidence to confirm Brundage's claim that Cushing was aware of the IOC's intent to manage the distribution of television revenue, a decision purportedly made in Paris concurrently with the award of the 1960 Olympic Winter Games to Squaw Valley. In fact, Brundage's letter to the Executive Board, dated 3 August 1955, makes it clear that the IOC's effort to secure control over the television rights revenue was not initiated until two months after the conclusion of the IOC's Paris Session.

While Prentis Hale was sympathetic to Brundage's desire for a portion of the television revenue, he confirmed that Squaw Valley had pledged the money to the state treasury. He informed Brundage that Squaw Valley's current forecast of expenditures for preparing facilities necessitated the receipt of "all revenues, from every source, including television."[99] Not surprisingly, Hale's message miffed Brundage.

Brundage asked Otto Mayer to review his correspondence files and lobbied John M. Peirce, director of finance of the State of California, for a reversal of the condition set out for state appropriations that required television revenue to be forwarded to the state treasury. This effort failed. Meanwhile Mayer's investigation revealed that the issue had not been discussed at the 1955 IOC Session. Even though the Executive Board had addressed television revenue and the possibility of distributing the money to the IOC, ISFs, and the OCOGs in a meeting during the course of the session, no action had been taken in June 1955. The absence of any evidence presented to Cushing confirming the IOC's intent to control television revenue was noted in Brundage's letter to the Executive Board dated 3 August 1955. Still, on the basis of Brundage's letter to Cushing dated 16 September 1955 (in which he stated that the IOC reserved the television rights) and a notation in the minutes of the 1956 session in Cortina to the effect that Brundage had reserved the rights from the 1960 Olympic festivals for the IOC, Mayer believed that the Squaw Valley organizers would have to yield.[100]

By September 1957 Brundage realized that there was little chance to secure control of the Squaw Valley television money. He informed the IOC

Session in Sofia that Cushing had ignored his communication in 1955 and had failed to apprise members of the restructured Organizing Committee of it. These actions left the IOC little choice but to sacrifice this revenue because of Squaw Valley's arrangements with the California state legislature.[101] The sole contract negotiated for Olympic entertainment programming entailed a modest $50,000 payment from CBS to Squaw Valley. Though the IOC's own financial loss was minimal, especially relative to its proposed share, any revenue at all would have been welcome in light of the organization's proclivity for operating in financial deficit.

THE ROME GAMES

Brundage drew even less satisfaction from his effort to enforce IOC television policy with respect to the 1960 Rome Olympics. He engaged in a similar prickly exchange of correspondence with Giulio Onesti, president of the Rome Organizing Committee, concerning Rule 49. Like Prentis Hale and Alan Bartholemy, Onesti did not accept Brundage's revisionist view of past events. "The Rome Organizing Committee, I assume," stated Brundage, "understands that the disposition of [all television money] rests in the hands of the International Olympic Committee" because he had apprised Rome officials of this fact at the Paris Session.[102] His confidence was misplaced.

Rome, protested Onesti, accepted the challenge of staging the 1960 Olympics in accord with the rules in place when the city had been awarded the Games in 1955. Rule 49, he wrote cheekily, reserved money from the sale of "live" television rights for distribution by the IOC.[103] Strict interpretation of Rule 49, noted Onesti, precluded an IOC claim to the revenues from the U.S., Canadian, and Japanese markets because contemporary technology did not permit live transoceanic coverage. All Olympic footage to be shown on television in those countries would have to be flown there for delayed telecasts. Onesti did not fail to impress this reality upon Brundage, who grudgingly settled for Onesti's earlier offer of 5% of the net proceeds from the sale of television rights with a guaranteed minimum payment of $50,000.[104] Onesti's determined stand compelled Brundage to reassess his first effort to construct and implement IOC television policy.

REFLECTIONS

In the end the 1960 Winter and Summer Olympic Games occurred without mishap—indeed, with much glamour. The Winter Games in

Squaw Valley opened in February with a dazzling ceremony including ice statues and fireworks displays orchestrated by Walt Disney. Organizers constructed the sport facilities and accommodations for participants in close proximity to one another, contributing to the general atmosphere of goodwill.[105] With the expanded infrastructure, able to accommodate more than two million visitors, the Games avoided the transportation and communication nightmares forecast by Brundage.[106] While CBS aired only fifteen hours of coverage, two of them in prime time, these Games will be remembered as the first seen live on American television.[107]

A combination of new sport facilities built specifically for the Olympic Games and the archaeological remains of buildings once resplendent in ancient Rome provided the backdrop to the Games of the Seventeenth Olympiad.[108] Described by one journalist in attendance as "the loveliest Games of the modern era," the Rome Olympics successfully blended the aura of the ancient with the demands of modern sport.[109] The opening ceremony on 25 August 1960 took place in front of some 100,000 spectators in the newly constructed marble Olympic Stadium. Among the other venues of note were the gymnastics facilities in the Baths of Caracalla and the wrestling venue in the Basilica of Maxentius. The marathon run started on Capitoline Hill and finished at the Arch of Constantine.

The Rome Olympics were the first Summer Games to be televised live to Europe; eighteen countries received the broadcast. The Games were also televised on a delayed basis in the United States, Canada, and Japan, continuing a trend that would forever change the way the public watched the Olympics.[110] EBU paid $667,967 for the live European transmission rights; CBS spent $394,940 for the U.S. television rights.[111] Rome generated additional income for staging the Games through an extensive sponsor/supplier program, including forty-six companies that provided key technical support and various "value-in-kind" products such as perfume, chocolate, toothpaste, soap, and maps of Rome's Olympic sites.[112]

The 1960 Winter and Summer Olympic festivals also featured the beginning of confrontational negotiations between an OCOG and the IOC. Brundage correctly forecast the potential for friction between the IOC and Organizing Committees as a result of the appearance of television revenue. Each stonewalled against his calculated attempts to gain control of the distribution of television revenue. Brundage's chronology of the discussion with the OCOGs in 1955 was fanciful. His paradoxical combination of Olympic idealism and desire for the pragmatic benefits of commercialism was never clearer than in these efforts to rewrite past events. On the one hand, he wanted the IOC, ISFs, and OCOGs to share the fruits from the sale of television rights; on the other hand, he also wanted to control how much each received. He was dedicated to shielding the IOC from media criticism by removing it from direct involvement in negotiations with commercial television networks. Squaw Valley signed one television agreement for $50,000. Onesti and his colleagues reached agreement with television executives in a number of regions (including the United States, Western Europe, Eastern Europe, and Japan) for a total of $1,178,257.[113] More than a year after the close of the Rome Olympic Games Mayer was still trying to exact from Onesti what he believed to be full and fair payment.[114]

Brundage's strategy for avoiding future conflict, pending a review of Rule 49, involved sacrificing control of future television revenue in exchange for a fixed payment from the OCOGs that could be shared by the IOC and the ISFs. The IOC Executive Board subsequently established specific financial figures for the 1964 Olympic Games and television. It demanded a sum of $150,000–$130,000 from Tokyo and $20,000 from Innsbruck.[115]

The limited financial returns to the IOC from the Rome television agreements (less than $60,000) precluded sharing television money with the ISFs. The ISFs, however, became stakeholders in future negotiations during the 1960s. In light of the expanded revenue potential of television resulting from the advent of satellite technology in 1962, the ISFs issued a demand for one-third of all television income. Representatives of the NOCs, who considered their call for financial assistance no less justified than the one voiced by the ISFs, petitioned Brundage to cede a share of future television revenue to their coffers. Finally, some members of the IOC relished the possibility of enhanced television revenue resulting from changes in the sports television market due to technological progress. The prominence of the word "money" in the lexicon of leaders of amateur sport left Brundage exasperated.

Brundage's move to accept a fixed payment from the Organizing Committees of the 1964 and 1968 Olympic festivals eased tension between the IOC and OCOGs. But the rapid expansion of the revenue possibilities from the sale of television rights due to the attractiveness of live transoceanic telecasts introduced new arguments involving the IOC, ISFs, and NOCs. Forced to address the financial aspirations of the ISFs and the NOCs and the legitimate needs of the OCOGs, Brundage brokered an agreement in 1966 that established a formula for the allocation of television money to the IOC, NOCs, ISFs, and OCOGs. Throughout that process he considered the encroachment of commercialism on the Olympic enterprise to be increasingly ominous.

A review of the Melbourne negotiations and their immediate aftermath provides a foundation for understanding the evolution of the IOC's relationship with the television industry and helps place the contemporary debate in historical context. The concept of Olympic television rights—payment in exchange for the privilege of covering the Games beyond the rights granted to news agencies—emanated from the Melbourne discussions.

Television money, supplemented in more recent years by corporate sponsorship revenue, provided an infusion of capital to the Olympic Movement over a period of some forty years. It permitted a vast expansion of the IOC's Lausanne operation, assisted National Olympic Committees and International Sport Federations, and contributed to the increasing grandeur of physical facilities established by successive OCOGs. These changes, however, have prompted questions concerning the direction of the Olympic Movement and its partnership with commercial agencies.

CHAPTER 4

CONFLICT IN THE OLYMPIC MOVEMENT

Avery Brundage, Television Money, and the Rome Formula in the 1960s

The 1960s marked the IOC's first confrontation with the altogether different but not too unpleasing matter of money earned and how it might be spent. The entire concept of a relatively well-endowed treasury was completely foreign to the IOC's experience. Suddenly becoming the beneficiary of even modest wealth, of course, raised the specter of what to do with it. All Olympic organizations believed they deserved a share of the earnings, which posed a vexing dilemma for IOC leaders, under whose authority decisions on "sharing the wealth" were vested. National Olympic Committees (NOCs), of course, provided the athletes who performed in the Games; they were certainly stakeholders. International Sport Federations (ISFs) supplied the expertise necessary for organizing and executing each sport at the great festival; they, too, were legitimate stakeholders. Olympic Organizing Committees (OCOGs), with heavier financial burdens than any other Olympic organizations, were also bona-fide stakeholders. And the IOC itself—faced with increasing administrative costs as the Games proceeded to grow alarmingly in numbers of athletes, officials, and administrators—needed money to meet the challenges.

Thus, it came as no surprise that the "parent" IOC was rapidly and repeatedly entreated by the imploring hands of its "children" for a share of the family income. Prior to the 1960s, when the IOC had no income, the voices of NOCs, ISFs, and OCOGs were silent. With the coming of television rights fees, however, all this changed. Each Olympic Movement member stridently insisted on receiving its perceived rightful share. Brundage expended significant energy in his attempts to temper the attitudes of his fellow amateur sport administrators. With the advent of the "Rome Formula" in 1966—the IOC's first policy governing the distribution of percentage shares of television revenue to OCOGs, NOCs, and ISFs—Brundage believed he had found the means to maintain peace. He was wrong.

Before examining the complex series of events that established the fundamental formula for sharing of income by Olympic constituents, a brief overview of the 1964 and 1968 Olympic festivals is warranted. During this period the OCOGs increased their efforts to muster financial and "in kind" resources from commercial enterprise.

When Innsbruck was defeated by Squaw Valley by two votes at the IOC Session in Paris in 1955, the mayor of the Tyrolean alpine resort immediately announced his intention to bid for the next Winter Games.[1] At its session in Munich in 1959 the IOC awarded the right to host the 1964 Winter Games to Innsbruck.[2] Television rights fees became an immediate concern. While television rights for the 1960 Winter Olympics in Squaw Valley had been limited to the CBS payment of $50,000, Innsbruck organizers negotiated contracts totaling $936,667.[3]

The Ninth Olympic Winter Games opened on 29 January 1964. Faced with a serious shortage of snow, the organizers turned to the Austrian army for assistance. With the help of local fire-brigade personnel and equipment, the army transported twenty-five thousand tons of snow from higher snow fields to the River Inn Valley to serve the needs of alpine skiing competitions.[4] As the Olympic torch entered the stadium, over one thousand athletes assembled.[5] Despite mild conditions and a lack of snow, the events ran smoothly. In summing up the 1964 Winter Games in Innsbruck, obviously impressed with their organization, Avery Brundage remarked at the closing ceremony that "the Innsbruck Games have shown how much the human will is capable of achieving."[6]

At its session in Oslo in 1935 the IOC confirmed Tokyo as host for the Games of the Twelfth Olympiad.[7] The outbreak of the Sino-Japanese war in 1937 spelled the end of Tokyo's hopes of organizing the 1940 Games. Twenty-six years later, however, Japan was once again named an Olympic host.[8] Tokyo set new standards in preparing for the 1964 Summer Games, investing heavily in new and architecturally impressive sport facilities.[9] Brundage called the swimming pool a "cathedral of sports."[10] Equally impressive was the judo hall, designed to resemble a traditional Japanese temple. Organizers invested in improving Tokyo's infrastructure to accommodate the influx of tourists as well as the city's 10 million inhabitants. The construction of a new subway system and further improvements to the transportation infrastructure required an additional investment in excess of $1 billion.[11]

The corporate marketing relationships associated with the Games of the Eighteenth Olympiad included 250 national and international companies.[12] Tokyo created its own marketing agency, operating twenty-three commercial ventures ranging from the sale of commemorative stamps to selling advertising in the public transportation systems. The agency marketed "Olympic" cigarettes bearing the symbolic brand names "Peace" and "Olympia"; each package was emblazoned with the Olympic rings.[13] The Olympia brand was so successful that it generated over $1 million in revenue for Tokyo.[14] Technical support from sponsors also began to take on a greater role in helping to stage Olympic Games. Companies such as Seiko, for instance, provided the most accurate timing system yet seen in any Olympic Games. Computers for timing and scoring made their first appearance in Tokyo.[15]

On the threshold of advances in telecommunications that would eventually revolutionize the television industry, Tokyo was the beneficiary of further escalation in fees paid for television broadcast rights to the Olympic Games.[16] For the first time broadcasts of the Games were transmitted via satellite to receiving stations located overseas.[17] A race run in Japan, for example, could be seen split seconds later in New Jersey. Yet satellite time was expensive, and a fourteen-hour time zone difference between Japan and the U.S. East Coast made programming difficult. Despite the potential of live Olympic telecasts in the United States, Canada, Latin America, and Africa, NBC made limited use of the live satellite feed during the Games. The network planned its Olympic coverage around the prime time slots (8:00 P.M. to 11:00 P.M.) that promised lucrative advertising revenues despite the delayed coverage.

Determined to recoup its $1.5 million fee for the 1964 Tokyo broadcast rights, NBC sold commercial time to companies such as Kent cigarettes and Schlitz, "the beer that made Milwaukee famous." Reacting to this form of sponsorship, irate viewers in the United States "inundated" the IOC with complaints. Attempting to "prevent a recurrence" of this form of corporate sponsorship, Avery Brundage brought his concerns to the attention of the IOC Executive Board.[18] As a result a clause was added to the *Olympic Charter* that banned the commercial sponsorship of Olympic telecasts by tobacco, brewery, and distillery companies.[19]

By most standards the Tokyo Games were enormously successful. The opening ceremony provided the 80,000 spectators and millions of television viewers with a combination of established rituals and contemporary elements charged with symbolism. From the traditional Japanese dancers seen at the opening ceremonies to the Japanese farewell "Sayonara" flashed in giant letters on the computerized scoreboard during the closing ceremonies, Japan signaled its return from the ravages of World War II as a full and respected member of the international community.

The decision to award the 1968 Olympic Winter Games was originally scheduled to take place at the IOC Session in Baden-Baden in 1963; but due to a heavy agenda it was postponed to the session in Innsbruck in 1964.[20] The candidate cities vying for the 1968 Winter Olympics included Calgary, Grenoble, Lahti, Lake Placid, Oslo, and Sapporo. In the third round of voting Grenoble emerged victorious over a strong bid from Calgary.[21]

Upon returning home, the French organizers immediately set to work transforming the industrial city of Grenoble into a suitable venue for the celebration of a Winter Olympic festival. The construction of new sport facilities and the overall improvement of the local infrastructure required large amounts of money. Grenoble faced another problem. Its size and physical characteristics limited the city's ability to support the venues necessary for the competitions.[22] Only the skating disciplines could be held in the city. Surrounding villages and ski resorts served as sites for other competitions. The substantial distances between competition sites forced many competitors to request housing at the venues themselves rather than in the Olympic village.[23] Although some critics complained that this meant the Games "were prejudicial to the Olympic atmosphere" and thus could not be considered a true meeting of the "youth of the world," these Games provided a triumph for the French.[24]

For Brundage and many others within the Olympic Movement, the 1968 Winter Games—opened on 6 February 1968 by French president Charles de Gaulle—were characterized by the rapid growth of commercialism. Commenting on the situation in *Skiing* magazine, one writer went so far as to state that "the Olympic idea died somewhere in Grenoble."[25] Brundage stewed. He fired off a circular letter to IOC members complaining of the rampant commercialism in Grenoble. "They had Olympic butter, Olympic sugar, and Olympic petrol," he grumbled.[26] Following in the footsteps of Tokyo, Grenoble licensed two brands of Olympic cigarettes, each named after an Olympic venue.[27] The growth of commercialism in various Olympic winter sports, particularly alpine skiing, also bothered Brundage. The commercial endorsement link between alpine skiers and ski equipment manufacturers prompted a feeling in the crusty IOC head that the sport had degenerated into a business and "did not belong in the Olympic Games."[28]

The continued refinement of satellite technologies throughout the 1960s resulted in a substantial increase in the value of telecast rights to the Winter and Summer Olympic Games as well as in the number of hours of Olympic programming.[29] The 1964 Innsbruck Olympic Winter Games worldwide television rights had sold for $936,667, an almost twentyfold increase from the $50,000 received by Squaw Valley in 1960. Though Grenoble could not match the astronomical percentage increase generated by Innsbruck, it did not do too shabbily, negotiating a total of $2,612,822.[30]

At the IOC Session in Baden-Baden in 1963 the IOC awarded the 1968 Summer Games to Mexico City by a clear majority.[31] Brundage and his IOC colleagues were pleased; this marked the first time that a developing country, not counted among the world's industrialized nations, would host the Olympic Games.[32] Their enthusiasm faded, however, as it became clear that Mexico would not be spared from the political turmoil gripping many countries of the world in the 1960s. In Vietnam the launch of the Tet Offensive produced fighting and devastation that the world viewed on television with shock. The seizing of the USS *Pueblo* by North Korea threatened to rekindle hostilities on the Korean peninsula into yet another war. Tensions rose between Israel and its Arab neighbors. And the Cold War reached a new climax with the march of 650,000 Warsaw Pact troops into Czechoslovakia.

Protests also erupted within the Olympic organizations following the IOC's decision to rescind its eight-year-old ban on South Africa's participation in the Olympic Games. Under threats of boycott by the majority of some fifty African countries, the IOC reluctantly ordered Mexico City to withdraw its invitation to South Africa's athletes due to its government's apartheid policy. In Mexico students angered by "the betrayal of the Mexican Revolution by an entrenched bureaucratic party" demonstrated openly in the streets.[33] As the Olympic Games approached, 300,000 Mexican students and teachers went on strike.[34] On the night of 2 October 1968 a crowd of 10,000 demonstrators marched into the sprawling capital city's Plaza de las Tres Culturas in protest of government policies.[35] In response the Mexican army moved against the protesters, killing and wounding scores. Concerned by the developments in Mexico and their possible impact on the Games, an alarmed Brundage flew to Mexico City. Following a meeting with Pedro Ramírez Vázquez, head of the OCOG, Brundage issued the following statement: "We have conferred with the Mexican authorities and we have been assured that nothing will interfere with the peaceful entrance of the Olympic flame into the stadium . . . nor with the competitions which follow."[36]

Although there was no attempt by the Mexican dissidents to interfere with the Olympic flame and the competitions that followed, considerable interference from two enterprising shoe manufacturers occurred. On 11 October 1968, one day before the opening ceremonies, Horst Dassler and Armin Dassler, according to British runner Christopher Brasher, began paying athletes who agreed to compete in Adidas and Puma shoes.[37] We shall hear more later of Horst Dassler and his energetic and highly successful sports marketing linked to the Modern Olympic Movement.

Despite myriad tensions the Mexico City Games opened with great optimism. Mexico City's marketing campaign generated 49% of its operating budget from various commercial transactions in foreign countries and at home.[38] Mexico City also benefited from advances in satellite technology, selling international television rights for $9.75 million, a sixfold increase over the amount received by Tokyo.[39] Capitalizing on emerging telecommunication technologies, the Mexico City Games were the first to be telecast live in color.[40] The dramatic increase in television revenue, combined with corporate sponsorship marketing income, ensured that the organizers met their financial goals.

THE ROME FORMULA: AN OVERVIEW

During the early and mid-1960s Avery Brundage's attempt to protect the image of the Olympic Movement in the face of persistent lobbying by representatives of the ISFs and NOCs, all of whom demanded a portion of the newfound wealth, dominated Olympic discourse concerning the distribution of television revenue. Satellite technology and the prospect and ultimate realization of live transoceanic telecasts altered the sport television marketplace, precipitating an increase in the dollar value of Olympic television rights. Brundage's trepidation concerning the commercial taint of television revenue was balanced against the fact that the dollars could help organizations committed to the promotion of Olympic ideals. "This increase in commercial value [of Olympic television rights] can be of great use to the Olympic Movement if it is distributed properly," wrote Brundage in 1966, but "it can also be of great danger if Olympic ideals are not maintained."[41] Between 1960 and 1966 he devoted a great deal of time and energy to developing a method of distributing television money acceptable to the ISFs, NOCs, and IOC members. At the same time he knew the critical importance of revenues for Organizing Committees faced with significant capital expenses. The distribution exercise was replete with challenges.

In 1966 the IOC approved a formula for allocating television revenue resulting from negotiations conducted by Organizing Committees entrusted with the 1972 Summer and Winter Olympic Games (Munich and Sapporo, respectively). The distribution equation, dubbed the "Rome Formula," guaranteed the OCOGs approximately two-thirds of the television revenue and mandated that the IOC, ISFs, and NOCs equally share the remaining one-third. The ISFs had received one-half of the fixed payments sent to Lausanne by the 1964 and 1968 Organizing Committees (Innsbruck, Tokyo, Grenoble, and Mexico City), but the Rome Formula enabled them to receive a percentage share of all television revenue for the first time. It also established the NOCs as stakeholders in the television negotiations process because they also received a percentage share of television revenue.[42] While Brundage steered the process toward an agreement acceptable to the majority, some ISFs opposed any arrangement that negated their claim to one-third of all television revenue.[43] The NOCs and ISFs, dissatisfied with their ability to influence IOC policy, threatened to establish independent collective lobby groups to enhance their input into future Olympic decision-making in an effort to leverage more television revenue. Brundage's presidential agenda, however, did not include the concept of power sharing.

THE FINANCIAL ASPIRATIONS OF THE ISFS AND NOCS

As a result of settlements reached with Squaw Valley and Rome organizers, the IOC received only a nominal amount (less than $60,000) from the sale of 1960 Olympic television rights.[44] It had been Brundage's intent to share this money with the ISFs, but the plan (and the sharing) was deferred until 1964. During negotiations with Giulio Onesti, president of the Rome Organizing Committee, Brundage had noted that IOC control of television revenue would "give us [the IOC] an opportunity to satisfy the legitimate demands of the International Federations."[45] As early as 1955, Bunny Ahearne, president of the International Ice Hockey Federation, had petitioned the IOC Executive Board to generate a policy that allocated equal shares of television revenue to the IOC, OCOGs, and ISFs.[46] Even though Brundage ignored Ahearne's proposal, he was committed to the principle of sharing television money with the ISFs.

Brundage understood the vital role played by the ISFs. Among their principal functions were (1) establishing and enforcing rules pertaining to their sports, (2) encouraging the development of their sports throughout the world, and (3) accepting responsibility for the technical control and governance of their sports at the Olympic Games. Only after persistent complaints from the ISFs concerning the amounts that he granted to them in the 1960s did Brundage change his mind about the efficacy of providing them with a share of the television money.

Brundage's discussions with leaders of the ISFs addressed such issues as "who would control the distribution of the ISFs' share of television money." Smaller ISFs lobbied for equal distribution of the ISFs' share. David Cecil, the Marquess of Exeter, an IOC Executive Board member and president of the powerful International Amateur Athletics Federation

(IAAF), argued successfully, however, that the IOC should control the distribution of money and that shares should be proportionate, based in some way on the contribution of each ISF to the Olympic Games.[47] In 1964 (Tokyo) and 1968 (Mexico City) the Summer ISFs received shares determined by the IOC, ranging from $2,400 to $18,000 and $5,700 to $35,000, respectively. These sums did not satisfy ISF leaders, who badgered Brundage for more money. In the 1960s he grew increasingly frustrated with the "commercial attitude" of the ISFs and the infighting that television money provoked.[48]

Armand Massard, IOC Executive Board member from France, championed the NOCs' right to television revenue. In 1960 he took issue with the exclusion of the NOCs from the plan generated for the distribution of the fixed payments from the 1964 Innsbruck and Tokyo Organizing Committees. Government subsidy provided the most prevalent form of income for the world's NOCs, Massard concluded. Very few NOCs, he argued, enjoyed financial independence through access to alternative sources of revenue such as those available in Italy (lottery) and England (public subscriptions). Massard envisioned television revenue as a means for NOCs, especially those struggling for financial independence, to ward off the specter of government control. He also questioned why ISFs, which had "no real needs," received grants from the IOC.[49] Brundage was sympathetic. "We hope it may be possible from the receipts of television to assist National Committees like yours [the French NOC]," he reported, "until they can establish their financial independence . . . Governmental subsidy too often means governmental interference which, of course, is quite contrary to the spirit of the Olympic Movement."[50]

Massard renewed his argument during the IOC Session in Athens in 1961. The ISFs, he noted, accessed revenue through the staging of yearly world championships, while many NOCs relied on government grants. Brundage, however, replied that the money available from the 1964 Organizing Committees "was not sufficiently large to allow the IOC to subsidize the NOCs as well."[51]

In 1965 the voices of other IOC members joined the chorus for change. Guru Dutt Sondhi (India) questioned the financial needs of the ISFs, which he referred to as "rule-makers," and termed the exclusion of the NOCs from any sharing formula "unfair." Echoing Massard's opinion, Sondhi concluded that "the nourishers of the Games [NOCs] are certainly more worthy of support than the mere regulators [ISFs]."[52] Giulio Onesti suggested that the IOC retain 50% of all future television revenue and cede 25% to the OCOGs to offset the travel expenses of judges and referees attending the Olympic Games on behalf of the ISFs. The remaining 25%, he offered, should be distributed to newly constituted NOCs and those experiencing financial difficulty.[53] Onesti's thoughts clashed with those of Exeter, who believed that, "in practice, no division [of television money] could make any real impression on [the NOCs'] expenses," considering the amount of money available and the number of NOCs.[54] The challenge for Brundage was clear. How could he manage these divergent opinions? Was there some middle ground for Ahearne, Exeter, Massard, Sondhi, and Onesti?

THE EVOLUTION OF THE ROME FORMULA

Brundage needed to revise Rule 49 in the aftermath of his failure to secure control of the distribution of Squaw Valley and Rome television money. In 1960 the IOC Executive Board and General Session affirmed the necessity for such action.[55] Two years before, the IOC had reserved the right to allocate the funds resulting from the sale of the "direct, or what is commonly called Live Television Rights." The text of Rule 49 was flawed; this fact allowed Onesti to deflect the IOC's claim on money received from U.S. and Japanese networks for the right to telecast tape-delayed coverage of the 1960 Rome Olympics. In its revised form appearing in the 1962 *Olympic Charter* Rule 49 said: "Rights to report the Games immediately on Television" belonged to the IOC. Therefore the IOC distributed revenue from both live and delayed coverage of the Olympic Games at its discretion. The IOC retained its prerogative to approve all contracts negotiated by the OCOGs with international television networks before the two signatories actually ratified the agreements.[56] These stipulations reserved the IOC's authority to supply the 1964 Organizing Committees with all television royalties (minus the respective indemnity payments totaling $150,000) and empowered the IOC to distribute 50% of the indemnity payment to the ISFs.

While Brundage understood the wisdom of providing financial support to the ISFs, he was unsure about the best method for distributing the money. He told Exeter in March 1961 that the issue "must be handled by us with great discretion." An arms-length approach might be appropriate, he believed: the IOC could transfer jurisdiction over the distribution of television revenue to the ISFs. Exeter, who was shocked that Brundage had wavered from his initial thought of leaving distribution to the discretion of the IOC Executive Board, replied swiftly to these musings. "Heaven forfend that the [ISFs] should have to decide on how to divide the donation from the IOC," wrote Exeter; "the result would make the Congo [the site of a contemporary civil war] look like a kindergarten."[57] Exeter lobbied

Brundage to accept that some federations deserved larger shares of the money based on their "contribution" to the Games, suggesting that attendance at sports organized by the ISFs at the Olympic festivals required consideration. He also recognized that his view could not possibly prevail in a discussion at an open meeting of the ISFs. Exeter and Brundage agreed not to include the International Football (Soccer) Federation (FIFA) in the distribution scheme because the "football people [were] full of money."[58] Exeter's self-interest in the matter was all too evident. Exeter considered the issue a potential powder keg in upcoming IOC Session and Executive Board meetings. Historically the IOC and ISFs enjoyed a significant amount of cross-membership. If the topic was placed on the agenda for the upcoming Athens Session in June 1961, Exeter predicted that it "would start the biggest dog-fight of all times with everybody pushing his own favourite." Members of the Executive Board might raise conflict of interest as an issue because he was president of the IAAF, speculated Exeter. Exeter's strategy focused on convincing the General Session to grant the Executive Board jurisdiction in the matter and answering any queries from the ISFs with respect to the IOC's plans in very general terms.[59] Brundage acquiesced.

Exeter's campaign proved successful. At the Executive Board meeting in Athens, Brundage informed members that Exeter was considering methods of distributing the television money received from the Innsbruck and Tokyo Organizing Committees.[60] When the General Session convened four days later, it empowered the Executive Board to act on the matter despite the protest of Armand Massard, who questioned the financial assistance given to the ISFs at the expense of the NOCs.[61] Brundage and Exeter had earlier agreed that eligibility for a portion of the revenue hinged on the ISFs' confirming the preeminence of the Olympic Games by designating the competition as their World Championship for that year. The IOC apprised the ISFs that a minimum payment would be established and that the allocated sums would reflect each ISF's "contribution" to the Games.[62] To this point Exeter had sidestepped an open confrontation with ISF leaders.

Exeter believed it imperative for the IOC to retain complete control of television revenue. The antics of Bunny Ahearne justified his opinion. As early as 1955 Ahearne had pushed the Executive Board to cede one-third of all prospective television revenue to the ISFs. Failing to win approval of this initiative, he considered placing a direct claim on a portion of the money acquired by the Innsbruck Organizing Committee from television rights negotiations. Otto Mayer instructed Friedl Wolfgang, secretary-general of the Innsbruck Organizing Committee, to reject Ahearne's claim.[63] Later the IOC learned that Ahearne had threatened to cancel the ice hockey program at Innsbruck if the Organizing Committee did not comply with his demand. "Blackmail," railed Brundage.[64] Ahearne capitulated. But he and a number of other ISF leaders shifted their focus to future television revenue, specifically the money from the sale of television rights to the 1968 Grenoble and Mexico City Olympics.

Meanwhile Exeter generated a method of distributing the Innsbruck and Tokyo television money to the ISFs. In an attempt to give meaning to the term "contribution," Exeter calculated the average attendance at each ISF event from the previous three Olympic Games. This "rolling average," he rationalized, protected those ISFs whose sport had been staged most recently in regions (Squaw Valley and Rome) where the sport enjoyed only limited popularity. Even though these calculations entitled the IAAF to 54% of the ISFs' total share of Tokyo television money, Exeter's established minimum payment scheme for the smaller federations reduced the IAAF's share to 26%. Similar sacrifices by the swimming, basketball, boxing, and equestrian federations in favor of a minimum payment to the smaller ISFs, explained Exeter to Rudyard H. Russell, president of the International Amateur Boxing Federation (AIBA), demonstrated "a praiseworthy spirit in the cause of the general welfare of amateur sport."[65]

Many ISF leaders argued that their portion of the television income at Innsbruck and Tokyo did not match their contribution to those Olympic festivals. Winter ISFs received a mere $10,000 of the $936,667 resulting from the negotiations with international television networks conducted by Innsbruck organizers. Of the $1,577,778 received by the Tokyo Organizing Committee from television networks in exchange for exclusive television rights, the Summer ISFs pocketed $65,000, which, in turn, was subjected to Exeter's distribution plan. The prospect of burgeoning television rights fees as a result of the advent of satellite technology fueled the ISFs' campaign for more television money.

In July 1962 U.S. citizens witnessed the first trans-Atlantic satellite transmissions from Europe (England and France). These telecasts heralded developments that would revolutionize the television industry, increase the television rights fees for the Olympic Games, and provide enhanced enjoyment for those interested in watching the Olympics. Even though neither telecast exceeded nine minutes in length, the potential of the new technology was undeniable. "The trans-ocean links are the beginning of a new order of global communications," wrote a correspondent for the *New York Times*. "They can radically alter many forms of cultural, business, and social activity and recast relations between nations."[66] Less than two months later Japanese and U.S. researchers, with the support of the U.S. State Department, launched a cooperative effort aimed at furthering satellite telecommunications. NASA (National Aeronautics and Space Agency) began a preliminary investigation concerning the possibility of telecasting the 1964 Summer Olympics.[67] Ichiro Matsui, director of international broadcasting for Japan's government-sponsored television agency, Nippon Hoso Kyokai (NHK), and his Japanese colleagues were intrigued by this possibility. Matsui regarded the landmark trans-Atlantic transmissions as a "hopeful sign," although he understood the shortcomings of early technology.[68]

Without further refinement of the technology, conceded Matsui, serious consideration could not be given to live trans-Pacific telecasts of the Tokyo Olympics. Transmissions were limited to ten minutes in duration and picture quality was substandard. The low orbits of early satellites restricted transmission times to periods when the satellites were in view of both coastlines. By early 1964 researchers and technicians had not yet situated a satellite in a high-altitude synchronous orbit. At high altitude, wrote Richard Witkin of the *New York Times,* "a satellite just keeps pace with the west-to-east rotation of the earth below. It is like a miler in the outside lane who keeps with the man on the inside by running somewhat faster."[69] Such an orbit offered permanent contact with both the U.S. and Japanese coastlines, thus producing an uninterrupted feed of the television signal. But tests of the Syncom II satellite (which had not been placed in a high-altitude synchronous orbit) in April 1964 discouraged NASA and NBC officials, who judged the transmitted images "below standard commercial quality."[70] Members of the Japanese government monitored these developments closely.

Japanese politicians regarded the Tokyo Olympics as an opportunity to elevate national prestige and reintroduce the country to the world political and economic stage.[71] The Japanese government dispatched a communications expert to the United States to witness the Syncom II tests.[72] The 1964 Olympic project represented an enormous financial investment for the Japanese, who expended "incalculable psychic energy" in order to impress the world audience.[73] They valued the favorable publicity afforded by the potential of live telecasts in the United States. Effective telecasts, however, hinged on the successful launch of the Syncom III satellite.

This satellite, the first placed in a high-altitude synchronous orbit, provided NBC with the opportunity to provide live telecasts from Tokyo.[74] Enthusiasm for the project reigned in Japan and in the halls of the U.S. State Department but not in the offices of NBC's executives. A program of tape-delayed telecasts during prime time hours, maintained NBC officials, provided the network with the best opportunity to recoup its financial investment.[75] In a fashion now familiar to many Olympic viewers in the

United States, including those who witnessed the recent American coverage of the 2000 Sydney Games, NBC packaged Tokyo event highlight programs in the evening hours. East Coast viewers watched the opening ceremonies live; but an NBC decision not to preempt Johnny Carson's *Tonight Show* on the West Coast in favor of live Olympic coverage elicited "ill-feeling" in Japan as well as disappointment at the State Department.[76] It also drew a reprimand from Jack Gould, television critic for the *New York Times*. The telecast on the East Coast lasted 105 minutes. It was the only live coverage provided to U.S. viewers. "For the sake of a few thousand dollars . . . what will be the effect of an opinion of American values when the rest of the world hears that this country makes a moment of history subordinate to the fate of a cluster of advertising spot announcements in California," groused Gould.[77]

Even though NBC's decision limited the impact of the first live transoceanic coverage of the Olympics, ISF leaders understood the future economics of satellite technology. In 1963 the ISFs again called on Brundage to provide them with one-third of television revenue in 1968 and beyond.[78] Brundage's "fixed payment" plan resulted in the Winter ISFs' receiving $10,000, or 1.07% of the television revenue from the Innsbruck Olympic Winter Games. The Summer ISFs fared a little better on a percentage basis since the $65,000 received represented 4.12% of all television revenue negotiated by Tokyo organizers. With the potential windfall from satellite telecasting hoving into view, the ISFs were unwilling to accept Brundage's meager handouts in the future.

Brundage's worst fears about television revenue and the threat to his Olympic ideals were becoming a reality. "Let us once and for all recognise the fact that our amateur sports are a colossal business," concluded Bunny Ahearne, "and no one, no one should deny us the right of making an honourable, justifiable and reasonable commercial approach, when we are talking millions of dollars." "Despite my amateur heart," he stated, Brundage's method of distributing television revenue "insults my financial brain."[79] An increasingly besieged Brundage retaliated. "One should be suspicious of any amateur organization that has money . . . the minute this occurs its complexion changes and not for the better."[80]

Brundage stalled action on the ISFs' entreaties. In 1965 Marc Hodler, IOC treasurer, apprised the Summer ISFs that they would share $100,000 of the Mexico City money. The ISFs pressed Brundage to reconsider. He entertained an agitated group of ISF leaders who challenged him on his seemingly precipitous decision concerning television money accruing to the ISFs. Rudyard Russell, president of AIBA, informed his colleagues later that Brundage had adopted a conciliatory approach. Brundage confessed to the group that he had "entirely overlooked our resolution of two years beforehand," observed Russell. "I think he was very embarrassed at the time . . . he realized that he had let us down, and that unfortunately the terms for Mexico [City] had already been made."[81] Brundage's performance was of an Academy Award–winning caliber.

Brundage's apology lacked credibility. While no correspondence exists confirming his determination to deny the ISF claim, his views expressed later in 1965 provide a better barometer of his true feelings. He was not inclined to meet their demand. The demand for one-third of available television revenue, noted Brundage, would "provoke trouble" when considered in concert with the rumblings from the NOCs that they, too, wanted a share of the television money.[82] "The IFs . . . are demanding one-third of all the money received from television, although it is the NOCs that have the expense of bringing the teams to the Games," Brundage wrote Guru Dutt Sondhi.[83] Sondhi, an avowed supporter of the NOCs' claim for financial assistance, castigated ISF leaders for their recent conduct: "As it is, the [ISFs] have assumed too much power and dignity to themselves and covertly, if not overtly, try to overawe the IOC."[84] Brundage's thinking expressed in advance of the upcoming IOC Session in Madrid gratified Sondhi: "There is undoubtedly going to be a battle on this subject [television money] at Madrid," wrote Brundage, "and we should support the NOCs, which are our agents."[85]

While members of the IOC Executive Board such as Sondhi, Massard, Ivar Vind (Denmark), and José de Clark Flores (Mexico) advocated on behalf of the NOCs,[86] Giulio Onesti was the most passionate spokesperson. Onesti's thoughts concerning the distribution of television revenue clashed with those expressed by ISF leaders. Their demand for one-third of all television revenue was "out of line with their principles of function which would appear to be purely that of a technical nature and the control over the regularity of sport events," said Onesti.[87] Brundage recognized that Onesti's proposal concerning television revenue would incite Bunny Ahearne and his colleagues. The OCOGs, according to Onesti's plan, would offset the travel expenses of officials and judges appointed by the ISFs to work at the Olympics. The ISFs would not receive a direct percentage of the television revenue.[88] By October 1965 Onesti had tempered his view. He accepted ceding some money directly to the ISFs if the legitimate needs of the NOCs, especially those experiencing financial difficulty, were addressed first.[89]

Brundage had a twofold motivation for reaching an accord with Onesti. First, Brundage resented the relentless badgering of the ISFs for one-third of the television money. In June 1965 Exeter informed him that some

ISF leaders had discussed a telecast ban of their events at future Olympic Games if the IOC refused to concede.[90] Brundage knew that the mission of the NOCs—promoting Olympism within their respective countries and managing the financial and logistical responsibilities of sponsoring an Olympic team on a quadrennial basis—deserved financial support if funds permitted. Recognition of this fact through a revised distribution formula might rein in the pretentious ISFs. Second, Onesti wanted to enhance the NOCs' involvement in Olympic decision-making. Believing in the axiom "united we stand, divided we fall," he lobbied for the establishment of a formally constituted association of NOCs. In 1964 he initiated a failed attempt to launch a NOC-sponsored Coordinating and Study Committee. Nevertheless, Onesti remained dedicated to the concept of an association of NOCs. Brundage, of course, opposed the proposed structure of an umbrella association for the NOCs. A "one country–one vote" statute would empower the NOCs in scores of developing countries and threaten the traditional Euro-American dominance of the Olympic Movement.[91] Brundage thought that some cash might placate Onesti and convince him to abandon the NOC unification project.

No longer could Brundage address concerns expressed by members of the Olympic organizations in dismissive fashion. Former IOC member Douglas F. Robey (U.S.A.) recalled Brundage's modus operandi in his prior dealings with the ISFs and NOCs on Olympic matters. When the IOC had meetings with the NOCs or ISFs, Brundage would state, "We'll take it under advisement. It was a brush-off . . . He just wouldn't listen . . . Let them talk, and then forget it," observed Robey of Brundage's approach.[92] This captures the atmosphere when Brundage met with representatives of the ISFs in 1963, but the issue demanded his attention two years later. The emphasis placed on television revenue by the ISFs and NOCs defied his concept of the foundation of amateurism and the Olympic Movement. The practical realities of the situation, however, necessitated action. Successful execution of the IOC's mission required the cooperation of the NOCs and ISFs. Independently of each other, the NOCs and ISFs were lobbying for 58% of all Olympic television revenue. Brundage understood the need for a resolution that protected the financial needs of future OCOGs that would bear the burden of increasing infrastructure costs. He arrived at an inspired solution.

Brundage appointed Giulio Onesti chairman of a seven-member committee charged with the responsibility of studying the distribution of television revenue from the 1972 Olympics. Other committee members named were Ryotaro Azuma (Japan), Gabriel Gemayel (Lebanon), Vladimir Stoytchev (Bulgaria), Mario Negri (Argentina), Reginald Alexander

(Kenya), and Guru Dutt Sondhi (India).[93] By tapping confirmed supporters of the NOCs such as Sondhi and Onesti, Brundage ensured that the financial aspirations of the NOCs received a fair hearing. Exeter, as a member of the IOC Executive Board, enjoyed ex-officio status on all subcommittees.[94] As the two heavyweights on the committee Exeter and Onesti had to work together to hammer out a solution that addressed the needs of the NOCs, ISFs, IOC, and OCOGs. Onesti pledged to present the committee's report at the Executive Board meeting scheduled for April 1966 in Rome.

Brundage's decision to grant the responsibility of chairing the committee to Onesti reflected considered thought. Onesti dismissed the exorbitant fiscal claims of the ISFs and favored providing financial support to the NOCs. His appointment sent a blunt message to the ISFs: their lobbying for one-third of all television revenue had failed. Still, Onesti understood that the ISFs must be considered in any revenue-sharing formula that might be constructed.[95] Brundage harbored some hope that Onesti, in arriving at an acceptable formula, would become convinced that the IOC and NOCs might work together under the current administrative structure without the need for a new and, in Brundage's mind, dangerous NOC-sponsored organization.

A sparring match ensued between Exeter and Onesti concerning the relative merits of the NOC and ISF claims for television money. Despite Brundage's instructions Onesti questioned the extent of the ISFs' need for financial support. In an exchange of correspondence that Onesti later characterized as "ample and intense,"[96] Exeter countered Onesti's position. "Your statement that the [IFs] incur no expenses is quite unjustified," stated Exeter. The IOC understood this fact, he argued, and had provided them with 50% of the indemnity payments provided to the IOC by Innsbruck and Tokyo organizers.[97] Onesti retreated. "I am sorry that the controversy has been brought to levels of exaggerated tension," he observed, "that do not conform to the reality and the Olympic nature of our conduct."[98] The committee continued to work toward a compromise arrangement satisfactory to all parties.

Onesti's committee produced a preliminary report to the IOC Executive Board that addressed distribution of future Olympic television revenue and the need for the IOC to be more proactive in its dealings with the television industry. Rapid changes in the television industry could be monitored if the Executive Board established a committee to deal with "the questions relating to television rights with competence and technical knowledge of the problem." Such a committee, suggested Onesti and his colleagues, might draw on the experiences of officials of past Organizing

Committees who had confronted the issue of negotiating television contracts. Open dialogue with representatives of Olympic bid committees enhanced the possibility of averting future disputes between the IOC and OCOGs with respect to television. The sliding scale that served as the template for the distribution of 1972 Olympic television money pacified Brundage. The OCOGs received the lion's share of the revenue. The committee believed that the 1972 Summer Games offered the possibility for $5 million in television revenue, and the anticipated value of television rights for the 1972 Winter Games was set at $1 million. The IOC retained the first million dollars from the television revenue of the Summer Games for equal distribution to the IOC, ISFs, and NOCs. Furthermore, $750,000 was earmarked for the IOC to distribute at its discretion. The OCOG would receive $3,250,000, 65% of the anticipated revenue. The same method of distribution was favored for the Winter Games revenue; however, the limited projected global sum required the committee to adjust the scale.[99] Still, the OCOG would receive 65% of the money.

While Brundage, Exeter, and Onesti as well as the members of the committee viewed the formula as a viable proposal, a number of ISF leaders considered it another attempt by the IOC to wield Ockham's Razor. "Pure parsimony. We are the bosses," Ahearne exclaimed at a closed door meeting of the ISFs in April 1966, convened in part for the purpose of studying Onesti's proposal.[100] Ahearne defended the ISFs' claim to one-third of the television money. A tense atmosphere prevailed. Berge Phillips of the International Amateur Aquatics Federation (FINA) and Oscar State of the International Weightlifting Federation (FILA) also opposed the formula. News of the recent signing of ABC's $4.5 million contract with the 1968 Mexico City Organizing Committee, in light of Brundage's earlier decision to supply the Summer ISFs with a paltry $100,000, angered ISF leaders.[101] It seemed reasonable to assume that the 1972 Summer Olympic television rights would exceed $5 million, yet Onesti's plan guaranteed the ISFs only $333,333. Any further monies would be distributed at the discretion of the IOC. Similarly, the Winter ISFs had been presented with a proposal that guaranteed them $66,666. The ISFs resolved to renew their demand for one-third of all television revenue.

Following a review of Onesti's report, the IOC Executive Board determined that recent developments in the sport television marketplace required analysis and consideration. The Executive Board sought to quell dissent among the ISFs with a number of changes to the distribution formula. Onesti's plan mandated the allocation of equal shares to the IOC, ISFs, and NOCs of the initial $1 million of Summer Olympic television money and one-third of the first $200,000 of Winter Olympic television revenue. Any further money was to be distributed by the IOC. But the plan established a ceiling for the IOC's share of the television money. The IOC had no claim on a percentage of any revenue in excess of $3 million for the Summer Olympic Games and $600,000 for the sale of the rights to the Winter Olympics. Such an arrangement prevented the ISFs from deriving any profit in the event that Summer Games television rights exceeded $3 million. When the 1968 Mexico City Organizing Committee concluded a $4.5 million contract for U.S. television rights, the problem became clear. The IOC Executive Board removed the ceiling and included the ISFs, NOCs, and IOC in the distribution of all television monies, while protecting the financial interests of the OCOGs.[102] This policy was also applied to the formula for the distribution of Winter Games television revenue. Yet these adjustments did not satisfy the ISFs' claim to one-third of all television money. Would it be acceptable to them?

At a heated debate during the ensuing meeting of the IOC General Session, Berge Phillips and Roger Coulon reiterated the ISFs' demand for one-third of all television revenue. Brundage stifled further discussion. Both he and Exeter were satisfied with the revised proposal. The ISFs, observed Brundage, enjoyed the opportunity to recover their yearly expenses through their world championships. The NOCs and IOC, he concluded, also had financial requirements. William Jones, whose name would become familiar to Olympic fans in the United States six years later because of his intervention in the controversial U.S./Soviet men's basketball final in Munich, convinced Phillips and Coulon to back down. They tied their acquiescence to the establishment of a "common committee" to review the issue of television money sharing for 1976 and beyond, however.[103] The parties reached an accord, but the subject posed a continuing challenge to Brundage's ideals of pure amateurism and Olympism.

With peace came a price. The IOC approved a plan that encouraged OCOGs to "obtain as much as possible from the television companies."[104] Under the new formula the Summer Organizing Committee received nothing from the first million dollars, one-third of the second million, and two-thirds of any revenue exceeding $2 million. The removal of the cap on the money accruing to the IOC for distribution among the IOC, ISFs, and NOCs encouraged OCOGs to extract maximum revenue from the international television networks. Brundage was mindful of the potential problems: "If we are not careful," he told Swiss IOC member Albert Mayer, "this television money can lead to disaster."[105] Within weeks of the Rome Session Brundage sounded out Exeter for his thoughts on whether there was a viable means for the IOC to control how the ISFs spent the television money.[106] This was tantamount to closing the barn door after the horse had bolted.

THE ROME FORMULA

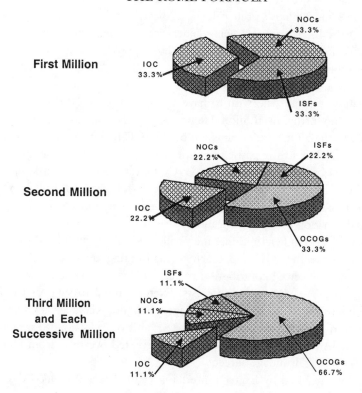

Roger Coulon, Berge Phillips, and Bunny Ahearne, three of the most vociferous critics of the IOC's treatment of the ISFs, determined that a new approach might assist the ISFs to achieve their financial goals. Their strategy mirrored the work of Giulio Onesti within the community of NOCs. The Rome Formula did not discourage Onesti from working toward the establishment of a Permanent General Assembly of NOCs (PGA). Similarly, Coulon and Phillips considered the Rome Formula to be a stepping stone rather than an end point in the ISFs' campaign for one-third of all television revenue. They resented Exeter's authority over the distribution of the ISFs' money, which negated a move to the assignment of equal shares for all ISFs.[107] Their determination to establish a General Assembly of International Sports Federations (GAIF), whose mission involved lobbying the IOC on issues pertaining to amateurism, site selection, and television money, alarmed Exeter.[108]

Exeter was not only convinced that the establishment of a GAIF would be harmful to the IOC; he was also concerned for his own federation, the IAAF. Coulon's activities, surmised Exeter, were motivated primarily by his dissatisfaction with the IOC's method of dealing with television revenue.[109] Coulon's and Phillips's principal allies, Ahearne and Thomas Keller, president of the International Rowing Federation (FISA), supported the GAIF initiative and called for the IOC to revise its approach to distributing television money.[110] If the IOC did not defuse this situation, warned Exeter, Onesti would become a greater threat: "We would be putting a sword in the hands of those who wish to have an association of NOCs."[111] Onesti required no further motivation. He interpreted the concession of television money to the NOCs as an admission by the IOC that it had not dealt fairly with the NOCs in the past. Attributing this policy shift to the increased pressure placed on the IOC by the NOCs, Onesti pushed forward in his efforts to galvanize support for the PGA.[112] His efforts bore fruit in 1968, when sixty-four NOCs met prior to the Mexico City Olympics and agreed to the formation of the organization.

Exeter also understood that the smaller ISFs might well band together and challenge the IOC's approach to distributing the television money based on a perceived contribution of each ISF to the Games. In order to protect the IAAF's financial interests, Exeter refused to support Coulon and Phillips. The IOC, he told Brundage, could not recognize any such organization if it did not include the IAAF and other major ISFs, among them AIBA and FIFA, which had similarly resisted overtures from Phillips and Coulon.[113] Brundage agreed.

While incensed by Exeter's interference, Phillips and Coulon did not abandon their efforts. In April 1967 GAIF staged its inaugural meeting at Lausanne's Continental Hotel, a short walk from the IOC's Mon Repos headquarters. In a letter to Brundage Coulon lashed out at Exeter: "The majority of the IFs [cannot] admit the fact that the [IAAF], whose President is also a member of the [Executive Board] of the IOC considers to have the right to oppose our decisions."[114] GAIF renewed the demand for one-third of all Olympic television money and called for the distribution of equal shares to the Summer and Winter ISFs from the sums derived from the sale of television rights to the respective 1968 Olympic festivals.[115]

Brundage received a barrage of correspondence from Exeter concerning GAIF. Any concession to Coulon and Phillips with respect to granting the ISFs autonomy over the distribution of their share of the television money, warned Exeter, jeopardized the working relationship between the IOC and the IAAF.[116] Brundage labored to quell a full-scale rebellion. He informed the ISFs that the distribution of 1968 Olympic television revenue had been approved by the IOC and defended Exeter's past efforts. He also invited a discussion with the ISFs about future television revenue but stressed that television money belonged to the IOC. Brundage censured

Coulon and his colleagues for their fixation with money: "I have deplored on more than one occasion, the idea of financial considerations being introduced into Olympic affairs." "For the first time," he noted, "serious arguments have been provoked and I do not like it!"[117]

In 1968 the ISFs revisited the television issue in meetings with the IOC Executive Board and the newly conceived Finance Commission. The process left Phillips, Coulon, Ahearne, and Keller disappointed. Even though GAIF enticed all ISFs with the exception of the IAAF to enter the fold, they could not move the IOC to cede control of their share of the television money. The IOC Finance Commission announced that a unanimously supported proposal from the ISFs was required for the IOC to transfer the distribution of the television money to them. The IAAF opposed GAIF's call for equal shares of the television revenue for the ISFs. The Finance Commission's stance reflected the practical reality of track and field as the showpiece sport on the Olympic program.[118] While the Winter ISFs concluded an agreement for equal distribution of television revenue from the 1972 Innsbruck Games,[119] it took the Summer ISFs four years to reach unanimity. They finally determined that 50% of the money should be distributed evenly, while the remaining 50% would be allocated on the basis of gate receipts.[120] In the end this preserved Exeter's approach, because he had enacted virtually the same distribution formula in determining the share of the ISFs' money from the 1968 Mexico City Games.[121]

As much as Brundage resented the increasing prominence of money as a topic of discussion at Olympic meetings, it was folly to ignore the need to improve the IOC's method of managing its financial resources. Even Brundage supported the establishment of the IOC Finance Commission in 1967 under the chairmanship of Lord Luke of England. The IOC authorized the Finance Commission to prepare quarterly financial statements.[122] Within a few months the Finance Commission established new expense policies in light of overspending on the part of some IOC staff members.[123] The changing nexus of sport and economics and the designs of some IOC members to enhance the organization's financial status, however, encouraged the rapid expansion of the Finance Commission's mandate to include control of the expenditures of IOC committees, budgeting, fund-raising, advising OCOGs on financial matters, monitoring television negotiations conducted by the OCOGs, and recommending formulas to the Executive Board for the allocation of television money to the NOCs and ISFs.[124] Brundage lamented this treacherous path. He considered some IOC members' fascination with money and the "obnoxious" attitude of the ISF leaders antithetical to their roles as advocates for amateur sport.[125]

REFLECTIONS

In 1955 Avery Brundage expressed mixed emotions about the prospect of television money. The potential impact on the image of the Olympic Movement and the articulation of the IOC and commercial television networks concerned him. His early efforts to harness television as a source of revenue for the IOC, as well as a means to increase the size of the Olympic viewing audience, reflected his reservations. He established a system that left negotiations to the OCOGs but retained IOC control over the distribution of the money.

Between 1955 and 1972 Brundage's disenchantment with his decision to embrace television revenue grew. Continual arguments ensued with OCOG leaders and advocates for the ISFs and NOCs who sought to assert their financial interests. The appearance of television money prompted uncontrolled spending by IOC secretary-general Johann Westerhoff's administration in Lausanne that left the IOC "broke."[126] Money prompted conflict between Westerhoff's successor, Monique Berlioux, and members of the Finance Commission who debated how the IOC finances should be managed.[127] The need to monitor the IOC's finances precipitated the formation of the Finance Commission, which soon abandoned the IOC's hands-off policy on television negotiations. After consulting entertainment industry executives for advice on television matters, the commission established target figures for Munich negotiators in their discussions with non-U.S. television executives.[128] These actions reflected the opinion of IOC members such as Kenya's Reginald Alexander, who referred to television money as the "lifeblood of [the IOC's] administrative existence."[129] "Distressed and disillusioned," writes Allen Guttmann, "Brundage watched as the IOC adopted first the financial procedures and then the fiscal attitudes of a modern corporation."[130]

By the time of his retirement at the Munich Olympics in 1972 Brundage's verdict was clear. The IOC "should have nothing to do with money," he concluded. Arguments between Olympic leaders and the amounts of money flowing into the coffers of the IOC and the ISFs imperiled the standing of the Olympic Movement. "Public respect is at stake," pleaded Brundage before members of the IOC Executive Board. "It has taken 75 years to build the present reputation, which could be ruined in 75 minutes if those responsible were not careful."[131] At the conclusion of the Munich Games, following the initial application of the Rome Formula, shares of television revenue allotted to the ISFs ranged from $44,597 to $424,239.[132] If he were alive today, it would not be difficult to gauge Brundage's consternation upon learning that the shares of the $86.6

million directed to the twenty-six ISFs participating in the 1996 Atlanta Olympics ranged from $2.17 million to $8.67 million. The seven ISFs that organized sports on the 1998 Nagano program shared in excess of $50 million.[133]

Brundage's message was in vain. His successor, Lord Killanin, was committed to improving the IOC's fiscal situation.[134] France's Jean de Beaumont, who served as Killanin's right-hand man on financial issues, mouthed the proper words for Brundage's sake, but his heart was elsewhere. "We are sliding slowly towards 'money business.' As you [Brundage] repeated it so many times, the Olympic Movement so far never had any money, and never needed any money," wrote Beaumont. "Our ideology, which is also a tremendous strength is chiefly based upon goodwill, spontaneity and enthusiasm, these three factors being sources of pure and honest energy."[135] Yet when Brundage proposed ceding all money to the OCOGs, in exchange for an agreement to fund the IOC's Lausanne operation, Beaumont fretted about the impact on the NOCs.[136]

Avery Brundage presided over the IOC during a period that witnessed a substantial philosophical shift in its approach to money, born of major changes in the television industry and years of amateur sport leaders' having operated without financial resources. Money enhanced their ability to promote amateur sport and the Olympic Movement throughout the world, argued IOC members and leaders of the ISFs and NOCs. These sport officials came to consider money vital to the execution of their mandates. "A younger Brundage might have . . . presented a more forceful argument to those within the IOC who wanted to chart a different financial course for the organization. In short, Brundage, an aging idealist, at odds with sport officials inside and outside the IOC chambers concerning financial matters, including the IOC's involvement with television, found the current of change too strong and was swept under."[137]

While Brundage viewed these changes as a major source of conflict within the Olympic Movement as well as evidence of a diminished Olympic ideal, Killanin took a different view. With respect to the ISFs, which had warred with Brundage over money and amateur regulations in the 1960s, he believed that television "played an extraordinary part in binding the Olympic Family together." A severe fracturing of the Olympic Movement was perhaps averted because television money proved a "compelling part of their need to stay within the Movement."[138] What could not be debated was the fact that the transformation of the IOC into a corporate entity was under way—and television money, more than any other factor, provided the impetus for this change.

CHAPTER 5

TELEVISION AND THE 1970s

Munich and Montréal

Two distinct phenomena influenced relations within the Olympic Movement in the 1970s. First, television rights fees spiraled due to continuing refinement of satellite technology; second, the popularity of sports television prompted OCOGs to claim greater shares of the revenue than afforded them by the Rome Formula. Burgeoning television rights fees and OCOG efforts to circumvent the Rome Formula strained the working relationship between IOC and OCOG officials. Avery Brundage's negotiating model for the 1960s proved altogether unworkable in the 1970s. Although Brundage had ceded responsibility for negotiating television contracts to the OCOGs in 1958 in order to keep the IOC above any commercial disputes, he had zealously guarded the IOC's right to distribute the money. Repeated clashes between Lausanne's Olympic nabobs and OCOG functionaries in Munich and Montréal inevitably drew the IOC toward compromising its "hands off" approach to negotiating Olympic television rights contracts with the world's networks. All parties understood the marketability of the Games as a television property. This scenario led to anger, confrontation, and frustration, sometimes straining or rupturing friendships.

THE MUNICH PRECEDENT: TELEVISION RIGHTS FEES VS. TECHNICAL SERVICES PAYMENTS

The Rome Formula did not prove to be the panacea for Brundage's struggles with ISFs and NOCs on the subject of sharing television money. As we have seen, the GAIF and PGA emerged as formally constituted organizations representing the interests and welfare of the ISFs and NOCs, respectively. Vigorous debates ensued between Brundage, members of the IOC Finance Commission, and representatives of the 1972 Munich and Sapporo Organizing Committees concerning the IOC's method of dispersing television money. The Sapporo and Munich organizers' approach to negotiations with U.S. television networks guaranteed friction between the IOC and the OCOGs. Willi Daume and Herbert Kunze, president and secretary-general of the Munich Organizing Committee, respectively, reached an agreement with ABC for $13.5 million, but the negotiating teams designated only $7.5 million of that sum as the television rights fee. ABC paid the remaining $6 million to Munich to offset costs of providing broadcast facilities.[1] Tomoo Sato, secretary-general of the Sapporo Organizing Committee, informed Lausanne officials that NBC had agreed to pay $5 million for the television rights to the Sapporo Winter Games and a supplementary technical services fee of $1,401,000.[2]

Brundage, Exeter, and Lord Luke, a key member of the Finance Commission, appalled by this arbitrary approach by both OCOGs, opposed the basis of these agreements. Broadcast facility costs, concluded Luke, must be considered in the same vein as stadium expenses—in other words, as an element of each OCOG's capital budget. The challenge of staging a festival, he said, entailed clear fiscal responsibilities.[3] If the IOC accepted the Munich and Sapporo contracts the IOC, NOCs, and ISFs would be contributing to the construction of telecast facilities. Exeter confirmed that this effort to skirt the IOC's allocation policy invited difficulties for the IOC. Specific Olympic organizations, for instance, would be quick to register displeasure over the Munich/Sapporo "technical fees" approach. First among the disgruntled would be the unsuccessful host city bid groups, each of which would argue that Munich and Sapporo had violated their pledge to cover *all* infrastructure expenses. The ISFs and the NOCs would take issue with the Munich/Sapporo approach because it deprived them of money.[4] Realizing this, the IOC Finance Commission and Executive Board withheld their approval of the contracts.[5] While Sapporo organizers debated the IOC's position on the "technical services" issue, eventually determining to transfer all television revenue to Lausanne, Munich officials stood firm.[6]

Willi Daume proved obdurate and refused to retreat from his position. "Our committee," he wrote, "has no intention of demanding anything that is not realistic."[7] While ABC paid $4.5 million for U.S. television rights to the Mexico City Olympics, cameras, videotape recorders, local and international television circuits, film processing, and telephone and telex costs required an additional outlay of $3.5 million. The Munich Organizing Committee and ABC, stated Daume, wrote these expenses into their contract.[8] This loophole concerned the IOC. "I do not think that any of us ever visualized that they [Daume and Kunze] would not pay the proceeds gross to us, and in fact help themselves to 2 million dollars of the IOC, [ISF,] and NOC money," wrote a perturbed Exeter.[9] Though the Finance

Commission approved the agreement following consideration of Daume's lengthy written submission in defense of the contract, the Executive Board balked.[10] After almost two years of bickering, Jean de Beaumont, an emerging force on the Finance Commission, reached a compromise agreement grudgingly accepted by all parties. In exchange for Daume's agreement to cancel a loan of $274,200 made to the IOC by Munich, the Executive Board approved the ABC contract in March 1971, two years after the conclusion of the initial negotiations between Daume and ABC.[11]

THE MUNICH AND SAPPORO GAMES

The "polite" friction existing between the Sapporo Organizing Committee and the IOC on the issue of "technical services" did not stand in the way of a Japanese Winter Olympic celebration on a par with Tokyo's Summer Games almost a decade earlier. At its session in Rome in 1966 the IOC awarded the 1972 Olympic Winter Games to Sapporo, the capital city of the Japanese island of Hokkaido.[12] Sapporo had been chosen host city for the 1940 Winter Games, which did not take place, and it had lost out to Grenoble as host city for the 1968 Winter Games. The Japanese government regarded the Games in Sapporo as an opportunity to expand the country's international reputation established as a result of the Tokyo Olympic project. Sapporo invested enormous sums of money in the construction of new sports venues. Huge expenditures made the 1972 Olympic Winter Games the most extravagant and expensive Winter Games thus far. A 300% increase over the Winter Games in Grenoble in the sale of television broadcast rights assisted organizers in meeting their budgetary needs.[13] The successful satellite transmission of images from the Tokyo Olympic Games in 1964 resulted in high expectations for broadcasting success in Sapporo.[14] To ensure success, NHK, a government-sponsored network, provided the television feed for broadcasters to choose the programming coverage they wished.

The day before the opening ceremony in Sapporo's Makomanai ice stadium, the OCOG suffered a major setback. The IOC ordered Karl Schranz, an Austrian alpine skiing idol, to leave the Olympic Village, allegedly for breaching the IOC's amateur regulations. At a time when many top skiers made money through product endorsements and sponsorships, the IOC, pressured by Brundage, decided to single out Schranz for punishment. His exclusion was meant to be a warning against the increasing encroachment of commercialization of sport. Alpine skiing was one of the worst offenders. According to Brundage, skiers "were more brazen than the other athletes in their subversion of Olympic rules."[15] The stubborn

Brundage demanded the ban of some forty other alleged "professional" athletes from competing at the Sapporo Olympic Winter Games. Saner heads prevailed; a majority of IOC members rejected his demand.[16]

On 13 February 1972 the Olympic flag was lowered in Sapporo's Makomanai ice stadium and ceremoniously folded, symbolizing the end of the Games. As the Sapporo Games passed into the annals of Olympic history, attention shifted to Munich and the Games of the Twentieth Olympiad.

At the IOC Session in Rome in 1966, members listened to presentations on behalf of Detroit, Madrid, Montréal, and Munich, the cities bidding for the 1972 Olympic Games. In the second round of voting the Munich contingent, led by Willi Daume, won the election, receiving thirty-one of the possible fifty-nine votes.[17] Almost immediately Munich set to work, determined to erase the unpleasant memories of Germany's "Nazi Games" thirty years before and highlight the city's emergence as "one of the most dynamic economies in the world."[18] These Games were intended to be, above all else, the "cheerful Games" (*heitere Spiele*).[19]

With considerable dedication and expense, Munich did its utmost to show the world a revitalized, prosperous, and friendly West Germany. Parkland just beyond the city limits provided the site for the Olympic Stadium, swimming hall, and basketball facilities. Each of the new facilities established new architectural standards for future Olympic venues. The OCOG and the government spent more than $3 billion on preparations for the Games, including the construction of new roads and a subway line to move people to and from the venues.[20]

One of the most flamboyant products for sale in Munich's "Olympic marketplace" proved to be the first official Olympic mascot, Waldi, whose canine image was licensed to private firms. A private advertising agency engaged by Munich organizing authorities carried on a vigorous campaign to sell a variety of products.[21] Munich secured further financial support through the establishment of a "Foundation for the Promotion of the Olympic Games," as well as a "Society for the Promotion of the Munich Games."[22] These organizations generated considerable direct and indirect revenues through the design and sale of commemorative coins and stamps, an Olympic lottery, licensed products, and donations in the form of cash, services, and equipment. As noted earlier, the revenue distribution scheme devised by the Munich organizers for U.S. television revenue added to the surety of substantial revenue for the Games.

The Munich Games opened on 26 August 1972. Athletes from 122 countries competed in twenty-one sports throughout the sixteen-day event. Shockingly, on 5 September 1972 the "festival of joy" was plunged into a disaster that will be remembered as the greatest tragedy in the history of the Modern Olympic Games.[23] Before dawn on the tenth day of the festival terrorist commandos of the Palestine Liberation Organization called Black September scaled a fence guarding the Olympic Village, forced their way into the dormitory housing Israel's team, killed two coaches, and took nine hostages, seven wrestlers and two Israeli undercover security officers. Twelve thousand German police immediately surrounded the village.

The terrorists demanded the release of 200 guerrillas from Israeli jails, but prime minister Golda Meir's refusal forced West German officials to negotiate with the terrorists, who finally accepted an offer of guaranteed safe passage to Cairo with their hostages. Helicopters carried the terrorists and their hostages from the Olympic Village to Munich's military air base at Fürstenfeldbruck, where a Lufthansa plane waited on the tarmac for their exit from Germany. Those who witnessed the following events, captured on camera, are not likely to forget them in their lifetime. During the attempted transfer of terrorists and hostages from helicopters to the Lufthansa aircraft German police and commandos opened fire. The terrorists employed grenades to kill the helpless hostages, who sat in the helicopters. Within minutes five commandos and one police officer lay dead as well as all the hostages.

With Munich's dream of a friendly and open Olympic Games shattered, Daume stated that "it would be difficult to resume the Games."[24] In a controversial decision, however, Avery Brundage declared that "the Games must go on." Following a one-day moratorium and a memorial service held at the Olympic stadium, the remaining members of the Israeli team returned home.[25] Indeed the Games did go on, but the appalling violation of the Olympic precinct overshadowed the startling and inspired performances of Mark Spitz, Valery Borzov, and Olga Korbut. In summarizing the Games of the Twentieth Olympiad in Munich, Richard Mandell wrote, "the Olympic Games reached a peak in terms of organization, public image, art and tragedy."[26]

THE AFTERMATH OF MUNICH: A POT BOILS

Willi Daume's success in lobbying for a technical services component in the Munich Organizing Committee's agreement with ABC provides the starting point for understanding how television matters impeded IOC/OCOG relations in the 1970s. The IOC's efforts at stonewalling his television agreement with ABC, argued Daume, betrayed a lack of understanding of the immense costs involved in providing the technical infrastructure needed to telecast Olympic events in the new era of satellite technology. IOC officials, who reluctantly agreed to the separation of television rights and technical services payments in the U.S. contract in order to resolve a two-year impasse, viewed Daume's approach as a naked attempt to limit the amounts of money payable to the IOC, ISFs, and NOCs. Though the actors changed, the IOC encountered this basic argument with successive Organizing Committees in the 1970s.

Daume's revolutionary initiative did not go unnoticed in Innsbruck and Montréal, host cities of the 1976 Olympic Winter Games and Summer Olympics, respectively. Though the IOC concluded a quick agreement with Karl-Heinz Klee (secretary-general of the Innsbruck Organizing Committee) on the distribution of U.S. television money and the basis of contracts for other markets,[27] Roger Rousseau, president of the Montréal Olympic Games Organizing Committee (COJO), bedeviled the IOC's new president, Lord Killanin, Jean de Beaumont, and Monique Berlioux with his persistent efforts to sidestep IOC television policy. Rousseau's defiance and the inability of the IOC to enforce its interpretation of the Rome Formula in advance of the 1976 Montréal Olympics posed severe dilemmas.

Rousseau's antics aimed at maximizing Montréal's share of television revenue at the expense of the IOC, ISFs, and NOCs troubled Lord Killanin. As early as 1973 he stated that the IOC could avoid this form of aggravation by managing all television negotiations in the future.[28] Brundage's system of claiming a fixed payment from the Organizing Committees and leaving television negotiations to OCOG personnel, noted Berlioux, offered an alternative means of averting these difficulties.[29] But Killanin could not turn his back on the boom in the sports television market and the promise of escalating television rights fees. Rousseau's actions prompted the IOC to establish a subcommittee on television dedicated to increasing the IOC's knowledge bank on the television industry. Killanin understood the folly in taking charge of negotiations without first expanding the organization's understanding of the negotiation process involved in the sale of television rights to sports events.[30] When the Lake Placid and Moscow Organizing Committees also proved difficult, the need for the IOC's enhanced involvement in future negotiations became obvious. Killanin and his IOC colleagues, seeking a means to protect the IOC's financial interests, approved a policy in 1977 whereby the IOC would negotiate television contracts jointly with the 1984 Olympic Organizing Committees.

The determined effort of the European Broadcasting Union (EBU) to prevent the escalation of its Olympic television rights payments provided a subplot to the tension between the IOC and the Organizing Committees in the 1970s. EBU succeeded in its campaign, paying $1,745,000 for the right to cover the 1972 Munich Olympics and $4,500,000 to Montréal for television rights (including technical services) to the 1976 Olympics. Moscow officials settled with EBU on a sale price of $5,652,500 for television rights (and technical services) for the 1980 Summer Olympics.[31] During the same period the price paid by the contracting U.S. network spiraled from $13.5 million (Munich/ABC) to $85 million (Moscow/NBC).

EBU executives employed two arguments to convince IOC officials that the Organizing Committees' demands for enhanced revenue from the European market were unrealistic. First, they maintained that EBU's status as a government-funded service prevented it from using commercial advertising as a means of generating revenue to compensate for expenses. Free of such shackles, U.S. television networks engaged in spirited bidding for Olympic television rights, while EBU operated on a fixed budget set by European governments. Second, if the IOC wanted blanket coverage in Western Europe, EBU represented its only option in the 1970s. This fact provided added negotiating leverage for EBU officials.[32]

The IOC was committed to a policy (then and now) that guaranteed widespread coverage of the Olympic Games. In the 1970s there existed no EBU competitor capable of ensuring widespread coverage of the Games throughout Western Europe. Despite Roger Rousseau's concerted effort to extract a larger sum from Western Europe, EBU held firm, refusing to yield to his demands. While Killanin appreciated the prospect of more revenue and indeed allowed Rousseau to pursue his agenda for an extended period, he feared the media and popular backlash resulting from a blackout in Europe. Killanin finally took a hands-on role to avert a crisis by advising Montréal to accept the final EBU offer.[33] Montréal was left with little choice but to settle on EBU's terms. EBU, fully understanding its competitive advantage, proved a stubborn negotiator with OCOGs in the 1970s.

UNSETTLING TIMES:
THE IOC, MONTRÉAL, AND THE SALE OF TELEVISION RIGHTS

IOC officials, whose memories of Willi Daume's negotiating approach remained vivid, shuddered at Roger Rousseau and Karl-Heinz Klee's plans for negotiations with U.S. television networks. Despite promises to abide by the IOC's legislation, Rousseau and Klee defended their right to separate television rights from technical services fees in the U.S. contract. The U.S. television rights contract represented a fundamental financial priority for OCOGs. While providing an early infusion of cash to the OCOGs, it also helped to establish targets for contract negotiations in other markets. From the perspective of IOC administrators, this money also provided a means of forecasting its own budgetary resources for the next four years. Rousseau and Klee viewed Daume's contract with ABC as a precedent and considered a technical services component in the U.S. contract a viable avenue toward maximizing early proceeds from television negotiations.

Within two months of the close of the Munich Olympics Killanin traveled to Montréal to gauge the city's state of preparedness. He learned that Rousseau and his colleagues planned to reserve money from the U.S. contract for technical services.[34] Montréal required this money, argued Rousseau, to deal with the heavy financial burden of providing equipment and space for the world's broadcasters. Killanin countered Rousseau's position, stating emphatically that the gross receipts from television negotiations would have to be forwarded to Lausanne. When Montréal accepted the responsibility of staging the Games, noted Killanin, it accepted the financial obligations involved in providing the sport complex and the facilities for transmitting the events to the world's television audience. "I personally believe that 'hardware' is as much a part of the installations as Press Boxes or Running Tracks," he stated, stressing that "this point will have to be fought hard by the Finance Commission."[35] Montréal's position ignored Mayor Jean Drapeau's pledge that gross television receipts would be subject to the Rome Formula, lamented Killanin.

Killanin turned to newly appointed Finance Commission chairman Jean de Beaumont to safeguard the IOC's interests in the stalemate. At a meeting of the Finance Commission in November 1972 Paul Desrochers, president of COJO's Finance Committee, revealed that Montréal was nearing an agreement for U.S. television rights with ABC for $25 million. Montréal anticipated an additional $25 million from the sale of television rights in other global markets. Of this $50 million, stated Desrochers in haughty fashion, Montréal would transfer $7 million to the IOC. Beaumont and fellow Finance Commission members Lord Luke and Marc Hodler registered their opposition to any such plan since the gross receipts were subject to distribution according to the Rome Formula. Gerald M. Snyder, vice-president of COJO's Finance Committee, argued that the Rome Formula applied to television rights only. His colleague Desrochers asserted that the IOC's policy was unacceptable to the provincial government of Québec. Beaumont quickly offered a compromise arrangement whereby the IOC would accept $12.5 million as opposed to the $18 million that it would receive if anticipated revenue ($50 million) was distributed according to the Rome Formula. No agreement resulted.[36]

Beaumont's preemptive offer to Montréal startled Killanin. He informed Monique Berlioux that the proposal required the Executive Board's consideration. The IOC had to be cognizant of the financial interests of the ISFs and the NOCs while at the same time providing financial security for the operation of the IOC's Lausanne headquarters in the event that an Olympic festival was canceled. Killanin also informed Rousseau of his dissatisfaction with the results of Desrochers's meeting with the Finance Commission. He reasserted the IOC's claim to the gross receipts from *all* television contracts.[37]

Before the parties resolved this matter Corydon Dunham, vice-president and general counsel for NBC, alerted Killanin that Montréal had concluded an agreement with Roone Arledge, president of ABC Sports, completely contrary to the concept of an open bidding process. During the recent Munich Olympics NBC had indicated its interest in bidding for the Montréal television rights. Montréal assured NBC executives that they would be granted an opportunity to bid and would be provided time to prepare the bid following the conclusion of a study of the television operation by Canada's host broadcaster, the Canadian Broadcasting Corporation (CBC). When NBC approached Montréal in mid-December, officials learned that ABC had obtained the "inside track" on an agreement. Arledge had been courting Montréal officials for two months. Rousseau pledged that the "matter was open" and granted NBC one week to structure its bid. Before NBC could present its bid, however, Montréal accepted ABC's offer and granted Arledge the right to match any competing offer. Concluded NBC's Dunham: "The bidding procedure has been made a sham."[38] Through communication with Rousseau Monique Berlioux attempted in vain to "get answers" for NBC's exclusion from the negotiations process.[39]

Rousseau contended that NBC and CBS had failed to initiate discussions concerning U.S. television rights and technical facilities with a Montréal task force established for this purpose. Roone Arledge publicly criticized NBC for playing "the wounded party." "Bidding is simply not the way rights are granted for most sports . . . Not a single sports event on NBC's schedule," he observed, "was gained through competitive bidding." Arledge further taunted his counterparts at NBC, chiding that their arguments reflected "the public relations stance you take if you're a disappointed suitor, and NBC often takes that stance."[40] While Arledge dismissed NBC's protest, ABC's legal department warned NBC that it risked legal proceedings if it interfered in the contractual relationship with Montréal.[41] Private negotiations with ABC defy logic when one considers that the presence of two other networks would have done nothing to limit ABC's bid and would probably have encouraged a higher sale price. Rumors surfaced—denied by all parties, including NBC—that ABC's privileged negotiating position resulted from NBC's refusal to pay a $5 million kickback to the provincial government of Québec.[42] These events marked the beginning of Killanin's troubles with Montréal concerning television. When he reviewed the contract, Killanin noticed that Montréal had deducted money from the global sum for technical services. Even though Montréal and ABC signed the television agreement on 3 January 1973, a copy did not arrive in Lausanne until 27 January.[43] At this time Killanin read that Montréal reserved one-half of the $25-million contract with ABC to assist in its effort to provide broadcast facilities. This action left only $12.5 million subject to allocation according to the Rome Formula. Killanin informed the members of the Finance Commission that the IOC would withhold approval of the contract until it received legal advice.[44]

In early February Killanin summoned Montréal officials to Lausanne for discussions on bothersome television matters. While members of the IOC Finance Commission and Executive Board met to consider their options, Montréal officials paced the halls uneasily, pondering Marc Hodler's reminder to them that the Organizing Committee did not *give* the IOC anything; the money belonged to the IOC, which would give the Organizing Committee its share. The Organizing Committee merely negotiated with the television companies on the IOC's behalf, Hodler pontificated.[45] Beaumont favored a rapid decision. The IOC could not afford to lose income sacrificed by delayed investment of its share of ABC's initial payment.[46] Still, Beaumont and his colleagues on the Finance Commission found Rousseau's terms unacceptable. Once again Rousseau dismissed Beaumont's proposal, which would have granted the IOC $12.5 million if worldwide television revenue totaled $50 million. With respect to the ABC contract, Rousseau maintained that the IOC was entitled to one-third of $12.5 million rather than one-third of $25 million. Killanin did not support Beaumont's proposal either, but for different reasons: he did not consider $50 million to be a realistic target figure for negotiations. Killanin sought a more concrete agreement concerning distribution of future television revenue. Following consultation with the IOC's three vice-presidents, he informed the Montréal delegation, including Rousseau, Drapeau, and Snyder, that the IOC had approved the ABC contract; however, its consent to the separation of television rights and technical services payments was limited solely to the U.S. contract.[47]

Within days of his return to Montréal Rousseau lobbied Killanin for the inclusion of a television services component in *all* future television contracts. Future negotiations must be discussed by the IOC and Montréal "in a spirit of partnership in the interest of the Olympic movement," wrote Rousseau, "rather than the highly pecuniary motives which animated the past meetings."[48] These two messages conveyed his belief that some sober reflection was required on the part of IOC officials. He implied that his approach was a practical method of dealing with the infrastructure challenges faced by Montréal and future OCOGs. The Rome Formula, countered Killanin, had been put in place with special consideration for the OCOGs. Of the four recipients of television money (OCOGs, IOC, ISFs, and NOCs), noted Killanin, the OCOGs received the largest share in recognition of their legitimate financial needs.[49] Further exchange of correspondence between the two antagonists failed to result in a concession by either.

Killanin also monitored Montréal's discussions with EBU concerning Olympic television rights for Western Europe. EBU tried diligently to temper Montréal's expectations. Georges Straschnov, EBU's delegate in attendance at the meeting of the Finance Commission in November 1972, informed Montréal officials that EBU's offer would not exceed the amount paid for Munich television rights. Contrary to the Munich experience, he commented, satellite costs involved in transmitting images from Montréal drained EBU's resources. Also, time zone differences precluded live coverage during peak viewing times in Europe.[50] Straschnov stated clearly that EBU would not deal with an agent hired to conduct negotiations on behalf of Montréal. Despite his pronouncement, Montréal hired Marvin Josephson, a former lawyer with CBS, to pursue maximum returns from the European market. Josephson's strategy aimed at fragmenting the strength of EBU by negotiating separate agreements with various member networks.

J. W. Rengelink, chairman of EBU's TV Programme Committee, testily informed Killanin that Josephson's stated goal of $25 million from the West European market was unrealistic.[51] When EBU expressed its displeasure with Josephson's effort to undermine the EBU, Killanin refused to alter the IOC's level of involvement. While it was critical for the IOC to remain informed of developments, he told Berlioux, "it is important that the IOC should not be caught between the EBU, which naturally wishes to pay the minimum, and COJO, which is endeavoring to obtain the maximum."[52] If Rousseau and Josephson squeezed more money from EBU, Killanin reasoned, then the IOC, ISFs and NOCs stood to benefit.

COJO'S TRICKERY

Montréal required a resolution to its standoff with the IOC concerning the basis of its future global television contracts before finalizing an agreement with EBU. Rousseau was adamant that all networks contribute to the cost of broadcast facilities through the inclusion of a technical services component. Despite Mayor Jean Drapeau's earlier pledge that

Montréal would not distinguish between television rights and technical services, Rousseau defended the ABC contract. The IOC finally consented to the ratification of the COJO/ABC contract in exchange for a promise by Montréal not to deduct a technical services fee from the gross sum of other global television contracts negotiated. Rousseau and his colleagues devised a plan to force the IOC's hand. They altered the memorandum of agreement concerning the ABC contract sent to Lausanne for the IOC's approval. In an annex to the document—one that the IOC's lawyer failed to read thoroughly before signing it on behalf of the IOC in May 1973— Montréal was authorized to separate television rights and technical services payments in *all* other television contracts.[53] When discovered, Rousseau's sleight of hand drew howls of protest from Lausanne in light of the gravity of the IOC lawyer's oversight.

In October 1973 members of the IOC Finance Commission convened in Varna, Bulgaria, to consider developments concerning television contracts related to the Games in Montréal and Innsbruck. Rousseau again locked horns with Beaumont, Hodler, and Luke, who resented his trickery. The IOC approved the ABC contract in consideration of Montréal's agreement to transfer the gross television receipts from other world regions to Lausanne for distribution. Montréal "repeatedly ignored" IOC television policy, charged an exasperated Lord Luke. Hodler concluded that Montréal "was trying to cheat the IOC out of money."[54] This tongue-lashing failed to shake Rousseau's resolve. If EBU wanted to use the broadcast facilities, the stoic Rousseau stated, it would have to contribute to Montréal's overhead costs.[55]

Karl-Heinz Klee and Alois Lugger, Innsbruck's mayor, also appeared before the Finance Commission to defend their signing of a $10 million U.S. television rights contract that contained a $2.2 million technical services component. Klee and Lugger departed Lausanne after the two sides compromised, agreeing to restrict the deduction for technical services to $2 million, subject to the approval of the Executive Board.[56] While subsequent negotiations were required in order to provide the Innsbruck Organizing Committee with a loan and a more favorable distribution key, these problems were overcome with minimal conflict. While the Innsbruck solution had been easy, Rousseau's continued posturing angered IOC officials—foremost among them Monique Berlioux.

In the early 1970s Berlioux's star was in ascendance in Lausanne. She was born in Metz, France, in 1925; her father was a tailor's cutter; her mother, a teacher. There is little doubt that the relationship with her mother helped to form Berlioux's independent and sometimes domineering qualities. Active in the French underground during the Nazi occupation, both she and her mother served as couriers in the Resistance. Following the war she became one of France's best swimmers, winning several national backstroke swim titles. Despite having undergone an emergency appendectomy three weeks before the opening of the 1948 London Olympics, she reached the semifinals of the 100 meter backstroke. Berlioux was well educated, with degrees in literature, language, and history from the Sorbonne as well as a master's degree. She became a journalist and married but refused to take her husband's name. Berlioux first met Brundage at the African Games in Dakar, Senegal, in 1963. Four years later he hired her to lead the IOC's Press and Public Relations Department. A steady rise in the corridors of power within the IOC's headquarters led to her appointment to a number of positions, including, finally, director-general. Usually absent from Lausanne's IOC headquarters, both Brundage and Killanin depended a great deal on Berlioux's assertive leadership, unquestioned dedication, and loyalty to the Olympic Movement and her almost superhuman capacity for work. She was a tough taskmaster, and with her rise to power she became even more so. Berlioux placed her formidable stamp on Olympic television rights negotiations in the 1970s and early 1980s.[57]

Monique Berlioux promoted a strategy designed to take some of the swagger out of Rousseau's step. Rather than offering a compromise solution as advocated by Beaumont, which might be interpreted by Montréal as a "sign of weakness,"[58] she counseled the members of the Finance Commission to delay in providing the IOC's consent to individual contracts. This might erode Rousseau's intransigence. Montréal's need for money would only increase as the weeks passed. Perhaps Rousseau might abandon his approach as financial exigencies rose. The Finance Commission concurred. Rousseau left Varna with the understanding that the IOC would consider each contract upon its submission to Lausanne. In February 1974, however, the IOC Executive Board completely reversed itself, on the recommendation of the Finance Commission, conceding to the deduction of 50% of the global sum of each contract for technical services.[59] Killanin sought closure to the debate. Rousseau, triumphant, pledged his silence on the nature of the accord.[60] Knowledge of Rousseau's terms had to be kept from Innsbruck officials.

THE MONTRÉAL/EBU STALEMATE

Killanin's decision reflected two considerations. First, the IOC lawyer's blunder rendered the situation problematic because the signed contract was a legally binding agreement. Second, with the IOC's quadrennial budget driven 98% by the returns from television, it was difficult to maintain Berlioux's approach indefinitely.[61]

Over the course of the next eighteen months Montréal unsuccessfully labored to unlock EBU's vault. Sir Charles Curran, president of EBU, steadfastly refused to yield to Montréal's demands. Curran's approach to negotiations reflected a smugness that EBU was the only network capable of providing widespread coverage of Olympic events to Western Europe. He also understood that from a public relations perspective the IOC would be loath to accept a blackout in the region because of Montréal's unwillingness to come to terms on a financial agreement. Nevertheless, Curran needed to bolster the resolve of executives employed by EBU's affiliated networks. His ability to convince his colleagues to resist Montréal's overtures to sign individual contracts, action potentially damaging to EBU's negotiating position, explains COJO's failed efforts.

Montréal's exorbitant demands, Curran wrote Killanin in December 1973, reflected a degree of naïveté and a disregard for the "financial [and] political realities of the situation."[62] Montréal's approach was doomed to fail, he noted, but the price of failure would be high. Unacceptable demands promised "the disappointment of millions of people throughout the world where television services cannot pay the sums now being demanded of them," he warned.[63] It was not EBU's responsibility to bail out Montréal from its financial problems. "I see no reason why broadcasting audiences should be soaked," Curran stated, "in order to provide amenities for cities who have overbid their resources in seeking to be hosts to the Games."[64] He characterized Marvin Josephson's effort to negotiate separate agreements with English and German television officials—his first initiative in compromising EBU's bargaining position—as a "bad bet."[65] A waiting game favored EBU. In March 1974 a confident Curran informed Lord Luke that EBU, if need be, was willing to wait until 1976 to reach an agreement.[66]

At his Dublin residence a disturbed Lord Killanin pondered the situation. Following a personal meeting with Curran in April, he dispatched a lengthy missive to members of the Executive Board. While he supported Montréal's efforts to maximize the returns from television in Europe, the demands, Killanin thought, were not realistic: "EBU is a buyer's union . . . [that] naturally desires to obtain the best and cheapest terms." Killanin believed that the two sides needed to find some middle ground. It was not his role to step into the situation unless there was a complete breakdown in negotiations. He assumed a low profile to shelter the IOC from media criticism in the event that the dispute became angry and prolonged. "It will be a slow game of poker," concluded Killanin.[67] Though he coveted television money far more than Brundage had at the time of his retirement, Killanin remained deeply conscious of the IOC's image.

ECONOMIC REALITY DRIVES
ADMINISTRATIVE CHANGE IN LAUSANNE

Prompted primarily by Rousseau's actions and the recognition of its dependence on television revenue, the IOC established a Television Subcommittee in 1973 charged with the responsibility of improving the IOC's management of television issues and augmenting its knowledge of the negotiation process. One of its early initiatives involved constructing a questionnaire on television facilities for bid committees pursuing the right to host the 1980 Winter and Summer Games.[68] The Television Subcommittee also recommended that the IOC hire an "expert" to act as a liaison with the OCOGs and the television networks. This expert's counsel to the IOC on financial and technical issues might prove valuable.[69] Quality of Olympic programming remained a high priority. It was important to avoid driving the costs of programming beyond the means of the television networks, which might "kill the goose that lays the golden eggs." The expert's proposed mandate included facilitating improved communication between the IOC and the OCOGs.[70]

While the early work completed by the subcommittee reflected a practical response to the IOC's situation, those involved refused to admit that this expansion of the IOC's bureaucracy marked a shift in its philosophical approach to revenue generation. The subcommittee avowed that the "expert" was not to be a "commercial agent."[71] It also confirmed that the "International Olympic Committee stands as the sole guarantor for the Olympic ideal and cannot be confused with a financial or commercial enterprise. There shall be no question of this."[72] The subcommittee began consultations with the Inter-Union Radio and TV Basic Facilities Advisory Committee, bodies stocked with European and U.S. executives willing to provide their expertise on technical matters.[73] The Executive Board delegated two members of the subcommittee, Luc Silance and Walter Schätz, to attend future television negotiations conducted by Innsbruck and Montréal officials.[74] Silance acted as an IOC legal adviser. Schätz, a former official with the Munich Organizing Committee, possessed vast knowledge in the area of sports television. These actions, according to the subcommittee, did not alter the IOC's administrative philosophy; rather, they permitted the IOC "to safeguard its autonomy."[75] Contrary to the subcommittee's posture, this action did indeed alter the IOC's administrative philosophy— it intruded IOC self-interests directly into television rights negotiations.

DÉJÀ VU: MONTRÉAL REWRITES THE RULES
FOR TELEVISION NEGOTIATIONS

"The Montréal years, from the time the Canadian city was awarded the Games of the 21st Olympiad to their opening in 1976," recalled Killanin, "were agonizing years for the Movement and, of course, for me."[76] Labor strikes and cost overruns marred preparations for the festival. The People's Republic of China/Taiwan and New Zealand/Africa issues provided political conundrums. Montréal's disregard for IOC television policy and its cavalier flouting of IOC regulations, however, irritated Killanin and his colleagues beyond measure.

Montréal again drew the ire of IOC officials when it revealed that it had granted Canadian host television rights to the government-owned Canadian Broadcasting Corporation for $1. The Canadian government, noted Rousseau, channeled $25 million to the host broadcaster to cover a significant portion of the anticipated $56 million required for the broadcast complex. He did not wish to ask CBC for a rights payment, money that would essentially burden Canadian taxpayers. Countering that argument, the IOC claimed that Rousseau's approach diminished the amount of money subject to the Rome Formula. Lord Luke summarized the opinion in Lausanne and Dublin, albeit in understated fashion, when he commented: "COJO's attitude in this affair was not in the spirit of a partnership."[77]

When the Finance Commission considered Rousseau's argument in October 1974, Beaumont and his colleagues registered their displeasure with the CBC contract on three counts. First, while Canadian taxpayers might appreciate Rousseau's largesse, the agreement compromised the financial returns for the IOC, ISFs, and NOCs. CBC paid $257,000 for Canadian television rights to the 1972 Munich Olympics. Marc Hodler ventured that the Canadian television rights for the Montréal Olympics might yield a figure in excess of $2 million.[78] Walter Schätz concluded that the *minimum* value of the Canadian rights was $910,000.[79] Second, the agreement would prejudice Olympic television rights negotiations in other regions. In the short term Hodler said CBC's $1 contract acted as a lever for EBU officials in their negotiations with Montréal. Monique Berlioux concurred with him.[80] Schätz shuddered at the thought of the financial impact of such a precedent on the value of domestic television rights when future Games might be staged in the United States.[81] Third, the Finance Commission realized that CBC might still sell advertising time. The sale of commercial time on its telecasts to a captive Canadian audience offered the prospect of a massive profit for CBC. Within months of finalizing its deal with Montréal, for instance, ABC's sales department peddled its advertising time for a sum in excess of $40 million.[82] Beaumont and his colleagues, resolving to set the value of Canadian television rights at $2 million, presented the results of their Finance Commission deliberations to the IOC Executive Board and Rousseau.

While the minutes of the Finance Commission are otherwise ambiguous, the record of Beaumont's presentation to the Executive Board clearly indicates that the $2 million figure represented the amount of money that the IOC felt it should receive. When given the news that the IOC Executive Board had set the value of the Canadian television at $2 million, Rousseau called an immediate recess to the proceedings.[83] He was shocked. Montréal had filed the contract in February. At that time the IOC had not registered any opposition to the terms of the agreement. Addressing Rousseau, Berlioux produced the IOC's copy of the agreement, revealing a blank space for the CBC payment to be entered.[84]

Jim Worrall, Canadian member of the IOC as well as a member of COJO, was the uneasy mediator for the next day's proceedings. Worrall reported Rousseau's reluctance to present an update on Montréal's preparations to the Executive Board until the CBC contract was settled. Rousseau offered to accept Schätz's estimate of the maximum value of the Canadian television rights ($1.8 million). When subjected to the standard method of separating television rights and technical services fees, this would yield $300,000 for the IOC. He would pay this money to the IOC within thirty days if Killanin and Beaumont approved the CBC/COJO contract. Worrall and Luc Silance, the IOC's legal adviser, subsequently brokered an agreement whereby the IOC would receive $300,000 on the day that EBU made its first television payment to Montréal. If Montréal's negotiating effort resulted in gross television receipts in excess of $37 million, however, an additional $100,000 would be transferred to Lausanne. If the total surpassed $40 million, an additional $200,000 would be directed to the IOC.[85] On the surface it appeared that the IOC had achieved a better deal; but Montréal fell short of the negotiation targets ($34,862,200), which canceled the prospect of supplemental payments. In addition, the IOC's decision to link the payment for Canadian rights to the conclusion of the EBU negotiations proved short-sighted. The IOC sacrificed a tangible amount of investment income because the EBU did not sign an agreement with Montréal until some twelve months later.

THE EBU/MONTRÉAL STANDOFF CONTINUES

When Walter Schätz and Luc Silance met with EBU and Montréal officials in October 1974, the discussion reinforced their opinion that their differences on the value of West European television rights remained a vexing issue. Montréal reconfirmed that it expected $20 million from EBU for the television rights/technical services package. EBU's Straschnov scoffed at Montréal's figure. EBU would pay Montréal $2 million, he replied. Straschnov's EBU colleague, Miro Vilcek, noted that EBU had acquired the rights to the 1974 World Cup, a global sporting phenomenon of similar stature to the Olympic Games, for $1.75 million. Montréal's demands revealed little insight into the European television market. Affably, Schätz noted that it was not unreasonable to expect that EBU would make a meaningful contribution to the costs involved in providing the broadcast facilities.[86] In his submission to the Finance Commission Schätz counseled the IOC to challenge EBU's position forcefully. "It is high time to put an end to the preferential treatment given to the big industrial nations in Western Europe, Eastern Europe, Japan, and Australia, especially since these countries are the most successful in the Olympic Games," he concluded.[87] Lord Killanin instructed Rousseau to seek a compromise.[88] The thinking in Lausanne was that although EBU was not able to match the buying power of U.S. networks it could do better than its current offer.

Meanwhile EBU aired its laundry in the international press. The *New York Times* informed its readership of Charles Curran's refusal to pay $20 million for the television rights and technical services package. An unidentified EBU official told a writer for the *Dublin Evening Press* that "[EBU] members do not have the money and we feel that they would rather not show the Olympics than give way on this. The prospect for a blackout in Europe is very real."[89]

Prior to the next negotiating session between Montréal and EBU Georges Straschnov warned Killanin that "the chances of agreement are slim, as the starting positions on the two sides are very far apart."[90] Following a late January 1975 meeting Luc Silance and Monique Berlioux concluded that neither Montréal nor EBU evinced a willingness to seek a compromise. "The parties separated without being able to decide on any point whatsoever," lamented Silance.[91] Marvin Josephson indicated that Montréal wanted $20 million from EBU and $10 million from OIRT (Intervision) in Eastern Europe.[92] Montréal's failure to provide a breakdown on its hardware costs, as had been requested by EBU, perturbed Straschnov. Negotiating on behalf of EBU and OIRT, Straschnov offered $5.5 million for television rights and technical services for all of Europe. He declined to engage in further negotiations because the tendered figure was a "final offer."[93] In a joint EBU/OIRT press communiqué Straschnov announced that "the answer to the question whether European audiences will be able to see the Olympic Games on their screens is now entirely in the hands of COJO."[94]

Montréal made the next move. In March 1975 it lowered its expectations from EBU ($14.5 million) and OIRT ($6.4 million). In defense of this grudging compromise Montréal reasoned that "the Games are no longer the private preserve of the handful of people wealthy enough to cross oceans to view them. Today everyone on earth with access to a television set has a front row seat. Fairness demands that the cost of facilities required to produce the signal be shared by all broadcasters carrying the Games to their viewers."[95] Even though Killanin remained hopeful of an improved offer from EBU and OIRT, he believed that Montréal had not improved its chances for a swift resolution to negotiations. Olympic coverage must remain accessible to European viewers, Killanin insisted. To Rousseau he wrote: "I do not completely share your views that a too high pitch to EBU will not terminate negotiations on the present basis." Killanin countered Rousseau's response—charging that he had been unwittingly "co-opted" by EBU—by arguing: "I can assure you that I have not been 'indoctrinated' by the EBU but look at this on the basis of someone resident in Europe, fully conscious of the economic situation affecting broadcasting overall."[96]

A series of meetings in August and September and Killanin's personal intervention, precipitated by increasing concerns within the Olympic Movement regarding the potential for a blackout or substandard Olympic coverage in Europe, brought a settlement. While Killanin considered letting negotiations play out a little longer, Jean de Beaumont and representatives of European NOCs convinced him that he needed to define a window for their conclusion.[97] At the end of May an aroused Killanin encouraged Rousseau to conclude an agreement with EBU within two months. The IOC, he stated, faced criticism from the ISFs and NOCs for permitting the separation of television rights and technical services in the television contracts.[98] There was also a legitimate concern in Europe that Olympic coverage would be compromised. Montréal's failure to conclude an agreement impeded negotiations with other networks, such as the Australian Broadcasting Commission and Nippon Hoso Kyokai (Japan). The Australians, distressed by Montréal's demands, had "reached the end of [their] negotiating tolerance," according to David McKenzie, IOC member from Australia.[99] Despite all this, when EBU and Montréal negotiators convened on 1 August they failed to resolve their differences.

Television executives representing EBU, OIRT, ABU (Asian Broadcasting Union: Australia, Philippines, Hong Kong, New Zealand), OTI (Organización de la Televisión Ibero-Americana), and ASBU (Arab States

Broadcasting Union) present at the meeting remained silent. On behalf of them all, Charles Curran addressed the Montréal negotiators. He achieved a degree of solidarity rarely witnessed among the international television networks. The networks offered $8.6 million for television rights and technical services for their collective regions, reported Curran. He indicated that another $600,000 was available, but only in the event that Montréal agreed to the financial terms by 1 September. Then he tightened the screws: if Montréal failed to meet the deadline, the resulting lack of lead-time for technical preparations precluded Olympic telecasts in these regions. Schätz, who represented the IOC at the recent meeting, sympathized with Montréal. Montréal officials, who sought $18,045,000 from the networks, had given much ground in the past few months. If successful, argued Schätz, Curran's strategy compromised the international market for Olympic television rights for the foreseeable future. The other broadcast unions were in lockstep with Curran and believed that his approach would destroy Montréal's resolve. Why else, queried Schätz, did the networks send officials to Montréal who merely nodded their approval of Curran's comments as if they were working from a script?[100] Once again Rousseau and his colleagues refused Curran's offer.

By mid-August Killanin's patience had disappeared. He did not share Schätz's opinion that the IOC should "risk a conflict with the unions" and support Montréal.[101] The media criticism resulting from a widespread television blackout, especially because of a dispute over money, provided too much of a public relations challenge for the IOC. With stalemate lurking, Curran improved his offer to $9.3 million. In a press release Killanin directed Rousseau to reconsider his position.[102] A hopeful sign, concluded Curran, but "there [was] no room for Canadian illusions" with respect to the availability of more money.[103] Killanin and the IOC Executive Board met with Montréal officials in Algiers in late August to impress upon them that the IOC would not accept a blackout. Meanwhile Curran relaxed on a holiday.[104] He had the upper hand.

Killanin tried to improve Curran's offer; but failing that he was prepared to inform Rousseau that he would have to accept $9.3 million. Georges Straschnov announced that EBU could increase the offer to $9.5 million. On 7 September in London Killanin huddled with Mayor Jean Drapeau, informing Jim Worrall of the revised offer. The list of networks covered by the agreement now included URTNA (Union des Radiodiffusions et Télévisions Nationales d'Afrique) and SABC (South African Broadcasting Corporation). On 11 September COJO's Board of Directors yielded and accepted the offer brokered by Killanin.[105]

Killanin breathed a sigh of relief and urged both sides to deal with the fine print of the contract in short order.[106] Predictably, Curran cast blame for the protracted and often unfriendly negotiations on Montréal's inexperience and limited understanding of the basis of television markets outside the United States. EBU's efforts, he boasted, ensured that the world's television audience would see the Games at a reasonable price. Montréal's excessive demands, noted Curran, galvanized the international networks against its plan to transfer the costs of televising the Games to the networks. "I do not think anybody else should take us on in the future," he stated boldly.[107] Curran intended his comments for Lake Placid and Moscow officials engaged in early stages of planning for television coverage of the 1980 Olympic festivals.

THE INNSBRUCK AND MONTRÉAL GAMES

The 1976 Olympic Winter Games were originally awarded to Denver at the IOC Session in Amsterdam in 1970.[108] The combination of the 100th anniversary of the state of Colorado and the 200th anniversary of the birth of the United States in 1776 had given Denver the edge over the other three candidates, Sion, Tampere, and Vancouver. A 300% increase in costs associated with hosting the Games, the construction of new sport facilities, and the anticipated environmental impact related to a projected increase in tourism, however, led to a public referendum on the protection of the environment in which, to the dismay of the Denver OCOG, a 60% majority strongly objected to the use of public funds to finance the Olympic Winter Games. Unable to host the Games without public funds and support, Denver reluctantly withdrew from its host city obligation on 15 November 1972.[109]

The IOC Executive Board awarded the 1976 Olympic Winter Games to Innsbruck in February 1973.[110] Utilizing existing sport venues with only minor refurbishment and modernization together with hasty construction of a freeway through the River Inn Valley and erection of publicly funded residential blocks (built to accommodate more than 1,250 athletes), preparations rushed ahead for opening the Games in February 1976. Organizers solicited donations and once again called upon the Austrian army to help with the construction work.[111] Innsbruck raised $11,627,330 from the sale of television broadcast rights, a sum that included $2 million in technical services from the U.S. contract.[112]

On 4 February 1976 athletes from thirty-seven nations gathered in the majestic setting of the Tyrolean Alps at Innsbruck for the opening ceremony. In the presence of Lord Killanin, at his first Olympics as IOC president, the Games opened in Bergisel Stadium with the lighting of two

Olympic flames, one to commemorate the 1964 Games and a new torch to represent the 1976 Games. The problem of security, a major concern following the tragedy in Munich four years earlier, was handled by members of the Austrian police (a contingent that almost doubled the number of athletes present). To ensure the safety of those attending the Games security personnel patrolled the entire site, paying special attention to the security of the Olympic Village.

When the Summer Olympic Games opened some five months later, Britain's Queen Elizabeth delivered the welcoming address. Construction cranes still dominated Montréal's skyline.[113] Industrial disputes, poor supervision, and severe cost overruns made it impossible to complete the necessary work on the Olympic venues in time for the opening ceremony. Eighty cranes and 2,000 workers working triple overtime were not enough to complete the 60,000-seat Olympic Stadium and its cable-suspended roof by the Games' opening.[114] As the competitions began, steel girders and a single crane jutted into the sky from the Olympic Stadium's unfinished roof.

Politics also played a major role in the Montréal Olympic Games: 24 of the 116 registered NOCs boycotted the competitions. Twenty-two African nations refused to participate in light of their objections to the IOC's decision to allow New Zealand's participation, arguing that a tour of South Africa by the All-Blacks rugby team violated the Olympic Movement's anti-apartheid policy. The Taiwanese team also withdrew after the Canadian government barred it from entering the country. Canada's expanding foreign relations with the People's Republic of China, Taiwan's arch political enemy, figured prominently in prime minister Pierre Trudeau's decision to exclude the Taiwanese.

Despite being faced by numerous problems, the Games of the Twenty-first Olympiad reflected near-perfect organization and strict security. The sporting competitions showcased the superb gymnastic skills of Nadia Comenici, the all-around track and field excellence of decathlete Bruce Jenner, and the introduction of women's rowing, now a center-stage Canadian Olympic event. At the closing ceremony on 1 August 1976, as the stadium lights were dimmed, five hundred young women in white entered the stadium infield forming five interlocking rings. Flag bearers for each country followed. "Brightly costumed Indians, representing all the tribes of Canada," entered the stadium accompanied by "native" music piped through the stadium sound system.[115] Entering the five interlocking rings formed by the young women in white, they erected a large tepee in the center of each. The flag of Greece was then raised and the Greek anthem was played, followed by the Canadian flag and anthem, and finally the flag and anthem of the Soviet Union, host of the 1980 Olympic Games.

Lord Killanin declared the Games closed and called upon the youth of world to assemble again four years hence. The Olympic flag was lowered and the Olympic flame extinguished, while two live satellite pictures of Moscow appeared on the giant scoreboards in the stadium. Finally, the scoreboards flashed a concluding message to those who had gathered, "Farewell Montréal—'Til We Meet in Moscow."[116]

REFLECTIONS

Avery Brundage preferred a policy that kept the IOC in the background regarding negotiations for television contracts. While Brundage consulted with television executives, Killanin—the first IOC president who actually brokered a television deal (Montréal/EBU), albeit with some reluctance—also advanced the IOC's knowledge of the television industry by establishing the Television Subcommittee. His actions underscored his determination to protect the IOC's financial interests. Killanin's agenda and the IOC's dependence on television money fueled this attempt to bring greater sophistication to the IOC's management of its relationship with the television networks.[117]

Infighting among the IOC, ISFs, and NOCs concerning the distribution of money from the sale of Olympic television rights dominated the 1960s; however, escalating television revenue in the 1970s shifted the primary locus of conflict to the IOC's relations with the OCOGs. OCOG leaders in Munich and Montréal argued that the IOC's distribution policy failed to address the rapidly expanding costs of hosting an Olympic festival, which, of course, included the need to provide television broadcasters with the means to transmit Olympic images throughout the world. The Rome Formula, countered IOC officials, recognized the OCOGs' need for revenue, providing approximately two-thirds of total television income money to the organizers.

Much of the IOC's aggravation with the Munich and Montréal organizers was self-inflicted, resulting from its own decisions and inexperience. Willi Daume's negotiations with ABC and the IOC's subsequent approval of the separation of television rights and technical services in the Munich/ABC contract provided the entry wedge for Karl-Heinz Klee and Roger Rousseau. The Munich Precedent steered IOC/OCOG discussions pertaining to the distribution of television revenue. Innsbruck and Montréal used Daume's deal to exact better terms from the IOC. Roger Rousseau also capitalized on the IOC's failure to execute due diligence in reviewing the Montréal/IOC agreement on the ABC contract. In the 1970s the IOC's primary method of resolving conflict with Olympic organizers concerning the distribution of television revenue was largely defined by the word "concession."

Despite the IOC's attempt to enforce its will by modifying the *Olympic Charter* and obtaining pledges from all bid committees that they would abide by the IOC's distribution policy if successful in obtaining the right to host the Games, OCOG leaders realized that the IOC's ability to stave off their challenges was compromised.[118] First, as the guardian of the Olympic Movement, the IOC bears responsibility for ensuring the celebration of the Olympic Games. The IOC could not threaten to remove the host privileges from cities when confronted by financial disputes with the OCOGs. An effort to transfer an Olympic festival one or two years into the mandate of an OCOG posed a logistical nightmare. Second, an angst continued to pervade Lausanne with respect to media criticism that would most certainly surface if the IOC became embroiled in prolonged arguments about money. A third factor forcing the IOC's hand was its own dependence on television revenue as the foundation for its operational budget. The IOC could not withhold approval of television contracts indefinitely because of the need to replenish its coffers. Reginald Alexander's 1969 verdict concerning television revenue was correct—it was the "financial lifeblood" of the IOC's administrative existence.[119]

In retrospect the 1970s witnessed three significant historical signposts concerning the IOC's management of television matters: (1) the Munich Precedent; (2) the establishment of the Television Subcommittee; and (3) the decision to join the OCOGs in negotiating contracts with the television networks, a change that made the IOC a formal partner in the negotiations. The movement toward a policy of "joint negotiation" represented a two-stage process. First, the Television Subcommittee under the direction of Monique Berlioux improved the IOC's knowledge of the television industry, the broadcasters' requirements at an Olympic site, and the process involved in negotiating contracts. Berlioux's subcommittee owed its genesis to Montréal's negotiating practices. Second, when negotiations conducted by Moscow and Lake Placid produced conflict, the IOC, through Berlioux, sought advice from U.S. broadcasters. They counseled the IOC to take a more active role in the negotiations process. This dialogue confirmed an opinion growing in Dublin and Lausanne. Further internal discussion and debate resulted in the IOC abandoning its arm's-length approach in favor of taking a seat at the negotiation table. Television contract discussions concerning Lake Placid and Moscow, and their role in pushing the IOC to the negotiation table, were the next step in the IOC's transformation into a corporate entity.

CHAPTER 6

CONFRONTATIONS GALORE

Lake Placid, Moscow, and the
1980 Olympic Festivals

Throughout the latter months of Montréal's negotiations with EBU Monique Berlioux kept one eye fixed on Montréal and the other on Lake Placid, the small upstate New York resort town nestled in the Adirondack Mountains preparing to host the 1980 Winter Olympic Games. Berlioux, an increasingly dominant figure in IOC matters, played a significant role in representing the IOC's financial interests when Lake Placid officials maneuvered for IOC concessions concerning the distribution of U.S. television money. The Munich Precedent, as well as separation of television rights and technical services in the U.S. television contracts for Innsbruck and Montréal, gave Lake Placid officials an incentive to pursue an agreement favorable to the Organizing Committee. In the end the dispute resolution concerning television revenue involved more than simply the IOC and the Lake Placid Olympic Games Organizing Committee (LPOC). A third party entered the scenario, the United States Olympic Committee (USOC), an emerging power broker in Olympic financial affairs.

Organizers of the Moscow Olympics similarly confounded IOC officials with their demands for modifications to the Rome Formula. Ignati Novikov, president of the Moscow OCOG, pressed IOC officials for and received a $50 million deduction for technical services from NBC's $85 million contract. Novikov's management of discussions with the U.S. networks and his failed attempt to peddle the television rights in a high-stakes auction in Moscow, however, provided a final impetus for the IOC to establish itself as a joint negotiator of television contracts for the 1984 Olympic Games and beyond. In 1977, with the Lake Placid and Moscow negotiations behind it, the IOC modified the *Olympic Charter* to reflect this new status.

The Finance Commission and Executive Board believed that joint negotiation furthered two of the IOC's objectives: to safeguard its financial interests, as well as those of the NOCs and ISFs, and to reduce conflict with the OCOGs. The IOC's learning curve regarding television in the 1970s accelerated rapidly. Officials possessed greater self-confidence in their ability to act as a constructive force in the negotiations. This practical approach, Killanin and his colleagues determined, was an improvement over the past practice resulting from Avery Brundage's philosophical misgivings with regard to the IOC's involvement in commercial negotiations. The transition from observer to negotiating partner marked an important step in the IOC's continuing corporate makeover.

MONIQUE BERLIOUX AND U.S. TELEVISION NEGOTIATIONS FOR THE LAKE PLACID OLYMPIC WINTER GAMES

Monique Berlioux's influence in television matters increased in the 1970s, due chiefly to three fundamental factors. First, she showed a good deal of initiative as chair of the IOC Television Subcommittee, using her position to enhance her knowledge of the television industry. Second, she often represented the IOC at negotiation sessions; her office also acted as the clearing-house for communication with the OCOGs. Third, Killanin delegated a great deal of authority in these matters to Berlioux and Finance Commission chair Jean de Beaumont.

Having sacrificed significant amounts of revenue to Montréal as a result of an administrative mistake in Lausanne, Berlioux, Beaumont, and the Finance Commission adopted a hard-line approach with Lake Placid. In early 1975 Art Devlin and Norman Hess, Lake Placid's vice-president and legal counsel, respectively, discussed LPOC's financial status with the IOC Finance Commission. With respect to the town's plans for funding the construction of broadcast facilities, Devlin and Hess presented uniquely American financial concerns. Because the host broadcaster would be a private network, bereft of government support, Lake Placid officials would have to shoulder all expenses. Devlin and Hess professed innocence of the fact that the network's contribution toward the construction of facilities *and* its payment for television rights were both subject to the Rome Formula. Marc Hodler reminded them of the Lake Placid bid committee's affirmative response to the question on the Radio-TV questionnaire distributed to all bid committees: "Can you confirm that the full receipts from television, less the proportion due to you as Organising Committee, will be handed over when received in conformity with the IOC formula for division between the IOC, International Federations and NOCs?" Though

Hess admitted awareness of the Montréal and Innsbruck agreements, he continued to argue Lake Placid's position. Hodler dismissed his arguments but indicated that the IOC might consider a loan. Such an idea, noted Berlioux, required IOC approval.[1]

Lake Placid and IOC officials also addressed the timetable for negotiations with the U.S. networks. Lake Placid officials were anxious to conclude an agreement because expenses had already begun to mount. The IOC Executive Board, however, wanted the negotiations delayed for a number of reasons.[2] First, the Executive Board desired some time to study Hess's arguments concerning the unique financial challenges faced by Lake Placid and an American host network. Second, IOC regulations did not permit publicity concerning an Olympic festival until the conclusion of the preceding Games. Third, and perhaps most significantly, "some of the contracts signed early on have been very advantageous to the company concerned, but not for the Organising Committee and therefore the IOC," noted Berlioux.[3] Within months of the signing of the Montréal/ABC contract the IOC learned that NBC had been prepared to offer $30 million for U.S. television rights, bettering ABC's accepted offer by $5 million.[4] Hess agreed to delay negotiations, but Lake Placid's TV-Marketing Committee proceeded to discuss technical issues with interested U.S. television executives.

During the summer months of 1975 ABC, NBC, and CBS officials inspected the Lake Placid site to gauge the challenge involved in telecasting an event in the small upstate New York resort community. Robert F. Wussler, vice-president of CBS Sports, visited Lake Placid in August and expressed concern about the financial burden of providing host broadcaster facilities. Nonetheless, he promised to send a production proposal within one month. NBC representatives toured Lake Placid in June and pledged to send their proposal "shortly." As autumn descended on Lake Placid, only ABC had completed follow-up inspections and maintained steady contact with the LPOC.[5]

Lake Placid informed Killanin on 1 October that it was prepared to begin "definitive preliminary negotiations with a specific United States TV network." Norman Hess requested a meeting with IOC representatives to discuss television issues; however, following consultation with Killanin, Berlioux scheduled a meeting for Daniel Mortureux and Silance with Lake Placid officials in Innsbruck in January 1976.[6] Berlioux's reply reflected the IOC's desire to stall the consummation of a U.S. agreement until after the Innsbruck Olympic Winter Games. Lake Placid, chafing at the delay, prepared to discuss financial terms with ABC. Was Berlioux aware of this? Killanin himself appeared confused. In early January he assured CBS and

NBC officials that "strict instructions have been given to [Lake Placid and Moscow officials] that no final negotiations should take place without the agreement of the IOC."[7] Lake Placid's discussions with ABC intensified as the Innsbruck Games approached, carried out without the knowledge of CBS, NBC, and the IOC.

When Mortureux and Silance met with Hess and John Wilkins in Innsbruck, they learned that Lake Placid had selected ABC as its choice to telecast the Lake Placid Olympic Winter Games. Mortureux reiterated that no contract could be signed without IOC approval. He also requested a complete record of Lake Placid's discussions with CBS and NBC.[8] Approval of the contract hinged in part on the IOC's verifying that ABC's competitors had been granted an opportunity to pursue the U.S. television rights. Silance also expressed his concern that whichever U.S. network gained the television contract might seek to limit the actual rights payment because of the expenses involved in fulfilling its responsibilities as host broadcaster. He counseled Hess and Wilkins "not to cheat the IOC in this respect."[9]

During the Innsbruck Games ABC and Lake Placid reached a tentative agreement for U.S. television rights that was guaranteed to rankle IOC officials. ABC pledged $9 million for U.S. television rights. One-third of this sum ($3 million) was to be paid to the IOC. The remaining $6 million was designated for Lake Placid. While there was no technical services component included in the $9 million contract, a plan conceived by Lake Placid and ABC to offset the latter's costs as host broadcaster eliminated the IOC as a recipient of money resulting from television contracts negotiated with non-U.S. networks. ABC was to receive the first million dollars from the non-U.S. contracts and Lake Placid would receive the second million. Additional revenue was to be divided equally between ABC and Lake Placid. The bottom line was a guaranteed $7 million for Lake Placid from the U.S. and non-U.S. contracts. The ABC/Lake Placid agreement also listed Canada as part of ABC's broadcast territory, a clear violation of IOC rules.[10] This clause forced Canadian networks to purchase domestic rights from a U.S. network. Considering Canada's often-demonstrated knee-jerk response to any effort by its southern neighbor to influence Canadian culture and/or sovereignty, this clause proved pregnant with negative overtones. In addition, Lake Placid permitted ABC to match any rival offer from NBC or CBS. The dictum issued by Silance less than two weeks earlier had been ignored completely.

During the later stages of the Innsbruck Olympic Winter Games Lake Placid officials implored Jean de Beaumont to approve the ABC deal. He turned aside Lake Placid's advances. "You will understand," Beaumont explained to Killanin, "that not knowing the terms nor the figures, I thought this to be too premature." Considering the prejudicial nature of the agreement from an IOC perspective, his decision to defer action was judicious. Beaumont conceded, however, that ABC was the favored suitor. He understood that Lake Placid needed money to push forward with preparations. "Being aware that their eagerness to treat rapidly with ABC was on account of their being short of money," Beaumont informed Killanin, "I advised them to make some private arrangements with ABC so as to obtain from them a kind of bona fide advance of funds."[11] Killanin expressed concern about Beaumont's advice. Rival networks remembered the Montréal television fiascoes. At that time they charged that ABC had secured the inside track on obtaining U.S. television rights by paying an advance to Montréal.[12] Killanin concurred with Beaumont that the IOC could not proceed without obtaining further details, including the nature of the bidding opportunities granted to CBS and NBC.

Meanwhile Lake Placid and ABC's Board of Directors studied the contract proposed jointly by Roone Arledge and Lake Placid's TV-Marketing Committee. Lake Placid approved the deal on 25 February and obtained a $250,000 advance from ABC, refundable in the event that ABC did not obtain the U.S. television rights (ABC gave its consent to the agreement on 6 March).[13] The IOC remained "out of the loop" with respect to the financial details of the agreement. In a letter to Berlioux dated 15 February Wilkins confirmed Lake Placid's preference to deal with ABC but did not mention the tentative agreement signed by the two parties two days earlier.[14] In fact, a copy of the contract did not arrive in Lausanne until 19 March. An anonymous source, however, perhaps a disgruntled CBS or NBC executive, revealed that ABC and Lake Placid had reached an agreement for $10 million. A competitive bid process might yield $15–20 million, opined the same source.[15] Monique Berlioux pursued confirmation of the existence of the ABC/LPOC contract.[16]

Lake Placid's activities highlighted the poor lines of communication between Lake Placid and Lausanne and the continuing struggle for authority over the negotiations process between the LPOC and the IOC. First, Lake Placid ignored the IOC's request to view the document before it was signed. Second, it did not address the IOC's call for information concerning bid opportunities granted to NBC and CBS. Despite John Wilkins's claim that Lake Placid's "depleted" treasury prompted the agreement with ABC, Berlioux reminded him that IOC approval hinged on a thorough review of the contract and LPOC's report concerning its discussions with ABC's rival networks.[17]

CBS AND NBC CAMPAIGN FOR A COMPETITIVE BID PROCESS

Confusion reigned at CBS headquarters. Compromised by Arledge's approach and their own inaction, CBS officials considered their options. On 21 February, eight days after the signing of the tentative ABC/Lake Placid deal, Hess informed Wussler that the TV-Marketing Committee had been authorized to negotiate a U.S. television rights contract. Hess requested a meeting with CBS to discuss "preliminary negotiation procedures."[18] On 27 February, however, Wilkins wrote to Wussler abruptly informing him: "Because of what we view as your extended lack of interest since our summer meeting, we are concentrating our television efforts on the American Broadcasting Company."[19] The conflicting messages from Hess and Wilkins—one seeking a meeting to open negotiations, the other stating that CBS was not in the television negotiating plans of Lake Placid—concerned Wussler. Wilkins's correspondence sounded an alarm in CBS's New York office, prompting a flurry of communication with Lake Placid, media outlets, and the IOC.

Though CBS officials pressed for a meeting with Lake Placid officials and crafted production plan proposals, the flurry of energy was "too little, too late." Before any meetings between CBS and Lake Placid could be arranged, LPOC and ABC reached an accord on 6 March. CBS officials were livid and immediately registered their anger at Lake Placid's action with New York senators James L. Buckley and Jacob Javits.[20] Meanwhile NBC called for the IOC to declare the ABC contract null and void and publicly enunciated its dissatisfaction in the U.S. media.

Wilkins's explanation of the negotiations process emphasized CBS's and NBC's limited contact with Lake Placid in the aftermath of their site inspections in 1975. It was only after ABC's successful telecasts from Innsbruck, he asserted, that CBS and NBC expressed any interest in dealing with Lake Placid. NBC vice-president of sports Carl Lindemann told Norman Hess on 18 February that "NBC had a renewed interest in televising the 1980 Games and could now open up the cash box." As for Wussler and his CBS colleagues, stated Wilkins, they had not maintained any contact with Lake Placid during the fall and winter months. CBS initiated communication after it received Wilkins's bombshell announcement concerning Lake Placid's agreement with ABC. Neither company had completed a meaningful study of technical issues. Specifically, neither CBS nor NBC had investigated the state regulations governing the construction of telephone and microwave communication lines. They did not forward production plans to Lake Placid despite their promise to do so within weeks of their site inspections in 1975. "Their continued complete silence and failure to pursue the further information we knew was necessary," argued Wilkins, "indicated to us that NBC and CBS felt that televising the 1980 Winter Games from Lake Placid was not a profitable business venture for them and therefore not worthy of their further time, expense or even the courtesy of a phone call or letter to explain their delay in their promised early reply to our summer meetings." ABC, in contrast, maintained contact with Lake Placid and provided periodic updates on its technical plans.[21]

The "big three" U.S. networks deluged Killanin and Berlioux with correspondence as they jockeyed for position. The dilemma remained unresolved. The IOC withheld its approval of the ABC contract, pending a review of its terms. Corydon Dunham of NBC charged that Lake Placid's "arrangements fall far short of accepted business practices in dealing with matters affecting the public interest and are clearly against the interests of the Olympic Games and the public."[22] Robert T. Howard, NBC's president, urged Killanin to judge the network bids on merit.[23] John Schneider, president of the CBS Broadcast Group, confirmed CBS's desire to bid for the U.S. television rights. He called on the IOC to order Lake Placid "to accept sealed bids."[24] Robert Wood, president of CBS, could not understand Lake Placid's refusal to pursue negotiations with CBS and NBC when the process assured the receipt of additional revenue. "Rather than continue a paper war," he wrote Ronald McKenzie, president of LPOC, "we will await the decision of the IOC."[25] Arledge defended ABC's actions, reconfirming his network's devotion to the Olympic Movement. "Everything we have done as a network," he told Killanin, "has reflected nothing but credit and distinction to the Olympic Movement." Expressions of outrage from CBS and NBC, offered Arledge, represented an attempt to "justify their own inadequacies by implying that there was something unethical in the way that the agreement was reached."[26] Marvin Josephson, ever the opportunist and always sensitive to developments in the U.S. television market, offered to manage the bidding process for the IOC.[27] The IOC ignored him.

In early April Mortureux and Berlioux completed a fact-finding mission concerning Lake Placid's management of the U.S. television negotiations. Meetings brought together Mortureux, Berlioux, American IOC member Julian Roosevelt, F. Don Miller, executive director of the USOC, and Lake Placid officials. Following a review of documentation supplied by Lake Placid Berlioux and Mortureux concluded that "the U.S. networks were treated in all fairness and had been given equal opportunity." They agreed with Wilkins's assessment that ABC's successful telecasts from Innsbruck had triggered sudden interest from NBC and CBS. The IOC broached four points of concern about the terms of the ABC/Lake Placid agreement, however. First, the IOC would not accept an agreement that limited its share of world television revenue to $3 million. Second, the IOC expected a minimum of $4 million, because Innsbruck contracts had reaped $3.8 million for the IOC, ISFs, and NOCs. Third, ABC's payments had to be sent to Lausanne for distribution rather than to Lake Placid. Fourth, ABC's planned expenditure of $20–30 million on technical facilities required elaboration. McKenzie, Wilkins, Berlioux, and Mortureux discussed these matters at length. Berlioux and Mortureux subsequently counseled the IOC Finance Commission to seek Killanin's authorization to renew negotiations with ABC for the purpose of seeking an additional $1 million from Arledge to be shared equally by Lake Placid and the IOC.[28]

A second round of negotiations with Roone Arledge yielded an additional $1.5 million from ABC, confirming the leverage afforded to the IOC and LPOC as a result of the interest expressed by CBS and NBC. Arledge deleted the revenue-sharing agreement from the contract and set the IOC's share of the $11.5 million at $3.75 million.[29] CBS and NBC officials, stymied in their effort to gain an opportunity to provide the IOC with formal bids, approached federal authorities.

Fred B. Rooney, chair of the Subcommittee on Transportation and Commerce of the Committee on Interstate and Foreign Commerce, expressed the reservations of the members of the U.S. Congress concerning the IOC's decision to deal exclusively with ABC. Rooney confirmed that CBS and NBC had presented documentation of their grievances to his subcommittee. He also expressed his colleagues' consensus that the IOC should invite offers from CBS and NBC in order to protect the public interest.[30] "It would seem that NBC and CBS have been engaged in congressional ear banging in addition to twisting arms of the IOC and [Lake Placid]," commented Val Adams of the *New York Daily News*.[31]

BEAUMONT'S AUCTION

During a series of meetings in Paris in late May Beaumont and the Finance Commission, with Killanin's approval, brought a significant measure of closure to the U.S. negotiations. On 24 May Berlioux, Mortureux, and Silance reviewed the second contract established by Lake Placid and ABC. They asked Roone Arledge to consider a modified distribution key that provided the IOC with $4.25 million and reduced Lake Placid's share of the $11.5 million to $7.25 million. At this point Arledge was less concerned with who received what than alarmed by the threat posed by CBS's and NBC's lobbying on Capitol Hill. He agreed to the revised distribution formula. On the following day Beaumont, Mortureux, and Silance met with

CBS, NBC, and ABC delegations led by Barry Frank, CBS vice-president–sports, Robert Howard of NBC, and Roone Arledge. CBS and NBC appealed for an opportunity to bid for the U.S. television rights. Killanin had been clear in his communication with CBS and NBC, argued Frank and Howard, that Lake Placid would not deal with its television negotiations until the conclusion of the Innsbruck Games. Subsequently Beaumont received bids from CBS ($14 million), NBC ($15.5 million), and ABC ($12 million).[32] In their effort to secure the U.S. television rights, concluded Val Adams, the networks "may have already exerted more energy than will be expended by athletes on the snowy slopes of the Adirondacks."[33]

Despite Beaumont's pledge that all bids would remain secret, he clearly granted ABC an opportunity to match NBC's offer. By the conclusion of the Paris meetings on 25 May ABC's bid was the lowest of the three offers. But a week later Arledge proffered a new figure. Prefacing his remarks with the message, "In follow-up to our meetings with you and your colleagues in Paris on May 25th, 1976 and subsequent events, we now wish to relate a decision which we hope will be received in the cooperative spirit in which we make it," Arledge offered Beaumont $15.5 million, on the expressed condition that the IOC solicit no further bids.[34] Beaumont promised rapid action from the IOC. He had managed this final round of financial negotiations without assistance from Lake Placid officials, who, despite their presence in Paris, were not invited to attend the meetings.[35] Within a week the ABC deal received approval from Beaumont and Killanin.[36]

Lake Placid agreed grudgingly but was not pleased. Wilkins vented his frustration with Beaumont's auction in Paris: "We mutually agreed at Lake Placid that while bidding was possible, commercialization of the Olympics was not a desirable goal for the IOC or for the Lake Placid Olympic Organizing Committee." Beaumont's auction departed from the IOC's previously articulated philosophy, he concluded. Lake Placid had been misled concerning the agenda of the Paris meetings: "Daniel Mortureux further advised us that our TV Committee was not to be invited to the IOC Finance Commission meeting to be held on May 25, 1976 in Paris, as all matters were settled and would merely be ratified on the basis of our last negotiation and agreement for division of payments." Wilkins and Lake Placid personnel present in Paris had been shut out of the final negotiations, probably an even greater sore point. An embittered Wilkins wrote to Berlioux decrying that they "had no input, were allowed no comment, were given no information as to your deliberations and were not consulted prior to your decision."[37] He demanded a meeting with Berlioux on 16 and 17 September in Lausanne to discuss the ABC contract. Berlioux brushed him off. "I am afraid at the moment I work for the IOC and am not under orders from [Lake Placid officials]," she retorted. Confrontationally, Berlioux told Wilkins that LPOC's management of the U.S. negotiations had created "turmoil" for the IOC and turned "the three American networks against us."[38]

Beaumont's management act marked a significant turning point in the history of the IOC and its relationship to commercial matters. It signified the end of the IOC as a "background" or "behind the scenes" adviser in negotiations proceedings and marked the beginning of its drift toward eventually assuming entire control of television matters.

Finally, it seems inconceivable that an element so fundamental to the contract as the manner in which the money would be divided between the IOC and Lake Placid was not fully vetted before the release of financial details of the ABC/LPOC agreement to the media on 11 June. This issue was not addressed until the end of July, however, when Berlioux informed Wilkins that the IOC expected to receive $6.25 million, leaving $9.25 million for Lake Placid. If she believed that Wilkins was grateful for Beaumont's efforts to improve ABC's offer and placate CBS, NBC, and U.S. federal authorities, she was mistaken. Berlioux and Wilkins sparred in an exchange of communication. Wilkins questioned the IOC's need for $6.25 million, considering Berlioux's comment in April that $4 million would suffice.[39] Berlioux challenged his recollection of the meeting in April when she replied that the $4 million represented "a minimum requirement in order to start negotiations."

The search for a method of distributing the money finally acceptable to both parties lurched forward as a result of two successive meetings in October and December. Even though ABC officials, representatives of the IOC, and Wilkins were able to reach agreement on many issues pertaining to ABC's responsibilities and rights, including the removal of Canada from ABC's broadcast territory, an acceptable method of dividing the money between the IOC and Lake Placid proved elusive. Wilkins refused to sign the contract if the IOC was granted $6.25 million. He indicated that he and Lake Placid would not sign the ABC contract unless the IOC agreed to provide them with a $1 million "gift" and an interest-free loan of $1.25 million (later revised to $1 million).[40]

The involvement of F. Don Miller, the USOC's executive director, in Lake Placid's latest decree disturbed Berlioux.[41] A 30% tax on U.S. network payments for Olympic television rights whenever the Games were staged outside the United States, noted Miller, represented a point of discussion for U.S. president Jimmy Carter's administration. If authorities in Washington did not follow through on Carter's "30% tax," and the IOC did not consent to supplement Lake Placid's share of the television revenue, the

USOC favored a second approach. It would call for the transfer of 10% of all television revenue to the NOC of the country in which the Games were staged. Julian Roosevelt, an American IOC member, supported Miller's position. The USOC, stated Miller, was willing to guarantee the IOC's loan to Lake Placid as well as an additional $1.6 million for the IOC from the sale of television rights to non-U.S. networks. If the IOC agreed to these terms, the USOC would withhold its support of federal legislation concerning an Olympic television rights tax and shelve its proposal to grant 10% of the television rights to the NOC of the country in which the games were held. "Blackmail," cried Berlioux.[42] Blackmail it may have been, but it proved not to be the last time that the USOC resorted to such tactics. This episode foreshadowed the USOC's employment of the congressional brickbat as a means of enhancing its own financial standing concerning television money in the 1990s. Julian Roosevelt telephoned Beaumont about the USOC offer.[43] Berlioux, in turn, contacted Killanin. IOC officials deferred a final decision pending a period of study and reflection.

Berlioux and Beaumont differed on the appropriate course of action. Berlioux resisted conceding the IOC's position. Based on the antagonistic tone of her correspondence with Wilkins, it is not difficult to understand why she opposed surrendering to Lake Placid's will. Her stand also reflected her fierce advocacy of the IOC's financial interests. Beaumont adopted a more conciliatory tone. "My personal feeling," he told Killanin, "is that we ought to appreciate somehow the great financial income we have had from the United States." The IOC's share of the U.S. television contract, after the deduction of the proposed $1 million gift, noted Beaumont, represented a 69% increase over the sum received by the IOC from the sale of world television rights to the 1976 Innsbruck Olympic Winter Games. If the IOC agreed to the terms proposed by Lake Placid/USOC, it was guaranteed $6.85 million. "There seems to be some disagreement with the Director [Berlioux] over my suggestions," conceded Beaumont.[44] Killanin, who had been confused and believed that Miller was seeking only the $1 million loan, accepted Beaumont's suggestion.[45] Later the Finance Commission clarified that the USOC was to receive the $1 million gift for the advancement of amateur sport in the United States; however, it was clear that the USOC would funnel the loan money to Lake Placid to offset some of its hardware costs. The Finance Commission supported Beaumont's recommendation.[46] The foundation for a settlement had been established.

Berlioux and Mortureux also met with ABC, NBC, and CBS officials in New York to discuss issues pertaining to future IOC policy governing Olympic television rights negotiations. Network executives pressed the

IOC to deal exclusively with the rights payments and leave the OCOGs to negotiate the technical services payments.[47] The IOC received legal counsel that such a solution represented a potential "house of cards." If the OCOG negotiated a hardware contract, the network might plead limited resources as a means of reducing its rights payment. It was suggested that future contracts (1984 and beyond) should contain both the television rights and hardware components. Negotiating these contracts jointly with the OCOGs offered the best opportunity for the IOC to protect its financial interests.[48] This plan was proposed and accepted at the IOC's Prague Session in 1977.[49] It marked a significant but predictable departure for the IOC from past practice. Difficulties encountered with the Innsbruck, Montréal, Lake Placid, and Moscow Olympic Organizing Committees led the U.S. networks and the IOC to seek a means of reducing conflict during the negotiations process.

MOSCOW

While Olympic enthusiasts focused their attention on the sporting dramas unfolding in Montréal's Olympic Stadium, U.S. television executives renewed their quest for television rights to the 1980 Moscow Olympic Games. These rights represented a treasured commodity for the American networks. Conversely, the Soviets were poised to exploit the networks' competitiveness as a means of bankrolling a significant element of the infrastructure costs inherent in hosting the Games. The Soviet ship *Alexander Pushkin,* docked in Montréal's harbor for the Games, provided the setting for a meeting between Moscow organizers and the representatives of the "big three" U.S. networks. Ignati Novikov, president of the Moscow Olympic Organizing Committee, hosted a typically lavish Russian feast. "The decks were awash with gallons of Stolichnaya vodka and Armenian cognac," observed William O. Johnson of *Sports Illustrated,* while "tables groaned beneath platters of cracked lobster, sliced sturgeon, [and] caviar."[50] The Americans, "who came from stately Manhattan skyscrapers, [were] quick-witted, supersophisticated salesmen given to Gucci shoes and manicured hands." They stood opposite "the burly, pallid, [and] somewhat grim bureaucrats who composed the Soviet negotiating team."[51] Following food and drink and the usual social amenities Novikov raised the eyebrows of his guests by announcing his initial bargaining position: the Soviets expected $210 million from the U.S. market. None of the television executives reached for their checkbooks. An NBC official deadpanned that 210 million pennies seemed more reasonable.[52] Novikov's demand was not taken seriously by his American audience.

Nevertheless, U.S. television networks ingratiated themselves with Soviet organizers well in advance of negotiations for television rights to the Moscow Olympics. CBS, for instance, engaged Mary Tyler Moore, star of the popular television sitcom *The Mary Tyler Moore Show*, to provide commentary for a program on the Bolshoi Ballet.[53] NBC pursued an agreement to televise the USSR Festival of Music and Dance.[54] ABC used its morning programming to court Novikov and his colleagues by producing a ten-hour series on life in the Soviet Union that caused some members of ABC's news division to wince. Referring to this "sanitized" view of Soviet life, one ABC official concluded ruefully that "we made Moscow look like Cypress Gardens without the skiers."[55] As a further means of currying favor all networks purchased Soviet films best described as propaganda, as evidenced by depiction of "the heroic efforts of farm labor, new production quotas at lumber mills, and the glories of life on the collective farm." These efforts accomplished little, concluded David Klatell and Norman Marcus, authors of *Sports for Sale,* because the Soviets viewed the "whole episode as a chance to tweak the Americans a bit, watch them squirm, and dump on them a bunch of worthless productions gathering dust in some Ministry of Culture film library."[56] Novikov's request for favorable coverage of the Soviet Union was hardly a departure from his script; his lavish and carefully staged party aboard the *Alexander Pushkin* was merely another orchestration designed to test the demeanor of American negotiators.

Why were the U.S. television executives content to act as marionettes in Novikov's production? The answer is money and Nielsen ratings. Roone Arledge's team at ABC demonstrated that an Olympic television rights holder in the U.S. could reap a profit and use the athletic drama as a springboard to enhanced network status.[57] The Cold War backdrop for Olympic competition served only to heighten interest in executive offices at NBC, CBS, and ABC. "The fact that the Games were taking place in the heart of the Soviet Empire was of great interest to network News as well as Sports," wrote Klatell and Marcus. "It represented perhaps an unparalleled opportunity to pierce, even in a limited way, the Iron Curtain with the all-seeing television lens."[58] Robert Wussler, CBS's vice-president–sports, and Carl Lindemann, his counterpart at NBC, along with Roone Arledge, understood the unique opportunity afforded by the IOC's decision to award the 1980 Games to Moscow.[59] The Moscow site, the perception of the Olympics as the pinnacle in athletic competition, and constant reminders of conflicting American and Soviet world views provided to Americans through domestic news coverage, television, and Hollywood fare proved a tantalizing combination for the U.S. networks.[60]

But once again poor lines of communication between the IOC and, in this case, the Moscow Organizing Committee dashed hopes for trouble-free negotiations for U.S. and European television contracts, the two most important financial agreements from the IOC's perspective. Novikov's elegant shipboard party transpired unbeknownst to Killanin, Beaumont, and Berlioux. They had not been invited. Less than two months after the conclusion of the Montréal Olympics Killanin queried Novikov concerning unofficial reports that discussions with U.S. networks were nearing the "final negotiation moment." He counseled Novikov not to sign any documents before the IOC reviewed them.[61] Killanin suspected that Novikov would seek an exemption from the Rome Formula.[62] He requested a report from the Soviets on the status of negotiations and the timetable for concluding an agreement with one of the U.S. networks.[63]

Vitaly Smirnov, Soviet IOC member, complied with Killanin's request. Prior discussions with U.S. executives, noted Smirnov, addressed technical issues. Proposals concerning production plans were forthcoming from the U.S. networks and would be discussed with members of the IOC Executive Board. Smirnov indicated that Moscow officials would then proceed to discuss "numbers" with U.S. television representatives.[64] At the Executive Board's meeting in October 1976 he reported that the U.S. networks wished to conclude an agreement before the presidential election on 2 November. In Smirnov's mind this was simply not feasible. He stated that a contract would be forwarded to Lausanne for review in the near future.[65]

At the Finance Commission's November meeting in Paris an IOC/OCOG dialogue began concerning the terms of the Rome Formula. During a discussion with Beaumont, Berlioux, and Mortureux, Vladimir Koval, executive vice-president of the Moscow Organizing Committee, estimated the cost of satisfying the needs of the world's broadcasters at 422 million rubles (1 ruble = U.S. $1.25). He boldly demanded 80% of the television money, not the 50% granted to the OCOG in the case of the Montréal contracts. Beaumont calmly reminded Koval that Moscow had agreed not to draw a distinction between television rights and hardware when the Games had been awarded to the city in 1974. Killanin, he stated, was unwilling to sanction such an agreement with Moscow.[66]

Later in November Novikov and Smirnov appealed to Killanin for concessions due to the Soviets' lack of foreign currency. Killanin sympathized but did not discuss how the IOC might assist Moscow in this regard. He informed Berlioux that the Rome Formula could be relaxed and that a $15 million share from the U.S. market for the IOC satisfied its needs.[67] Killanin realized that the Munich Precedent, the Montréal contracts, concessions to Innsbruck, and the impending deal with Lake Placid demanded concessions for Moscow. The need to maintain control of the process to avoid a repeat of the fiasco with Montréal dictated Killanin's stance.

In early December Mortureux and Georges Straschnov, EBU's former head of Juridical Affairs, who had recently been engaged by the IOC as a television adviser, booked passage to Moscow in order to bring closure to this aspect of the negotiations process. While the Soviets lobbied for the same terms granted to Roger Rousseau, they soon tendered a compromise proposal. On the basis of their discussions with U.S. networks they considered a $90 million contract to be a realistic goal. In exchange for a $70 million deduction from the U.S. contract for technical services the Soviets agreed not to separate television rights and hardware costs in the remaining global contracts. Mortureux, Straschnov, and the Soviets arrived at an agreement, subject to Killanin's approval. If the Soviets reached a deal with one of the American networks for a minimum value of $80 million, the IOC would accept the classification of $50 million as a technical services payment.[68]

The Soviets also apprised Mortureux and Straschnov of the preliminary offers received from the three major U.S. networks and a fourth player, the Soviet-American Trading Company (SATRA). SATRA focused its business efforts on the import/export trade but solicited advice on the Olympic initiative from major entertainment giants Metro-Goldwyn-Mayer and Viacom. SATRA proposed to establish a temporary network of television stations throughout the United States specifically to telecast the Games. ABC's bid of $73 million exceeded those forwarded by CBS ($71 million), NBC ($70 million), and SATRA ($70 million). None satisfied Novikov and his colleagues. They envisioned an auction in Moscow, with a minimum bid of $80 million. If more than one of the competing networks offered the minimum, then subsequent rounds of bidding would be held, with each new bid increasing by a minimum of 5%.[69] Beaumont and Killanin approved this course of action.[70]

The U.S. networks resented the Soviets' blatant effort to drive up the price of U.S. television rights. A limit placed on the size of the network negotiating delegations (three persons, including an interpreter) also irritated them. The Soviet Embassy in Washington refused to issue more than three visas for each network. Considering the stakes involved and the amount of money being discussed, the network officials did not relish a process necessitating constant communication with their head offices in New York. "What the Russians didn't say," wryly noted Val Adams of the *New York Daily News,* "is whether they accept American Express or other credit cards."[71] Perhaps the most confused and angered of the American travelers was Robert Wussler, CBS's newly appointed president. In November he and CBS chairman William Paley engaged in private discussions with Novikov in Moscow. They departed the Soviet capital thinking they had outfoxed Roone Arledge as well as NBC, having reached a handshake agreement with Novikov.[72] Given the circumstances the pre-auction reception at the Hotel Sovietskaya in December 1976 exuded feelings of mutual distrust.

Karl Ryavec, author of *United States Soviet Relations*, provided a commentary on the strained discussions between Soviet and American politicians and diplomats during the Cold War that may help us to understand this encounter. He observed that "negotiations and interactions between rivals are always difficult, but they are especially troublesome and frustrating if the parties to the negotiations think differently, have different conceptions of normalcy, govern themselves and run their economies by opposing principles, and view each other as either enemies or untrustworthy or odd."[73] Embarrassed by Novikov's evident grasp of capitalism and humiliated by their own earlier groveling, U.S. executives opted out of Novikov's auction. "They want us to be like three scorpions fighting in a bottle," complained Arledge; "when it's over, two will be dead and the winner will be exhausted."[74] The Soviet demand for $50 million of the contracted sum to be paid within two years of signing the television contract agitated U.S. network officials. Novikov's antics disturbed NBC's Carl Lindemann, who later commented that his approach reflected the thought that "there was no limit to the manic competitive zeal of the networks." "But what bothered me even more," observed Lindemann, "was the fact that this wasn't just another ball game . . . this was the United States against the Soviet Union—and we couldn't let this happen."[75] The American executives left Moscow (after showing each other their plane reservations as a sign of good faith) to seek a waiver from the U.S. Justice Department that would permit them to tender a pooled bid.

This display of solidarity shook Novikov. "If any of you leave Soviet soil this day," he railed, "you will never, never be allowed to return."[76] Arledge took some satisfaction in Novikov's frustration when he recalled that "he could practically see the steam coming out of [Novikov's] ears."[77] Novikov failed to entice Arledge to sign an agreement during a private meeting called after the announcement of the decision of the U.S. networks. His effort to seal an agreement with William Paley by telex also failed.[78] Novikov's decision to sign a letter of intent to finalize a contract with SATRA, subject to the IOC's approval, failed to elicit the desired response from the U.S. executives, who in essence believed that they had turned the tables on the wily Novikov.

U.S. executives expressed confidence that the IOC would not sanction an agreement with SATRA, an unproven entity in terms of its ability to deliver quality Olympic coverage in the U.S. market. The Americans viewed Novikov's move as a face-saving measure. Arledge shrugged off the SATRA/Moscow agreement. Wussler stated that it was simply another stage in the negotiations. "I don't think the story is over," he asserted. "I think [the process] will go on for weeks."[79] Meanwhile SATRA dismissed doubts concerning its ability to cover the Games and anticipated the IOC's approval. "The only people in the United States who feel that the networks are the only ones who can do it are the networks themselves," noted a SATRA official. Ralph M. Baruch, president of Viacom and one of SATRA's consultants, warned that any effort on the part of the "big three" networks to assert that SATRA's project hinged on Pay-TV as a means of offsetting its costs was a "red herring" designed to force the Soviets back to the table.[80]

IOC approval of the SATRA initiative, however, was not possible without the IOC having access to details concerning the letter of intent. Without the benefit of a report from Novikov the Finance Commission discussed the failed auction at its meeting on 5 January 1977. Committee members pondered various press reports and rumors that SATRA was willing to pay $100 million for rights and technical services. Berlioux advised deferring any further discussion until the IOC received a report. Marc Hodler suggested that the SATRA accord might result in improved offers from the U.S. networks.[81]

Two weeks later Moscow organizers signaled their intent to cast SATRA aside. Once again the Soviets invited proposals from CBS, NBC, and ABC. "We are most sincerely interested to concede these television rights to a competent body that enjoys a good professional reputation," commented a Soviet negotiator.[82] Within days CBS withdrew from the process and informed the Justice Department that it was no longer interested in the pooled bid. NBC and ABC were left to contest for the U.S. television rights. CBS's own doubts about dealing with the Soviets and the activities of a mysterious West German named Lothar Bock triggered the withdrawal.

Bock served as CBS's intermediary in negotiations with the Soviets that resulted in the handshake deal between Novikov and William Paley in November 1976. U.S. film producer Bud Greenspan had introduced Wussler and Bock. Bock enjoyed a good relationship with the Soviets, notably through his past efforts to negotiate appearances for Soviet entertainment groups and dance troupes in Western Europe. He had purely financial motives for working for CBS's benefit. Following the failed Hotel Sovietskaya proceedings, Bock had continued to lobby on CBS's behalf. Roone

Arledge, aware of Bock's extended behind-the-scenes work, challenged Wussler about Bock's association with CBS and his dealings with the Soviets. Bock had proceeded on his own without CBS's consent, replied a worried Wussler. CBS, of course, was party to the joint appeal to the Justice Department for a pooled bid. Subsequently Bock returned triumphantly to the United States with an $81 million contract. Wussler, faced with the conundrum, removed CBS from all television negotiation proceedings. Bock's actions, known to Arledge, threatened Wussler's and CBS's reputation if he signed the contract. With CBS's withdrawal from the entire process, the pooled bid option crumbled. Meanwhile Bock had a contract, but his employer was unwilling to sign the deal. CBS's decision endangered any financial gain he sought from this process. When Wussler released Bock from his contract, he wasted little time in approaching NBC's Carl Lindemann.[83]

Lindemann seemed less informed than Arledge about Bock's role in CBS's negotiations with the Soviets. The two shared breakfast at the Plaza Hotel in Manhattan. "The conversation was remarkably low-key, considering its substance," recalled Lindemann. Bock recounted to Lindemann his recent discussions with Novikov and the nature of the contract. "We ordered something to eat," said Lindemann. "He kept talking. We drank our orange juice, then it dawned on me what he was saying." A clear opportunity to break ABC's stranglehold on U.S. Olympic television rights presented itself. "We left without eating," noted Lindemann. NBC capitalized on Bock's free-agent status and Novikov's need to deal with one of the "big three" networks. Robert Howard, Lindemann, and an NBC lawyer left New York for Moscow the next day, unbeknownst to Roone Arledge. He soon learned of their departure, however. Ignoring a message from the Soviets not to bother coming to Moscow, he rushed there anyway.[84] ABC offered $85 million in a last-ditch attempt to obtain the rights, but the Soviets settled for NBC's $82 million offer, primarily because of a much more favorable payment schedule. Howard left little to chance: he matched Arledge's offer of $85 million.[85] Novikov stimulated "a Pavlovian reaction in capitalist dogs," lamented one *New York Times* editorial writer.[86] Bock walked away from the process with a king's ransom, $1 million in cash, NBC's pledge to purchase fifteen television programs that he would produce, and a four-year contract as a special consultant.[87] The IOC approved the NBC contract in short order, relieved that a proven broadcast network owned the rights.

The book was not yet closed on U.S. television negotiations for the Moscow Games, however. SATRA launched a $275 million legal action against NBC, citing interference with contract, conspiracy, international impairment of economic relations, conversion of contract rights, unfair competition, and restraint of trade.[88] Novikov conceded video cassette and official film distribution rights and $3 million to SATRA as a means of settling the dispute. Even though the IOC succeeded in its efforts to convince court authorities that Novikov signed the letter of intent with SATRA without its knowledge and approval, it had incurred over $32,000 in legal fees. That amount was recovered from the Soviets.[89]

Despite his earlier pledge to accept the distribution of all future U.S. television revenue according to the Rome Formula, Novikov appealed to Killanin to grant the IOC's share of the EBU contract to the Moscow organizers. He pleaded a lack of foreign currency, but his real motivation was accommodating the $3 million payment owed to SATRA. Killanin refused on the grounds that the IOC's share of television money also belonged to the ISFs and NOCs.[90] Beaumont and Killanin concluded that the $50 million deduction from the U.S. contract for broadcast facilities was a significant concession.[91] They were not moved to sacrifice additional IOC revenue.

By August 1978 Novikov and EBU had settled on a figure of $5.95 million. Still, Novikov renewed his attempt to finesse better distribution terms from the IOC. He noted that Moscow was able to provide only three unilateral channels to EBU, even though EBU had requested six. Considering the additional cost of $250,000–300,000 for each additional channel, Novikov sought a deduction of $950,000 for technical services. Killanin and Beaumont were dismayed but linked their approval to television revenue from Eastern Europe (OIRT). According to Eastern European television policy, Soviet-bloc nations selected as hosts of international events were required to provide programming free of charge. Killanin had refused to sanction CBC's proposed $1 sweetheart deal with Montréal for Canadian television rights. While this situation did not provide a direct analogy, both threatened the IOC's bottom line. Killanin demanded (and received) $300,000 from the sale of Canadian television rights to the Montréal Games. The IOC, he announced, required $500,000 from the sale of television rights in Eastern Europe.[92] The Soviets agreed; but unfortunately for the IOC, the contracted currency was the ruble, which forced the IOC, ISFs, and NOCs to spend their revenue share in the Soviet Union or risk losing most of it on the international money exchange market.[93] IOC officials hoped that the decision to establish the organization as a full partner with future OCOGs in the television negotiations process offered some relief for aggravations stemming from the IOC's prior arm's-length involvement in contract discussions.

FALLOUT FROM AFGHANISTAN

In late December 1979, practically on the eve of the opening of the Lake Placid Winter Games and scarcely six months before the Moscow Games, the Soviet Union launched an invasion of Afghanistan, which in the end prevented U.S. participation in Moscow and compromised the results of television negotiations in the United States and Europe. President Jimmy Carter, already the target of severe media criticism because of perceived foreign policy gaffes, searched for a means to counter the Soviets' activity in the volatile Persian Gulf region. He imposed economic sanctions and canceled scheduled Strategic Arms Limitation Treaty (II) talks. Soviet prestige, determined Carter, would suffer a grievous blow if U.S. athletes did not travel to Moscow for the Olympic Games. He established a 20 February 1980 deadline for the withdrawal of Soviet forces from Afghanistan. His administration launched a diplomatic campaign for support from other governments aimed at pressuring the IOC to move, cancel, or delay the Moscow Games. Killanin's efforts to dissuade Carter or convince the Soviets to appease the Americans and their allies failed.[94]

The U.S.-led boycott compromised the caliber of competition in Moscow and disrupted the financial plans of the Moscow Organizing Committee and the IOC. Four months prior to the Opening Ceremony the U.S. Department of Commerce (DOC) placed an embargo on NBC's payments to Moscow. In May Carter extended this policy to NBC's payments to the IOC. In terms of the television rights component of the NBC contract, $22.33 million and $12.67 million were due to Novikov's committee and the IOC, respectively. When the DOC imposed the regulatory measure, Moscow had already received $10.66 million; $6.83 million had been sent to Lausanne. NBC officials pledged to meet their financial obligations to Moscow and the IOC. In August 1981 the Reagan administration permitted NBC to forward money to the IOC. The IOC received $5.82 million, representing a principal payment of $4.83 million, plus interest. NBC's payment was $1 million short of the original sum, but this amount had been contingent upon the participation of the U.S. Olympic team. This clause had been added to the U.S. contract without the IOC's knowledge, which provided Berlioux with an additional source of frustration. The IOC, though irritated, elected not to pursue the matter in court. Similarly, EBU argued that it should be allowed to renegotiate its contracted sum because it claimed that the boycott had altered the structure of the Games. Seeking a means to avoid a tangled and grievous legal dispute, the IOC agreed to reduce EBU's rights payment by $297,500.[95]

THE LAKE PLACID AND MOSCOW GAMES

As the IOC worked to gather the necessary political support to stave off the threatened boycott, it also struggled to respond to the mounting doubts "over just what the Olympics was all about."[96] The enormous deficit of the 1976 Olympic Games in Montréal, combined with the threat of further boycotts, had left many questioning the very future of the Olympic Games. When the IOC selected Moscow to host the Games of the Twenty-second Olympiad at the IOC Session in Vienna on 23 October 1974, "East-West relations were tense," but there was little concern over the development of an international crisis.[97] The USOC had every intention to send a full team to the 1980 Olympic Games. Funds were being raised, team trials had been scheduled, and squads were being selected.[98]

Everything changed on 28 December 1979 when Radio Moscow reported that the Soviet Union had been asked by the government in Kabul to intervene in Afghanistan.[99] Before invading the Afghan interior to combat the Mujahidin guerrillas, the Soviets ousted Hafizullah Amin and installed Babrak Karmal as president.[100] Although the foreign policy options available to President Carter were limited, his government succeeded in achieving a boycott of the Moscow Olympics by the United States. On 21 January 1980 the U.S. House of Representatives endorsed the president's boycott proposal by a vote of 386–12. Although the decision was not binding on the USOC, the American NOC followed suit two days later, reassuring Congress of its patriotism. On 29 January 1980 the U.S. Senate voted 88–4 to support Carter's boycott initiative.[101]

As Jimmy Carter called on all U.S. allies to join the American boycott of the Moscow Games, Lake Placid opened its second Olympic Winter Games on 12 February 1980. Lake Placid officials encountered difficulties financing the necessary preparations. In 1976 the organizers estimated the total cost of hosting the 1980 Olympic Winter Games at $156 million.[102] But a combination of inflation, administrative problems, insufficient television revenue, and poor publicity as a result of the announcement of the boycott of the Moscow Olympic Games extended Lake Placid financially, almost to the point of bankruptcy.[103] As the Olympic Winter Games closed on 24 February 1980, Lake Placid had accumulated expenditures totaling some $178 million, leaving a shortfall of almost $8.5 million.[104] But there had been some dividends for the United States. Still entrenched in American Olympic legend are the five gold medals won by its superlative speed skater Eric Heiden and, at an even more epic level, the "Miracle on Ice" gold medal achieved by the ice hockey team in defeating the highly favored Soviets in the semifinal and the Finns in the final.

Overshadowed by the largest boycott in Olympic history, the Games of the Twenty-second Olympiad in Moscow were attended by only eighty countries.[105] Yet the Soviet organizers did all they could to make their Olympic Games memorable in the minds of those who attended. In an effort to market the Games Moscow created a commission to manage the production and sale of various products bearing the Olympic emblems. In all the commission issued 6,972 certificates in the USSR granting the right to manufacture Olympic merchandise. These companies alone manufactured approximately 17,500 different items. The commission also approved the production of an additional 1,633 Olympic items by companies located in seventeen different countries for sale within the Soviet Union. Moreover, Moscow signed representation contracts with nineteen marketing and advertising firms throughout the world to distribute licenses in over forty foreign countries.[106]

When the Olympic Games opened on 19 July 1980 in the 100,000-seat Lenin Stadium, the conundrum presented by the mass boycott and its associated protests faded.[107] Soviet president Leonid Brezhnev declared the Games open. A lavishly staged opening ceremony followed, with groups dressed in traditional costumes representing all the Soviet republics. According to the official Moscow report, the total expenditures incurred during the preparation for the Games approximated $1.304 billion (861.9 million rubles).[108] Other authors have estimated the total expenditures for the Olympic Games at an astonishing $9 billion.[109] The total revenues generated by the various programs and activities in Moscow totaled approximately $1.127 billion (744.9 million rubles). Unlike the case of Lake Placid, the state assumed the balance.

As the Moscow Olympic Games came to a close on 3 August 1980, the flag of Los Angeles, as host of the Games of the Twenty-third Olympiad, was hoisted next to those of Greece and the USSR. A huge bear representing the official mascot, Misha, with large helium balloons attached, entered the stadium infield. It was released and drifted slowly out of the stadium. Misha's likeness was then depicted by cardholders in the grandstands—a tear fell from his eye as the Games closed. Fireworks illuminated the Moscow sky as the Games of the Twenty-second Olympiad ended.[110]

REFLECTIONS

Lord Killanin altered the IOC's modus operandi concerning television negotiations in the 1970s. Troubled and frustrated by numerous arguments with OCOG representatives from Munich, Montréal, Lake Placid, and Moscow, Killanin understood the necessity of becoming a more active partner in the television negotiations process. Unlike Brundage, he accepted change, as evidenced by his efforts at shuttle diplomacy during the boycott era, his decision to liberalize outdated amateur rules, and his conclusion that better relations with the ISFs and NOCs strengthened the Olympic Movement.

Killanin delegated much authority regarding television to Jean de Beaumont and Monique Berlioux. The pair's management of the IOC's relations with the OCOGs on television matters in the 1970s translated into a "good cop/bad cop" approach, although not necessarily by design. Berlioux, though thoroughly efficient, often angered OCOG leaders with her strident attitude, inflexibility, and arrogance. Beaumont, in contrast, while no less concerned about the OCOGs' attempts to enhance their share of television money, often adopted a conciliatory approach and sought compromise. Beaumont also tempered the strong feelings of Finance Commission members such as Lord Luke and Marc Hodler, who bristled when the IOC was asked to sacrifice television revenue to the OCOGs.

The IOC's dependence on television revenue and conflict with OCOGs concerning terms of U.S. and European contracts convinced Killanin, Beaumont, and Berlioux that they could no longer support a policy that forced the IOC to react to the negotiations conducted by the OCOGs. The organization's long-term financial security demanded that the IOC abandon its arm's-length approach to managing television negotiations. Despite nagging concerns about the impact on the IOC's image due to a growing involvement in television negotiations, a full partnership role at the negotiation table offered a means to assert greater control over the entire process.

For Monique Berlioux, whose power base expanded in the 1970s and whose iron grip on the IOC's Lausanne operation remained firm, there was the prospect for even more influence. She prospered in an environment that she controlled as a result of decisions by Brundage and Killanin to maintain their principal residences in the United States and Ireland, respectively. It is easy to understand why Berlioux, having represented the IOC at numerous discussions with OCOG representatives concerning television contracts and gained recognition and familiarity with key television industry executives in the United States and Europe, considered herself in a position to add more responsibility to her portfolio. Her mistake, as the early 1980s proved, was her belief that Juan Antonio Samaranch, whose presidential candidacy she endorsed, accepted her vast sphere of power and influence.

New actors shouldered much responsibility in representing the IOC's interests during television negotiations in the 1980s. The partnership of Juan Antonio Samaranch and Richard Pound replaced the tandem of Beaumont and Berlioux. Samaranch, Pound, and their fellow IOC members learned that joint negotiation was not the answer for the IOC in its search for a means to reduce conflict with the OCOGs concerning the management of television negotiations. In advance of the 1992 Albertville and Barcelona Olympics the IOC finally decided to forego joint negotiation in favor of assuming sole authority over the process. As an element of the IOC's continuing transformation into a corporate entity in the 1980s, however, Samaranch's move to establish a second revenue stream for the IOC by courting corporate executives and presiding over the marriage of the Olympic rings to multinational corporate logos overshadowed this change in the IOC's managerial approach to revenue generation.

1. Pierre de Coubertin (ca. late 1890s), founder/architect (1894) of the Modern Olympic Movement and conceiver of the five-ring Olympic symbol (1913). The five rings have become one of the most visible "brand logos" in the world, generating billions of dollars for the treasuries of the IOC and its Olympic constituents through its links with television advertisers and multinational business firms. (Courtesy: International Centre for Olympic Studies)

2. The 1924 Paris Olympic Games: in the Colombes Stadium in Paris, against the backdrop of a commercial signboard advertising Ovalmatine, 3000-meter steeplechase competitors complete the race's last hurdle en route to the gold medal victory of Ville Ritola of Finland (Katz of Finland second, Bontemps of France third). The Paris Games marked the first and the last time that commercial product advertising appeared in the Olympic Stadium. (Credit: IOC/Olympic Museum Collections)

3. The 1924 Paris Olympic Games: the finish of the 800-meter run in the Colombes Stadium (won by Douglas Lowe of Great Britain), with commercial signboards advertising women's perfume: "Chenine Niger, parfum sublime." (Credit: IOC/Olympic Museum Collections)

4. Paul H. Helms (ca. 1950), Olympic Bread impresario and punching bag for Avery Brundage's insistent pummeling on the issue of Olympic commercialism. (Courtesy: Amateur Athletic Foundation of Los Angeles)

5. *(below)* The controversial Helms Bread wrapper with distinguishing Olympic rings and Olympic motto, initially registered by Paul Helms in 1932 to market his bakery firm's Olympic Bread. (Courtesy: Personal photo archives of Scott G. Martyn)

6. Avery Brundage (ca. 1946), czar of the American Olympic Movement (1928–52) and zealous proponent of commercial-free Olympic Games. (Courtesy: International Centre for Olympic Studies)

7. Counselor John T. McGovern (ca. 1950s), critical mediator between the legal rights of bakery entrepreneur Paul Helms and the "my way or the highway" dictum of Avery Brundage. (Courtesy: International Centre for Olympic Studies)

8. During a visit to Los Angeles in 1951 IOC president Sigfrid Edström (center) meets with Paul H. Helms (left) and his son, Paul Helms Jr. (right). (Courtesy: Amateur Athletic Foundation of Los Angeles)

9. Avery Brundage (ca. 1952), at last triumphant in the USOC's bid to wrest control of American Olympic symbols from Paul Helms, stands resplendent in a hat adorned with the officially registered United States Olympic Committee shield. (Courtesy: International Centre for Olympic Studies)

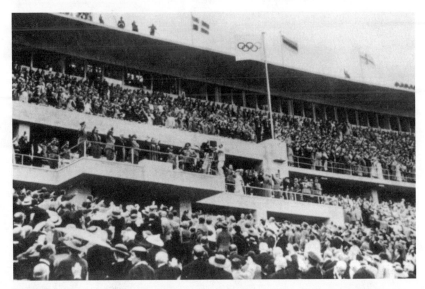

10. Reich chancellor Adolf Hitler's pavilion box at the opening ceremonies of the 1936 Berlin Olympic Games. Images of Hitler's familiar countenance (middle of pavilion) and IOC president Count Henri Baillet-Latour (to Hitler's right) are captured by an early version of the television camera (far right). (Credit: IOC/Olympic Museum Collections)

11. 1936 Berlin Olympic Games: a television camera films (from left to right) Hitler, Prince Umberto of Italy, Reich minister for propaganda Joseph Goebbels, and Luftwaffe commander Hermann Göring. The resulting image was beamed via closed circuit to various television viewing venues located in the immediate Berlin area. (Credit: IOC/Olympic Museum Collections)

12. 1936 Berlin Olympic Games: a television camera and crew prepare to film the final of the 200-meter sprint. Finish-line judges are arranged on an elevated stand. In all some 162,000 Berliners watched Olympic events both "live" and delayed over a period of 138 telecast hours. (Credit: IOC/Olympic Museum Collections)

13. IOC President Killanin and his closest adviser, Madame Monique Berlioux, visit with Soviet state and Olympic officials on the eve of the 1980 Moscow Games. From left to right: Berlioux, Vitaly Smirnov (IOC member in the Soviet Union), Killanin, the interpreter, Leonid Brezhnev (president of the Soviet Union), Ignati Novikov (president of the Moscow OCOG), and an unidentified Soviet. (Courtesy: International Centre for Olympic Studies)

14. "Her feet effectively under the [IOC] President's table . . . her hand on every doorknob, every appointment, every contract, every decision" (David Miller, *Olympic Revolution: The Biography of Juan Antonio Samaranch* [London: Pavilion Books, 1992], p. 252): IOC director-general Madame Monique Berlioux receives an appreciation gift, a Waterford crystal globe, from Michael Morris, the Lord Killanin, upon his retirement in 1980. In the early summer of 1985 Berlioux was abruptly and summarily discharged from IOC duties. She returned to her native France, where she assumed a post in the civic government of Paris. (Courtesy: International Centre for Olympic Studies)

15. In pursuit of television gold: ABC's Roone Arledge (ca. 1970s), zealous Olympic TV rights impresario. No American television official, including NBC's Dick Ebersol, did more than Arledge to make the Olympic Games a television spectacle and thus a rich source of IOC revenue. (Courtesy: Amateur Athletic Foundation of Los Angeles)

16. Peter Ueberroth (ca. 1984), architect of commercial Olympic Games. Ueberroth's largely privately funded 1984 Games became Olympic history's watershed event in creating determination by cities the world over to bid for the right to host an Olympic festival. (Credit: Amateur Athletic Foundation of Los Angeles/LPI)

17. Lausanne, 28 May 1985: Juan Antonio Samaranch shakes hands with ISL's Horst Dassler, setting in motion TOP, the IOC's corporate sponsorship program. The TOP initiative added corporate sponsorship to a two-decade history of television marketing to form the twin pillars of Olympic commercialism. Pictured in background is IOC administrative staff member, Alain Coupat. (Credit: IOC/Olympic Museum Collections)

18. Richard W. Pound (ca. 2000), the IOC's revenue production point-man. In the critical American television and corporate sponsorship marketplace Pound's tough, face-to-face North American style of doing business produced billions of U.S. dollars for both the IOC and, indirectly, the USOC. (Courtesy: Stikeman Elliott/Montréal)

19. John Krimsky (ca. 1998), the USOC's revenue production point-man. Krimsky, as uncompromising as Pound in the arena of Olympic commercial negotiations, transformed the USOC from a modestly endowed organization in the 1980s to one of immense wealth and vast assets by the end of the millennium. (Courtesy: International Centre for Olympic Studies)

20. The Sunset Television Contract signing (5 March 1997) that secured U.S. television rights for NBC to three Olympic festivals: 2004 Summer Games, 2006 Winter Games, and 2008 Summer Games. Seated: Dick Ebersol of NBC (left) and Juan Antonio Samaranch (right). Standing (left to right): Richard Pound, Don Petroni (IOC outside legal counsel), Howard Stupp (IOC legal affairs director), and Bill Hybl (USOC president). (Credit: IOC/Olympic Museum Collections)

PART II

THE IOC BECOMES
A CORPORATE ENTITY

In the commercial history of the Olympic Games, events of the decades of the 1980s and 1990s are of benchmark importance. For instance, critical changes in IOC statute principles relative to television rights negotiations led the IOC to shed the encumbering and often difficult alliance with OCOGs and to establish itself as the sole authority in the rights negotiation process. Consequently the IOC became not only wealthier beyond its most optimistic expectations but extraordinarily more powerful in the context of global sport. Indeed, as the process of business enterprise mushroomed inside the decision-making venues of the IOC's Lausanne headquarters, the organization began to assume the trappings of a global business giant headed by a quasi–chief executive officer (CEO), Juan Antonio Samaranch.

Television matters aside, it was in the world of product advertising and consumer sales, often referred to as marketing, that the IOC became linked indelibly to what most people refer to as commercialism. The corporate sponsorship link, as noted in the preceding chapters, was explored and at times modestly exploited by OCOGs dating from the earliest history of the Games. Conventional wisdom, of course, reports that Peter Ueberroth "wrote the book" on how an OCOG should go about the fund-raising project. After all, had he not produced a profit of over $200,000 million by wedding television and corporate sponsorship to "his" 1984 Summer Games?

It was not Ueberroth who led the IOC into the world of corporate marketing, however, but an earlier sports marketing impresario who provided the impetus for the corporate marketing of the five-ring Olympic symbol. That individual was Horst Dassler, son of Adi Dassler, godfather of the global sporting goods empire known as Adidas. Horst Dassler's influence on Juan Antonio Samaranch, who was elected to the presidency of the IOC in 1980, was a critical factor in forging the now well-developed and highly visible link between the Olympic Games and corporate sponsorship.

(Although their discussions on the subject of commercial sponsorship of sport were informal and unrecorded, IOC marketing officials corroborate that they took place.) At the same time, the 1980s and 1990s witnessed the rise of the USOC as an aggressive pursuer of the revenues previously reserved exclusively for the IOC, OCOGs, ISFs, and collective body of the world's NOCs. In the end the USOC—wealthy, powerful, politically aggressive, thirsting for new levels of achievement in the world's most important international sports festival—challenged the IOC's very authority as a ruling body.

Finally, undergirding the acceleration of matters commercial in the Modern Olympic Movement was a factor that had already played a role in the past—protection of Olympic marks and symbols from the marauding expeditions of those intent on manipulating the name and global mystique of the Games for their own business means and, of course, without paying for the privilege to do so. As noted in the Helms case, the process of protection originally began with initiatives taken by NOCs, usually with some prodding by the IOC. The IOC has never owned its marks and symbols within the borders of any country except Switzerland, the nation in which it is physically located. Nevertheless, the IOC has made a crucial contribution to NOC initiatives that sought to protect by law the Olympic symbols, which have brought riches into the hands of their owner, the Modern Olympic Movement. The second part of this book begins with the subject of protection, a bedrock issue in marketing.

CHAPTER 7

PROTECTING AND EXPLOITING
THE OLYMPIC MYSTIQUE

The Emergence of TOP

The IOC's contemporary success in generating revenue by courting multinational corporations and granting them an exclusive opportunity to link their marketing programs to the five-ring Olympic logo—the most recognized symbol in the world, according to polls commissioned by the IOC—is contingent upon an ability to protect the mark from being unlawfully used. Olympic moguls believe that they have "a legal and moral right to protect the intangible elements and properties that are attributes of its name and symbol and it would be remiss for the good of the movement if it were not vigilant and aggressive in enforcing those rights."[1] As one Olympic official observed, "one of our greatest sources of revenue is licensing companies to call themselves the 'Official Olympic Company' or 'Official Olympic Supplier' in a particular category"; if they did not protect these "official marks," "[we] would be cutting our own throats."[2] Given what is at stake for the Modern Olympic Movement in today's world—literally billions of dollars generated by the Olympic five-ring symbol alone—it is appropriate to revisit the efforts to establish jurisdiction over use of Olympic words and marks.

From the first public appearance of the Olympic symbol at the twentieth anniversary of the Modern Olympic Movement in 1914, the IOC has relied primarily on a reactive policy in identifying violators and registering protests against those seeking without authority to exploit an affiliation with the globally recognized five-ring Olympic mark.[3] The first reactive campaign initiated by the USOA (later known as the USOC), as noted earlier with regard to the Helms case, occurred in the late 1940s. For almost a quarter of a century the subject of insignia protection lay largely latent in the boardrooms of NOCs, OCOGs, and the IOC. The subject was raised in IOC General Session discussions from time to time in the 1950s and

1960s, only to disappear rapidly in the press of more urgent business. Even the advent of selling television rights, which included the "understood" use of Olympic marks by television networks and by companies purchasing advertising, failed to focus interest on this problem. It was not until the late 1970s that an association with the Olympic marks and logos sought by commercial business firms at last stimulated initiatives by the IOC to establish laws of protection. As approved at the Seventy-ninth IOC Session in Prague in 1977, a by-law to Rule 6 of the *Olympic Charter* announced that the IOC "shall take every appropriate step possible to obtain legal protection of the Olympic symbol on a national and international basis."[4]

The need for symbol protection was noted well before 1977, however, in the face of alarmingly increased costs associated with putting on the Games, particularly the 1972 and 1976 Games. Those responsible for funding the Games had to explore every revenue-generating possibility. Sales of Olympic event tickets, commemorative coins, and stamps, though important, represented minor revenue sources in the greater scheme of production. Although television revenues provided impressive financing opportunities, they fell far short of the total funding required. This fact led in time to energetic expansion of an experimentally modest OCOG fund-raising initiative of the past, corporate sponsorship, but with a twist—selling exclusive rights to commercial firms to link products and services to the Olympic mystique and protect these rights by law. This phenomenon did not originate with the IOC but rather with a member of its constituent NOC family charged with the responsibility of hosting and paying for the 1976 Olympic festival. Among the first definitive contemporary examples of symbol protection is the case of the Canadian Olympic Association (COA) and its adjunct affiliate, the Montréal Olympic Games Organizing Committee (COJO).

CANADIAN PROTECTION OF OLYMPIC INSIGNIA

Montréal's successful bid for the Games of the Twenty-first Olympiad acted as a catalyst for the COA's energetic attempts at protecting Olympic insignia. Understanding the commercial forum in which the Games would be held, the COA lobbied the Parliament of Canada to pass legislation that would protect Olympic insignia. On 27 July 1973 Parliament passed what it called the "Olympic Act," which related only to protection of trademarks and symbols with respect to the 1976 Summer Olympic Games.[5] Two years later Canadian federal authorities approved extensive amendments to the original "Olympic Act," specifically relating to "Trade Marks and Symbols."[6] The act created an "Olympic Corporation" (i.e., the Montréal

Organizing Committee),[7] which was omnipotent with regard to authorizing use of Olympic trademarks and symbols within Canada.[8] The Olympic Act defined the Olympic Corporation's existence, and thus its power, for a period beginning on 13 June 1975 and terminating on 1 January 1977.

Capitalizing on this Olympic trademark and symbol protection, COJO established the foundation for a vast expansion of marketing programs aimed at facilitating its goal of "self-financing the Games." Efforts included (1) selling rights to official suppliers and sponsors, (2) exploitation of official emblems of the Games (including those purchased from Munich), (3) production of commercial publications, and (4) establishing numerous concession opportunities around Olympic venues. At its height the marketing program included signed agreements with no fewer than 628 companies, each for a fee of $50,000 (CDN). Forty-seven companies were multinational in scope; forty-two of them were designated "official sponsors." The total corporate sponsorship initiative netted revenues of barely $5 million after the deduction of administrative and management costs, however, obviously only a small share of the monies needed to underwrite the cost of the Games.[9] Even though COA had been proactive in terms of protecting Olympic symbols by federal law, the OCOG's strategy of enlisting a large number of sponsors, each for a relatively small fee, failed to produce significant revenues. Peter Ueberroth heeded the negative lessons of Montréal concerning the marketing of corporate sponsorships when he began his Los Angeles Olympic Games organizational odyssey in 1979.

Though COJO ceased to exist after 1 January 1977, the activities of the COA went on indefinitely. Thus the 1 January 1977 restriction imposed by the Olympic Act left many within the COA concerned about its ability to protect all Olympic insignia from unlawful use beyond the period of the Games. Yet another concern was the definition of "Olympic Corporation" defined within the act, leaving in question continued ownership of all Olympic-related insignia by the COA.

Such anxieties were real; professional help was needed. The COA sought counsel from lawyer Kenneth McKay of the Toronto law firm Sim, Hughes, Ashton & McKay. McKay explored avenues of trademark protection for the COA's "Official Marks" as well as a quest to confirm the COA as a public corporation. Referring to the tenets of the Canadian Trade-Marks Act, McKay initiated formal procedures to register the COA trademark as a public authority.[10] To the consternation of the COA, the Registrar of Trade Marks refused the application on the grounds that the COA did not meet the three-part test to qualify as a public authority: (1) there must be a duty to the public, (2) there must be a significant degree of governmental control, and (3) any profit earned must be for the benefit of the public, not for private gain.[11] McKay appealed on behalf of the COA. On 12 November 1981, in federal court, Trial Division Judge Patrick Mahoney heard the COA's appeal, ultimately confirming it as a public authority. In his ruling Judge Mahoney stated:

> The appellant [COA] is a public authority within the contemplation of subpara. (iii) of s.9(1)(n) of the Trade Marks Act. The appellant [COA] is a non-profit organization which pursues objects of a public nature. The Canadian community wants those objects pursued. The appellant is, in fact, the only entity exercising the power to pursue those objects and is accepted by the community as exercising that power as a right.[12]

This victory was short-lived. The Registrar of Trade Marks launched a counterappeal. The issue boiled down to the question of whether or not the COA was considered a "public authority" that had the right to have its mark given public notice. In a subsequent ruling the court upheld its original decision, finding that the degree of control exercised by the government over the activities of the COA was sufficient to establish its character as a "public authority."[13] After this ruling the COA itself began to ponder its "marks" ownership in the context of future marketing initiatives.

WIPO AND THE NAIROBI TREATY

Within the IOC the almost subliminal attempts begun in July 1949 to censure misuses of the Olympic words and symbols had been largely forgotten or ignored. When little money was at stake the matter was consistently brushed aside in the face of more critical issues such as budget matters, organizational crises, and boycotts. Yet, as previously stated, in spite of Rule 6 of the *Olympic Charter* expressly stating that the IOC "shall take every appropriate step possible," the IOC had done little to establish legal protection of Olympic symbols in either a national or international context. In lieu of attempting to gain legal protection for its marks itself, the IOC shifted the responsibility to each NOC to ensure protection in its respective nation in observance of Rule 6, identifying the Olympic flag, symbol, and motto as the "exclusive property of the IOC."[14]

With the Helms case a distant memory, the IOC was at last galvanized to take action on the symbol protection issue. Events of the 1970s, particularly the 1972 and 1976 Games, dictated renewed vigor and a new approach to the issue of international symbol protection. The IOC focused its attention on the power of the World Intellectual Property Organization (WIPO).

WIPO evolved in the latter part of the nineteenth century, prompted by a need for protection of intellectual property throughout the world.[15] In 1974 WIPO became one of sixteen specialized agencies in the system of United Nations (UN) organizations, with a specific mandate to administer intellectual property matters recognized by the member states of the UN. In accord with its growing importance, the WIPO Secretariat moved into the organization's current Geneva headquarters in 1978.[16] WIPO expanded its role, forming an alliance of cooperation with the World Trade Organization (WTO).[17] The agreement, which entered into force on 1 January 1996, provided for cooperation between the two organizations concerning the Trade-Related Aspects of Intellectual Property Rights (TRIPS) Agreement. Membership in WIPO is open to any state that signed the Paris or Berne intellectual property agreements of the late 1800s or to any other state satisfying one of the following conditions: (1) it is a member of the United Nations, any of the specialized agencies brought into relationship with the United Nations, or the International Atomic Energy Agency; (2) it is a party to the Statute of the International Court of Justice; or (3) it has been invited by the General Assembly of WIPO to become a party to the Convention.[18]

The objectives of WIPO are (1) to promote the protection of intellectual property throughout the world through cooperation among states and, where appropriate, in collaboration with other international organizations; and (2) to ensure administrative cooperation among the intellectual property unions—that is, the "unions" created by the Paris and Berne Conventions and several subtreaties concluded by members of the Paris Union.[19] WIPO encourages the conclusion of international agreements that promote the protection of intellectual property throughout the world, in two main branches (1) industrial property, focusing on inventions, trademarks, industrial designs, and appellations of origin; and (2) copyright, focusing on literary, musical, artistic, photographic, and audiovisual works.

As a specialized agency of the United Nations WIPO is responsible for taking appropriate action in accordance with the treaties and agreements it administers.[20] WIPO is also charged with promoting creative intellectual activity and facilitating the transfer of technology related to industrial property to developing countries in order to accelerate their economic, social, and cultural development. According to Kamil Idris, its director-general, "WIPO's fundamental function may be broadly, but fairly, said to be the promotion of the progress of humankind."[21]

Because the five-ring Olympic logo constituted a "service mark," it was not possible to place the symbol on WIPO's international register without the request of a national administration under whose jurisdiction the body seeking to have its mark protected resided. The Swiss government did not recognize the Olympic logo as a trademark and refused to make the request on the IOC's behalf. The IOC appealed to the government, pointing out that it used the five-ring symbol on its publications, notepaper, and numerous other media, thereby making the symbol a trademark. After deliberation the Swiss administration accepted this point of view, and the Federal Intellectual Property Office in Berne, Switzerland, registered the symbol as an IOC mark. This action protected the Olympic symbol in Switzerland against unauthorized use in reviews, periodicals, and books as well as any photographic or graphic reproduction. The IOC requested that the Swiss government petition WIPO to register the symbol internationally, such registration being valid in the twenty-four member states of the Madrid Agreement concerning the International Registration of Marks.[22] The Swiss administration advanced the petition on the IOC's behalf.[23]

The limited number of countries that signed the Madrid Agreement, however, perturbed the IOC. The IOC searched for a government willing to propose to WIPO that an agenda item discussing specific protection for the Olympic Symbol should be added to the conference, as had been done in 1949 for the Red Cross.[24] The government of Kenya, with the support of its NOC, presented the IOC's appeal.[25]

In order to succeed the IOC required the support of other states. To achieve this the IOC used the by-law to Rule 6 in the *Olympic Charter* that required the Executive Board's approval of all NOC official marks.[26] Having been asked to submit its emblem to the Executive Board for approval, each NOC was requested to petition appropriate state authorities to secure legal international protection of the Olympic symbol. Several NOCs, among them India, the Netherlands, and Tunisia, reacted immediately by securing the backing of their respective federal governments in the form of a letter in support of the international protection of the Olympic symbol.[27]

With the Moscow Olympic Games concluded and a new president at its helm, the IOC renewed its efforts to secure protection of the symbol. By the autumn of 1981 the IOC had gathered the necessary political support to introduce a Treaty on the Protection of the Olympic Symbol through its agent, the Kenyan government, at WIPO's conference scheduled for Nairobi in September 1981. On another political front, only a few months earlier, the IOC had been issued an exceptional decree from the Swiss Federal Council acknowledging the general rights of the IOC as well as a formal decision granting certain privileges in the areas of taxation and immigration. According to Howard Stupp, the IOC's director of legal affairs, "the Swiss Federal Council has raised the IOC above . . . other nongovernmental institutions."[28]

As the Nairobi conference approached, Reginald Alexander, IOC member in Kenya, prepared the IOC's case.[29] Alexander's report, submitted to the IOC Session in Baden-Baden on 29 September 1981, indicated that in a vote taken on 26 September twenty-two nations had agreed to sign the convention to protect the IOC emblems.[30] Predictably, given the exclusive rights assigned by Congress to the United States Olympic Committee regarding the words "Olympic," "Olympiad," and *Citius, Altius, Fortius* as well as Olympic-related symbols by Public Law 95-606 (the Amateur Sports Act), the delegate from the U.S. government attending the conference did not sign the treaty, refusing to state a rationale for his position.[31] Adoption of the convention by the United States government would have formally acknowledged the IOC's exclusive rights to the Olympic emblems, thus establishing a conflict with those rights previously assigned by Congress in the Amateur Sports Act.

FIFTY YEARS OF PROTECTION COME TO AN END

Following the adoption of the Nairobi Treaty, the issue of the protection of the Olympic symbol assumed heightened urgency. In early December 1982 (after informal discussions between Juan Antonio Samaranch and Horst Dassler) Klaus Jürgen Hempel, managing director and director of the board of Dassler's firm International Sports Leisure Marketing Aktiengesellschaft (ISL) in Lucerne, Switzerland, sent a letter to the Château de Vidy.[32] Hempel confirmed his company's interest in expanding its sports marketing activities beyond the sphere of World Cup Soccer, at the time its major client. Discussions soon ensued, aimed at implementing a new worldwide sponsorship program that was eventually known as The Olympic Program (TOP).[33]

As ISL began the formidable task of preparing a proposal to organize and market the IOC's first worldwide corporate sponsorship program, the IOC awarded the 1984 Olympic Winter Games to Sarajevo at the IOC Session in Athens in May 1978, providing the organizers six years to prepare.[34] The sale of television rights, sponsorship, and advertising contracts as well as the private efforts of the citizens of Sarajevo complemented government funding. The Sarajevo report set the costs of the Games at $72 million (17,285 billion Yugoslavian dinars). In the end Sarajevo stated that its revenue generation efforts exceeded expenditures by approximately $10.6 million (2,543 billion Yugoslavian dinars).[35]

The Games of the Twenty-third Olympiad, awarded to the City of Los Angeles at the IOC Session in Athens in May 1978, marked a "turning point in the Olympic Movement."[36] Though the driving force behind the

Los Angeles bid was the city's mayor, Tom Bradley, in the end it was the entrepreneurial genius of Peter Ueberroth that led to the great success of the Games. Ueberroth mounted an impressive marketing program that attracted thirty-five commercial "partners," sixty-four "suppliers," and sixty-five companies holding licenses.[37] Each commercial product category enjoyed designated rights and exclusivity. In most cases the sponsor companies were large multinational corporations. The Los Angeles marketing program alone generated some $157.2 million in the form of cash, equipment, goods, "value-in-kind" products, and services provided.[38] Some companies even funded the building of new sport facilities, a deal that allowed them to advertise on the admission ticket.[39] Television rights fees more than doubled those paid for the 1980 Moscow Olympic Games, eventually equaling $286,914,000.[40] More than 2.5 billion people from the 156 nations that acquired television or radio broadcasting rights followed the action in Los Angeles.[41]

Although a boycott imposed by the Soviet Union and many of its allies in retaliation for the mass U.S.-inspired boycott of the 1980 Games compromised the festival, the 1984 Olympic Games ushered in the formalization of relations between the world of business and the Modern Olympic Movement. From this point forward the IOC would openly encourage all OCOGs and NOCs of the host cities and countries to establish joint marketing programs.[42]

The protection of the Olympic symbol took on added urgency within the IOC following the successful staging of the 1984 Summer and Winter Olympic Games. Responding to an IOC request, ISL submitted a confidential report on the protection of the Olympic symbol that included a number of comments.[43] ISL pointed out that with the exception of the United States and Canada, where local laws existed, the Olympic symbol was protected only under international copyright law in a limited number of countries, most of them not particularly important in envisioned marketing endeavors. The report also noted that under international copyright laws the Olympic symbol created by Pierre de Coubertin in 1913 would expire on 31 December 1987, fifty years after the baron's death.[44] Although the Nairobi Treaty offered some protection for the Olympic symbol, not all countries within the Modern Olympic Movement had signed the treaty, and very few governments had ratified it internally. After 2 September 1987 any individual or firm might use the Olympic symbol to market an initiative in a country that had not ratified the Nairobi Treaty. Finally, ISL suggested that the IOC consider modifying the Olympic symbol and having it copyrighted as a new logo for the International Marketing Program.[45]

In response to ISL's report of 20 November 1984 Monique Berlioux echoed ISL's comments at an Executive Board Meeting in Calgary on 25 February 1985. In strong terms she called for the IOC to encourage every NOC to seek its government's ratification of the Nairobi Treaty. Canada's Richard Pound, an emerging force in the IOC's marketing operation, thought that few people were aware of the danger involved. Understanding the importance of this situation and its potentially dangerous impact on the IOC's new marketing initiatives, Samaranch directed that the IOC lawyer, legal adviser, and adviser for marketing prepare reports on the legal status of the Olympic symbol in thirty major countries.[46]

At an Executive Board meeting in Berlin on 31 May 1985 Samaranch referred to two reports on the protection of the Olympic symbol written by IOC legal advisers and informed the members that the question of copyright was extremely complicated. Concerned about the possible damage to the IOC/ISL marketing initiative, Pound reflected that the "circle of knowledge" in this matter was uncomfortably wide and that the IOC should be careful about raising this matter in any publications or documentation or at press conferences.[47] Further, he added that it was unlikely that many of the developed countries would ratify the Nairobi Treaty due to their internal copyright laws that assigned the rights to the Olympic symbol to the respective NOC. In those cases and in those countries, Pound noted, "even the IOC needed the NOC's permission to use the rings." Following a lengthy discussion, the Executive Board asked Pound and Kéba M'Baye, IOC member in Senegal, to study the question of copyright and at a future Executive Board meeting present their views on the situation as well as a written proposal on how to protect the symbol.[48]

Due to the fact that the copyright protection afforded the Olympic symbol would be substantially weakened after 31 December 1987, Pound and M'Baye suggested to the Executive Board that the IOC create a new emblem and seek its protection by registering it as a "mark." The Executive Board directed Pound and M'Baye to prepare a recommendation for the creation of a new IOC emblem containing the Olympic rings that might be commercialized and to seek specialist designers for its creation before 1986.[49]

At the IOC Executive Board meeting in Lisbon in October 1985 M'Baye submitted a lengthy "note on the protection of the Olympic Symbol." His note provided a synopsis of two studies presented to the IOC by "eminent specialists" in the area of international trademark protection and the law. Both studies addressed the "theoretical and practical aspects of all the legal problems posed by the protection of the Olympic Symbol."[50] The Pound/M'Baye report, submitted at the Executive Board meeting in Lausanne on 11 February 1986, presented two possible approaches for the

IOC: (1) create a new emblem that could be commercialized, as were the NOC emblems in certain cases, which meant abandoning a symbol to which the Olympic Movement was sentimentally and commercially attached, or (2) keep its present symbol and claim that it was an element of its personality. Pound and M'Baye said that the IOC might "try to make more countries ratify the Nairobi Treaty," but both admitted that "there was little hope in this respect." Other options were debated, including changing the order of the five interlocked rings from their blue, yellow, black, green, and red arrangement. Something similar had been attempted previously (inverting the rings—two above and three below) but had been abandoned because it risked confusion on the part of the general public.[51]

Based on the results of a study it commissioned, ISL supported one of the conclusions offered by Pound and M'Baye. The study, undertaken by the lawyer K. Vorwerk of Gerenberg-Gossler and Partners, was distributed to the Executive Board at a meeting in Seoul on 22 April 1986.[52] The IOC's use of the current five-ring symbol for official business could continue, Vorwerk concluded; but he added that for commercial reasons and in order to guarantee effective protection for a longer period the IOC required a new symbol. This, he warned, posed a complex task, because problems relating to the IOC's exclusive authorization to use the new symbol might impinge on the rights of some NOCs, particularly those in the larger, developed countries. Responding to Vorwerk's warning, Pound stated that he "did not know whether the creation of a new symbol would be useful to the IOC as the market would be extremely confused, particularly if the IOC continued to use the current symbol for official internal purposes."[53] Samaranch shared Pound's doubts and voiced his reluctance to proceed with the "new symbol" project, even though "the IOC had already commissioned certain artists for the design."[54] In the interim the Executive Board directed Pound to discuss the problem with major sponsors who had enjoyed long-term affiliations with the Modern Olympic Movement.[55]

As the debate regarding the protection of the Olympic symbol continued, Pound, M'Baye, and IOC legal adviser François Carrard proposed a solution for the protection issue that might lead to a final decision at a forthcoming meeting of the Executive Board.[56] In February 1987 they forwarded two possible courses of action: (1) maintain the present Olympic symbol—it was part of the legal personality of IOC, and this point would be defensible to a certain extent even after the symbol entered the public domain with the expiration of the copyright; or (2) create, only if the need became apparent, a new symbol easily recognizable as belonging to the IOC: for example, the rings with the initials IOC/CIO.[57] They recommended the first option. Following an open debate the Executive Board approved their report as submitted and asked them to examine national legislation concerning the Olympic symbol in a number of specific countries where problems could arise.[58] Furthermore, it was reemphasized that the IOC must respond energetically to those who sought to "abuse" the Olympic symbol, "whether they are unauthorized third parties without a link of any kind with the Olympic Movement, or even sponsors or licensees of the IOC who exceed the limits which have been assigned to them."[59]

In the final analysis, whether or not the Olympic symbol fell into the public domain after 31 December 1987 really had no bearing on the IOC's continued use of its Olympic trademark. The IOC had invested almost a century of energy and money into the promotion of the five-ring mark since its initial public release in 1914 but had long neglected its protection. Once in the public domain the Olympic mark might well become the object of unauthorized commercial exploitation. The Nairobi Treaty offered limited security. If the treaty had been unreservedly ratified in a large number of economically developed countries, it would have provided the IOC with sufficient protection for the Olympic symbol. Ratification of the Nairobi Treaty by Olympic nations, however, has proven to be disappointing for the IOC. Few of the Western industrialized countries have acceded to the treaty or are expected to do so in the near future.[60] Thus the IOC acknowledged that it cannot rely exclusively on the treaty for the protection of the Olympic symbol. Instead it adopted the steadfast position that it must urge its NOCs to pursue strong internal protection programs for the ultimate security of the Olympic symbol, particularly as the protection awarded its author, the Baron Pierre de Coubertin, ended on 31 December 1987, fifty years *post mortem auctoris*.[61]

EXPLOITING THE OLYMPIC MYSTIQUE:
LICENSING AND THE RISE OF CORPORATE SPONSORSHIP

To protect the Olympic marks was one thing, to exploit them in the international marketplace was quite another. More than one IOC member was concerned that the Modern Olympic Movement derived some 98% of its revenue from the sale of television rights in the early 1970s. Well before the IOC finally formed a commission to investigate new sources of revenue generation the subject engendered discussion inside the halls of IOC decision-making. The organization's almost complete dependence on the whim of television executives to continue to pay millions of dollars for TV rights made many nervous. Some pundits predicted a leveling off of spiraling rights fees, if not a decline. In response the IOC experimented with the international marketing of its symbols. Its initial exercise, though educational, failed in that regard.

Licensing Horror:
Intelicense and the IOC's First International Marketing Program

For all its efforts, and aside from the euphoria produced by much of the otherwise glorious 1976 Olympic festival, the City of Montréal reeled from a deficit of $990 million (CDN). The government of Québec called on the city of Montréal to assume 20% of the shortfall through property tax increases.[62] A series of medium-term loans from the Québec government provided the means for retiring the remaining balance of the deficit, some $792 million.[63] Although the IOC was not directly responsible, the massive shortfall did little to enhance the reputation of the IOC in particular and the Modern Olympic Movement in general.[64]

Attempting to recover money spent on the Games, Montréal contacted Stanley R. Shefler, president of Intelicense Corporation SA. Shefler had been involved in the marketing efforts surrounding the 1976 Olympic Games. Montréal officials asked him to establish a licensing program for stylized Olympic pictogram figures originally designed and used by Munich during the Games of the Twentieth Olympiad. Montréal purchased the figures after the 1972 Games and used them extensively throughout the 1976 Games, licensing them to a variety of companies for display on consumer products and employing them liberally in the *Official Report* of the Games.[65] Shefler embarked on an ambitious plan to market the pictograms to firms for display on manufactured products.

Upon learning of Shefler's Intelicense initiative, IOC director Monique Berlioux wrote a letter to all NOCs instructing them to avoid doing business with Intelicense; she reminded them that COJO's legal authority was due to expire on 1 January 1977, and according to the *Olympic Charter* COJO would soon be liquidated. Therefore, she argued, Intelicense's activities as the marketing agency for the Montréal Organizing Committee were illegal. Shefler informed Berlioux that he intended to take legal action against the IOC. Prior to the initiation of formal proceedings in the Swiss courts, however, he agreed to a meeting between the two parties. The IOC believed that a face-to-face meeting would avert legal proceedings. By the end of the meeting the IOC had agreed to purchase the pictograms from Montréal for the purpose of establishing its own licensing program. The IOC then asked Shefler's company, Intelicense, to consider managing the newly proposed IOC licensing initiative. Shefler accepted, and Intelicense and the IOC agreed on a seventy-year marketing contract.

Berlioux directed Shefler to design a series of new pictograms; Shefler immediately contracted graphic designer Van Der Wal, who set to work to create completely new stylized athletic figures. Upon completion of the project Van Der Wal signed his "creation rights" over to the IOC. With the pictograms now the property of the IOC, Berlioux wrote to all NOCs: "This letter will certify that Intelicense Corporation SA of Switzerland has been appointed by the International Olympic Committee to act as exclusive world licensing agent for the copyrighted official I.O.C. Summer Olympic pictograms. The agent is authorized to grant licensing rights on behalf of the I.O.C. and to receive royalty revenue for the support of the International Olympic movement."[66] Shefler subsequently distributed "cooperation agreements" to all NOCs requesting them to survey the use of the pictograms in their territory. He also announced that each participating NOC would receive a share of the total IOC income from the program as well as an additional 10% of the total income derived from manufacturers in its specific country. Ten NOCs signed agreements immediately, including Greece, Mexico, and China, each a significant prospective consumer market.

As the Moscow Olympics approached, a large cloud hovered over the Modern Olympic Movement. The boycott, in protest against the December 1979 Soviet invasion of Afghanistan, weighed heavily on the Intelicense-IOC marketing initiative. As the licensing program evolved, the USOC wrote to the IOC registering apprehensions about doing business with Intelicense. In response the IOC voiced its support for Intelicense and the work it was doing for the benefit of the Olympic Movement. Protecting its own domestic interests, the USOC refused to cede territorial access to the United States to Intelicense for the purpose of licensing the Olympic pictograms. In fact, it launched a suit against Intelicense as well as its two licensees in the United States, International Sports Marketing (ISM) and Millsport. In formulating its case against Intelicense the USOC cited Public Law 95-606, the Amateur Sports Act of 1978, which protected the emblems of the IOC and the USOC and gave the USOC exclusive rights in the United States to all Olympic-related terminology and designations. Responding to the suit, Intelicense and ISM countersued the USOC, citing their official authority as exclusive world licensing agent for the copyrighted official IOC Summer Olympic pictograms.[67] The legal controversy raised other issues, such as why the ISFs were not consulted on the design of the pictograms. Shefler responded quickly to these questions, personally visiting each of the ISFs. Upon returning to Intelicense, he designed a set of new and improved pictograms incorporating the five interlocking rings.

Concern soon surfaced within the IOC over Shefler's use of the five interlocking rings combined with the pictograms. Berlioux informed him that the *Olympic Charter* prohibited the inclusion of the five interlocking rings. Shefler challenged Berlioux, citing the USOC's contract with LEVI's that allowed the company's logo to be incorporated with the rings alone. Undaunted by Berlioux's bluster, Intelicense exercised its rights and continued to sign license agreements on an international basis. Due to the pending litigation involving the USOC, however, Shefler was forced to sign with "less powerful licensees" than he would have desired.[68]

With the appearance of yet another official Olympic marketing firm, International Sports and Leisure Marketing (ISL) of Lucerne, Switzerland, intent on marketing the five-ring symbol, Intelicense launched a court case against the IOC.[69] Shefler contended that the IOC had no right to grant anybody other than Intelicense the sole rights to market the Olympic rings alone, citing restrictions outlined in the *Olympic Charter*. The firm further argued that even if the *Charter* was changed the agreement would only be legally valid if it did not contain rights for any kind of sports design resembling in any way the official pictograms in combination with the Olympic rings. As the argument portion of the *Intelicense-ISM vs. USOC* cases concluded in the United States, and with a preliminary judgement still a week away in the *Intelicense vs. IOC case*, Shefler approached ISL in hopes of establishing a formal agreement of cooperation. Given the continued deterioration of his company's relationship with the IOC, Shefler proposed the possibility of ISL purchasing Intelicense. Concerned over the outcome of the pending litigation involving Intelicense and the lack of a signed contract with the IOC, ISL responded to Shefler's overture by stating that any decision on his proposals could take up to a year.[70]

By November 1984 the case brought by the USOC against Intelicense and ISM had not yet been settled. Although the USOC prevailed in the lower court and the Court of Appeals, Intelicense lodged a final appeal to the U.S. Supreme Court. IOC lawyer Samuel Pisar, in reviewing the status of the case, did not expect Intelicense to succeed. He noted that the USOC had claimed substantial monetary damages from the two companies as well as full disclosure of all documents. The preliminary judgements also stopped Intelicense and ISM from conducting any pictogram business.[71] In the early months of 1985 the United States District Court in Vermont, to which the case had been assigned by the Supreme Court, issued an award totaling $212,000 in favor of the USOC.[72]

When the *Intelicense vs. IOC* case was filed in April 1983 in Geneva, the court first focused on matters of procedure. On 9 October 1984 the presiding judge asked both counsels whether it might not be useful to summon the parties to appear personally in order to attempt a form of conciliation. The judge pointed out that whatever the outcome of the trial it appeared to him that both parties would incur heavy financial costs. Both resisted the judge's suggestion.[73] The IOC, in particular, felt there was no great urgency for action of any kind given the mounting legal costs accruing to Intelicense.[74]

On 3 January 1986 Intelicense asked the court to impose a number of new provisional measures on the IOC. The first was to forbid the IOC from licensing ISL or a third party to use the Olympic emblem without specifying in the contract that the "licensee forbids himself to affix the five Olympic rings on any pictogram representing one of the thirty-five sports as stylized on the pictograms given in license by the IOC to Intelicense Corporations S.A. by agreements of October 1st and 23rd, 1979." Second, Intelicense asked the court to forbid the IOC from licensing the use of "other" Olympic pictograms to ISL or a third party, as they would create confusion with Intelicense's official pictograms.[75] Finally, the court was requested to garnish agreements or draft agreements between the IOC and ISL or a third party in order to ascertain their possible contradiction of the existing Intelicense contracts. In support of its requests and claims Intelicense raised the IOC's recent agreement with ISL aimed at the commercialization of pictograms or Olympic emblems. The firm further argued that the IOC had intended to design and exploit other pictograms, rather than utilizing the official pictograms licensed by Intelicense, within the framework of the Olympic Games in Seoul in 1988.

At a hearing on 27 January 1986 in Geneva the IOC's attorneys requested that the court reject all claims and requests filed by Intelicense.[76] After reviewing Intelicense's claims and requests, the court rejected them outright. Shortly before the hearing, however, Intelicense filed a new seventy-four-page petition requesting that "the IOC be sentenced to pay amounts exceeding 60 million Swiss francs" in damages for the years 1983 and 1984.[77] Essentially, Intelicense argued that due to the actions of the IOC it had been unable to exploit the pictograms covered by the original agreements of 1979. The main portion of the damages, 55,770,630 Swiss francs, consisted of an alleged loss of profit in connection with the nonperformance of an agreement between ISL and Intelicense.[78] At the hearing attorneys for Intelicense asked that the new claim be joined with the claims already pending before the court in Geneva.

The court decided to consider this new claim as a new case; it would be tried separately from the case originally filed in April 1983, in which no claim for damages had been submitted. The judge, as he had done in October 1984, once again stated that he would welcome a personal appearance of the parties in order to reexamine the possibility of some form of conciliation or settlement. This time the counsels for the IOC signaled that it might be appropriate for the IOC to show some consideration of the judge's offer.[79] At the IOC Executive Board meetings in Seoul in April 1986 François Carrard, IOC legal adviser,[80] informed Samaranch of counsel's suggestion. Carrard advised that the IOC be represented by the highest level at the meeting scheduled for 20 May 1986 in Geneva. Responding to Carrard's suggestion, Samaranch confirmed his intention to attend the meeting, accompanied by Judge Kéba M'baye, remarking that "the whole affair was utterly regrettable" and that "he could not understand how the IOC had ever signed such a contract." He further chastised those involved, stating that "the signatories had demonstrated a high level of incompetence." In making this charge Samaranch obviously had Monique Berlioux in mind. The entire affair nettled the IOC president.[81] Assigning personal responsibility, according to Carrard, was a "fairly delicate subject," however, as the IOC Finance Commission and Executive Board had approved the original 1979 agreements.[82]

At the IOC Executive Board meeting in Stockholm in April 1988 Carrard reported that the IOC had successfully defended its position in court against Intelicense's claims. A conflict that had developed between Shefler family members over the ongoing legal proceedings benefited the IOC.[83] Responding to the court's decision, Intelicense's legal counsel filed an appeal in the Geneva courts.[84] As the antagonisms within the Shefler family escalated, Carrard announced that the owners of Intelicense were "ready to meet with the IOC President in order to end this conflict."[85] Finally, at the IOC Executive Board meetings in Belgrade in April 1990 Carrard announced that "the Intelicense affair had . . . been resolved."[86]

The prolonged litigation took its toll on Intelicense and the Shefler family. At the IOC Executive Board meetings in Barcelona in June 1990 Carrard reported that Intelicense neared bankruptcy.[87] A few months later the IOC settled the claims with Intelicense for $2 million Swiss francs, a far cry from the original damages sought by the firm that parented the first true international Olympic marketing program. The IOC paid 50% of the agreed settlement immediately, with the remainder being paid when it was "sure it would not be exposed to any indirect claims from the creditors of the now bankrupt company."[88] In Lillehammer in December 1990 Carrard informed the IOC Executive Committee members that the liquidation of Intelicense was proceeding smoothly.

The IOC and the Establishment of TOP

In early December 1982, four months after soccer's World Cup tournament concluded in Madrid, a courier departed the newly created offices of ISL in Lucerne, Switzerland, bearing a package addressed to Juan Antonio Samaranch at the IOC headquarters at Château de Vidy in Lausanne.[89] The parcel contained a specially commissioned limited edition lithograph entitled *The Case against the Bourgeoisie* by Franz Borghese, one of Italy's most celebrated modern satirical artists. Accompanying the package was a letter from Klaus Jürgen Hempel, managing director of ISL, who was entrusted with the future development of ISL. Hempel's letter and gift were designed to capitalize on a series of informal talks held previously between IOC president Samaranch and ISL's founder/owner Horst Dassler, head of the vast global Adidas sporting goods empire. The thrust of their discussions was aimed at marketing the value of the Olympic Games and their identifying logo/symbols. An appreciative Samaranch quickly responded to Hempel, thanking him for "the nice lithograph by Franz Borghese" and offering his personal salutations and best wishes for "a happy and fruitful new year."[90] Indeed, 1983 proved to be fruitful beyond any prediction: it ushered in an era of lucrative Olympic commercialism tied to the affairs of business marketing.

Created shortly after the finals of the 1982 Soccer World Cup, ISL, which specialized in sports sponsorship marketing, obtained exclusive contracts with the International Football (Soccer) Federation (FIFA) and two of its continental subfederations, the European and South American Football Unions.[91] In an effort to expand its global operations, ISL identified the Modern Olympic Movement's five-ring symbol as "the most powerful and visible symbol in the world of sport." ISL envisioned a worldwide sponsorship marketing program involving various multinational corporations, "most of them from North America, Japan or Western Europe," that would generate sufficient revenues to provide a regular income for the Olympic organizations and, of course, enhance its own company resources and power in the world of sport business.[92]

Samaranch's increasing anxiety over the IOC's nearly sole reliance on revenues generated from the sale of television rights prodded his support for ISL's vision of Olympic marketing.[93] Continued dependency on television money posed serious ramifications.[94] Samaranch urged the organization of a new IOC commission responsible for identifying areas of opportunity for the generation of revenues and for recommending a strategic direction for their acquisition. Television rights revenue alone, though impressive, did not satisfy the IOC's rapidly expanding needs and responsibilities. The late Louis Guirandou-N'Diaye, IOC member in the Ivory Coast, chaired the new administrative body, entitled the Commission of New Sources of Financing. The commission set to work on its mandate. At its second meeting in New Delhi in late March 1983 it approved in principle the concept of a worldwide sponsorship program along the lines of a plan forwarded to the IOC by ISL's team of marketing experts.[95]

As the Olympic Movement prepared for the 1984 Games in Los Angeles, the USOC and its marketing agency, Spencer Marketing Services (SMS), received word that the IOC had initiated discussions with ISL aimed at marketing the Olympic five-ring symbol. SMS had a "long history of association with the USOC," having been fundamentally responsible for the development of the American NOC's corporate marketing program. Concerned about the possible implications for their client of an IOC/ISL marketing agreement, Muriel Cohen, vice-president of SMS, dispatched a letter to the IOC's Monique Berlioux, requesting a meeting with ISL officials. "I read with great interest," wrote Cohen, "that [the] International Olympic Committee intends to market its five-ring emblem. Our company has a long history of association with the United States Olympic Committee, having developed their corporate marketing program for them . . . I will appreciate it if you would put us in touch with International Sports Leisure as we would like to arrange to meet with them, either here or in Switzerland."[96]

Berlioux, whose personal and administrative style was abrupt and businesslike, sent Cohen ISL's postal address and telephone number in Lucerne.[97] Within weeks of Cohen's letter to Berlioux other parties contacted the IOC's headquarters in Lausanne to register their concerns about the IOC's rumored association with ISL. For example, Walter Tröger, secretary-general of the West German Olympic Committee, wrote to Berlioux concerning "rumors regarding an agreement between the IOC and a certain company in Switzerland for the marketing of Olympic Symbols." Tröger reminded Berlioux that it was he and two of his colleagues, Drs. Ritter and Pilsl, who had "started the whole business . . . of transferring national actions and egotism into international cooperation, having in mind, the interests of the IOC as well as that of the NOCs." Tröger also noted that Ritter and Pilsl had previously submitted a detailed analysis and proposal to the IOC and NOC Assemblies in Europe to market Olympic symbols worldwide.[98] Berlioux's response to Tröger was brief. She simply reiterated the IOC Executive Board's decision made in New Delhi on 24 March 1983 to support in principle the concept of an international Olympic marketing program as recommended by the Commission of New Sources of Financing.[99]

In March 1983, on the recommendation of the Executive Board, the IOC Session (New Delhi) assigned ISL the task of developing an international sponsorship/marketing program "aimed at commercializing the Olympic emblem." Tröger's letter prompted Berlioux to send a message to all Olympic organizations with the information that ISL had been retained because of the "comprehensive program it prepared and submitted to the entire Olympic Movement, and . . . because its partners (Dentsu and Interpublic) represent 70% of those companies in the world likely to collaborate in such a project."[100] Other key considerations in the Executive Board's recommendation included (1) development of a program that could benefit all NOCs worldwide, (2) IOC control of the commercial development of sponsorship in a manner that did not contradict the ideals of the Olympic Movement, and (3) negating the arduous task of requiring each multinational company to negotiate one-on-one with every individual NOC across the world.[101]

SETTING A PRICE: ESTABLISHING THE VALUE OF USOC INVOLVEMENT IN THE OLYMPIC PROGRAM

Within a month of the decision in New Delhi IOC and ISL officials convened an in-camera meeting with representatives of the USOC and the British Olympic Association (BOA).[102] They sought to convince the USOC and BOA of the benefits of a worldwide marketing program and to reassure them that they would not experience a decrease in revenues from their own domestic marketing efforts by agreeing to take part in the IOC's proposed worldwide sponsorship marketing program. It was far from a pleasant encounter. Of all the NOCs the USOC and BOA possessed the most effective domestic marketing programs. Each expressed deep reservations about any initiative that would clearly "milk the countries with the most potential."[103] The USOC in particular saw the IOC/ISL effort as an attempt to encroach on its territory, envisioning—correctly as it turned out—that most of the multinational corporations approached would be those with head offices based in the United States. After lengthy and sometimes painful discussions all parties, including the USOC, agreed on product categories and target dates for concluding an agreement regarding the development of a worldwide Olympic sponsorship program.[104] This outcome marked a major compromise on the part of the USOC.

As early as March 1983 a preliminary draft agreement between ISL and the IOC "to assist the IOC in the financing of the Olympic Movement" had been produced.[105] Though the international sporting community knew that discussions had been ongoing, the fact that the process had developed well beyond the discussion stage was newsworthy. In early April Monique Berlioux wrote to Horst Dassler reconfirming that the IOC and ISL "agreed to conclude a *final agreement* by 31st December 1983 at the latest."[106] To formalize the relationship between the IOC and ISL "with respect to the licensing and merchandising of certain Olympic emblems, including the five Olympic rings, throughout the world," Berlioux, representing the IOC, and Ems Magnus, ISL's marketing manager, signed a letter of understanding on 2 June 1983.[107] The next day a pleased Magnus wrote Berlioux, expressing her "great pleasure in meeting [you] for the first time . . . on such an important occasion." Added Magnus: "[Y]ou can rest assured that ISL will work hard to meet the expectations of the IOC and the Olympic Movement."[108]

In accordance with the preliminary accord ISL began the process of pursuing agreements from all NOCs for the marketing rights in their respective countries with regard to the IOC's worldwide sponsorship program to be known as TOP (The Olympic Program). The process proved much more complex than originally expected, however. Some NOCs proved hesitant, and the most obdurate was the USOC. With time running out on the IOC/ISL agreement deadline Hempel and Jürgen Lenz, ISL's deputy managing director, wrote to Samaranch in late November 1983 requesting an extension in signing the final IOC/ISL agreement. Reassuring Samaranch that an extension would allow ISL "to complete the project to everyone's satisfaction," they requested that the "signing" date be advanced by nine months, from 31 December 1983 to 30 September 1984.[109] The USOC's intransigence precipitated the request.

In its own opinion the USOC had the least to gain and the most to lose by joining the prospective TOP initiative. Aware of the fact that for any worldwide Olympic marketing program to be successful it must include the USOC, the world's richest and most powerful NOC, Lenz wrote Don Miller, secretary-general of the USOC, requesting a "rapid decision on a presentation date and conclusion of an agreement between USOC/ISL." Referring to the USOC as the last "major stumbling block" in bringing about solidarity on TOP among NOCs worldwide, Lenz reemphasized ISL's position, stating that it did not want "to be burdened with the blame of the project not being realized only because the USOC is not joining in on the project."[110] Miller responded quickly. Though the USOC was reluctantly disposed toward the ISL project, he stated that the Eastern European boycott situation developing around the upcoming 1984 Los Angeles Olympic Games prevented for the time being a rapid USOC decision on the matter.[111]

As the USOC focused its attention on boycott matters, the stalled ISL/USOC negotiations elicited concern in Calgary and Seoul, host cities for the 1988 Olympic festivals. On 22 June 1984 Tae Woo Roh, president of the Seoul Olympic Games Organizing Committee (SLOOC), wrote William E. Simon, president of the USOC, expressing his hope that the

USOC would soon complete negotiations with ISL. "We are anxiously waiting for the conclusion of these negotiations," Roh wrote, "in order that we may finalize our trademark registration program in the U.S., which is of key importance to the Seoul Olympic Organizing Committee."[112] American law restricted Seoul's access to the large and financially lucrative U.S. market. The Amateur Sports Act gave the USOC exclusive rights to all Olympic-related terminology and designations marketed in America. Seoul needed the USOC's approval to market in the United States. Ultimately a massive payment of dollars would be the price for such approval.

Several days later ISL's Lenz received a telex from William H. Wardle, senior vice-president of marketing for OCO'88 (Calgary Olympic Games Organizing Committee), outlining the difficult predicament in which Calgary found itself—a situation caused by the failure of ISL to conclude an agreement for the USOC to join TOP. The delay compromised Calgary's efforts, he stated. The feeling in Calgary was that the USOC might never join TOP. After all, what did the USOC have to gain? Wardle and Calgary did not understand "why an NOC with an effective marketing program [USOC] would participate in such a program . . . and [we] have become increasingly concerned that our view is supported by the lack of progress that you have made . . ."[113] A frustrated Lenz assured Wardle that he was "convinced that the benefits for the USOC of participation in our scheme will be the decisive factor . . . [and] the disparity between local marketing programs vs. exclusive, worldwide opportunities for major sponsors will be very apparent, particularly in the U.S., once the L.A. euphoria has subsided."[114]

Sensing an impasse between ISL and the USOC, Samaranch dispatched a letter to the USOC's president Simon, stating that the entire program was being "blocked because of delays your NOC is causing in signing an agreement." Samaranch appealed to Simon "to help the Olympic Movement as a whole by giving this matter [his] closest attention."[115] Soon after, ISL made its first formal presentation to the USOC, outlining the benefits of ISL's marketing program to the entire Olympic Movement. ISL attempted to sell the message that "there is in fact no valid reason for any NOC to decline to participate. ISL's marketing program will provide a significant increase in income for all NOCs."[116] Although ISL officials appreciated the opportunity to present the IOC Worldwide Sponsorship Program with the USOC, the position taken by some USOC officials disturbed them. For example, Larry Huff, a USOC Executive Committee member, suggested that the Olympic organizations in socialist countries be excluded from sharing in sponsorship funds generated on the strength of Olympic properties. This position, argued ISL, "by its sheer partisan nature [is] incompatible with what the Olympic Movement stands for."[117]

Disturbed by the limited progress made in the USOC case, and acknowledging that without the USOC's membership ISL stood "no chance of gaining unanimous agreement from all NOCs" for the program, Lenz sought help from Samaranch.[118] With no chance of concluding the negotiations for the IOC/ISL agreement before the already extended deadline of 30 September 1984, ISL once again requested a "further extension of the deadline for the conclusion of the Final Agreement" to 31 March 1985.[119] Samaranch, though increasingly perturbed by lack of demonstrable progress, agreed to the request.[120]

THE COST OF USOC PARTICIPATION IN TOP

Almost two months after ISL's presentation to the USOC Don Miller recommended approval of the IOC/ISL proposal on the condition that the USOC receive "appropriate assurances of legal indemnification as well as a minimum monetary return of at least thirty percent" (after all was said and done, the USOC received 15%) to be "derived from the gross revenues received worldwide from each sponsorship agreement approved by the USOC prior to distribution or deduction of any commission." Miller's assertive demand also set forth other provisos: (1) approval by January 1985 of an acceptable ISL agreement with the respective Olympic Games Organizing Committees responsible for conducting the 1988 Summer and Winter Olympic Games; and (2) finalization of the IOC/ISL agreement by April 1985.[121] An aura of distrust pervaded negotiations to develop a blueprint for the proposed marketing agreement between the USOC and ISL.

As a result of mounting concerns within the IOC Executive Board over Monique Berlioux's ability to conclude the ongoing Marketing Program negotiations, combined with the delays that continued to plague the process, Samaranch instructed Richard Pound, the rising star in IOC financial matters, to take over all negotiations from Berlioux. By the 1980s the complexities of Olympic finance had clearly advanced beyond her capabilities.

Samaranch instructed Pound to conclude negotiations so that the IOC could enter into a contract for TOP. Two weeks after the deadline of 31 March 1985 had passed representatives of the IOC and ISL met in Lausanne to establish the dates for the signing of the Seoul/ISL, Calgary/ISL, and USOC/ISL agreements. They were to be signed in Washington, D.C., on 22 May 1985. The signing of the IOC/ISL agreement was to take place in Lausanne on 28 May 1985.[122] On that day in Lausanne, at the 148th meeting of the IOC Executive Board, relief and commensurate celebration ensued as Juan Antonio Samaranch, representing the IOC, and Horst Dassler, representing ISL, signed the TOP-I (1985–88) agreement.[123]

Reflecting on the USOC's financial return from TOP-I after almost two years of participation in the program, George D. Miller, who succeeded Don Miller as secretary-general of the USOC, expressed his belief that the USOC's decision to participate in TOP-I was at the time the correct one.[124] But, as Miller reported to Samaranch four months later, the program had not added to the USOC revenues beyond what might have been achieved had they "not been involved in [the] worldwide marketing program."[125] In thinking ahead to the prospect of a TOP-II (1989–92), Miller informed Lenz that if the existing terms could be "renegotiated to the satisfaction of the USOC and the IOC" the USOC would be prepared to continue the program for the next quadrennium.[126] Three months later Samaranch dispatched a letter to the USOC expressing his hope for their continued participation.[127]

PREMIUMS AND ROYALTIES: AN IOC/USOC CONUNDRUM

With its participation in TOP-II still in question the USOC forged ahead with its own marketing initiatives with the help of K Promotions. Chief among such initiatives was the USOC's premium program: "Premiums are items that are provided free of charge or sold at a subsidized price for advertising or promotion in connection with the purchase of a sponsor's designated products. An Olympic premium bears the sponsor's trademark together with an official Olympic mark or marks."[128]

The sponsors involved in the USOC's premium program provided items such as coffee cups, T-shirts, key chains, and lapel pins free of charge to give away or sell at a subsidized price in return for advertising their association with the USOC. Giving away premium items involved no payment of royalties to the USOC by the sponsor; but premium items sold, even at a subsidized/reduced price, resulted in royalty payments. The sponsor and the USOC often used premium items in cause-related marketing programs. Each premium item displayed both the sponsor's trademark or logo and an official Olympic mark or marks. The premium program defined and promoted the relationship between sponsors wishing to align themselves with the USOC and the Olympic Movement in the United States.

Upon learning of the USOC's premium program initiatives (and under pressure from numerous TOP sponsors to resolve the premium royalties distribution issue within the United States), Andrew Craig, ISL's executive vice-president, dispatched a letter to John Krimsky, deputy secretary-general of the USOC, proposing "the possibility of K Promotions handling five ring [premium] items for all TOP sponsors."[129] Then Craig unloaded a bombshell, suggesting to Krimsky that all royalties on premium items sold in the United States, previously paid entirely to the USOC, henceforth be split 50/50 between the IOC and the USOC. Craig's rationale was that the IOC, as the licensor of the five-ring mark, would no longer accept anything less than an equal share of all future royalties. Krimsky responded immediately to Craig's suggestion. He reiterated the USOC's feeling that TOP-I had eroded its revenue base; consequently, the USOC was unwilling to accept further deterioration of its remaining sponsorship revenues. "The USOC respectfully rejects this newest proposal and recommends that ISL/IOC continue its current agreement," he concluded.[130] In the wake of Krimsky's rejection ISL again turned to the IOC for help. Richard Pound, bristling at Krimsky's out-of-hand rejection, contacted George Miller from his Montréal law office and negotiated a 70/30 split between the USOC and the IOC, the greater proportion remaining with the USOC.[131] Thrust and parry was Pound's strategy. Give a little, but not all. The IOC must not be seen to weaken in the face of a strong challenge, even if the challenge emanated from a family member.

John Krimsky proved an especially formidable opponent for Dick Pound in the USOC's battle to gain what it felt was its rightful share of American-generated corporate sponsorship and television revenues. Experienced, knowledgeable, a tough negotiator, Krimsky arrived at the USOC as deputy secretary-general in early 1986, at almost the same time that the USOC began to joust with the IOC on financial matters. He brought with him lengthy experience in the competitive world of marketing. For twenty-six years Krimsky had served Pan-American World Airways, with various portfolios from marketing analysis and implementation to revenue control. Near the end of his career at Pan-Am he was senior vice-president–marketing, responsible for the air carrier's $4 billion annual passenger and cargo revenue.[132] From 1976 to 1980 Krimsky served the firm as vice-president–federal affairs. In Washington he formed the Pan-Am Political Action Committee, directed at securing major tax legislation and regulatory reform. His activities on Capitol Hill armed him for his orchestration of lobbying USOC causes in Congress. By the time he left the USOC in early 1999 he had raised well over $2 billion for the organization.[133]

Although Pound settled the IOC/USOC premiums dispute, he informed Miller that the IOC was dissatisfied with the current distribution of royalties and "that for [all] future programs of this nature, the matter of income split is an open issue." Pound, after thanking ISL's Craig for his "efforts to protect the interests of the IOC in [the] matter," counseled him that "it is more important for our sponsors to be well and efficiently served than to waste time on disputes as to how premium income should be divided among us."[134]

IOC/ISL/USOC NEGOTIATIONS
AND THE CONTINUATION OF TOP

With the premium/royalty negotiations involving the USOC now concluded, ISL began the task of completing the remaining Seoul and Calgary TOP-I agreements. On 15 September 1987, in an effort to "once and for all close this nightmare," ISL sent the IOC/ISL/Seoul and IOC/ISL/Calgary draft agreements to the appropriate parties for approval.[135] ISL also began to compile a detailed outline of the various provisions that would constitute the basis of the IOC/ISL TOP-II agreement. As with TOP-I, ISL knew that the USOC would again play a central role in the successful staging of future TOP initiatives. By December 1987 the USOC had agreed in principle to continue its participation in TOP.[136] In a letter to ISL Baaron Pittenger, successor to George D. Miller as secretary-general of the USOC, stated that his NOC was "looking forward to its participation in TOP-II" and supported the early implementation of the program. Progress made in "recognizing the unique contributions of the American market" to the International Olympic Marketing Program delighted Pittenger.[137] The USOC's participation, however, would not come without a price attached.

Although the USOC had agreed "in principle" to participate in TOP-II, it qualified its participation. Pittenger wrote Samaranch demanding 20% of the total gross compensation paid in cash or provided as a benefit-in-kind by each international TOP sponsor.[138] In effect the USOC, though originally demanding 30% for TOP-I revenues, had settled for 15%. It had not been happy. The majority of the multinational corporation participants in TOP-I maintained their corporate headquarters in the United States, which underscored the rationale for the USOC's new demands. Given these realities, the IOC's position in negotiating with the USOC was compromised to some extent. On one hand, a perturbed Richard Pound, now chair of the Commission of New Sources of Financing, suggested that Pittenger's new demand for TOP-II was yet another indication of the USOC's "exaggerated view of its importance in the world." On the other hand, if the "USOC did not want to participate neither would the major TOP sponsors" such as Coca-Cola and 3M, conceded Pound, "because the US market was so important to them."[139] Samaranch forwarded a copy of Pittenger's letter to the IOC's director of legal affairs, Howard Stupp, requesting his reaction. Stupp responded quickly. TOP, he noted, raises "money for certain NOCs who have limited, if any, marketing programs of their own." Also, the program provided the IOC with a certain level of visibility as well as control within the Olympic Movement while at the same time effecting an alignment with internationally respected corporations. With respect to the USOC, Stupp remarked that the availability of a "worldwide package helps increase the value of Olympic-related rights in the USA," thus increasing USOC revenues. For these reasons Stupp predicted that the "USOC will agree to participate in TOP-II."[140] Five days later his reflections on Pittenger's letter prompted still another thought. "Pittenger's hardline tactics," Stupp wrote Samaranch, reflected his intent "to negotiate the best deal possible."[141]

Concerned that the USOC would once again delay the implementation of the IOC's TOP initiative, ISL decided to plan on the basis of the USOC receiving 20% of all revenues on TOP-II up to a gross income of $100 million. Income in excess of $100 million would be subject to separate future review.[142] Although TOP-II contracts were substantially the same as those of TOP-I, ISL felt that the primary deterrent for USOC participation in TOP-II lay in the language of the agreement.[143] Eager to proceed with negotiations on the USOC/IOC and USOC/ISL agreements, ISL scheduled a late June 1988 preliminary meeting with USOC and IOC officials at its offices in Lucerne. Twelve days before the scheduled meeting ISL's Craig informed Stupp that John Krimsky and USOC counselor Richard Kline would be unable to attend because of conflicting "Olympic business" in Barcelona.[144] Krimsky, however, proposed an alternative, requesting that the negotiations instead take place in Malta a few days prior to the date proposed for the meeting originally scheduled for Lucerne. Without hesitation Stupp agreed. The Malta meeting produced little progress on the actual language of the agreements, however.[145]

Ongoing negotiations with the Barcelona Olympic Organizing Committee (COOB'92) lurched forward. The problems, according to Richard Pound, were due in part to "an exaggerated idea of what COOB'92 [thought it] was entitled to gain from the program." Further problems developed when Spain's NOC awarded Olympic sponsor rights to direct competitors of TOP sponsors, violating the guaranteed right of first refusal to TOP sponsors. Commenting on the situation, Pound stressed the importance of being more specific at the time when the Games were awarded to a host city as to what products would be included in the International Marketing Program, how the revenue derived would be shared, and exactly what responsibilities would be assigned to the host NOC.[146]

Responding to Pound's concerns associated with the growing complexity of the IOC's marketing programs currently in place, the IOC Executive Board decided in January 1989 to initiate a search for a full-time marketing director. The search was carried out for the most part by Richard

Pound. On 1 February 1989 the appointment of Michael Payne took place. Payne came to the IOC from ISL's marketing staff. His primary job responsibility was to supervise and coordinate all IOC revenue-generating activities. His tenure at ISL armed Payne with a thorough understanding of the IOC's marketing initiatives.

A DIFFICULT TRANSITION: CLOSING THE BOOKS ON TOP-I

Attempting to close the books on the TOP-I premium program royalties, Payne called for all outstanding accounts to be paid by 13 April 1989 (the TOP-I quadrennium closed on 31 December 1988).[147] In response Krimsky stated tersely that the USOC had concluded nothing with respect to a final accounting of the premium royalties from TOP-I, adding that Seoul still owed the USOC in excess of $150,000 in payments. Krimsky stated that he had received no response from Seoul despite frequent communications on the subject. Also, Coca-Cola and Kodak, two original TOP sponsors, refused to provide the USOC with any data pertinent to the U.S. premium program, arguing that the original agreements did not warrant release of the information requested. Other TOP-I sponsors were seeking "some kind of credit" from the USOC to offset unliquidated premium items, a request consistently rebuffed by the USOC. Krimsky refused to "place an immediate priority on settlement of premium royalties" in the face of more pressing issues.[148]

Frustrated by Krimsky's position with regard to TOP-I royalties, Payne reminded him that in Malta the previous June Krimsky had mentioned that the IOC entitlement (30% of all U.S. territory premium royalties) was already $300,000. To Payne it was "only proper that those monies that can be identified, and have already been paid to the USOC, should now be paid to the IOC," particularly now that TOP-I was clearly over.[149] Krimsky responded by fax that same day, suggesting that the "combination of Maltese wine and sun" must have caused Payne "some selective hearing on the issue of TOP-I royalties." According to Krimsky, the $300,000 royalty figure discussed was an estimation resulting from a combination of "TOP-I sponsor premium [royalties], U.S. territory premium/royalty designations, Coke and Kodak that never paid or reported directly, and the anticipated value of royalties through the end of the quadrennium."[150] Miffed at Krimsky's response, Payne retorted that "the wine and sun must have got to the other members of the IOC/ISL delegations in Malta [as well]," as he was not alone in understanding that the IOC's entitlement of TOP-I premium royalties was $300,000. Based on "total premiums usage around the world by TOP-[I] sponsors," Payne concluded that he would find any figure less than the $300,000 royalty estimate for the U.S. market "out of proportion to reported sales throughout the rest of the world."[151]

As Payne and Krimsky continued to square off in the debate on TOP-I premium royalties, ISL proceeded with negotiations on the subject of royalties with the USOC for TOP-II. "Be prepared to be smoked," wrote Krimsky to Payne concerning the USOC's intended TOP-II premium royalty demands.[152] The USOC had previously rejected a number of premium royalty distribution plans suggested by both the IOC and ISL.[153] On numerous occasions it had submitted its own premium royalty distribution plan, only to have it rejected by ISL. On 4 May 1989 Krimsky closed the door on further negotiations by stating that "the USOC feels strongly it has provided ISL all the concessions under this agreement that are warranted." Krimsky stated that the agreement previously submitted by Richard Kline represented "the final USOC position" on the matter.[154]

Krimsky's uncompromising stance caused a further deterioration of the USOC's already strained relationship with the IOC. Accordingly, Pound reported to his IOC Executive Committee colleagues that "the situation is such that it looks as if no solution can be found without recourse to legal means." IOC president Samaranch was less pessimistic, however, stating the importance of settling "this affair amicably in view of the key position which the United States occupies on the Olympic stage."[155] As a result of Samaranch's personal intervention, the USOC and ISL soon concluded negotiations in favor of USOC demands.

Intent on concluding all TOP-II agreements, Andrew Craig wrote Stupp on 30 April 1990, offering ISL's assistance in closing the remaining IOC/USOC agreement.[156] Stupp, weary of the entire matter, elected to proceed without Craig's help; seven days later he scribbled a quick note on Craig's letter and returned it to him: "I am having the agreement updated and typed on the IOC word processor."[157] Having concluded all TOP-II agreements and established an acceptable revenue distribution model, Michael Payne and John Krimsky met in late May 1990 to continue negotiations on various Olympic marketing issues. During that two-day meeting they reached tentative agreements on a number of issues, including the USOC's participation in TOP-III (1993–96). Despite these agreements "in principle" on TOP-III, the specter of USOC/IOC disharmony was destined to rise yet again.

CHAPTER 8

MONIQUE BERLIOUX'S ZENITH

Sarajevo and Los Angeles Television Negotiations

"Over a period of twenty years," observed David Miller, "[Monique] Berlioux not only had her feet effectively under the [IOC] President's table, but could and did lay her hand upon every doorknob, every appointment, every contract, every single decision that was made."[1] During the latter stages of the tenure of IOC president Avery Brundage (1969–72) and throughout the subsequent term of Lord Killanin (1972–80), IOC director Monique Berlioux brought a sorely needed degree of efficiency to the operation of the organization's Lausanne headquarters.[2] Berlioux acted as the IOC's link with the world media, established agendas for IOC sessions, prepared presidential speeches, and constructed an effective and unique position of influence within the IOC's administrative structure. Along with Jean de Beaumont, chair of the IOC Finance Commission (1972–88), Berlioux also spearheaded the IOC's efforts to improve its troubled financial status through a more informed and vigorous approach to monitoring Olympic television rights negotiations.[3]

In this role Berlioux's fierce advocacy of the financial interests of the IOC and its affiliated organizations, the ISFs and NOCs, often conflicted with the goals of Olympic Organizing Committee leaders faced with burgeoning budgetary demands for hosting the Games. In the years prior to 1985, before the development of the IOC's sophisticated and highly successful corporate sponsorship program (known simply as TOP), the IOC's budget was almost wholly secured by television money.[4] Prior to the Los Angeles experience in 1984 Organizing Committees also relied heavily on television money and government subsidy. All Olympic parties (IOC, ISFs, NOCs, and OCOGs) had vested interests in the size of the television contracts and the disbursement of funds.

Television rights negotiations conducted by Munich, Montréal, Lake Placid, and Moscow Olympic organizers often left the tandem of Berlioux and Beaumont at loggerheads with those entrusted to stage the Olympic

festivals.[5] Organizing Committees confounded IOC officials on those occasions when they signed preemptive agreements with television companies, especially networks in the highly competitive and lucrative U.S. market. Such agreements, while they maximized the OCOG share of the
contracts at the expense of the IOC, NOCs, and ISFs, involved sidestep-
ping the Rome Formula.[6] Realizing that the Rome Formula mandated the
receipt of one-third of the television rights fee by the IOC (shared equally
with the NOCs and ISFs), the Organizing Committees followed Willi
Daume's lead and consummated contracts with two revenue components—the rights fee shared by the Organizing Committee and the IOC
and a technical services payment retained exclusively by the Organizing
Committee.[7] The IOC, argued leaders of the Organizing Committees, did
not understand the magnitude of the costs involved in providing the technical infrastructure required to address the needs of the world's broadcasters. The IOC, expecting to receive one-third of the gross value of the contract, resented this means of compromising the amount of money due to
Olympic organizations.

In addition to the decisions of Organizing Committees to sign contracts incorporating technical services payments, the 1976 Montréal and
1980 Lake Placid Organizing Committees consummated deals with ABC in
the absence of an open bidding process.[8] Embittered officials at CBS and
NBC threatened legal action as a means of redress. The sense of frustration
in Lausanne resulting from these negotiations, and the organization's determined effort to improve its knowledge base concerning television in the
1970s, dictated a change in policy.

In 1977 the IOC abandoned its "oversee at a distance" approach to
television rights negotiations and legislated changes in the *Olympic Charter* by which, in theory, it became a full partner in the process. Though the
IOC's full-partner status was supposed to have guided the television negotiations concerning the 1984 Olympic festivals, in essence it did not.[9] Peter
Ueberroth saw to that. His plan was to negotiate the contracts subject to
the IOC's approval. Ueberroth successfully lobbied for the lead role in negotiations. Without the promise of public funds, private sector revenue was
critical to the Los Angeles operation. Following troubled U.S. television
negotiations conducted by Sarajevo officials, Monique Berlioux controlled
television negotiations for rights to the Winter Games in other regions.

Berlioux coveted the opportunity to expand her portfolio by virtue of
the IOC's decision to take a more active role in television negotiations, but
winds of change in Lausanne limited her impact beyond the short term. In
the television rights negotiations process for the Calgary and Seoul Games
in 1988 Berlioux's presence was hardly noticeable. By that time IOC pres-

ident Juan Antonio Samaranch had entrusted Canada's Richard Pound with the leadership of the fledgling Television Rights Negotiations Commission, due in large measure to his desire to curb Berlioux's power.[10]

SARAJEVO

Fast approaching the zenith of her influence in Olympic affairs in the late 1970s, Berlioux anticipated an opportunity to wield an increased measure of authority in the negotiations arena. The IOC soon relaxed its new policy governing television negotiations with respect to the 1984 Los Angeles Olympics, however, even though it did retain final approval of all contracts. The IOC accepted the request of the Los Angeles Olympic Games Organizing Committee (LAOOC) for authority in this area of its business operations because of its status as a privately funded organization bereft of public funding. Adverse media reports concerning the financial debacle of the 1976 Montréal Olympics contributed to the IOC's decision on the matter as well.[11] Berlioux, though maintaining observation of the work of Los Angeles, focused her efforts on working collaboratively with Ahmed Karabegovic, secretary-general of the Sarajevo Olympic Games Organizing Committee (SOOC), who represented Sarajevo in television negotiations.

Far from being friendly collaboration, U.S. television rights negotiations drew Berlioux and Karabegovic into adversarial roles. The consummation of a U.S. television agreement was an early priority for Organizing Committees. The U.S. contract provided the largest single infusion of operating capital into Organizing Committee coffers. From a revenue standpoint the U.S. contract was also central to the IOC's budget process. Further, it provided both the Organizing Committees and the IOC with a reference point for initiating financial discussions with the world's other television networks. The IOC, which had in the past made many concessions to Organizing Committees concerning the distribution of television money, envisioned joint negotiation as a means of leveling the playing field in its dealings with the OCOGs. Ahmed Karabegovic preferred the status quo. Monique Berlioux soon realized that joint negotiation was not a panacea for alleviating frustration concerning Olympic television rights negotiations.

A lack of communication between Berlioux and Karabegovic concerning where and when U.S. television negotiations would be held foreshadowed future problems. Karabegovic scheduled contract talks with U.S. television executives between 17 and 20 December 1979. Initial negotiations would be held in Sarajevo. After that, noted Karabegovic, final negotiations with the successful company would be held in Lausanne. He failed to vet these dates with Berlioux before approaching American executives.[12] Even though the decision to begin negotiations in Sarajevo and conclude them in Lausanne was in keeping with her wishes, Berlioux flatly refused the proposed dates because they were not convenient for IOC officials. She also noted that a final decision on the winning network required the approval of Killanin and Beaumont.[13] Later Berlioux maintained that she had been clear in discussions with Karabegovic that representatives of all three U.S. companies would have to proceed to Lausanne for the final phase of discussions.[14] Both parties finally agreed that negotiations would be held in late January 1980.

Karabegovic and Berlioux also discussed the method of distributing U.S. television money. Killanin and Beaumont, she noted, would recommend to the Executive Board the same method of dividing the money as in the U.S. contract adopted by the IOC and Los Angeles. This agreement reserved five-ninths of the contract's value as the technical services component and set aside four-ninths of the revenue as the rights payment subject to the Rome Formula. Berlioux stated that the IOC expected a minimum share of $13 million.[15] While Berlioux was clear that this represented a recommendation, Karabegovic, with some justification, assumed that the Executive Board was a rubber stamp. The lack of a firm agreement proved problematic.

Karabegovic offered a format for the discussions to be held on 22–24 January 1980. Each U.S. company would be afforded three hours to present its respective telecast plans and financial proposals to the Sarajevo and IOC representatives on the twenty-second. A one-hour follow-up discussion with each group would be scheduled for the next day. Karabegovic then planned to announce the results of the competition for U.S. television rights on the twenty-fourth, with the successful U.S. delegation subsequently proceeding to Lausanne.[16] Berlioux concurred with the agenda set for the twenty-second and twenty-third in Sarajevo but wrote: "As for the 24th, I think we need to have a meeting among ourselves to review the matter and to take a decision prior to any kind of announcement."[17] She implied that all interested parties would have to be present in Lausanne because the final decision was to be made on the twenty-fourth. Karabegovic responded favorably by noting that Sarajevo accepted "the 24th of January for the finalization of discussions in Lausanne."[18]

On the other side of the Atlantic U.S. television executives at CBS and NBC struggled with the dates for far different reasons. CBS successfully appealed for a one-day postponement for its initial presentation because high-ranking executives needed in Sarajevo would be delayed in the United

States due to the network's coverage of the Super Bowl.[19] NBC, however, petitioned for a 30–60-day moratorium until the unsettled situation involving U.S. participation in the 1980 Moscow Olympics became clearer.[20] Sarajevo badly needed money "up front," which it was likely to get only if it concluded a television deal quickly. Delay was anathema. Sarajevo rejected NBC's petition. Arthur Watson (president, NBC Sports) and Geoffrey Mason (executive vice-president, NBC Sports) flew to Sarajevo but returned to the United States before presenting a formal offer.[21] On 23 January Yugoslavian negotiators, led by Karabegovic, hijacked the negotiation process.

Karabegovic's subsequent action startled Daniel Mortureux and Alain Coupat, the IOC's representatives attending the meetings in Sarajevo. Monique Berlioux, occupied with IOC affairs in Lausanne, was equally concerned. When Mortureux and Coupat arrived on 22 January, they received a document entitled "Programme of Visit" that had been sent to the competing networks but not to the IOC.[22] The most contentious element of Karabegovic's plan involved the determination of the contracting network in Sarajevo and the formalization of the agreement in Lausanne with the successful bidder.[23] When Mortureux and Coupat challenged this scheme, Karabegovic held firm. Amid some misgivings, preliminary negotiations proceeded.[24]

When Arthur Watson and Geoffrey Mason appealed for a one-day extension on 22 January, Karabegovic demanded that NBC proceed with its presentation or he would postpone all presentations until the next day. Watson and Mason, who lobbied NBC executives in New York for permission to proceed with negotiations, accepted Karabegovic's counterproposal. Having lost the debate with their fellow executives, however, they withdrew from the discussions on the morning of 23 January. Mortureux and Coupat reiterated that they had no authority to approve a contract on behalf of the IOC and cautioned Karabegovic that NBC's withdrawal greatly complicated the negotiation process.[25]

Mortureux and Coupat, frustrated by Karabegovic's dismissive attitude toward their concerns and their inability to deal with him except through an interpreter, pressed Sarajevo on two issues. First, they asked for Sarajevo's anticipated share from the U.S. contract based on its budget projections. Second, they queried Karabegovic on the manner in which negotiations would proceed, given that NBC had withdrawn and that the final negotiation session was to be held in Lausanne. Karabegovic stated that Sarajevo expected approximately $67 million but refused to modify his position about where the final decision on the contracting network would be rendered. The negotiations resumed with the question of the final procedure still unresolved.[26] CBS and ABC made their presentations and tendered initial offers.

CBS's ($52.7 million) and ABC's ($70 million) offers did not impress Mortureux and Coupat. Deeming these offers unacceptable, they pressed Karabegovic to proceed to Lausanne because they themselves "had no power, even in principle, to take a decision, and that the final decision had to be taken by the IOC in Lausanne."[27] Ljubisa Zecevic, a member of SOOC and an eyewitness to Sarajevo's dealings with IOC representatives, notes that Karabegovic was the principal spokesperson but accepted extensive counsel from Sarajevo's marketing director, Mirza Kulenovic.[28] Karabegovic, with his resolve stiffened by Kulenovic, proved defiant and stated that "the Games were to be held in Sarajevo, not in Lausanne, and that, as long as he was in charge of the OCOG, he would not accept any order from the IOC."[29]

Karabegovic's recalcitrance was not at odds with attitudes exhibited by key officials of past Organizing Committees or those that championed the interests of local organizers in the future. Samaranch has characterized the period spent by a prospective Organizing Committee pursuing the privilege of hosting an Olympic festival as the "Yes, Yes, Yes" phase of the IOC's relationship with an Organizing Committee.[30] Compliant and cooperative local organizers, still basking in the celebratory mood that grips a newly appointed Olympic host city, work together with IOC officials toward mutual goals. Conversely, Samaranch has stated, when the organizers are forced to translate their Olympic vision into reality, and the magnitude of their responsibilities is brought into sharp focus, local officials sometimes prove far more protective of local concerns and less conciliatory during the "No, No, No" stage in IOC/Organizing Committee relations.

Any semblance of formality soon disappeared from the proceedings. ABC representatives sought to negotiate directly with the Organizing Committee and stated that they planned to better any offer forwarded by CBS. Mortureux and Coupat withdrew from the discussions. Karabegovic reduced the procedure to an auction and simply approached the ABC and CBS delegations with the other's most recent offer.[31]

A flurry of communication provides an indication of Berlioux's frustration. Apprised of Karabegovic's actions, she contacted Killanin to register her concern. Berlioux also warned Karabegovic that the IOC would not approve any contract negotiated contrary to IOC policy.[32] One can imagine Berlioux's agitation when Anto Sucic, president of SOOC, implored Killanin to authorize a trip to Lausanne by representatives of the U.S. company offering the most money or invite Sarajevo representatives to Dublin for face to face discussions. Sarajevo was going over her head. The unsettled political situation vis-à-vis Afghanistan and the 1980 Moscow Olympic Games, argued Sucic, dictated the consummation of an agreement. "I strongly believe," he wrote, "that quite more important for the Olympic movement is the date of signing the TV rights contract [than] the way it was done and what were the funds in question."[33] Seeking to defend IOC interests and resentful of the challenge to her authority, Berlioux telephoned Killanin in order to emphasize her concerns.[34] Karabegovic's actions confirmed that the IOC and Sarajevo had progressed to the "No, No, No" phase of its relationship. Sarajevo solicited an offer of $91.5 million from ABC, which exceeded CBS's final offer by $1.5 million.[35] Sucic complained that Sarajevo employed procedures agreed upon by Berlioux and Karabegovic. Berlioux's demand that all networks send their delegations to Lausanne was not acceptable to the networks, he added. Sucic believed that Berlioux's attitude and the withdrawal of the IOC representatives from the process implied that the IOC did not trust Sarajevo.[36]

Mortureux and Coupat, disgusted by Karabegovic's conduct, advised the IOC to take a firm hand in its future dealings with Sarajevo. Specifically, they recommended that the IOC send procedures directly to Sarajevo and the television networks for all future negotiations and that the IOC host all future proceedings in Lausanne. They also noted that Sarajevo anticipated receiving $78 million from the contract, with the remaining $13.5 million payable to the IOC. While these amounts reflected the prospective distribution if the IOC applied the Los Angeles distribution key, stated Mortureux and Coupat, if it employed the Lake Placid formula the result would be more favorable to the IOC.[37]

The IOC's Finance Commission, under the leadership of Jean de Beaumont, met during the course of the 1980 Lake Placid Olympic Winter Games to consider the Sarajevo situation. The minutes of these sessions reveal reports submitted by Berlioux concerning two meetings between Berlioux and Karabegovic held in Lake Placid. Berlioux reported that Karabegovic sought $45 million from the $91.5 million U.S. contract to cover the anticipated cost of supplying the international signal to television broadcasters. This was an element of the $102 million required to satisfy the physical space and technical requirements for television broadcasters. Karabegovic proposed that they divide the remaining $46.5 million according to the Rome Formula, resulting in the IOC's receipt of $15.5 million.[38] When ABC representatives confirmed that the offer had been $91.5 million if the basic feed was provided, both Berlioux and Killanin believed that the $91.5 million stood alone as the rights payment. They expected the receipt of a full one-third share or $30 million.[39] While Beaumont argued that receipt of 28% of the U.S. contract by the IOC, as had been the case with respect to the ABC/Lake Placid agreement, might prove acceptable, Berlioux's opinion held sway during discussions.[40] She convinced members of the Finance Commission to adopt a hard line.[41]

When informed of the Finance Commission's decision, Karabegovic responded firmly. He said that the application of the Los Angeles distribution key translated into $13.5 million for the IOC. Having understood that the IOC expected a minimum of $13 million from the U.S. contract, he believed his counteroffer of $15.5 million to the IOC to be generous. He confirmed this offer and asked that it be forwarded to Killanin.[42] Karabegovic complained that Berlioux had agreed to extend the same treatment to Sarajevo accorded to Los Angeles with respect to the distribution of U.S. television money.[43] If the IOC did not accept his offer, he stated, Sarajevo would cancel the previous negotiations and renew discussions with the U.S. networks. Berlioux advised Karabegovic that this approach placed Sarajevo in a precarious position and that ABC might take legal action.[44]

Karabegovic, understandably, felt slighted. On 7 December 1979 Berlioux informed him that Beaumont and Killanin favored classifying five-ninths of the U.S. contract as a technical services payment in keeping with the agreement reached between the IOC and Los Angeles. The remaining sum would be subject to the Rome Formula. This plan would form the basis of their recommendation to the Executive Board. Karabegovic, assuming Beaumont and Killanin to be in agreement, expected this formula to be accepted with little discussion. He pressed Berlioux on this point. Berlioux, in her report to the Finance Commission and the Executive Board, "denied having accepted the formula mentioned by Sarajevo and added that she had only stated that the said proposal would be reported to the Finance Commission and to the President."[45] It appears that Berlioux overstepped her authority and did not clear the proposal with Beaumont and Killanin. The differences in Berlioux's semantics seem linked to Karabegovic's conduct during the U.S. negotiations, to Sarajevo's attempt to undermine her authority through direct appeals to Killanin, and to the advice of Mortureux and Coupat that the IOC needed to exert an enhanced measure of authority over the negotiations process. Berlioux, there is little doubt, bore much of the responsibility for the impasse.

A lull in developments regarding the U.S. contract ensued, but Berlioux proceeded with negotiations in other markets. Her unilateral decision to send copies of negotiation procedures to international television executives, along with a stern reminder that "contracts concerning radio and television may only be negotiated and concluded by the IOC jointly with the Organising Committee and to the IOC's benefit,"[46] miffed Karabegovic. Berlioux did not want a repeat of the U.S. contract negotiations that spun out of control. Her letter, stated Karabegovic, reflected an intent to "expropriate the OCOG all its competences [*sic*]" with respect to television negotiations.[47] When she expressed confidence in his abilities and denied his charge, a wry smile must have crossed his face.[48] Karabegovic, concerned that the U.S. contract situation was not resolved, pressed for a meeting.[49]

Berlioux and Karabegovic met in Lausanne in May to discuss the impasse. Bolstered by the infusion of money from the U.S. television rights deal contract for the Los Angeles negotiations, the IOC played hardball. The delay in resolving this outstanding matter, noted Karabegovic, impaired Sarajevo's financial planning. Berlioux replied testily that "the case was identical for the IOC and this would not have arisen had Sarajevo accepted the IOC's rules . . . it was not for the IOC to bow to the rules of the Sarajevo OCOG."[50] Of course, Berlioux also realized that Karabegovic's position was compromised, because he had previously stated to Mortureux and Coupat in Sarajevo in January that Sarajevo anticipated $67 million from the sale of U.S. television rights. Berlioux reiterated that the Executive Board had accepted the Finance Commission's recommendation that the IOC retain a full one-third share.[51]

Karabegovic rejected this arrangement but provided a counteroffer. He was confident that he could lobby the government of Bosnia-Herzegovina for $22.5 million; however, Sarajevo required a technical services component of $22.5 million in the contract. That would leave $69 million for distribution, according to the Rome Formula. Karabegovic had in effect presented a proposal that would elevate IOC revenue from $15.5 million to $23 million. Sarajevo would collect a total of $68.5 million. Karabegovic stated that if the IOC dissented he would reconvene U.S. companies for another round of negotiations because the IOC had recanted on its prior agreement for the distribution of U.S. television revenue. The Finance Commission and Executive Board considered Karabegovic's plan in early June.[52]

On 6 June in Essen, Germany, the Finance Commission deliberated on the means of resolving the financial issues concerning the ABC contract. Berlioux presented Karabegovic's proposal, but Beaumont, seeking a distribution like that applied to the U.S. contract for Lake Placid, indicated that the IOC should receive $25 million.[53] A worried Karabegovic queried Berlioux on 9 June about the IOC's response.[54] Berlioux, unable to respond until the Executive Board considered Beaumont's proposal, nevertheless replied to Karabegovic:

On account of the answers given by the city of Sarajevo as a candidate city and in consideration of the terms of the contract
signed between the IOC and the city of Sarajevo on 18th May
1978, the IOC shall receive its share amounting to 1/3rd (one
third) of the total sum i.e. 30 million U.S. dollars as it has already
been reported to you. However, the Executive Board of the IOC
agrees to restrict its share to US dollars 25 million. Out of the
first instalment [$20 million] US dollars 10 million shall be paid
by ABC direct to IOC 30 (thirty) days after the signature of the
contract.[55]

The formal tone of the message, in keeping with Berlioux's writing
style, reflected her desire to place Karabegovic on the defensive. She also
confirmed her planned meeting with Karabegovic on 12 June in Lausanne.

During the meeting on 12 June Berlioux wrestled Karabegovic into a
submissive position. "The Executive Board's decision was final—the Games
belonged to the IOC and this should not be forgotten," she noted.[56] The
IOC's demand for one-half of ABC's initial $20 million payment con-
cerned Karabegovic. Kulenovic, who was also present, protested that Sarajevo was not afforded an opportunity to discuss the distribution key: the
Executive Board was simply imposing its will.[57] Berlioux offered Sarajevo a
loan from the IOC's portion of the $20 million payment. Karabegovic, in
desperate need for an agreement to assist Sarajevo's flagging resources,
asked for a $10 million loan and a reduction of the IOC's share to $24 million.[58] Several days later Beaumont's position remained unchanged with respect to the IOC's total share ($25 million), but he indicated, subject to
Executive Board approval, that the Finance Commission would lend Sarajevo $10 million at 8% interest to be repaid in 1984. The $10 million was to
be loaned over four payments between 15 October 1980 and 15 February
1983.[59] Despite significant haggling, and Karabegovic's position that Sarajevo required the loan in 1981, the two sides could agree only that the
IOC's total share would remain at $25 million and that the first payment
would be shared equally. The parties placed loan arrangements in abeyance
(Samaranch proved supportive of Sarajevo's needs and eventually convinced the IOC Executive Board to grant a loan of $8 million). While an
agreement had been reached some five months after Karabegovic signed
the ABC deal, joint negotiation provided little satisfaction for Sarajevo and
the IOC. Most of the proceedings had been a nightmare.

Joint negotiation had been conceived as a means for the IOC to protect its financial interests and alleviate past friction with OCOGs concerning television negotiations. U.S. television rights negotiations for the 1984

Sarajevo Olympics, however, revealed that the prospect for problems remained. Karabegovic did not willingly relinquish the degree of autonomy enjoyed by previous Organizing Committees. He realized the central importance of U.S. television revenue to Sarajevo and sought to retain control over the negotiations process. In the end, however, Karabegovic yielded because the IOC's need for money was not as acute as Sarajevo's in light of the IOC's earlier windfall from ABC's contract for the Los Angeles Games.

The four levels of IOC bureaucracy involved in the process also proved troublesome and contributed to the escalation of the problem. Mortureux and Coupat, acting as Berlioux's representatives in Sarajevo, were unable to influence Karabegovic's decision to proceed with negotiations. Berlioux's presence in Sarajevo may have tempered his conduct. Her status as a negotiator on behalf of the Finance Commission also caused difficulties, however. She gave Karabegovic reason to believe that the IOC Finance Commission, more specifically Jean de Beaumont, as well as President Killanin himself, favored extending the same distribution method for U.S. television money as that accorded to Los Angeles. Karabegovic approached the U.S. negotiations with this formula acting as a guide for the contract value sought. One can imagine his anger when he learned of the subsequent decision of the Finance Commission and Executive Board to forego the formula employed for the distribution of U.S. television money for the 1984 Los Angeles Olympics. Karabegovic, of course, committed the cardinal sin of trying to usurp Berlioux's authority by concluding an agreement in Sarajevo.

These difficulties prompted spirited action on behalf of the IOC. Berlioux played a prominent and energetic personal role in negotiating contracts with Canadian, Australian, European, and Japanese television executives in the ensuing months.[60] Her approach was fortified by the entire Sarajevo experience.[61] Berlioux's effort reflected her desire to exert greater authority in discussions as a means of protecting (and advancing) the IOC's financial interests. The IOC also refined its approach to future negotiations by inserting the joint negotiation policy in the contracts signed by the IOC and the host cities for the 1988 Winter and Summer Olympics at the time the awards were made.[62] It was no longer limited to inclusion in the *Olympic Charter.* The IOC also established distribution keys for U.S. television money with Calgary and Seoul representatives before negotiations with the networks were opened.[63]

SAMARANCH: SARAJEVO'S WHITE KNIGHT?

On the surface, protracted discussions about the $8 million loaned by the IOC to Sarajevo in two installments (1981 and 1983) appear to be a mere footnote to the tangled U.S. television rights negotiations process and Berlioux's activities. Yet, when reviewed in concert with other unfolding issues concerning the IOC's management of financial affairs and its new initiatives in revenue generation, they speak to the rapidity with which Juan Antonio Samaranch established himself as a "hands-on" leader. Berlioux's and Beaumont's days as the IOC's power brokers in this arena were numbered.

Ahmed Karabegovic understood that the IOC Finance Commission would recommend to the Executive Board that the IOC extend a $10 million loan to Sarajevo over the course of the next two and a half years. Daniel Mortureux had delivered this information to Karabegovic when the two sides concluded a final agreement with ABC in June 1980. With no firm loan terms established, Karabegovic pressed the IOC for the $10 million in the fall of 1980.[64] Documents reviewed are unclear as to whether he sought the entire sum up front or the staggered payments in line with the proposal tendered by Mortureux in June.[65] Between June and October 1980 Beaumont had a change of heart concerning the wisdom of loaning Sarajevo such a substantial amount of money. Instead he recommended, and the Executive Board approved, a $3 million loan contingent upon the receipt of a bank guarantee. Samaranch played an integral role in convincing Beaumont of the wisdom of extending this loan.[66] Still, it was another bitter disappointment for Karabegovic, who believed once again that he had been misled.

Nonetheless, Samaranch moved quickly to shore up financial aid for Sarajevo and exert his authority over IOC financial policy. He dismissed Beaumont's concerns about the risks involved in extending a second loan of $3 million to Sarajevo in 1982 and ensured that the Executive Board approved such a policy in principle.[67] This loan was eventually extended in 1983 but was increased to $5 million.[68] By the end of 1981 Samaranch had engineered the movement of substantial IOC financial reserves from a bank owned by Beaumont in Paris to two Swiss banks. This action made it abundantly clear to Beaumont and members of the Finance Commission that they were sitting on an advisory rather than a decision-making body. Samaranch also shifted responsibility for investigating new sources of revenue from the Finance Commission to a working group headed by Louis Guirandou-N'Diaye that reported directly to the president.[69] While Beaumont retained the post of chair of the Finance Commission until 1988, he never again enjoyed the same degree of latitude with respect to decision-making that he possessed under Brundage and Killanin. Samaranch also convinced the Executive Board that Lance Cross, a member of the Executive Board and the chair of the IOC's Television Commission, should join

Berlioux in negotiations for television rights to the Calgary and Seoul Olympic Games.[70] Later Samaranch turned to Richard Pound to lead the IOC/OCOG teams in negotiating television contracts.

A direct correlation existed between the occasional appearances of Presidents Avery Brundage and Lord Killanin in the IOC administrative precincts of Lausanne and the rising influence of the organization's director, Monique Berlioux. With the arrival of Juan Antonio Samaranch in Lausanne as an "in-residence president," Berlioux's power began to decline.

LOS ANGELES

Peter Ueberroth, president of the Los Angeles Olympic Games Organizing Committee (LAOOC), was but one of the vast majority of Californians who opposed the use of taxpayers' money to underwrite the 1984 Los Angeles Olympics. "I believed then, as I do now," wrote Ueberroth in 1985, "that there are many important programs much more deserving of government support than a sports event, even one as special as the Olympic Games."[71] Ueberroth's philosophy, wary taxpayers, and tight-fisted politicians who feared a reincarnation of the financial sinkhole that had swallowed the city of Montréal underscored the evolution of a different method of financing the Olympic Games.

Following the award of the Games to Los Angeles in 1978, the city amended its charter in order to prevent the use of public funds for the project. Because Los Angeles had been the only serious bidder for the 1984 Summer Olympics, the IOC was left with little choice but to reach a unique accord with Los Angeles organizers in light of the absence of public funds. Heretofore the IOC had awarded the Games to a city. Los Angelenos did not embrace the Olympics in 1978, and the lack of public financing forced the IOC to renegotiate the standard terms of award. The 1984 Los Angeles Games would not be organized by the city but rather by a private organization.[72] To provide the fuel for their financial engine Ueberroth relied on the private sector rather than different layers of government.

As the newly named president of LAOOC, Peter Ueberroth understood that television money and corporate sponsorships were central to the successful staging of the Los Angeles Games.[73] Arthur Young and Company and Peat, Marwick and Mitchell collaborated on a study of revenue streams employed by the Organizing Committees of the Munich, Montréal, and Moscow Summer Olympic festivals. It revealed that Los Angeles required "a six-fold increase in revenue from non-public sources, primarily in sponsorship programs, television sales, and ticket revenue" in order to compensate for the loss of government funding.[74]

One of the early priorities was the consummation of a U.S. television rights agreement. Day-to-day expenses incurred by Los Angeles in the short term also necessitated action, however. Ueberroth and Hollywood impresario David Wolper devised an innovative method of generating operating capital months in advance of opening formal negotiations with the networks. In April 1979 Ueberroth and Wolper called on all interested bidders for U.S. television rights to provide Los Angeles with a refundable $500,000 deposit. Los Angeles could operate on the interest for a number of months before opening negotiations. When a date for formal negotiations was established, all bidders would have to provide an additional $250,000 deposit. When five parties—NBC, CBS, ABC, ESPN, and Tandem Productions, a company led by Norman Lear, Bud Yorkin, and Jerry Perenchio—proffered the checks required to reserve a seat at the negotiation table, Los Angeles collected the interest of approximately $1,000 per day.[75]

Los Angeles's "innovative" revenue generation scheme aggravated Killanin and Berlioux, both of whom took issue with Ueberroth's decision to pursue this course of action without notifying the IOC. They reminded him that the IOC had the right to send an observer to all negotiations sessions.[76] Ueberroth ignored IOC criticism and, while confirming the networks' deposits, stated that discussions with the networks had been limited to "informal fact-finding sessions."[77] "I am afraid," stated Killanin, that Los Angeles's activities are "quite unacceptable to the International Olympic Committee."[78] Berlioux's voice joined Killanin's in chastisement: "It seems strange to consider as fact-finding sessions negotiations culminating in deposit of dlrs 750,000—at least to our usual practice."[79]

The presence of Tandem Productions at the negotiating table, an "unknown" player in the world of Olympic television, also concerned the IOC. Berlioux advised Ueberroth that "only an existing nationwide network should be considered, the games are not a lever for anybody to set up a 'fourth network' in the USA."[80] She aired her concerns during a meeting with Wolper.[81] Ueberroth listened politely to Berlioux's call for Los Angeles to transfer one-third of the deposit money to the IOC and then ignored her request. There were other concerns on the part of the IOC. Berlioux could not have been pleased by Los Angeles's jaundiced assessment of negotiations conducted by previous Organizing Committees with European television executives. Los Angeles, observed Wolper, would not "give away" television rights to EBU and the Japanese networks.[82] Berlioux's expression of disapproval of Los Angeles's actions did not shake Wolper. The IOC, he replied, would be given one month's notice before Los Angeles commenced negotiations with the U.S. networks.[83] Wolper's conduct revealed his view that the IOC was only a junior partner in all television negotiations.

While some members of Los Angeles's Television Advisory Committee forecast a sale price of $100 million, media analysts believed that the U.S. deal might reach $175 or $200 million.[84] Ueberroth was optimistic that a $200 million contract might be feasible. He was proven correct. In September 1979 Wolper's Bel-Air mansion provided the setting for Los Angeles's negotiations with the U.S. networks. Los Angeles reached a tentative agreement with ABC that outlined a payment of $100 million for rights and $125 million for technical services. Ueberroth understood that the deal was indeed tentative until it had been approved by the IOC.[85]

Ueberroth prepared for Berlioux's visit to Los Angeles, confident that her approval was forthcoming. After his perusal of an IOC financial balance sheet provided by David McKenzie, IOC member from Australia, Ueberroth was even more assured that the IOC would be satisfied with the negotiated terms. Leaving nothing to chance, however, he fêted Berlioux in royal fashion. He delegated preparations for Berlioux's visit to Joel Rubenstein. "The checklist for her impending visit was encyclopaedic," recalled Ueberroth. "We had to make sure that a swimming pool was available, that Evian water was supplied, that there were exquisite flower arrangements, that the room service met her French tastes, that restaurant arrangements were made at the finest eateries, that appointments were not scheduled either early in the morning or late at night, and that her traveling staff received equally impeccable treatment."[86] On the heels of this treatment, Berlioux accepted the contract terms.

The IOC approved the $100 million U.S. rights fee, a vast improvement on the rights fee ($35 million) negotiated by Ignati Novikov for Moscow in 1977. Ueberroth's strategy to negotiate contracts whose terms of payment were front-end–loaded benefited the IOC as well. Within weeks the IOC received $25 million from ABC, improving its financial state considerably.[87] This money permitted Berlioux to squeeze Sarajevo for maximum revenue from the U.S. contract for the 1984 Olympic Winter Games.

Los Angeles's effort to revisit Marvin Josephson's strategy of maximizing television revenue in Europe, however, drew Peter Ueberroth into conflict with the IOC's newly elected president, Juan Antonio Samaranch. In May 1981 EBU was prepared to discuss financial terms for West European television rights following completion of an extensive investigation of technical arrangements. As early as 1979 David Wolper had informed Berlioux that Los Angeles planned to wield a big stick in its discussions with EBU. When the negotiating teams convened at New York's Park Lane

Hotel, Ueberroth delivered the perfunctory pleasantries and then issued Los Angeles's demand for $100 million.[88] Los Angeles's demand of $100 million for West European rights correlated to a formula of its own design of $1 per television set in the territory.[89] Berlioux was present for the meeting but, contrary to her authoritative management of Sarajevo's negotiations with non-U.S. networks, offered few comments. Los Angeles was the dominant partner in this set of negotiations.

EBU dismissed Los Angeles's negotiating position as unrealistic when one considered the union's noncommercial status. EBU's Albert Scharf stated that the demand for $100 million "was utterly out of consideration." Ueberroth retorted that the "Olympic Movement had been undervalued." Scharf offered $8.33 million for Los Angeles television rights, based on a 40% increase on the price paid for Moscow television rights ($5.95 million). In an effort to characterize Ueberroth's position as unreasonable he underscored the fact that EBU had paid $5.27 million for rights to the 1982 World Cup.[90] Berlioux agreed with Ueberroth's opinion that networks (presumably non-U.S. networks) had not been paying fair market value for television rights. Stymied, the two sides agreed to a short recess.[91]

When the parties returned to the negotiating table, Ueberroth presented EBU officials with a new offer. He reduced Los Angeles's demand by two times Scharf's offer of $8 million (rounded-off). Therefore, Los Angeles valued EBU rights at $84 million, "the year of the Games," as Ueberroth stated. Scharf, scoffing at Ueberroth's proposal, sought Berlioux's support, asking her whether she backed Ueberroth. "Being well aware of the possible consequences and the fact that there might be no more negotiations," Berlioux signaled her support of Los Angeles. Stymied once again, the two parties agreed to meet in the fall after both negotiating teams had reviewed their positions. Ueberroth informed EBU officials that he would file the following report with LAOOC's Board of Directors: "We found this group [EBU] to be well informed, very sincere and very professional. Financially, we are far apart."[92]

Following the publication of an article in the *Stuttgarter Zeitung* less than a month after the EBU/IOC/Los Angeles meeting in New York, Ueberroth and EBU's secretary-general, Regis de Kalbermatten, exchanged letters. Kalbermatten was agitated because both groups had agreed to avoid discussions with the media. The *Stuttgarter Zeitung* wrote that Los Angeles might view an offer of $65 million with favor.[93] Ueberroth, discussing the situation with the *Stuttgarter Zeitung* reporter, reiterated his determination to find an agreement acceptable to both parties.[94]

Within months Ueberroth's posture changed. Italy's Channel 5, an independent network, offered Los Angeles $10 million for Italian Olympic television rights. At the IOC's Eighty-fourth Session in Baden-Baden Ueberroth reported Los Angeles's interest in pursuing negotiations with Channel 5 because of the disparity between the two European offers. EBU's offer of $8.33 million for a territory covering thirty-two countries, including Italy, paled in comparison to the Channel 5 bid. Although he understood that it was important "for the whole world to see the Olympic Games on television," he refused to dismiss the Italian offer out of hand.[95] Samaranch took a low-key approach and reminded Ueberroth of the need for the two parties to work jointly on television contracts. Though he confirmed that the receipts from television were important to the IOC, it was "essential that everyone be able to see the Games through television."[96]

In November Ueberroth reiterated Los Angeles's position on the Channel 5 offer when he stated that its television advisory committee, stocked with people familiar with the television industry, supported negotiations with the Italians. "We feel it is very important to both short and long range revenue potentials for Organizing Committees, the IOC, the IFs, and the NOCs," observed Ueberroth in a message to Samaranch, whom he correctly perceived as the principal road block to any deal.[97] Samaranch delegated Berlioux to attend Los Angeles's upcoming negotiations with EBU and asked her to "explain the IOC's position."[98] Samaranch, who was beginning to affect policy in the negotiations arena, refused to consider an offer from an entity other than EBU. It was a protectionist approach that he promoted zealously throughout the 1980s.

When Los Angeles Olympic officials caucused with EBU representatives in mid-November, Ueberroth, agitated by Samaranch's attitude, was emphatic that EBU would have to move from its earlier negotiating position. If Samaranch did not support Los Angeles's efforts to maximize revenue through negotiations with individual European networks, then Ueberroth did not feel committed to an earlier agreement with the IOC that precluded the inclusion of a deduction for technical services in non-U.S. contracts. Ueberroth informed EBU that Los Angeles expected $30 million for television rights in Western Europe. EBU tendered a counteroffer of $12 million. The two sides reached an agreement at $19.8 million, but Ueberroth and EBU arbitrarily decided that the rights portion of the contract was $12 million. Los Angeles, therefore, would receive $15.8 million. The terms of the agreement reduced the IOC/NOC/ISF share of the sum from $6.6 million to $4 million. When Berlioux reminded Ueberroth that the IOC and Los Angeles had agreed not to include deductions for technical services in contracts other than the one for U.S. territory, Ueberroth was unmoved, citing Samaranch's refusal to support his plan to negotiate with Channel 5 and other individual networks.[99]

Ueberroth dismissed Berlioux's request to revisit the negotiated terms. Defending his actions in a sternly worded missive to Samaranch, he wrote: "Because the IOC wishes to protect EBU, the LAOOC will be prohibited from receiving maximum amounts." Los Angeles, stated Ueberroth, would not accept less than $15.8 million. In blunt fashion he concluded that "if the IOC wants more [than $4 million], it must get it directly from EBU." Though Ueberroth believed EBU had worked hard to improve its offer, convinced as he was that EBU was best prepared to present the Games in Europe, he nevertheless did not sanction signing a deal "under unfavorable terms," as had been the case with previous Organizing Committees.[100] The ball was in Samaranch's court.

Two weeks after Ueberroth and EBU reached their tentative accord Berlioux briefed the IOC Executive Board on the recent discussions. While not pleased with the decision to limit the IOC's share of the television contract, Samaranch believed that if the IOC received its money up front and invested it immediately "the difference" could be recovered. Lance Cross, however, was convinced that the purchase of European rights by individual networks would result in additional revenue for all parties. He thought that Channel 5 and RAI, the government-sponsored member of EBU, might be able to work out an arrangement whereby the revenue in the Italian market was maximized. Cross also warned that the NOCs and ISFs were aware of Channel 5's offer and might question the IOC's decision to sacrifice the additional revenue. Samaranch was committed to a deal with EBU. He emphasized the need to guarantee widespread coverage of the Games in Europe.[101]

Samaranch massaged the result of Los Angeles's negotiations to make it more satisfactory to the IOC. He argued for acceptance of the contract if Los Angeles agreed to provide the IOC with its total share of $4 million when EBU transferred $12 million of the sum in February 1982. The Executive Board approved the plan, but Samaranch required Ueberroth's consent to modify the payment schedule.[102] In a subsequent telephone call from Samaranch the two discussed the matter until the IOC president persuaded Ueberroth to accept the proposal.[103] The outcome on this issue underscores the persuasive diplomatic skills of Samaranch, especially in light of Ueberroth's earlier refusal to adjust the terms of the deal, including the payment schedule.

THE EBU MONOPOLY

Historically EBU's privileged status in European negotiations reflected market realities. As a government-sponsored consortium within an environment devoid of private commercial networks, EBU was the IOC's only option until the emergence of private networks capable of paying substantial prices for Olympic television rights offered the IOC and Organizing Committees an opportunity to improve television revenues in the European market in the 1980s. Samaranch eschewed negotiations with EBU's rivals. He defended his approach in the face of charges of favoritism, stating that EBU was the only entity capable of ensuring blanket coverage in Europe. In the 1980s there is no doubt that EBU continued to be treated differently than other networks interested in acquiring Olympic television rights. True, ABC had enjoyed a privileged position in Olympic negotiations in the 1970s. Roone Arledge was often apprised of his rivals' bids by individuals representing the IOC and/or Organizing Committees.[104] Arledge, however, also considered the Olympics to be a major element of the network's sport programming package and outbid his NBC and CBS counterparts. In short, he paid market value.

Prior to IOC/Los Angeles negotiations with Australian networks IOC member Kevan Gosper reminded Monique Berlioux of the close relationship of Channel 7 (Australia) with the Australian Olympic Committee, its ownership of the Sarajevo rights, its "history of televising Games in Australia," and its losses with respect to Moscow telecasts. He noted that Channel 7 was not seeking "special treatment," but he wanted Berlioux and Los Angeles officials to understand the sentiments of the "Olympic Movement here in Australia."[105] In late January 1982 Los Angeles signed a major deal with Rupert Murdoch's Channel 10 for $10.6 million.[106] The network that bid the most money walked off with the Australian television rights.

The IOC also supported Los Angeles's effort to maximize revenue in the Asian territory through negotiations with networks in Korea, New Zealand, and the Philippines, each of which had been previously represented by the Asian Broadcasting Union (ABU).[107] ABU appealed to Samaranch for redress in light of the IOC's policy of negotiating with EBU.[108] Samaranch noted the Los Angeles/IOC agreement that left LAOOC in control of television negotiations. His support of Ueberroth's approach only served to highlight EBU's privileged status, however. "Finally," wrote Samaranch, "as head of the Olympic Family, the IOC is responsible as well for all NOCs and those ISFs with sports on the Olympic program and accordingly can only concur with the position taken by the LAOOC to deal in the open marketplace in order to obtain the most favorable agreements possible."[109] These words did not govern his approach to television negotiations in Europe.

Samaranch resisted using rival bids as a meaningful lever to obtain improved offers from EBU until the 1990s and even then only after repeated badgering from Richard Pound. Samaranch and Marc Hodler managed the IOC's interests in discussions with EBU beginning with the negotiations for Calgary and Seoul. "He did not want ripples with [EBU]," noted Pound in explaining why he was not given responsibility to negotiate with European television executives when Samaranch appointed him chair of the IOC Television Rights Negotiations Committee in 1983.[110]

The IOC's protectionist approach in Europe, warned Pound, angered U.S. television executives. For the Los Angeles Olympics, despite the fact that Ueberroth tripled the sum paid by EBU for rights and technical services for the Moscow Games, the sale price translated into a rate of $0.14 per TV household in the 32-country territory. In the United States ABC's $225 million contract for the Los Angeles Olympics reflected a payment of $1.69 per TV household.[111] This disparity confounded Pound's sense of logic. His agitation reached a new level of exasperation when EBU acquired the rights for the 1988 Calgary Olympic Winter Games for $5.7 million more than two years after ABC purchased the U.S. television rights for $309 million. EBU obtained the rights to the 1988 Seoul Olympics for $28 million and paid $75 million for West European rights to the 1992 Barcelona Olympics.[112] While the numbers revealed incremental increases from the $19.8 million rights and technical services package negotiated by Ueberroth, the Barcelona deal represented a figure of slightly less than 20% of the sum paid by NBC ($401 million). Feelings of resentment, observed Pound, might push the U.S. networks to seek a waiver from the U.S. Justice Department that would allow them to submit a pooled bid, as had been considered in the aftermath of Novikov's failed 1976 auction of U.S. television rights to the 1980 Moscow Games. A pooled bid, he noted, would greatly compromise television revenue in the U.S. market, a potential financial disaster for the IOC. "It was not something he [Samaranch] would want to see unfold on his watch," Pound warned the president.[113]

In time, Samaranch listened. When Universum Film-AG (UFA), a German network, offered $300 million for the European rights to the 1996 Atlanta Olympics, EBU submitted a somewhat comparable bid of $250 million. Following the IOC's decision in 1995 to seek long-term financial security by packaging a number of Olympic festivals for sale to networks, media mogul Rupert Murdoch offered $2 billion for the European rights to the 2000, 2004, and 2008 Summer Olympics and the 2002 and 2006 Olympic Winter Games. EBU tendered a substantial bid of $1.442 billion.[114]

Samaranch displayed an obvious preference for dealing with EBU, but the network no longer held the clout of exclusivity at the negotiating table because the IOC had shown a willingness to consider rival European bids. Charles Curran, EBU's president, scoffed at Marvin Josephson's demands prior to the 1976 Montréal Olympic Games, marginally improving his initial offer during negotiations that extended for two years. He knew that EBU was the IOC's only option and that Lord Killanin would force Montréal to accept EBU's terms in order to avoid a blackout in Western Europe. Meanwhile Killanin, who fretted over the media backlash resulting from a blackout, lobbied Montréal to accept EBU's offer. Such arrogance on the part of EBU officials was at least partially attenuated as a result of two factors: (1) the emergence of viable private television networks in Europe; and (2) Richard Pound's ability to convince Samaranch of the need to improve European television revenue and the possible consequences in the American market if he did not.

UEBERROTH'S NEGOTIATION EFFORTS AT A GLANCE

Four markets proved critical in Los Angeles's successful effort to secure a tangible increase in the television revenue generated through negotiations conducted by Moscow prior to the 1980 Olympics. The U.S. networks engaged in a bidding war for television rights to the Moscow Games. NBC secured them for $85 million. The possibility of promoting the network's image and programming, however, and the prospect for significant advertising revenue as a result of the Games being in an American city in 1984 pushed NBC's best offer for the Los Angeles Games to $225 million. Rupert Murdoch's bid of $10.6 million was a pleasant surprise for Ueberroth, especially when one considers that Channel 7 had acquired Australian television rights for the Moscow Olympics for $1,360,284. Japanese television rights for the Moscow Games sold for $4.5 million, but Ueberroth adopted a tough approach in his negotiations with the Japanese and squeezed $19 million from that market.[115] While disappointed with the IOC's refusal to permit Los Angeles to entertain a bid from Italy's Channel 5, Ueberroth succeeded in tripling the price that EBU had paid for the Moscow Games. In the end Los Angeles negotiated television contracts totaling in excess of $286 million, nearly a threefold increase over the revenue obtained via negotiations conducted by the Soviets.[116]

THE WINDS OF CHANGE

The Sarajevo and Los Angeles negotiations represented the high-water mark for Monique Berlioux's influence in the IOC's financial dealings. Berlioux and Jean de Beaumont figured prominently in representing the

IOC in television negotiation sessions in the 1970s; however, Richard Pound and Samaranch swiftly replaced them as the architects of the IOC's television negotiations strategy regarding the sale of television rights to the 1988 Calgary and Seoul Olympics. Samaranch's appointment of Richard Pound as chair of the IOC's Television Rights Negotiation Commission in 1983 spelled out a changing of the guard in Lausanne. With Samaranch now a permanent fixture in Lausanne and the sound of his steps echoing in the halls of the IOC headquarters on a daily basis, Berlioux's former administrative autonomy disappeared. The pace of the IOC's transition to a corporate entity quickened.

CHAPTER 9

THE GUARD CHANGES IN LAUSANNE

Richard Pound, Television Negotiations, and the 1988 Olympic Festivals

Despite his youth and lack of experience in television negotiations Richard Pound, an international tax lawyer and relatively new member of the IOC Executive Board, offered Samaranch the prospect of aggressive leadership relative to the IOC's interests in television negotiations. Pound's ascent in the area of television negotiations in 1983 also gave Samaranch the opportunity to reduce Berlioux's profile. Samaranch, elected IOC president in 1980, immediately moved into Lausanne's Palace Hotel to become the first on-site resident IOC executive officer since the days of Pierre de Coubertin in the first quarter of the twentieth century. Samaranch respected Berlioux's knowledge and experience but soon realized that her influence and conduct hampered his efforts to function effectively in Lausanne. Berlioux mistakenly believed that she would be able to operate in much the same fashion as she had during the tenures of Brundage and Killanin. Samaranch's paranoia about Berlioux's interference, according to David Miller, reached the point where the IOC president had his Palace Hotel suite searched for listening devices.[1]

Tension in Lausanne rose to new levels as Berlioux and Samaranch engaged in heated debates. Some of these arguments involved the most significant element of Samaranch's plan to restructure the financial basis of the Olympic Movement—the development of a second major revenue stream through the establishment of a corporate sponsorship program. Within two years Berlioux's deteriorating relationship with Samaranch and a number of Executive Board members necessitated action. The Executive Board jettisoned Berlioux at the IOC's session in Berlin in 1985. "You couldn't have two crocodiles in the same pond, and Samaranch didn't want another one behind him," offered Beaumont as an explanation for Berlioux's departure.[2]

Pound quickly emerged as a major power broker. In addition to serving as chair of the Television Rights Negotiations Commission with responsibility for the IOC's interests in Calgary and Seoul television negotiations, he was appointed chair of the New Sources of Finance Commission in 1988, one year after having been elected IOC vice-president in 1987. His leadership of the New Sources of Finance Commission furthered the evolution of the IOC's TOP initiative. Pound's approach to revenue generation reflects a heavy dose of pragmatism. Without the financial support of corporate sponsors, television networks, and their advertisers, he reasoned, the Olympics faced a severe challenge, considering the reluctance of governments to accept the lion's share of the financial commitment required to stage an Olympic festival. Thus commercial relationships needed to be nurtured. While cognizant of critics who decry the Olympics as a diminished spectacle because of overcommercialization, Pound argues that the successful pursuit of television contracts and the IOC's marriage with multinational corporations empowered the Olympic Movement and facilitated the promotion of the Olympic message throughout the world.[3]

Change was not limited solely to the personalities representing the IOC at the negotiating tables in the 1980s. By the end of the decade ABC no longer boasted of its status as "America's Olympic Network." ABC obtained the U.S. television rights to the Sarajevo, Los Angeles, and Calgary Games but in the case of Calgary paid a whopping $309 million and incurred a significant financial loss. Television network ownership changes and the Calgary experience deterred ABC from aggressively pursuing television rights for Seoul and beyond. Consequently, CBS and NBC executives contested to become "America's Olympic Network" in the late 1980s and early 1990s. Organizing Committees, no longer afforded the benefits of the IOC's previously lower profile in television negotiations, sought the advice of professional consultants on the value of television rights. Even Pound relied on some of their suggestions concerning negotiation procedures. Barry Frank, a former CBS and ABC executive and corporate vice-president of TransWorld International (TWI), a subsidiary of International Management Group (IMG), emerged as a new player, much to the chagrin of network executives.[4] The United States Olympic Committee also forced the IOC to adopt a new method of distributing American television money. In 1985 the USOC claimed exclusive authority over the use of Olympic emblems in U.S. territory through the Amateur Sports Act (1978), a U.S. federal statute.[5] This claim translated into a demand for financial compensation in exchange for permitting the use of the Olympic rings by sponsors of Olympic television broadcasts in the United States, a privilege that heretofore had never been challenged.

The USOC's initiative, launched after the U.S. rights negotiations for the Calgary Games had been completed and at a critical juncture in the troubled negotiations with the U.S. networks concerning the sale of the television rights to the Seoul Olympics, provided Pound with a stiff test. The USOC claimed that the use of the Olympic rings by these sponsors infringed on its own domestic corporate sponsorship program. If U.S. sponsors of Olympic television broadcasts were not permitted access to the Olympic rings in their commercial advertising, they would refuse to pay a premium price for advertising time, thereby reducing the amount of money that U.S. networks would offer for future Olympic television contracts. The USOC's claim threatened the financial result of the Calgary negotiations. It also endangered the prospects for the Seoul negotiations. Pound's task was to find a solution acceptable to the USOC and his IOC colleagues. He had to sell the plan to members of the Executive Board and IOC members from countries other than the United States, who well recalled the profit in excess of $200 million from the Los Angeles Olympics that the USOC was unwilling to share with members of the Olympic Movement worldwide. Samaranch's heated request for $7 million of the profit, a sum that would have offset the extra expenses incurred by participating NOCs due to the Soviet bloc boycott, was denied.[6]

CALGARY

"When the biggest prize of the Winter Olympics was handed out," wrote Bill Abrams of the *Wall Street Journal* in February 1984, "no television cameras recorded the moment, no band played a national anthem and no gold medal was draped over the winner."[7] Abrams was not describing an event at the recently completed Sarajevo Olympic Winter Games. He was referring to the grueling eleven-hour U.S. television negotiations conducted by the IOC and the Calgary Olympic Games Organizing Committee (OCO'88) at Lausanne's Palace Hotel two weeks before the opening of the Sarajevo Games. Exhausted ABC executives who captured the U.S. rights with an eye-popping bid of $309 million were in no mood to celebrate. Roone Arledge, ABC's executive vice-president James Spence, and a number of colleagues slumped in their chairs in Arledge's hotel suite somewhat glassy-eyed, realizing that they had exceeded the maximum bid established by ABC's upper management team by $34 million.[8] Media analysts speculated that ABC risked a loss of $50–60 million. Poor Nielsen ratings revealed in the aftermath of ABC's coverage of the Sarajevo Olympic Winter Games compounded the anxiety pervading ABC's Sports Department.[9]

ABC's precedent-setting contract and the willingness of NBC and CBS executives to bid more than $250 million resulted from a number of factors: (1) the format for negotiations based on a series of sealed bids developed by Richard Pound, Bill Wardle (vice-president, marketing, for OCO'88), and OCO'88's television consultant, Barry Frank (corporate vice-president of TWI); (2) the competitiveness of the networks; (3) projected network advertising sales resulting from Calgary's location in a favorable time zone; (4) ABC's self-proclaimed status as "America's Olympic Network" and its need to maintain that status; and (5) U.S. executives' misty-eyed reflections on the U.S. hockey team's "Miracle on Ice" in Lake Placid. CBS bowed out when the bidding passed its maximum offer of $257 million, leaving NBC and ABC deadlocked with identical offers of $300 million. A final round of head-to-head bidding yielded an NBC offer of $304 million, which Arledge topped with ABC's $309 million bid.

Calgary officials flew home exhilarated beyond measure, having far exceeded even their loftiest expectations. Before Pound, Frank, and Calgary opened negotiations with the networks, Frank had offered the most optimistic forecast: $287 million.[10] An embittered Jim Spence labeled the effort to exploit the U.S. television market the "most demanding, frustrating, infuriating, nonsensical and historic negotiations in the saga of American television sports."[11] CBS and NBC officials, while not saddled with the financial risk accepted by Arledge and his associates, also resented the process. They refused to participate in negotiations for Seoul television rights if the IOC employed the same method.

The sale of U.S. television rights for the Calgary Olympic Winter Games marked a turning point in the history of Olympic television rights negotiations. For the first time the IOC and an Organizing Committee acted as co-negotiators in the truest sense of the term. This arrangement had been mandated in 1981 as a result of the host city contract signed by Calgary (and Seoul) at the IOC's session in Baden-Baden. Even though the *Olympic Charter* had been modified in 1977 in order to establish a policy of joint negotiation in advance of the 1984 Sarajevo and Los Angeles Games, collaboration between the IOC and the respective Organizing Committees did not reflect this reality. First, Los Angeles controlled television negotiations for its 1984 Summer Olympics; following the troubled negotiations for the sale of U.S. television rights to the Sarajevo Olympic Winter Games, the IOC (represented by Berlioux) was the dominant partner in negotiations for the sale of non-U.S. television rights to the Winter Games. Second, even though Monique Berlioux was present for the Calgary negotiations Richard Pound managed the process. Third, while the IOC retained people such as Maurice Louvet and Georges Straschnov as advisers on technical and financial matters pertaining to television and Marvin Josephson and Lothar Bock had played roles in past negotiations on behalf of the Montréal and Moscow Olympic Organizing Committees, respectively, Calgary's decision to retain Barry Frank as its television consultant altered the dynamics of the negotiation process.

THE ROAD TO LAUSANNE

One of the significant sources of conflict between the IOC and past Organizing Committees was the method of distributing television money. The lack of a firm agreement between the IOC and the Sarajevo Olympic Organizing Committee concerning the division of U.S. television money before Ahmed Karabegovic entertained U.S. television executives is central to understanding the ensuing struggle between Karabegovic and Monique Berlioux. Despite assurances that Los Angeles would not include deductions for technical services in non-U.S. contracts in exchange for the deduction of five-ninths of the gross value of the U.S. contract for hardware costs, Ueberroth signed contracts with EBU and Japanese negotiators that contained technical services components. In order to avert difficulties of this nature with OCO'88, Berlioux traveled to Calgary in the summer of 1983 to reach a negotiated settlement on the distribution of television money. The IOC agreed to allow Calgary to deduct 20% from all television contracts for technical services in recognition of the spiraling costs involved in providing the technical infrastructure required by the world's broadcasters.[12]

The next step in advance of the U.S. negotiations scheduled for November 1983 involved the establishment of the format for negotiations. This dialogue provided the first indication that Richard Pound would not be a "paper" chairman of the IOC Television Rights Negotiations Commission. Pound supported Calgary's desire to have identical, detailed draft television contracts signed by all bidders before negotiations opened. Implementing this, Pound and Calgary officials agreed, would give the networks a better understanding of what they were purchasing. Berlioux's dissent reflected her desire to force Calgary to the negotiation table before the end of December 1983. She was not opposed to the concept of a draft contract but did not want the negotiation process slowed.[13]

Barry Frank believed that the U.S. rights would increase in value after the Sarajevo Games, but Berlioux, Pound, and Samaranch were adamant that the talks should be staged before the Games began. They did not believe that the U.S. Winter Olympics team could replicate its glorious success in Lake Placid in 1980. Disappointment in the United States and lower ratings in Sarajevo, they agreed, translated into reduced offers from the

U.S. networks. Pound did not envision any impact on the offers, however, if the IOC received the bids in January 1984 as opposed to December 1983.[14] He permitted Calgary and Barry Frank to proceed with the development of a draft agreement.

Pound also desired to establish a procedure for negotiations involving a series of sealed bids submitted simultaneously to the IOC/Calgary negotiations committee. Again he overruled Berlioux when she countered that the bids should be presented in serial fashion following discussions with the individual networks. Pound replied bluntly that his thoughts on this matter, and those of Calgary, took into account input from ABC's rival networks indicating that leaks had occurred in past negotiation sessions. Berlioux said that sealed bids did not prevent leaks at the end of each round of bidding. Even though he agreed with this point, Pound stated that simultaneous bids removed the appearance of any advantage for the network that provided the final presentation.[15] When Pound and Calgary attempted to include a provision in the negotiations format that barred all private communication between network representatives and members of the IOC/Calgary negotiations committee once financial discussions had been initiated, Berlioux vehemently dissented.[16] Following a conference call between IOC officials and Calgary representatives on 9 January 1984, this provision was removed from the negotiations format.[17]

Jim Spence admitted that ABC had "privileged information" in the negotiations held in Lausanne. Did Monique Berlioux oppose provisions regarding confidentiality in order to permit her to play a role as ABC's source of inside intelligence? Spence blamed Barry Frank for the events in Lausanne, which were analogous to putting two proud fighting cocks (ABC and NBC) into a confined arena.[18] On 20 January 1984 the "big three" networks submitted four signed copies of identical contracts to Pound's Montréal office. Four days later, when financial terms were reached with one of the networks in Lausanne, the sum would be added to the contract submitted by the winning network.[19] According to Spence, the successive rounds of bidding yielded the following offers from the three U.S. networks:

> Round One
> > ABC $208 million
> > CBS $182 million
> > NBC $200 million
>
> Round Two
> > ABC $261 million
> > CBS $195 million
> > NBC $250 million

Round Three

ABC $280 million

CBS   ————

NBC $267.5 million

Round Four

ABC $300 million

CBS   ————

NBC $280.5 million

Round Five

ABC $300 million

CBS   ————

NBC $300 million.[20]

With the exception of the first round, the bidders submitted offers equal to or in excess of a minimum bid. Frank, stated Spence, misled ABC when he assured officials even as late as the morning of the negotiations that clearly outbidding its rivals provided a network with the opportunity to close a deal with the IOC/Calgary negotiators. Spence asserted that this promise should have been fulfilled after round three but most assuredly after round four. ABC, he charged, had clearly outbid NBC. He also resented the committee's decision to provide the continued appearance of CBS as a participant in the negotiations after it withdrew from the process following the second round.[21] But Spence's anger reached its peak when he described the method used to break the ABC/NBC deadlock—the flip of a coin.

IOC and Calgary officials informed the NBC and ABC delegations that the winner of a coin flip would determine whether to bid or defer to its rival, reserving the opportunity to better the tendered offer by a minimum of $1 million. Both NBC and ABC appealed for a final round of sealed bids. Pound's team refused. Though Spence was liberal in his criticism of Barry Frank, he reserved his most vitriolic comments for the IOC. "I could not believe that this august and historic body had turned the process into nothing short of a carnival," he recalled.[22] Arthur Watson, NBC's president of sports, offered to make the call; but when Pound flipped the coin, nerves got the better of Watson—he did not call the toss. Somewhat embarrassed, Watson pledged to make a call on a second toss of the coin. He called "heads." "Heads" it was. Watson elected to submit the first bid. ABC was smug; its preference had been to defer. NBC officials caucused for thirty minutes and returned with a bid of $304 million. Following a hurried phone call from Arledge to ABC's president, Fred Pierce, ABC countered with $309 million. NBC folded.[23]

Was the format for negotiations unfair? It is difficult to muster sympathy for U.S. network executives who at any time could have called it a day once the bidding exceeded the point where the network, based on its own projections, believed the risk was no longer acceptable. Personal and network reputations rise and fall on the basis of ownership of certain sports events, however. The Olympic Games are one such property. Pound, Frank, and Calgary officials understood this reality. These were playing a high-stakes game of poker. And in this case the dealer (IOC/Calgary) held all of the cards. The IOC and Calgary officials devised a procedure that left the negotiating team in complete control of the negotiations. Though CBS's Neal Pilson folded when the bidding soared past his limit of $257 million, Arthur Watson and Roone Arledge found the "pot" too tantalizing. Seven years earlier the U.S. networks had walked away from a similar bid process established by Ignati Novikov. It is interesting to speculate how Pound and Frank would have reacted if the networks had employed a similar approach in 1984.

Calgary leaders drew much less satisfaction from negotiations with EBU. Juan Antonio Samaranch and Marc Hodler closed a deal with EBU for $5.7 million. In an article entitled "European TV Receives 'Bargain' Deal from IOC," *Calgary Herald* writer Crosbie Cotton related OCO'88 chairman Frank King's severe disappointment with the contract. King's comments expressed in a public forum agitated Samaranch. "I am extremely annoyed by the contents of this article," he snapped in a letter to King, "particularly in view of your statements."[24] The windfall from the U.S. negotiations, however, tempered Calgary's disappointment with the EBU contract. It provided an attractive financial cushion.

Pound knew that the terms of the EBU deal would draw little favor in Calgary. Even he had severe misgivings. Due to the insistence of Samaranch, the IOC continued to provide the EBU with a privileged position in negotiations for West European television rights. While aware of expanding revenue possibilities due to the emergence of private commercial networks in Europe, Samaranch maintained that European viewers' access to Olympic coverage should not be compromised by selling the rights, admittedly for more money, to a series of individual networks. These networks could not guarantee blanket coverage of the European market. Samaranch's refusal to explore other avenues, thereby suppressing the value of West European television rights, concerned Pound. He understood the resentment of U.S. television executives who for years had engaged in spirited bidding wars for Olympic television rights.[25] Samaranch's "most favored status" for EBU smelled of politics.

In a report submitted to the Executive Board during the latter stages of Samaranch's negotiations with EBU, Pound wrote:

Members of the Executive Board should be aware that, in financial terms, the Organizing Committees and Olympic Movement would realize far more by selling the rights to one or two commercial networks in Italy and the U.K. than to EBU. There are, of course, other considerations than merely financial which we must take into account, but so long as EBU is convinced that we will not go elsewhere, it will make no serious effort to reduce the gap between its payment and the rights fees paid for U.S. television.[26]

During a meeting of the Executive Board in April 1986 Pound lamented EBU's willingness to pay more for American soap operas than for Olympic television rights.[27] Samaranch's decision to sign an "EBU-IOC Cooperation Agreement" that outlined means by which the two organizations might collaborate to promote the Olympic Movement in the future was another source of irritation for Pound.[28] Samaranch was unmoved. Following the signing of the EBU television contract in February 1987, he observed that the "signing of the television rights agreement between the IOC, OCO'88 and the EBU constituted another step forward in the friendly relationship between the Olympic Family and the EBU, a relationship already made concrete by the Co-operation Agreement entered into in 1986 between the IOC and EBU."[29] Still, Pound's campaign to improve television rights offers from EBU had begun.

ENTER THE USOC

The "USOC has apparently given indications to both OCO'88 and SLOOC [Seoul Olympic Games Organizing Committee] that it will insist on some compensation from both organizations in order to give its 'consent' for Olympic telecasts to occur in its territory using Olympic symbols, emblems, network composite logo and general 'Olympic' designations." Richard Pound's message landed with a resounding thud on Juan Antonio Samaranch's desk in late September 1985. The current and future implications of this USOC initiative, exclaimed Pound, were "extremely serious."[30] The USOC's grenade threatened revenue from the ABC/OCO'88/IOC contract signed the previous year and made Pound's job of closing a deal for U.S. television rights for the Seoul Olympic Games fraught with difficulties.

Seoul's U.S. lawyer, Don Petroni, studied the situation. The USOC's claim based on the Amateur Sports Act, he reported, was sound from a legal perspective.[31] Follow-up conversations between Pound, the USOC's president, Robert Helmick, and its lawyer, Richard Kline, were discouraging. Kline's pugnacious attitude concerned Pound. The USOC claimed that the use of the Olympic emblems in commercial advertising on U.S. telecasts compromised its domestic sponsorship program. The USOC did not challenge the IOC's right to sell U.S. television rights; nor did it take issue with the use of commercials by telecast sponsors that did not include Olympic emblems. The USOC's position focused squarely on what it perceived as potential endangerment of advertising revenues from the U.S. networks because the link with the Olympic rings was one of the primary reasons why sponsors paid a premium price for advertising time during Olympic telecasts. The possible shock waves at ABC Sports, which already faced losses in the neighborhood of $50–60 million, alarmed Pound. He was willing to seek an agreement with the USOC for the future but opposed any deal for the 1988 Winter and Summer Games.[32]

In Lausanne the IOC's director of legal affairs, Howard Stupp, provided Samaranch with a preliminary legal opinion on the USOC's claim. He confirmed Petroni's earlier belief that the USOC possessed legal grounds for the claim. He also believed, however, that the USOC could launch the claim on the basis of the *Olympic Charter* without having to rely on the Amateur Sports Act. The financial repercussions of the USOC's initiative, noted Stupp, were severe: "The claim being put forth by the USOC can . . . be raised by any other NOC with respect to Olympic telecasts in such NOC's territory." The pertinent clauses, he observed, had been added to the *Olympic Charter* in 1972. The timing of the USOC's action puzzled him. "Why is the USOC now making the claim?" asked Stupp. "Are they genuinely concerned with the well being of their marketing program and are they trying to protect what is rightfully theirs? Or, are they just being greedy?" Stupp understood the need to negotiate with the USOC, however. It was "neither realistic nor practical," he noted, to prevent telecast sponsors from using Olympic emblems in their commercial advertising. It was not "desirable" to rebuff the USOC either, he stated. Stupp shared Pound's opinion that the USOC's claim for a share of 1988 U.S. television revenue was exceedingly troubling. "In my opinion," wrote Stupp, "they are unjustified, morally and perhaps even from a legal point of view (despite the USASA), in asserting such right with respect to the telecast of the 1988 Olympic Games at this point in time."[33] The apparent hypocrisy of the USOC's claim, in his mind, sprang from its refusal to share a portion of the profit from the Los Angeles Games with the NOCs who participated in the 1984 festival.

Earlier in the year the USOC had resisted Samaranch's request for the distribution of $7 million to the NOCs to reimburse them for accommodation costs stemming from their participation in the Los Angeles Games. Some NOCs extended themselves financially to send additional athletes in order to compensate for the absence of competitors from the Eastern bloc countries that had chosen to boycott the Games. The USOC was under no obligation to accede to this request because Lord Killanin had signed an agreement with Los Angeles permitting profit from the Games to be retained in the United States. Accordingly 40% of the profit was dedicated to the promotion of amateur sport in southern California, 40% went to the USOC, and 20% was distributed to National Sport Governing Bodies by the USOC at its discretion (Group A members of the USOC). While Los Angeles favored reimbursing the NOCs, the USOC did not. Instead the USOC discussed the possibility of establishing a "Friendship Fund" that would assist athletes in other regions of the world by offsetting some of their training expenses in the United States.[34]

Samaranch delegated the responsibility of finding a solution to this conundrum to Richard Pound. Despite Pound's forthright expression of his feelings on matters where their opinions differed, such as EBU's privileged status, Samaranch appreciated his competence and enthusiasm for his work on television and corporate sponsorship matters. "I quite understand your concern," wrote Samaranch, "and my personal view is that we should try to reach an agreement with USOC before the respective postures become tougher. I believe you are the right person to propose a project of agreement for which I rely completely on you."[35] Pound's administrative juggling act continued as he dealt with the USOC file while he sought closure for the protracted, tedious, and extremely frustrating negotiations for the sale of U.S. television rights to the Seoul Olympic Games.

SEOUL

Juan Antonio Samaranch cleared his throat and approached the microphone. "Today we are reaching the end of a long and difficult path, with the signature of a contract which gives NBC Sports Inc. the exclusive rights to broadcast the Games of the XXIVth Olympiad in Seoul upon the territory of the United States of America," he told the assemblage of IOC representatives, NBC executives, and Seoul officials.[36] The date was 26 March 1986, nearly four years after the IOC Executive Board had encouraged the rapid signing of a U.S. television contract for the Seoul Games.

Samaranch's original timetable for U.S. negotiations was unrealistic. The protracted discussions resulted from (1) the networks' concern about the political instability of the Korean peninsula, (2) the 14-hour time zone difference between Seoul and New York and the refusal of the networks to negotiate before they received a complete event schedule that permitted live coverage of leading events in prime time, (3) the difference of opinion between the Koreans and U.S. television executives on the value of the rights, and (4) the fact that a policy of joint negotiation prevented the IOC from concluding an agreement without Seoul's consent. In the wake of negotiations for U.S. television rights to the Sarajevo Olympic Winter Games the IOC wrote the policy of joint negotiation into the host city contracts for the 1988 Calgary and Seoul Games. This experiment proved short-lived because the "long and difficult path" described by Samaranch in March 1986 led the IOC to exert sole authority over television negotiations as a means of reducing conflict with future Organizing Committees.[37]

In September 1983 Samaranch reached a draft agreement with Seoul president Tae Woo Roh on the method of distributing television money. Pound realized that Seoul faced difficult financial challenges, but the result of Samaranch's unilateral negotiations with Roh startled him. He believed that Samaranch, who was committed to nursing Seoul through the critical early years of planning, overplayed his hand. If the total proceeds were less than $500 million, Seoul would receive 20% of the money in the form of a technical services payment. If the sum exceeded $200 million but was less than $500 million, however, Seoul would receive a minimum of $125 million for technical services. Pound registered his concern about the formula with Samaranch. If the contracts totaled $200 million, the IOC would cede 62.5% of the money for technical services and would be entitled to only one-third of $75 million (the money to be shared with the NOCs and ISFs). The Seoul rights, he stated, required a sale price of $300 million for the IOC to receive the same amount it was due if the Calgary rights sold for $200 million.[38]

A progressive scale that allowed Seoul to claim an increased percentage for technical services if the total proceeds exceeded $500 million concerned Pound. For each extra $100 million, Seoul would receive an additional 5% claim for technical services on the total proceeds (e.g., SLOOC would receive 25% for technical services if the total proceeds were $500 million or more but less than $600 million). Pound was willing to consider using the progressive scale on the increase in revenue but not on the total proceeds. For instance, he could envision granting 25% "on the increase from dlrs 500–600 million and 30% on increase from dlrs 600–700, but not on whole total price."[39] Above all, the precedent of this agreement concerned Pound. Samaranch held firm but did accede to Pound's request to raise the threshold for the payment of $125 million for technical services from $200 million to $225 million. In effect this deal (assuming the proceeds did not exceed $500 million) replicated the arrangements made between the IOC and Los Angeles. The Executive Board duly approved the agreement at its November meeting.[40]

Even though Roh and Samaranch cleared a hurdle that had impaired relations between the IOC and Organizing Committees in the past, conflict between the IOC and Seoul concerning the U.S. television contract emerged four months later at the first meeting of IOC officials with SLOOC representatives and U.S. network executives. In early April 1984 IOC vice-president Ashwini Kumar and Monique Berlioux traveled to Seoul for a series of meetings with the U.S. network officials and SLOOC personnel. On this mission Kumar replaced Pound, who was detained in Montréal due to commitments with his law firm.[41] Kumar, Berlioux, and their Seoul partners listened to Neal Pilson (CBS), Arthur Watson (NBC), and Jim Spence (ABC) extol the virtues of their respective production teams. The "big three" networks also used these meetings to raise their concerns on several issues: (1) the recent bid process for the U.S. rights to Calgary's Olympic Games, (2) the need to include suitable insurance arrangements in the Seoul contract, and (3) the problems for U.S. networks imposed by a 14-hour time difference between Seoul and New York. Kumar and Berlioux agreed that the presentations provided by the CBS and NBC delegations were superior to that of ABC and promised to relay concerns about the prospective bid process to the Television Rights Negotiations Committee.[42]

Seoul's attitude concerning television negotiations displeased Kumar and Berlioux. Seoul, reported Kumar, showed little regard for the IOC's policy of joint negotiation. Barry Frank, SLOOC's adviser, had distributed a proposed schedule of events to the networks without the knowledge of the IOC and the ISFs. "SLOOC has kept us in the dark about these 'private' negotiations," stated Kumar. The schedule distributed by Seoul, he informed the networks, should be ignored because the IOC and the ISFs had not been consulted. Seoul argued that the agreement between Roh and Samaranch, subsequently approved by the Executive Board, failed to mention the IOC's role as a co-negotiator.[43]

Kumar and Berlioux, in firmly asserting the IOC's rights as a co-negotiator in accordance with the host city agreement signed in 1981, rebuffed Seoul's secretary-general Sang Ho Cho's desire to maintain exclusive control of financial discussions with the world's broadcasters. Cho's attempt to "usurp the chairmanship" of the first meeting with one of the U.S. networks (CBS) disturbed Kumar, who, along with Berlioux, "firmly and politely" made it clear that he had been delegated to chair the meetings on behalf of Richard Pound.[44] SLOOC also invited representatives of the U.S. cable industry to Seoul for separate discussions without the IOC's knowledge. Kumar and Berlioux stayed in Seoul for an extra day in order to represent the IOC at this meeting.[45] Despite the firm hand exhibited by the IOC representatives, Seoul would not abandon its attempt to manage television negotiations without the IOC, predicted Kumar. "If we are not careful," he warned Samaranch, "[Seoul] will gallop away with our primary and inherent rights, and therefore, we have to be very firm with them, and treat them as no more than a 6-year phenomenon, which the IOC creates for the generation of revenues."[46]

Kumar also sounded a cautionary note concerning the involvement of Barry Frank. "I would also like to state in the most positive terms," he wrote, "that in getting the maximum of revenue we should not be the butt end of any accusation that we twisted the networks' arms to a degree that may hurt our dignity, and become counter-productive in the future . . . A few more dollars extracted per the advice of the 'consultants' may appear to be an attractive proposition, but would in the end kill the goose that has so far laid the golden egg."[47]

Berlioux and Kumar submitted reports highlighting Seoul's efforts to circumvent the IOC's joint negotiation policy. They provided interesting reading for Richard Pound but did not offer any revelations. "I am not surprised to learn that SLOOC wishes, in effect, to exclude the IOC from television negotiations," he wrote Berlioux. "This has been apparent from the very beginning of discussions with them." Pound admitted that the networks' unease with the prospects for the Seoul Games in light of the two Koreas issue was problematic and might necessitate altering the negotiations process. The negotiations format would have to leave the IOC/Seoul team in control, however, "even if the networks are not happy."[48]

SAMARANCH AND THE SEOUL EVENT SCHEDULE

For multiple reasons the IOC and the U.S. networks agreed to conduct negotiations for the Seoul television rights after the Los Angeles Games were concluded. The ISFs' immediate agreement to Seoul's request to stage a significant number of events in the morning hours in Seoul in order to appease the U.S. networks' desire to maximize the number of hours of live prime time programming precluded the networks' receipt of a complete events schedule until June. Also, ABC's heavy commitment to Calgary severely compromised its ability to compete with its rivals; in the event that ABC did not win the Seoul rights, its commentators and production crew would be demoralized mere days before trying to mount coverage of the Los Angeles Games.[49] A post–Los Angeles timetable satisfied NBC and CBS because they appreciated having a reasonable amount of time to study the event schedule before establishing their bidding strategies. When Kumar, Berlioux, U.S. network executives, and Seoul officials parted company, however, nobody envisioned a time lapse of seventeen months before the IOC/Seoul team received bids from the U.S. networks.

The sticking point for the IOC/Seoul team and the U.S. television networks was the networks' demand for a complete event schedule before offering bids for U.S. television rights. While Roone Arledge did not lobby aggressively for an event schedule customized for American television, CBS and NBC awaited a schedule that would afford them an opportunity to provide extensive live coverage of major events in prime time.[50] In this regard Seoul and TWI's Barry Frank targeted gymnastics, swimming, and track and field events for special attention. Pound conceded later that the ISFs "were not slow to recognize the bargaining power which the situation afforded."[51] IAAF president Primo Nebiolo stalled any agreement on altering the traditional pattern of staging finals in track and field in the afternoon and evening hours. International Amateur Aquatics Federation (FINA) officials agreed to shift diving finals to the morning hours but resisted staging preliminary swimming heats in the evening and finals on the following morning.[52] An appeal from Michael O'Hara (a former Los Angeles official employed by TWI) to Robert Helmick, president of the FINA, provides an indication of TWI's approach:

> May I reiterate the import to the U.S. television rights sales for Seoul '88 of the opportunity to present swimming finals to U.S. sports fans during prime time. It will also be the finest chance to secure new swimming participants, as occurred during the '84 Olympics. We recognize that this calls for the early determination and announcement of the flip flop of preliminary and final competitions but feel that the cause is sufficiently just to make this happen.[53]

Meanwhile the International Gymnastics Federation (FIG) protested moving events to the morning because it would force athletes to rise in the early morning hours to ensure proper preparation and warm-ups for competition.[54] Samaranch pushed the federations on this issue because of the potential loss of income if the schedule was not geared to U.S. television.

During a meeting of the Executive Board during the Los Angeles Olympics Samaranch indicated that a favorable schedule for U.S. television offered the prospect of a contract for $400 million. If the IOC failed to convince the federations to dispense with the traditional approach to staging finals in the afternoon and evening hours, the value of the contract might plummet to $200 million. It was imperative for the IOC to obtain the cooperation of the federations in drafting a schedule tailored to the needs of the U.S. networks.[55] Samaranch's pragmatism was impaled between an understanding that U.S. television executives paid heavily for television rights and the need to maximize revenue from the U.S. market for Seoul and the NOCs, ISFs, and IOC.[56]

Samaranch adopted a far different public posture. He was reluctant to give the impression in the public arena that the IOC was willing to bow to the demands of U.S. television executives. In October and November 1984 he made a number of public pronouncements of the IOC's intent to finalize a schedule in keeping with the wishes of the ISFs. Kenneth Reich, dispatched by the *Los Angeles Times* to cover a media symposium in Lausanne co-sponsored by the IOC and EBU, informed his reading audience back home in the United States that Samaranch's remarks during the final session indicated that "American television's push to change the time of key Olympic finals at the 1988 Seoul Games to morning hours [would] be turned aside." Reich also reported that "even if this decision costs the Seoul organizing committee and the IOC $300 million to $400 million in reduced American rights payments, the finals will still be at the traditional times preferred by the sports federations, mainly in the afternoon and evenings."[57] In updating members of the IOC concerning his efforts to effect changes in the Seoul event schedule Samaranch downplayed his role.[58] His approach reflected his appreciation of the sensitivity of some members to the thought that the U.S. television networks possessed the power to influence the event schedule. Pound understood Samaranch's dissembling, but Barry Frank was frantic because Samaranch's comments cast a pall over the negotiation environment in the United States.

Samaranch's attitude concerning the event schedule alarmed Frank, who feared that his efforts to cull maximum revenue from the U.S. market on behalf of Seoul were being compromised. "President Samaranch's statements regarding his unwillingness to change event times in Seoul are having a very negative effect on U.S. networks," Frank informed Pound. The afterglow of ABC's solid ratings in Los Angeles, which led him to view the American market for Seoul with optimism, had been snuffed out. He appealed for Samaranch's neutrality on the scheduling issue in light of the effect that his comments had on nervous U.S. executives.[59]

Pound pledged to contact Samaranch but assured Frank that Samaranch was working toward a solution beneficial to Seoul and the IOC. "Do not confuse what [Samaranch] says with what he does," he cautioned. Pound told Frank that Samaranch had a two-pronged strategy. He wished to protect the IOC from media criticism and avoid open conflict with the ISFs:

It would be foolish of him to say he is trying to browbeat the federations and also counter-productive. Privately, he is working very hard for our mutual objective. It does no good to anyone to rub in the fact that the U.S. networks are strong enough to influence the scheduling of events. It is far better to pursue one-on-one discussions, come up with a schedule and negotiate quietly on the basis of the schedule than to pursue everything through the press. Ideally we want happy federations who will have responded to SLOOC's needs, not the idea of an artificial schedule imposed by IOC or U.S. networks.

"Let's not over-react at a critical time," counseled Pound.[60] His response appeased Frank, who confessed that his panic resulted from not having been privy to Samaranch's strategy.[61]

Even though Samaranch supported the plan to increase the schedule's appeal to the U.S. networks, he was less optimistic that the ISFs would consent to the changes in November than he had been earlier in the year.[62] Samaranch's parallel plan aimed at ensuring a favorable schedule had failed.

At the IOC's session in New Delhi in 1983 Samaranch proposed to the Executive Board that ex-officio member status be offered to Mario Vázquez Raña, president of the Association of the National Olympic Committees (ANOC) and a key contributor to his campaign for the IOC presidency, and Primo Nebiolo, president of the Association of Summer Olympic International Federations (ASOIF).[63] Nebiolo was determined to expand the IAAF's World Championships into an event rivaling the Olympic Games in stature. Samaranch believed that IOC membership might bridle Nebiolo's ambition. The proposal met with opposition at the Executive Board level, but Samaranch persisted. He maintained that the IOC's need for good relations with members of the Olympic Tripartite prevailed over the qualms of some IOC members who believed Nebiolo and Raña had designs on the presidency of the IOC in the future. Samaranch, sensing that the session opposed the rule change, did not risk putting the proposal to a vote.[64]

David Miller, Samaranch's biographer, is incorrect in stating that the IOC president backed away from his proposal in Sarajevo in February 1984 when he sensed that some IOC members had great difficulty with Nebiolo and Raña's personalities. It is true that the efforts of Executive Board members to "sound out" IOC members revealed opposition to Samaranch's proposal, due mainly to the individuals involved rather than the concept itself of granting ex-officio status to the presidents of ASOIF and ANOC.[65] Discussions continued at the Executive Board level during the

Los Angeles Olympics, however, and by this time Samaranch believed that Nebiolo's appointment could be used as an effective lever to obtain concessions from the federations concerning Seoul's event schedule.

In order to support this conclusion, it is necessary to examine in detail discussions concerning Nebiolo and Raña during the Executive Board meeting in Los Angeles. Under the agenda item "Rule 12—Ex-Officio Members," the following nonverbatim comments are attributed to Samaranch:

> With regard to television contracts, negotiations were in hand for Seoul. At the Winter Games in Sarajevo, ABC had obtained very low viewer ratings owing to the time difference; the public had known results before seeing the events on television. In respect of Seoul, the three major American networks were not interested in final negotiations until they knew the exact events timetable for the main sports, again owing to the problem of the time difference. Finals would have to be held in the morning, in order to be broadcast direct at peak viewing time in the United States. If this was achieved, the contract could amount to US$ 400/500 million, otherwise the figure was likely to be in the region of US$ 200 million. The most important IFs, like athletics, were reacting, emphasizing the tradition of holding finals in the afternoon and evening, athletes' conditions etc., and therefore it was essential to reach a mutual agreement and maintain good relations with the IAAF President [Nebiolo].

The Executive Board sounded out IOC members to ascertain whether the session would accept the proposal. Samaranch was anxious to avoid another rejection of the rule in the session.[66]

The prospect of a quid pro quo is implied. When Berlioux suggested putting forward a motion that would permit the IOC to elect ex-officio members without naming Nebiolo and Raña (or the positions of president of ASOIF and ANOC), however, Samaranch's response left little doubt about his thoughts: "This is not a bad idea, but the same problem will arise when actually electing the ASOIF and ANOC Presidents . . . Following the failure of the Sarajevo broadcasts, the Seoul contract negotiations are vital. The major sports [ISFs] like athletics, swimming, football, gymnastics, boxing, and basketball have to be convinced on the events timetable," he concluded.[67]

Romania's Alexandru Siperco, a member of the Executive Board, suggested a crafty means of opening the door for Nebiolo and Raña. If the session passed a rule that enabled the IOC to grant ex-officio status to certain nominees, then a by-law proposal could follow that mentioned the ASOIF and ANOC presidents in particular. A rule change required a two-thirds majority vote, but a by-law could be added with a simple majority, observed Siperco.[68]

Pound dissented. He was cool to the original proposal but willing to support Samaranch. He did not approve of the move to pull an end run on the session, however. This transparent scheme would disappoint IOC members, concluded Pound. He believed that the proposal needed to be directed to the session in its original form. Pound also understood the improved value of the U.S. television contract if the ISFs permitted Seoul to schedule major events in the morning hours; but "the proposed rule change," he said, "should not be advocated simply to boost the Seoul negotiations."[69] When the Executive Board revisited the issue before the close of the Los Angeles Olympics, Pound, Belgium's Prince Alexandre de Merode, and the Ivory Coast's Louis Guirandou-N'Diaye doubted the session's support for the proposal.[70] Samaranch did not risk a second defeat. He shelved his plan until the early 1990s, at which time he set the political tone necessary for the appointment of Nebiolo and Raña as full members of the IOC.[71]

U.S. TELEVISION RIGHTS NEGOTIATIONS: ROUND 1

IOC, Seoul, and U.S. network officials convened in Lausanne in September 1985 for financial negotiations. Seoul's inability to provide the networks with a complete schedule until a year after the close of the Los Angeles Olympics delayed the talks. The size of the gap between the Koreans' expectations and the anticipated bids from the networks threatened to derail the discussions.[72] Barry Frank boasted of the possibility of obtaining $700 million for U.S. television rights.[73] The Koreans knew that tradition dictated that the OCOGs peddled the Summer Games television rights for over two times the contract price obtained for Winter television rights.[74]

Pound cautioned Seoul deputy secretary-general Sei Young Park, however, that the U.S. networks had been quite vocal about their refusal to consider the sale price envisioned by Korean organizers.[75] Despite Pound's attempt to temper Seoul's expectations, Young Ho Lee, Korea's minister of sport and chair of the SLOOC Executive Committee, boldly stated before traveling to Lausanne that Seoul would "take a very hard line with the TV networks—$600 million and not less."[76] When IOC and Seoul representatives met prior to opening discussions with the networks in Lausanne, Samaranch "emphasised the need for the IOC and SLOOC to be united in their position, and for the negotiations to be concluded as postponement would result in a reduced rights fee." Lee replied that Seoul concurred with Samaranch's view but reserved the right to "re-consider its position if the offers were substantially lower than anticipated."[77]

Marathon negotiations the following day, complete with "enough lobby intrigue to fill a Sydney Greenstreet movie," wrote William Taaffe of *Sports Illustrated,* left the Koreans "stunned and demoralized." "The days of astronomical bidding wars and open checkbooks are apparently over," Taaffe concluded.[78] The collective antipathy of the networks toward the sealed bid process employed by the IOC/Calgary negotiating team led Pound and his negotiating partners to settle on a set of ninety-minute meetings with the networks concerning contract issues. Each network submitted a bid, but Seoul and IOC officials did not discuss the financial offers until the completion of the three conferences. At this point the IOC/Seoul team was free to pursue negotiations with one or two of the networks or to adjourn the negotiations.[79] NBC provided the best offer— $325 million.[80]

Throughout the protracted negotiations network executives such as ABC's Georges Croses (vice-president of European affairs) and NBC's Alex Gilady (vice-president of European planning and development) maintained a vigilant watch for signs that one of the rival networks was closing in on a deal. Croses and Gilady monitored the movements of network executives, keeping a close watch on "doors, elevators and house phones."[81] Contrary to past negotiation sessions, however, there was little activity to monitor.

Seoul officials rejected the offers provided by the U.S. networks. Young Ho Lee, the highest-ranking Seoul official in attendance, absented himself from all discussions. Lee's Seoul colleagues present at the meetings refused to take responsibility for concluding an agreement because the bids were so far below expectations. Pound grew frustrated with the Koreans, none of whom had "power to negotiate." Seoul's bargaining representatives in Lausanne declined to pursue negotiations further without guidance from SLOOC leaders in Seoul. Nobody wished to accept the blame for signing an agreement with one of the networks under the disappointing financial terms offered.[82] Pound had requested Roh's presence in Lausanne because he anticipated this type of impasse; however, Roh's domestic duties in Korea prevented his attendance.[83] "At one point," reported Taaffe, "[Pound] took the SLOOC members aside for a lengthy private lecture. It was the Olympic equivalent of being taken to the woodshed."[84] His arguments concerning the depressed economics of sport television in the United States, low ratings, and reduced advertising rates failed to move the Koreans. If discussions did not yield an agreement in Lausanne the Koreans and the IOC would lose money, Pound explained.[85] Even though Samaranch interceded with Roh in order to expedite an agreement, the Seoul representatives in Lausanne had already called it a day, insisting on a second round of bidding in New York in October.[86]

Following Pound's return to Montréal, ABC, NBC, and CBS forwarded their "revised" offers. Roone Arledge stuck with ABC's original offer of $225 million plus a revenue-sharing agreement with respect to the sale of cable rights. CBS offered $300 million, but concerns about political instability in the region translated into an end-loaded offer whereby $246 million of this sum was payable after the closing ceremony. Only $13.5 million was to be transferred at the time of a signed agreement. NBC, which was willing to include a revenue-sharing agreement on its gross advertising sales, offered $300 million and was willing to make a payment of $50 million when the contract was consummated.[87] Pound informed Sei Young Park that the offers were "regrettably, self-explanatory." Seoul's intransigence proved costly. Pound urged Seoul to work toward finalizing an agreement.[88]

Pound recommended to Samaranch that the IOC negotiate with NBC at the earliest possible time. He doubted the prospect for a turnaround in the U.S. television market. An early agreement offered the IOC the opportunity to deflect some of the media criticism resulting from the failed negotiations in Lausanne. "If negotiations can be handled quickly and concluded," cabled Pound, "IOC can emerge in good position, as responsible and reasonable organization faced with unrealistic partner, but essential that situation not be allowed to drag on any further."[89]

U.S. TELEVISION RIGHTS NEGOTIATIONS: ROUND 2

When the five parties renewed discussions in early October the U.S. networks avoided a bidding war. Barry Frank, frantically attempting to improve the guaranteed sum payable to IOC/Seoul, pushed ABC and CBS officials to reenter the fray. His effort failed. Neal Pilson feared the future implications of the type of profit-sharing agreement offered by NBC. ABC president Fred Pierce vetoed any move to improve his network's bid because of an earlier pledge to ABC's new ownership group, Capital Cities Communications, to limit ABC's best offer to $225 million. NBC provided Seoul the only means to trumpet the figure $500 million in the press because the contract value could reach this point if NBC's gross advertising sales reached $900 million.[90] Un Yong Kim, Seoul's lead negotiator, Pound, and Arthur Watson shook hands on the financial terms of the agreement, leaving some of the fine points for future discussion.

During the ensuing six months Pound managed parallel negotiations with Seoul/NBC and the USOC. Signing a final contract with NBC and Seoul before the resolution of the USOC's claim was folly. Indeed, the immediate and long-term impact of the USOC claim required intricate negotiation. The USOC demanded 20% of the gross value of both the Calgary and Seoul contracts plus 20% of all future U.S. television contracts signed.[91] The deteriorating relationship between NBC and Seoul, however, posed a far larger short-term problem.

NBC's demand that Seoul would have to provide insurance for NBC's rights fee, production costs, and capital equipment stalled progress. Un Yong Kim canceled the signing of the contract scheduled for early December. This act elicited a swift response from Pound, who charged that the Koreans had reneged on the agreement reached in New York. Seoul's action promised a renewed wave of media criticism, he warned. Leaks emanating from Seoul had already resulted in preliminary reports in the press. If Seoul did not proceed with the signing, observed Pound, the media would interpret SLOOC's conduct as a vote of nonconfidence. Kim pledged to try to reach a mutually acceptable accord with NBC on the issue.[92]

Seoul's foot dragging angered Samaranch. In long and oftentimes laborious discussions with Eastern bloc nations and North Korea, he had supported Seoul and its hopes for a successful festival. In his book *Five Rings over Korea* Richard Pound provided an insider's view of Samaranch's diplomatic efforts to ward off a boycott of the Seoul Games. Samaranch asked Tae Woo Roh to intercede with Seoul negotiators whose action threatened to torpedo the agreement reached in New York. The insurance clause, he observed, was a fundamental prerequisite for NBC's involvement in financial negotiations. Stated Samaranch:

> I am greatly concerned with the negative effect of SLOOC's disclosure of the negotiation difficulties and with the failure to execute the NBC agreement. Such disclosures will strongly affect the prestige of the Seoul Games and also jeopardize the great efforts undertaken within the Republic of Korea. These Games are of course important to the IOC, but they are even more important to your country, and I urge you to make every effort to ensure that public confidence around the world is maintained.[93]

Media reports emanating from Korea reflected a consistently negative view of the IOC, lamented Samaranch. "It is difficult for me to continue to express confidence in the Seoul Games under these circumstances."[94] Roh, whose domestic political agenda forced him to adopt an arm's-length management approach, nevertheless replied swiftly to the president to "reaffirm our mutual trust and friendship we have built together."[95]

CLOSING THE DEAL: 26 MARCH 1986

In the waning months of negotiations NBC replaced Seoul as Pound's primary source of irritation concerning U.S. television rights. NBC threatened to renege on a previous agreement to pay interest on the initial $50 million payment from 4 November 1985 on. The network, cognizant of its negotiating leverage, presented Pound and Seoul with a draft contract filled with clauses prejudicial to Seoul's interests that had not been subject to discussion in previous meetings. NBC's experience with the Moscow Olympics translated into an aggressive approach with respect to cancellation and insurance clauses.[96] On numerous occasions NBC's actions led to the suspension of discussion. As he flew from Montréal to Switzerland in March, Pound harbored doubts about whether a deal would be signed in Lausanne. Seoul, by contrast, became more compliant after it realized that the NBC offer was the best available. Pound was satisfied that Un Yong Kim and Seoul's lawyer, Don Petroni, had made an honest effort to conclude an agreement.[97] They were faced with a difficult task in light of the domestic disappointment resulting from the initial round of negotiations.

The three parties (IOC/Seoul/NBC) closed the deal on 26 March 1986 after months of acrimony. The Broadcast Marketing Agreement (BMA) signed on the same day possessed greater historical significance. Samaranch delegated the responsibility of concluding an accord between the USOC and the IOC to a three-person commission composed of Pound, U.S. IOC member Julian Roosevelt, and senior Canadian IOC member Jim Worrall. They resolved, subject to the approval of the Executive Board, that the USOC would grant permission to ABC (Calgary), NBC (Seoul), and their telecast sponsors to use the Olympic rings for promotional purposes in exchange for $15 million (the cost to be shared equally among the IOC, Seoul, and Calgary). The second part of the agreement involved ceding 10% of the gross value of future U.S. television contracts to the USOC.[98] Pound believed the agreement to be a far better settlement than the passage of a proposed tax bill circulating on Capitol Hill that would keep 10% of the U.S. television money in the United States. Even though the proposed legislation would result in funneling the money to the USOC, it would be the government that controlled the revenue source as opposed to the USOC itself. Pound posed the thought that a government tax might escalate in time. Samaranch accepted Pound's logic. He encouraged Executive Board members to "sell" the agreement to their IOC colleagues. The Executive Board duly approved the BMA.[99]

EBU AND JAPAN POOL TELEVISION NEGOTIATIONS

The U.S. negotiations did not preclude discussions between IOC/SLOOC and other members of the international broadcast community, but the squabble between Seoul and NBC delayed the consummation of any television agreements. Even though Seoul was stymied by its inability to employ the dollar value of the U.S. contract as a lever to reap massive increases in other regions, Un Yong Kim believed he had one more card to play. Seoul turned its attention to the Japanese market. Kim exploited the Korean/Japanese relationship as a means of establishing a financial precedent for dealing with the other networks, including EBU. Samaranch had ceded the lead role in negotiations with Japanese television executives to Seoul in 1985 in exchange for retaining IOC control of negotiations with EBU.[100]

Kim met with Japanese television executives in September 1986 and pressed them to consider that their nation's Gross National Product was one-third that of the United States. The Olympic Games possessed a special importance for the Japanese people, lobbied Kim, and Japanese television networks would be able to reduce their production and travel costs because of the proximity of Seoul to Japan.[101] Kim wanted to improve the fee paid by Japanese television for the Los Angeles Olympics ($19 million).

Even though Kim and Japanese officials did not discuss financial terms, he remained optimistic that a $40–50 million fee was possible. The Japanese protested that negotiations were occurring in the absence of IOC representatives, in particular Pound. The status of Seoul's negotiations with EBU remained a mystery to the Japanese, which raised a second area of concern. Knowledge of the financial terms of EBU's contract would enhance their ability to resist Kim's demands. Understanding the mindset of the Japanese negotiators, Kim asked the IOC to delay concluding a deal with EBU until the Japanese television rights had been finalized.[102]

EBU negotiations had been percolating for some months. When the IOC Executive Board convened in February 1986, Samaranch confirmed holding two meetings with EBU executives.[103] By April Samaranch had reached a tentative agreement with EBU for $28 million.[104] Barry Frank continued to work behind the scenes, however, to improve the amount of money from the European market. Meanwhile Pound cultivated contacts with the community of EBU rivals in order to pressure EBU to improve its offer. It was precisely at this time that Pound was offered $1 million in exchange for his influence in effecting a change in IOC negotiations policy whereby EBU's stranglehold on European television rights would be loosened.[105] Offended by this approach, Pound spurned the offer. News of this bribe attempt did not become a public issue until January 1999 during the early stages of the Salt Lake City scandal when Pound himself recalled the event to three startled Canadian newspaper reporters while being interviewed before a speaking engagement in Kitchener, Ontario.[106] While some questioned why he had not raised this issue when it occurred, Pound recalled that he had informed Samaranch. Neither Samaranch nor Pound considered it a matter requiring public airing. Others wondered if Pound had invented the scenario for the purpose of self-aggrandizement. Pound replied that he had raised the issue simply to demonstrate that temptation is something often faced by IOC members. A handwritten "Note to File" dated 22 July 1986, located in Pound's personal files by the authors in late November 1998, discusses the bribe offer.[107] Though neither individuals nor organizations were named, the note proves that Pound did not "create history" in his aside to the press. When asked by the reporters in Kitchener if anyone had ever attempted to bribe him in the past, he provided an off-the-cuff, frank response.

As a result of his European wanderings Barry Frank drafted a proposal for investigating the value of the European television rights on the open market. He advocated a sealed bid process for Calgary and Seoul television rights in each European country. This approach forced EBU member networks to bid against private television networks. If the sum total of these bids exceeded EBU's offer, then the individual bids would be accepted and negotiations would follow in those countries where no bid had been forthcoming. It was a variation on Marvin Josephson's plan to eliminate the negotiating advantage enjoyed by EBU devised during negotiations for European television rights to the 1976 Montréal Olympics. Even though Frank believed that the private networks would be perturbed if the IOC gave EBU the final right to match the sum of the individual bids, such a scenario remained a possibility.[108] Pound understood that Samaranch would not accept this arrangement, but he did think that further discussions with representatives of Reteitalia, the chief sponsor of a major consortium of private European television networks controlled by Italian magnate Silvio Berlusconi, "might stir the pot" enough to improve EBU's offer.[109] Nothing tangible resulted from these discussions. Despite the efforts of Frank and Pound, EBU acquired the rights for its 32-country territory for $28 million when the three parties signed the contract on 18 March 1987.[110]

Seoul stalled progress toward a final contract with EBU until the financial terms of the Japanese contract were finalized. The Japanese offered

$40 million, but Kim asked for $60 million. To Samaranch the Japanese expressed their dissatisfaction with Seoul's approach and Kim's limited understanding of the Japanese market. In a meeting in Lausanne on 15 January 1987 representatives of the consortium of Japanese networks told Samaranch that the Koreans' demands reflected an effort to "[mix] the Olympic Games with politics."[111] The Japanese also believed that they had been "especially targeted" because Seoul dealt with them without IOC representatives present at the negotiations. The Seoul event schedule, complained Samaranch's visitors, favored the U.S. television network. Samaranch replied that Seoul's duties included conducting the Japanese negotiations. He hesitated to intervene. With respect to the event schedule Samaranch dissembled when he noted that the "IOC merely approved the times that had already been agreed upon between SLOOC and the respective International Sport Federations."[112] The Japanese retreated from Lausanne to renew discussions with Seoul. In April 1987 these negotiations resulted in the signing of a contract for $52 million, with $2 million of that sum reserved for technical services.[113] Seoul celebrated, one of the few occasions it had cause to do so with respect to television rights and South Korea's Olympic Games.

THE HAZARDS OF JOINT NEGOTIATION

The always awkward, sometimes rancorous scenarios underscoring the conflict between the IOC's interests and those of the OCOGs demanded change. The U.S. television negotiations for the rights to the Seoul Olympic Games triggered the IOC's decision to claim sole authority over future negotiations. Even though Pound knew that U.S. offers in the aftermath of the Lausanne negotiation session would be less attractive, a unilateral deal with one of the U.S. networks proved elusive. Pound and Samaranch understood the prospect for conflict between the IOC and OCOGs, which wanted to extract the last possible dollar from the U.S. market. The IOC, however, needed to maintain a relationship with U.S. television executives in order to secure the Olympic Movement's long-term financial interests. Other episodes confirmed the difficulties inherent in a policy of joint negotiation.

The lion's share of Pound's time with respect to the sale of Seoul television rights was spent dealing with the U.S. negotiations and the USOC problem. He also invested a significant effort, however, to conclude a favorable agreement with an Australian network. When Kim reached a tentative pact with Channel 10 for $7.4 million, Pound registered his displeasure to Samaranch that he had been shut out of the final discussions.[114] He believed a better offer had been forthcoming from one of Channel 10's rivals and that Kim's premature action had squandered the opportunity for a better contract. Seoul also signed an agreement with Hong Kong's ATV (Asia Television Ltd.) network for $900,000, prompting rapid legal action from ATV's primary rival, TVB (Television Broadcast Ltd.). TVB officials cited a prior verbal agreement with ATV that Hong Kong rights would be shared.[115] Hong Kong's High Court heard TVB's argument, ruling in favor of ATV. TVB won the case on appeal, however.[116] The IOC resolved the dispute one month before the opening of the Seoul Games when it designated ATV and TVB as joint rights holders.[117] These difficulties resulted from Samaranch's decision to cede authority in the Asian territory to Seoul in exchange for IOC control over negotiations in Europe.

REFLECTIONS

The 1980s marked a significant break from the past concerning the IOC's management of and approach to revenue generation. Samaranch established Richard Pound as chair of the Television Rights Negotiations Committee, a position of immense influence. Pound's task involved not only dealing with representatives of Organizing Committees and television networks but also the thorny issue of the USOC's claim for a share of U.S. television revenue. As Pound's star rose, Monique Berlioux's fell. Samaranch delegated primary responsibility for television negotiations to Pound partly as a means of diminishing Berlioux's power base. Berlioux's conflict with Samaranch and some members of the Executive Board who believed that she assumed too much power in Lausanne led to her formal resignation in 1985.

In the 1980s the IOC searched for a means of diminishing conflict with OCOGs concerning television negotiations. Brundage's policy of ceding authority over negotiations to the Organizing Committees gave way to joint negotiation in the 1970s as a means of reducing conflict between the IOC and OCOGs. The IOC's experiences with Sarajevo and Seoul, however, proved that joint negotiation did not offer a solution. In 1985 the IOC moved to avert future problems by claiming complete authority over television negotiations for the 1992 Summer and Winter Olympics.

The 1990s brought further change and conflict concerning television negotiations. The IOC negotiated long-term television agreements with networks in different regions of the world. Pound, Samaranch, and members of the Executive Board believed that long-term deals provided the

Olympic Movement with a measure of financial security while assisting future leaders of Organizing Committees to establish their budgets. Meanwhile the USOC's financial aspirations provided a vexing issue for Pound. He sparred repeatedly with U.S. Olympic officials who demanded changes in the terms of the BMA.

CHAPTER 10

THE IOC'S NEW CORPORATE FACE

The Rise of Meridian Management

In the late 1980s and early 1990s the IOC and its partner, ISL, collaborated successfully as TOP generated impressive revenue for successive Organizing Committees in Barcelona, Albertville, Lillehammer, and Atlanta. The IOC/ISL relation ended in 1996, however, because of the USOC's growing dissatisfaction with the competence of ISL's executives in dealing with major U.S. companies and the IOC's own reservations concerning ISL's operational efficiency due to a string of personnel changes. The IOC established a new company called Meridian Management (assuming stockholder status). Meridian Management's task, as had been the case with ISL, was to lead the IOC's efforts in the generation of corporate sponsorship dollars. With the emergence of Meridian Management the IOC took a further step in its transformation to a corporate entity. This chapter focuses on this transitional phase in the history of the IOC's involvement with corporate sponsorship.

THE CALM BEFORE THE STORM:
CORPORATE SPONSORSHIP IN THE 1990S

Olympic marketing grew beyond all expectations during the 1980s. The initiatives of the IOC and of the New Sources of Finance Commission ensured the development of an orderly marketplace with the creation of specific programs targeted to meet the interests of all the Modern Olympic Movement's partners. TOP-II generated $175 million for the Olympic Movement and established itself as the premier sports sponsorship program in the world. The program diversified the IOC's revenue base and provided technical and promotional support the IOC had long sought.[1]

In April 1991 the Executive Board noted that the changes in the Winter Games cycle necessitated the development and planning of the TOP-III program at a much earlier stage in the quadrennium than was the case with its predecessors. Ideally, according to Richard Pound, ISL needed to begin presentations to the TOP sponsors before the end of the year.[2] Recent changes in the management of ISL, however, and concerns over the stability of the firm resulting from the resignation of Klaus Hempel and Jürgen Lenz hampered the program's progress. In an effort to stabilize the situation the IOC held a number of meetings with Christoph Malms, ISL's new president, to discuss future collaboration between the IOC and ISL. On the basis of these meetings ISL and IOC Marketing Department officials developed a structure for TOP-III.[3]

In order to increase the overall value of TOP a number of recommendations were submitted to the Executive Board for review. Among them was a suggestion to reduce the number of sponsors from twelve to a maximum of ten companies with a proposed payment range of $25–40 million each. Such a move offered the prospect of an estimated $355 million for the 1993–96 quadrennial. To justify the suggested increase in TOP fees the recommendations included an enhancement of the overall sponsor rights package, increased hospitality opportunities, and the implementation of special centennial activities for sponsors surrounding the Games of the Twenty-sixth Olympiad in Atlanta. The IOC sought an increase in its revenue share of the program from 6.5% to 10%.[4] Finally, it was suggested that the ISFs be invited to participate in TOP, with the option for sponsors to acquire a special IOC/ISF extension package.[5]

As discussion concerning the implementation of TOP-III progressed, Juan Antonio Samaranch continued to establish personal contact with senior executives of current and prospective sponsors. In April 1991 he visited five of the TOP sponsors' headquarters. The visits fostered a closer relationship between the IOC and its partners, leading, it was argued, to the prospect of greater financial support for the Olympic Movement and better understanding of the "ideas and goals of the Olympics."[6] The IOC's Executive Board and the New Sources of Finance Commission deemed such efforts on the part of the president necessary, especially with regard to those corporations based in the United States. Preservation of the American corporate sponsorship market was paramount.

At the IOC Executive Board meeting in Seville in May 1992 Richard Pound reported that during the Olympic Winter Games in Albertville Coca-Cola had become the first sponsor to sign a TOP-III Agreement.[7] He expected to sign an additional four agreements before the Olympic Games in Barcelona, generating a "total of $200 million in revenue." This figure exceeded the proceeds from the entire TOP-II.[8] Pound also recommended "that participation in TOP be made mandatory for all newly-recognized NOCs," thereby greatly facilitating the administration of the program.[9]

ISL informed the IOC that it expected to complete all TOP agreements by the end of 1992.[10] Difficulties with various sponsor contracts and poor economic conditions in the United States, Europe, and Japan, however, forced ISL to defer its completion date to the end of March 1993.[11]

In September 1993 ISL presented a detailed report to the IOC Executive Board on the sales and NOC participation in TOP-III. Despite depressed economic conditions, seven companies signed agreements for TOP, generating approximately $250 million. But all was not completely rosy. A sponsor representative warned ISL that the Modern Olympic Movement risked "killing the goose that laid the golden egg" by dint of its excessive financial demands, "particularly those of certain NOCs."[12] In an attempt to address this concern the IOC established a Sponsor Advisory Group. Its primary responsibilities included providing existing sponsors with insight into future marketing policy and listening to their concerns in an effort to avoid a recurrence of problems.[13] The group held its first meeting in New York on 26 April 1993.[14] According to Michael Payne, the gathering was "a long but therapeutic meeting, enabling the sponsors to air their grievances."[15]

With TOP-III more than half completed, the Executive Board recommended that the IOC consider the development of "a successor program for the 1997–2000 quadrennial." In analyzing the future direction of the IOC's International Sponsorship Program the Executive Board focused on a number of issues. It considered whether or not the "major NOCs really wanted a TOP program."[16] Given the numerous benefits derived by the Modern Olympic Movement, Pound found such questions "unsettling."[17] The Association of the European National Olympic Committees (AENOC), he noted, had voted unanimously to demand that the IOC continue the program.[18] Also, AENOC recommended that the IOC amend the *Olympic Charter*, making participation in the IOC's International Sponsorship Program compulsory for all NOCs.[19]

The IOC also initiated preliminary discussions with ISL on prospects for the future of TOP and the resources that would accrue to the program in light of senior management changes at the agency. ISL had taken the important step of opening an office in Lausanne to facilitate overall Olympic coordination. Paramount to these discussions were the recommendations received from the Sponsor Advisory Group's meeting in New York, which included a desire to implement TOP-IV (or its successor) at the earliest possible opportunity.[20] At the conclusion of TOP-III total revenues generated had increased by approximately 360% over TOP-I and 200% over TOP-II. In terms of total revenue, excluding International Business Machines (IBM), TOP-III generated $299 million.[21] With IBM included, this amount eventually increased to $359 million. Various members of the Olympic Movement were the happy beneficiaries.[22]

TOP-IV AND THE FUTURE OF THE PROGRAM

When the Games of the Twenty-fifth Olympiad closed on 9 August 1992, the attention of the Modern Olympic Movement turned to the celebration of the 1994 Olympic Winter Games. The IOC awarded host city rights to the Norwegian town of Lillehammer.[23] These would be the first Winter Games celebrated according to the IOC's new schedule. In 1986 the IOC amended its procedures, stipulating that beginning in 1994 the Olympic Winter Games would be held during the second calendar year following the year in which an Olympiad begins.[24]

Before its selection as the site of the 1994 Olympic Winter Games, Lillehammer's residents numbered 21,000. Within four years, however, the Norwegian organizers had transformed the small town into a "first-rate Olympic site."[25] They refitted existing sports facilities, built new ones where necessary, and developed the required infrastructure to stage a modern Olympic Winter Games. The Organizing Committee also implemented an elaborate program of sponsorship and licenses.[26] Of course, officials also cultivated the traditional sources of revenue from the sale of television rights, tickets, coins, and philatelic items.

The Lillehammer licensing program, in particular, resulted in three times the revenue forecast and set new standards of organization and quality for future OCOGs to emulate.[27] The strength of the licensing operation resulted from a concerted effort "to capture the culture of Norway beyond the cliché image of Vikings" and "express this concept in visual terms."[28] According to Ase Kleveland, minister of culture, the Games were seen as "a unique opportunity to profile Norway."[29] More than one thousand companies approached Lillehammer in hopes of winning the right to manufacture licensed products for the 1994 Olympic Winter Games. The most salable items of official merchandise included pins, T-shirts, knitwear (sweaters, hats), key rings, table settings in porcelain and crystal, "Ludvig" backpacks (a kind of Norwegian backpack), postcards, ties, and mascots.[30] In all Lillehammer generated in excess of $520 million from all revenue sources, breaking almost every major marketing record for an Olympic Winter Games.[31]

AMBUSH MARKETING:
SUPPORTING THE EXCLUSIVE RIGHTS OF THE IOC'S SPONSORS

A typical TOP Agreement involves a sponsor purchasing the exclusive worldwide Olympic marketing rights and opportunities within its designated product or service category and promoting its support to draw further public attention to its involvement. The practice whereby another company, often a competitor, intrudes upon public attention surrounding the event, thereby deflecting attention toward itself and away from the official sponsor, is known as "ambush marketing." This term was initially created to describe the activities of companies that sought to associate their goods and services with an event, such as the Olympic Games, without paying for the privilege.[32] The term was first used in connection with the highly competitive promotional programs surrounding the Games of the Twenty-third Olympiad in Los Angeles in 1984.[33]

The issue of ambush marketing escalated during the 1992 Olympic Winter Games in Albertville, France, where a surge of "attacks by American Express on VISA's exclusive Olympic rights" took place.[34] American Express's advertising campaign, in the IOC's opinion, deceived the public into believing that it was an Olympic sponsor. Such activity threatened to undermine the value of Olympic sponsorship, thereby endangering the prospective revenue base for the entire Olympic Movement.[35] During preparations for the Games of the Twenty-fifth Olympiad in Barcelona in 1992 the IOC mustered an "ambush marketing patrol" composed of representatives from the IOC, ISL, USOC, and Barcelona OCOG. The IOC alerted official sponsors to report any instances of ambush marketing in Barcelona.[36]

Prior to the Olympic Winter Games in Lillehammer the IOC's Commission for New Sources of Financing warned that an increasing number of companies opted to present themselves as Olympic sponsors without any support for the Modern Olympic Movement, thus undermining the exclusive rights of a bona-fide sponsor by running parallel marketing programs.[37] The desire of marketing communicators to open new and cost-efficient lines of access to the millions of spectators watching the Olympic Games manifested itself in a shift of emphasis from traditional "above-the-line" advertising to an array of practices categorized as "below-the-line."[38] It is within the latter milieu that ambush marketing finds both its classification and its justification.

By implementing a sponsorship program as part of its marketing communications mix a TOP sponsor desires to gain the benefits of the public attention generated by the Olympic Games. TOP can also benefit its sponsors by transferring certain image connotations inherent in the Modern Olympic Movement to the company or brand. One such example of image transfer occurred during the 1988 Olympic Games in Seoul. Maximizing its official status as a TOP-I sponsor, Kodak developed a highly effective campaign utilizing the "Go for the Gold" theme.

The question of whether ambush marketing is an unethical or imaginative practice is widely debated within the sponsorship industry. Arguments for or against ambush marketing vary widely depending on whether one adopts a narrow or broad view of the practice itself. One thing remains certain, however: the growth of Olympic sponsorship expenditure worldwide has been accompanied by a parallel growth in the practice of ambush marketing. The promotional opportunities available within the Olympic Movement and the possibility of low-cost association by highly creative ambushers make it clear that ambush marketing activities will continue well into the new millennium. The IOC and its constituents risk losing continuing sponsorship unless the exclusive rights of international marketing partners are protected.

TOP-IV: THE EROSION OF THE IOC/ISL RELATIONSHIP

Although there seemed to be considerable interest within the Sponsor Advisory Group in continuing with TOP, the IOC Marketing Department in a confidential report to the Executive Board in December 1994 warned those involved that they "should not under-estimate the size of the challenge in continuing, let alone achieving growth, of the TOP program beyond its current levels."[39] The challenge, according to Richard Pound, was not only to maintain the current level of economic support but also to obtain a commitment from each TOP sponsor for TOP-IV in 1995. Nagano required this timetable in order to navigate the months of preparation for the 1998 Olympic Winter Games. Delays only offered problems, noted Pound. The biggest hurdle, however, remained the question of NOC participation in the program, even though ISL secured the participation of all NOCs in TOP-III.[40] The problems of international promotional and advertising strategies as well as multiterritory packaging and promotional campaigns compromised a sponsor's Olympic involvement if some NOCs opted out of TOP.[41] In preparing for TOP-IV many sponsors "informed the IOC that they were only willing to continue with Olympic sponsorship provided that the IOC could guarantee the participation of all NOCs."[42] It was hoped that the necessary commitment by all NOCs to TOP would be secured through the efforts of the Association of National Olympic Committees (ANOC).[43]

In view of the critical importance of TOP in the overall financing and promotion of the Modern Olympic Movement the IOC, on the basis of the recommendation of the Commission for New Sources of Financing, resolved that all NOCs be required to participate in the program. This critical resolution followed a period of consultation with ANOC, AENOC, commercially active NOCs, and continental NOC associations. In announcing its resolution to ANOC the IOC indicated that all NOCs would be notified of the "international product categories" reserved in TOP by 31 December 1996. Only those NOCs that "can prove severe disadvantage and prejudice, and that their release from a given category would not prejudice the overall interest of all the other members of the Olympic Movement," stated IOC officials, were exempt from participation.[44] Responding to the IOC's resolution, ANOC voted its support, thereby committing all NOCs to take part in TOP-IV and at the same time removing the biggest challenge facing the successful continuation of the IOC's International Sponsorship Program.[45]

The continuation of TOP also presented an opportunity to reassess the existing relationship between ISL and the Modern Olympic Movement. Richard Pound offered some thoughts to ISL's Christoph Malms on IOC/ISL relations and the future of TOP.[46] The continued deterioration of the ISL/USOC relationship and the lack of action on the part of ISL to repair the damages concerned the IOC. According to Pound, the USOC did not respect ISL, continually complaining about the agency's inability to deal with U.S. business leaders at the appropriate levels. He also noted a strong vibration emanating from the USOC "that only an American organization can deal with U.S. companies." Although the IOC wanted "to make every effort to continue the relationship," the involvement of ISL in TOP-IV depended on reaching a "mutually agreeable agreement to carry on forward."[47]

While discussions continued between the IOC and ISL, the IOC Marketing Department received commitments for TOP-IV from existing sponsors. Within the existing TOP-III sponsor group IBM committed through the year 2000 by virtue of its long-term contract with the IOC. Two other TOP sponsors also indicated a commitment to continue participation. Kodak signed a TOP-III agreement on 18 October 1994. By then negotiations with Coca-Cola had entered the advanced stages. The remaining TOP sponsors also declared an interest in continuing their participation in the program.[48] Given the lack of definitive progress on the part of ISL, however, the IOC doubted ISL's ability to deliver anything of significance.[49]

As the IOC's dissatisfaction with ISL's level of service grew, it explored means of changing the nature of the IOC/ISL relationship. At a meeting of the IOC's Marketing Liaison Committee for TOP-IV held in December 1995 Pound announced that in his opinion ISL should not be associated with the TOP initiative in the future. It was not a good time to be "changing horses," he stated, but ISL left the IOC no choice.[50] Following the resignation of Klaus Hempel and Jürgen Lenz, the quality of ISL's management team assigned to TOP had deteriorated. Since the departure of the agency's former managing director, Andrew Craig, "almost all staff in the ISL Olympic Department had quit or had been fired," and Craig's replacement had been unsatisfactory.[51] Pound informed the members that another key ISL staff member, Laurent Scharapan, had tendered his resignation and would be leaving the organization at the end of 1995. Scharapan's liaison role with the NOCs was critical to the existence of TOP.[52] Further support for Pound's thinking came from the Sponsor Advisory Group. In November 1995 the sponsors registered their dissatisfaction with the leadership and service provided by ISL, suggesting that the agency's Olympic Department was "suffering from an obvious leadership void." In the face of vast resources applied to membership and maintenance in TOP by sponsor companies, a strong feeling persisted that the return on investment to them was "extremely low."[53] According to Pound, this feedback prompted the IOC to face the inevitable. "The TOP Program would have to get along without its creator, ISL."[54]

Following discussions with Christoph Malms and Jean-Marie Weber, chairman of the Board of ISL, the IOC agreed to let the agency embark on gaining contracts for TOP-IV. But ISL would be paid only for contracts signed before 30 June 1996. Further, their sponsor service obligations would cease altogether by September 1996. If the IOC was not satisfied with the level of sponsor service during that period, it would supplement such service at ISL's expense.[55]

In an effort to minimize the damage to ISL's public image Pound recommended that "an exit scenario" be devised for the agency.[56] ISL was engaged in bidding for renewal of its FIFA contract. If the IOC jettisoned ISL, the agency's existing reputation and future business opportunities might be seriously damaged. It was agreed that a formula be put in place whereby ISL would recommend that the IOC assume responsibility for NOC coordination for TOP. The IOC's close relationship with the NOCs, enabling it to facilitate this aspect of the program, offered a satisfactory explanation for ISL's clients. In addition, it would be suggested that the need for a closer relationship between the sponsors and the IOC left the IOC itself best suited to manage sponsor service.

For the public record ISL would receive credit for the suggested changes. ISL would make a public statement identifying TOP as one of the finest sports marketing programs in the world and recommending that the IOC deal directly with the NOCs and sponsors. The IOC would then respond with its own public statement that it accepted ISL's recommendation.[57] Referring to ISL's understanding of the changes, Pound noted that only Weber truly comprehended the situation and the resulting possible impact on both organizations, while "Malms did not seem to grasp the seriousness of the situation." Developments were on a "fast track," added Pound, and required rapid resolution with or without ISL's acceptance of the IOC's conditions.[58] Given the accelerated deadline, Pound approached Scharapan and requested that he continue the NOC liaison role, even though Weber did not like the idea of direct cooperation between the IOC and Scharapan. The IOC hoped to reach an agreement to improve the financial efficiency of the IOC-agent relationship.[59]

In an effort to ease the transition John Moore, marketing director, Sydney Olympic Games Organizing Committee (SOCOG), offered his support. John Krimsky, the USOC's deputy secretary-general, informed the IOC Marketing Department that "the USOC was committed to taking up any slack" resulting from ISL's removal. He also indicated that "the USOC was prepared to play an expanded role in this field," should that be required.[60]

With respect to ISL's remuneration for contracts signed before 30 June 1996, it was proposed that ISL receive a fee of $500,000 per sponsor contract signed.[61] Pound noted that the proposed fee "would save money" for all parties involved with TOP and that it was still a reasonable level of remuneration. If ISL were to try to bargain, he warned, the fee would be reduced by $25,000, to $475,000 for each contract. The longer the delay continued, the greater the reduction in the fee.[62]

The IOC took its actions "more in regret than in anger," observed Pound. In his opinion the link provided by TOP to the Modern Olympic Movement "should have been a wonderful opportunity for an agency to be present at the highest levels of international business." "In the most objective view," Pound argued that TOP "had got to where it was because of the value of the 'property' and not because of the agency involved."[63]

One aspect of the ISL relationship "that had been working particularly well," according to Michael Payne, had been the cooperation with Dentsu, Inc. Dentsu, affiliated with TOP since its inception and the world's largest advertising company in terms of both gross income and billings, fulfilled a valuable liaison role with the OCOGs and facilitated a good relationship with Olympic sponsors located in Japan.[64] "To ensure continuity in Japan," the IOC Marketing Department determined that the "Dentsu team would be part of whatever direction was taken in the future."[65]

Following notification of the IOC's position, Weber expressed his agency's concerns to Pound regarding the IOC's "hurry to conclude the matter when so many points need to be discussed in the interest of the IOC, the sponsors, and the TOP-IV marketing program."[66] Having reviewed Weber's correspondence, Pound believed that Weber was "under orders to drag things out."[67] Unwilling to allow considerations of this nature to stand in the way of a speedy resolution, Pound expressed his disappointment in Weber's position. He further noted that if ISL did not "meet the deadlines" established by the IOC, it would "bear the risks which flow from failure to do so."[68] Reacting to Pound's letter, Brigitte Baenkler-Dassler wrote Samaranch on 21 December 1995 requesting his assistance:

> We hereby appeal to you to reciproke [*sic*] some of the support and assistance to ISL, which you and the IOC have always enjoyed from our family and its businesses in the many decades of our trustful relationship which we have had with the aim to jointly develop the Olympic movement and its ideals. To repeat myself: we do not ask for any change in direction of whatever decision the IOC deems appropriate—but we cordially ask you to proceed and implement these changes in a spirit, time frame and with a business arrangement for ISL which shields the company from [the] high losses the Group is now facing.[69]

According to Baenkler-Dassler, the IOC's representatives (Pound and Payne) "appear not to appreciate" that "ISL and its shareholders will incur substantial losses, both financially and in terms of reputation and goodwill."[70] Although the IOC made some accommodations, the die was cast. The IOC/ISL relationship was doomed.

On 5 January 1996, employing the "exit scenario" previously devised for ISL's departure, Pound distributed a letter to all NOCs informing them of the changes in the management of TOP.[71] He also told the members of the IOC's Commission of New Sources of Financing that "ISL will focus exclusively on the sales and negotiations for TOP-IV, with the objective of closing all negotiations before the Centennial Games."[72] Following extended discussions between the IOC and ISL and a telephone conversation between Payne and Weber on 12 September 1996, the two sides reached a final settlement on 13 September 1996.[73]

BECOMING A STOCKHOLDER: THE IOC ESTABLISHES ITS OWN MARKETING FIRM

The erosion and eventual rupture of the IOC/ISL relationship removed the existing barriers concerning the ongoing discussions with Scharapan. The IOC commenced formal discussions with Scharapan and Christopher Welton, senior vice-president of the Atlanta Olympic Games

Organizing Committee (ACOG), to evaluate the possibility of establishing a new organization to manage TOP.[74] These discussions resulted in the formation of Meridian Management SA (MM) in March 1996.[75] The IOC provided funding for the establishment and initial operations of the new agency. It also commanded a powerful share position in the company, holding 25% of the equity value and 50% of the voting power. Scharapan and Welton were allotted the balance of the equity and voting shares.[76]

The IOC assumed a shareholding position to safeguard its needs regarding TOP as well as "to ensure that the NOCs were comfortable with the new management of the program." Another consideration was to eliminate the possibility of other organizations "staking a claim" in MM.[77] MM reported "directly to the IOC Marketing Director." Its focus was the enhancement of the service support to both the sponsors and the NOCs.[78] The initial mandate of MM and of Scharapan and Welton was to concentrate their efforts solely on TOP and certain other Olympic-related assignments directed by the IOC. It is expected that in the future MM will expand its activities in the sports marketing field. But, given the IOC's

TOP PROGRAM HISTORY: SPONSORSHIP FEE AVERAGES
(All Amounts Shown in Millions—U.S. Funds)

	Total Revenue ($)			Percentage Increase (%)			Cumulative Increase (%)		
	Dollars	VIK[1]	Total	Dollars	VIK[1]	Total	Dollars	VIK[1]	Total
TOP-I	10.44	0.21	10.65	-	-	-	-	-	-
TOP-II	12.66	1.70	14.36	21.3%	709.5%	34.8%	21.3%	709.5%	34.8%
TOP-III	22.72	10.65	33.37	79.5%	526.5%	132.4%	117.6%	4971.4%	213.3%
TOP-IV	29.52	10.77	40.29	29.9%	1.1%	20.7%	182.8%	5028.6%	278.3%
TOP-V[2]	37.70	12.09	49.79	27.7%	12.3%	23.6%	261.1%	5657.1%	367.5%

1. VIK = Value-in-kind (contributions that are provided in the form of products and service).
2. Based on Preliminary Estimates for TOP-V.

TOTAL REVENUE

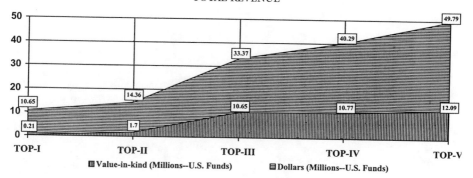

■ Value-in-kind (Millions--U.S. Funds)   ▤ Dollars (Millions--U.S. Funds)

position in MM, it will "always be the 'Number-One' client of Welton and Scharapan, and receive the particular attention that comes with such positioning."[79]

Assisted by ISL, MM and the IOC finalized all agreements for participation in TOP-IV.[80] The program involved the participation of eleven Worldwide Olympic Partners and generated approximately $500 million by the end of the quadrennium (31 December 2000). Each NOC participating in the 2000 Sydney Games received "a minimum of $40,000, and $400 per athlete" from the revenues generated by TOP-IV. Those NOCs in "larger developed markets" had received "several million dollars each" by the conclusion of the quadrennium.[81]

The TOP-V marketing program, encompassing the Salt Lake City Olympic Winter Games and the Athens Olympic Games, is already well under-way. The proposed TOP-V sponsorship fee of $55 million is expected to "yield a 22% increase from the base amount charged during TOP-IV."[82] The IOC also considered the "possibility of signing long-term contracts with TOP sponsors," similar to those signed with television networks.[83] As of January 2001 nine Worldwide Olympic Partners had renewed their sponsorships. The British conglomerate SEMA Group joined TOP in 2001 as Systems Integration, Operations Management, and Applications Delivery Partner.[84] With the addition of this British firm the IOC has taken another step toward the implementation of a truly worldwide sponsorship program, which in the future may be less dependent on U.S. financial sources.[85]

CHAPTER 11

TURF WAR

The USOC, IOC, and
Olympic Television in the 1990s

As the value of television rights soared in the 1980s and 1990s, the conflict management skills of Richard Pound and Juan Antonio Samaranch were sorely tested. The IOC sought to protect its financial interests and maintain what it considered a fair and equitable means of distributing television money to its constituents, OCOGs, ISFs, and NOCs. Its decision to abandon joint negotiation in favor of assuming absolute control of television negotiations beginning with the 1992 Albertville and Barcelona Games altered the tenor of discussions with OCOGs. Conflict was reduced but not eliminated. A second initiative, the negotiation of long-term television contracts by the IOC through 2008, also reduced the friction between the parties regarding television revenue.

The 1990s also ushered in a shift in the primary locus of conflict concerning the distribution of television money to the ongoing power struggle involving the IOC and the USOC. The USOC employed a two-pronged approach in its attempt to enhance its authority in the negotiation arena and add to its already substantial wealth. In the aftermath of the signing of the Broadcast Marketing Agreement (1986) that ceded to the USOC a 10% share of U.S. television contracts beginning with the 1992 cycle the USOC sought to increase its percentage share for future Games. Parallel to this lobbying with the IOC, the USOC spawned surreptitious efforts in Congress to establish new rules for the negotiation of U.S. television contracts. The goal for the USOC was congressional approval to conduct Olympic television negotiations in the United States. If the USOC secured the right to control negotiations with U.S. networks, it could structure the contracts and subsequent revenue sharing to its financial benefit at the expense of the IOC and other constituents of the Olympic Movement.

In the 1990s escalating friction between Pound—who acted as the

IOC's point-person in negotiations with the USOC—and its negotiating officials—Harvey Schiller, John Krimsky, and Dick Schultz—can be attributed in part to a clash of egos. Representatives of the two most powerful organizations in the Olympic Movement carried out discussions that centered on the distribution of millions of dollars, each harboring a burning desire to protect their turf—and in the USOC's case expand its turf. Alarmed at the extent to which U.S. television money bankrolled the development of non-American Olympic athletes and by the IOC's unwillingness to extract fair market value from major non-U.S. television markets such as Europe and Japan, Schiller, Krimsky, and Schultz argued that the USOC was entitled to 20% of the U.S. television revenue.

Pound was amenable to discussion concerning the USOC's share but was unyielding in his assertion of the IOC's right to negotiate directly with the U.S. networks. He invoked legal claim to the IOC's intellectual property rights, which included the authority to grant television rights in the United States and all other territories. Pound resented the USOC's efforts to diminish the IOC's authority.

Even though Pound fiercely defended the IOC's rights, he understood that his organization bore some responsibility for the creation of the USOC's bellicose attitude. As a U.S. television network sports property the Olympics possess a unique value. The IOC squeezed the "big three" U.S. networks for maximum revenue by capitalizing on their competitiveness. The Sherman Anti-Trust Act precluded a collaborative bid, which would have permitted the networks to collude in setting a price. Samaranch and Marc Hodler, however, who retained an iron grip on European negotiations, refused to press EBU to pay sums even remotely close to the figures paid by U.S. networks on a per household basis. From the halls of power at Château de Vidy in Switzerland they repeatedly stated that EBU was the only broadcast entity in Europe capable of delivering blanket coverage in the region. Although EBU's status as a government-sponsored network made the negotiating environment in Europe much different, the emergence of private European networks provided Pound with a lever to push forward his agenda in the 1990s. As a means of undercutting the USOC's argument for changes in the distribution of U.S. television money, appeasing disgruntled U.S. network officials, and mollifying agitated OCOG leaders who considered Samaranch's approach prejudicial to their financial bottom lines, Pound sought to increase European television revenue.

An examination of Pound's role in three interrelated developments concerning television revenue in the 1990s demonstrates how the IOC/EBU and IOC/USOC dilemmas were finally resolved. First, as a means of addressing the European problem that aroused USOC officials, Pound worked diligently at the IOC Executive Board level to change the IOC's approach to European television negotiations. During deliberations of the board he constantly badgered Samaranch and Hodler with the threats posed by U.S. congressional action. The emergence of viable competitors to EBU weakened their stonewalling and aided Pound in his mission. Evolving market realities and storm clouds in Washington forced Hodler and Samaranch to consider rival bids. Leveraging a $300 million bid from UFA (a German network) for European television rights for the 1996 Atlanta Olympics, the IOC pried a $250 million contract from EBU.[1] This set a new benchmark in European negotiations and represented a substantial increase on the $94.5 million combined sum for television rights and technical services fees received from separate agreements with EBU (Western Europe), TVE (Televisión Española, Spain), and OIRT (Eastern Europe) for the 1992 Barcelona Olympics.[2] Even though EBU retained favored status with Samaranch, the threat of doing business elsewhere had a noticeable impact on European television revenue in the post-Atlanta era. Second, Pound played a pivotal role in negotiations with the USOC concerning changes in the distribution formula for U.S. money. This drawn-out process resulted in a shift in the USOC's share of the U.S. television contract from 10% to 12.75% beginning with the 2004 Athens Olympics. Third, Pound and NBC's Dick Ebersol devised the "Sunset Project," a negotiations process culminating in the signing of a U.S. television contract for the 2004, 2006, and 2008 Olympic festivals with NBC.

The Sunset Project served four purposes. First, it prompted similar contracts in other regions, resulting in improved relations between the IOC and television networks possessing a longer-term commitment to the Olympic Movement. Second, advancing the time line for the negotiation of television deals permitted the IOC to provide financial data to prospective OCOGs. These data have been important tools for those who bear the responsibility of constructing budget plans. Cities that competed for (and won) the 2004 Olympics (Athens), 2006 Olympic Winter Games (Turin), and 2008 Games (Beijing) factored this information into their bids. Third, these deals provided financial security for the IOC and the Olympic Movement in the medium term. Finally, Pound's decision (approved by Samaranch and the Executive Board in 1995) to conclude negotiations with NBC for the U.S. television rights to the 2004, 2006, and 2008 festivals prior to a resolution of the debate concerning the USOC's share proved astute. Because the USOC had agreed in 1986 that its share of U.S. television contracts for 1992 and beyond would remain at 10%, Pound's Sunset Project initiatives greatly improved his negotiating position with the USOC.

THE EUROPEAN SCENE

Shortly after Winter Olympians left Calgary in February 1988 negotiations for U.S. television rights for the 1992 Albertville Olympic Winter Games intensified. Within four months Pound concluded a $243 million deal with CBS that marked the network's return to Olympic broadcasting for the first time since 1960.[3] This sum represented a significant decrease from the $309 million contract that Pound and the Calgary organizers had reached with Roone Arledge and his colleagues at ABC four years earlier. But Albertville officials understood the realities of the sport television property marketplace in the late 1980s.[4] ABC withdrew from negotiations, and NBC was more interested in pursuing the rights to the Barcelona Olympics, leaving CBS little competition.[5] The IOC subsequently turned its attention to extracting a much improved contract from the European rights holder. In April 1988 Hodler informed his fellow IOC Executive Board members of informal discussions concerning European rights and Albertville's demands for "higher rights payments than were traditionally made from the EBU."[6] Albertville's consultant, TransWorld International's (TWI) Barry Frank, advised a delay in negotiations for thirty months in order to capitalize on an improving European market.[7]

Meanwhile EBU understood that the price of delayed negotiations might be steep. EBU negotiators presented to Samaranch and Hodler the idea of a multi-Games agreement for the Albertville and Lillehammer Winter Games. Pound, recognizing that EBU wanted to suppress the value of the European rights, counseled Samaranch and Hodler that such an agreement would compromise future U.S. negotiations and stall any benefits to the Olympic Movement from the rapidly evolving competitive market in Europe. Samaranch was not wedded to EBU's proposal, but he was intent on eliminating consultative roles in the negotiations played by OCOG officials. Hodler concurred with Samaranch. UFA's $75 million bid for European television rights compromised their ability to sign a contract with EBU. Not surprisingly, Albertville officials had not scrambled to find a pen when EBU presented its last offer of $11 million. Samaranch expressed his concern about the interference of OCOG officials who sought maximum revenue, ignored EBU's proven record, and discounted the IOC's need to maintain a positive relationship with the television networks for the future.[8]

Pound grew weary of Samaranch and Hodler's defense of EBU's resource situation due to its status as a government-funded agency and the difference in the acceptability of commercial advertising in the U.S. and European markets. He reiterated his position that EBU had consistently been awarded "sweetheart deals." The $18 million deal for the Albertville

Games granted to EBU by Samaranch and Hodler did not impress Pound. EBU seemed to have enough money for American television programming, but the cupboard always seemed bare when EBU got around to Olympic television negotiations. "The amount EBU paid to cover the Games [was] derisory in comparison with large amounts made available for events comparatively less important," Pound argued.[9] He also championed the right of future OCOGs to be involved in television negotiations, albeit in a consultative role. Their presence, he suggested, forced IOC negotiators to seek the best possible agreements.[10] Pound believed that it made little sense to banish OCOGs—as the entities assuming the financial risk to host the Games—from the negotiations process.[11] Damaged relations between the IOC and the OCOGs might result from a decision to exclude OCOGs from the process. OCOGs expended significant energies in providing the technical infrastructure for the broadcasters. In the event that they did not perform this task well, in part because they were not involved in the process of negotiating the shared responsibilities of the OCOG and the broadcaster, future negotiations with the networks would be affected.[12] Pound's view proved to be the minority opinion, and the Executive Board approved the change in future host city contracts.

The IOC's decision to stage Winter Games and Summer Games on a two-year cycle beginning with the Lillehammer festival in 1994 prompted a flurry of negotiations in 1989. EBU acquired the West European rights to the 1992 Barcelona Olympics for $66 million plus an additional payment of $9 million in technical services fees. Though the $75 million package paled in comparison to the $401 million NBC shelled out for U.S. television rights, it represented an increase on EBU's $28 million contract for the 1988 Seoul Games. Meanwhile CBS, in an attempt to carve out a reputation as America's Winter Olympic network by building on the prospect of its Albertville coverage, agreed to a $300 million contract for the Lillehammer Games. EBU obtained the West European rights for Lillehammer for $24 million, a marginal increase on its Albertville contract. The limited return on European television rights did not go unnoticed in Washington, D.C., Colorado Springs, and Montréal.

THE McMILLEN BILL:
THE OLYMPIC TELEVISION BROADCAST ACT

While the world's attention was riveted on President George Bush's showdown with Saddam Hussein in the Persian Gulf in January 1991, Pound flew to Washington to discuss the Olympic Television Broadcast Act with its sponsor, Tom McMillen, a Democratic member of the House of

Representatives from Maryland. McMillen, a former National Basketball Association player, had been a member of the 1972 Olympic team that lost the gold medal match to the Soviet Union in one of the most controversial events in Olympic basketball history. The bill, which was introduced in October 1990, had three major thrusts. First, the legislation, if passed, granted the right to negotiate U.S. television contracts to the USOC, thereby empowering it to determine its share of Olympic television revenue from the U.S. territory. Second, the networks would receive an exemption from the Sherman Anti-Trust Act, permitting them to form a consortium. Third, the consortium would be prevented from interrupting live coverage with commercials.[13]

All three components of the bill concerned Pound. The USOC had approached the IOC in 1989 and 1990 seeking an increase in its percentage share of future U.S. television contracts.[14] The McMillen bill opened the door for the USOC to establish this percentage independent of discussion with the IOC. Contrary to the USOC's assertion that it had no involvement in the legislative initiative, the USOC envisioned the McMillen bill as a means of squeezing the IOC in relation to ongoing IOC/USOC negotiations concerning an increase in its share of television revenue. McMillen confirmed that USOC officials had been involved in crafting elements of the bill. The antitrust exemption threatened the overall amount of revenue available from the United States. Unfettered by any serious competitors, a consortium of the "big three" networks could control the bid process. The IOC's and USOC's inability to grasp the harm certain to accrue to each of them from such an eventuality puzzled Pound greatly.[15] Limitations on commercial advertising would most certainly reduce the networks' offer because of a drastic reduction in potential advertising revenue.[16]

McMillen's motivation was threefold. U.S. consumers shouldered excessive financial shares of several global initiatives, he stated, including "the current exercise in the Persian Gulf and other institutions such as NATO."[17] A reduction in Olympic advertising costs would have a trickle-down effect on U.S. citizens, who would no longer pay the premium added to the cost of products sold by Olympic advertisers. The transfer of control of negotiations to the USOC was designed to provide greater financial assistance to the USOC. A number of U.S. television executives, who were concerned about spiraling rights fees, suggested the antitrust exemption.

Pound characterized his discussion with McMillen as "cordial" and "worthwhile." He informed McMillen of the IOC's financial concessions made to the USOC. He also bought some time to deal with the situation. The proposed legislation might tarnish Salt Lake City's chance in the 1998

Olympic Winter Games bid process, he reflected to McMillen: Salt Lake City might feel the backlash in the final vote in June from IOC members who were cognizant of the USOC's unique television revenue-sharing agreement. Inaction, Pound told Samaranch after his meeting with McMillen, was anathema. "My main concern," wrote Pound, "is that it would take very little, at this moment, for any process which may involve Congress, to acquire a life of its own and become completely unmanageable." The involvement of the U.S. networks and the USOC in the process reflected the balance sheet concerning global Olympic television revenue. "If the networks are really involved in this, then our problem will be exacerbated and until we can show that other parts of the world are approaching U.S. levels on a per capita or other appropriate measure, we can expect little sympathy from within the U.S. If, however, we can at least demonstrate significant progress in this direction, things may improve," he concluded.[18]

At the IOC Executive Board meeting in June Samaranch quizzed Robert Helmick on the status of the U.S. television market. Offering his opinion on McMillen's initiative, Helmick alluded to the unrest in the United States concerning amounts paid by U.S. networks compared to networks in other regions. Recent data, he noted, indicated that when the populations of the U.S. and European markets were compared "revenues from the USA relating to the Summer Games were about four and a half times greater per household and for the Winter Games they were approximately ten times greater." Helmick called for the IOC and USOC to work together to find a solution.[19] He criticized a suggestion from Pound that the IOC consider hiring a professional lobbyist to safeguard the organization's interests in Washington.[20] It was important that the two organizations collaborate, Helmick emphasized. As for the U.S. television market, he expected satisfactory revenue for Atlanta.[21] Pound's concerns abated somewhat. Perhaps, he mused, the USOC finally understood the potential impact of the antitrust exemption and limitations on commercial advertising.

At a meeting of the IOC Executive Board in September 1991 Pound sensed that little had really changed in Hodler's and Samaranch's approach in negotiations for European television rights for the 1996 Atlanta Olympics. Samaranch valued the IOC's long-term relationship with EBU and dismissed the idea of abandoning "EBU for private companies which would not cover the Games properly."[22] Hodler desired more revenue from Europe but emphasized the importance of "full coverage." Pound scolded his colleagues by highlighting the "disproportionate" amount of money paid by the U.S. networks compared to EBU and Japanese networks. The newly competitive European market could not be ignored, he insisted.

"The worlds of television and business have changed, everything has changed, except for the IOC, which is still selling TV rights as in the 1960s," he stated, at the same time raising the specter of U.S. government legislation if the EBU inequity was not addressed.[23] The combination of Pound's call for change, the hovering ramifications of the McMillen bill, and the whopping $300 million offer from UFA pushed Samaranch and Hodler's hand, forcing EBU to structure a meaningful offer ($250 million).[24] The McMillen bill disappeared from Washington's legislative agenda later in 1991.

ATLANTA, NAGANO, AND THE U.S. AND JAPANESE TELEVISION MARKETS

In September 1990 the IOC awarded the right to host the 1996 Centennial Olympic Games to Atlanta, Georgia. The Atlanta Olympic Games Organizing Committee (ACOG) and its president, Billy Payne, convinced IOC members that a major city in the United States could stage an Olympic festival without public sector support. Although Payne's team benefited greatly from the shift in the European television market, Atlanta needed to score high in the IOC's negotiations for U.S. rights. Atlanta's construction schedule and its dependence on private-sector money, however, forced the IOC to negotiate a U.S. television contract in 1993 before the American television market's recovery was complete. Even though CBS, NBC, and ABC pursued the television rights, U.S. television executives refused to enter into a "three scorpions in a bottle" scenario. Such a competitive situation had paid handsome dividends to the IOC and Olympic organizers who negotiated with the U.S. networks in the late 1970s and early 1980s.

During the final preparations for the U.S. television negotiations in New York in July 1993 Pound reviewed the anticipated negotiating approaches of the three networks with Samaranch and members of the IOC's Television Rights Negotiations Committee. CBS, commented Pound, engaged in preliminary technical discussions but seemed more intent on securing the rights to the 1998 Nagano Olympic Winter Games. ABC held discussions concerning the conceptual elements of televising the Atlanta Games in partnership with ESPN. Turner Network officials were also "anxious" to capture the U.S. rights. Pound predicted a conservative bid, however, because none of the competitors would accept a financial loss on the project. NBC clearly stated that its ceiling was $450 million.

NBC structured its $401 million bid for the Barcelona Olympics with the expectation that U.S. viewers would support its "Triplecast" pay-per-view package that supplemented the "free" coverage on the main network. The "Triplecast" experience and its poor financial returns, noted Pound, "had a sobering effect on its [NBC's] approach" to the Atlanta negotiations. He concluded that a revenue-sharing plan might be incorporated into the contract. Atlanta considered that any figure below $550 million was "low."[25] Pound preferred to delay the negotiations for Atlanta, but Atlanta's budget plans precluded this option.[26]

A proposal from Barry Frank received fleeting consideration in the weeks before formal negotiations with the U.S. networks for Atlanta rights. Frank did not forecast great enthusiasm in the United States for the Nagano rights considering the time zone difference and recent financial losses suffered by the U.S. Olympic rights holders. The negotiating environment for Pound with respect to the Atlanta Olympics was not favorable. Why not sell the Nagano and Atlanta rights as a package? As the U.S. Olympic broadcaster for two successive festivals the network would benefit from the extension of the period of cost recovery, said Frank. The package possessed greater appeal to the networks and offered better returns for both Organizing Committees and the Olympic Movement. The IOC proceeded with the conventional format for negotiations, however.[27] CBS seemed anxious to maintain its status as the U.S. Winter Olympics broadcaster, and with the Atlanta negotiations only six weeks away Pound decided "to stay the course."[28] NBC acquired the U.S. rights for the 1996 Atlanta Centennial Games for $456 million plus a revenue sharing agreement (50-50) between NBC and the Olympic Movement on advertising revenue exceeding $615 million (after the Atlanta Games, the two sides divided $30 million).[29]

In December 1993 the IOC Executive Board convened in Lausanne. One of the agenda items involved a discussion of the negotiation timetable for U.S. television rights for the 1998 Nagano Olympic Winter Games. A successful Lillehammer festival in two months promised an improved U.S. market, commented Samaranch. Anita DeFrantz lobbied to conclude the Japanese rights deal for Atlanta before the consummation of the U.S. television contract for Nagano. If this timetable did not prevail and the U.S. contract for Nagano was high and the Japanese deal for Atlanta was low, there could be some hard feelings in the United States. The U.S. networks wanted to move forward with negotiations for Nagano, replied Pound. He also believed that a good result for Nagano might place some pressure on Japanese negotiators to reciprocate with a favorable offer for Atlanta.[30] He was mistaken.

One week after the Executive Board meeting in Lausanne Pound and IOC marketing director Michael Payne met in New York with Makoto

Kobayashi, director-general of the Nagano Olympic Games Organizing Committee (NAOC), Nagano's television consultant, Barry Frank, and USOC officials Harvey Schiller and John Krimsky. The agenda focused on the negotiations with the networks scheduled for January. Representatives of each U.S. network also met with the group to discuss negotiation procedures. They all expressed interest in the Nagano Games, but NBC was unlikely to engage in a bidding war. In addition to meeting with representatives of the "big three" networks, Pound's team met with Rupert Murdoch, CEO of the FOX Network. Murdoch requested a meeting to discuss the bidding process. Even though Pound was willing to receive a bid from FOX, he questioned FOX's lack of experience in sports telecasting.[31] Nonetheless, Murdoch's interest proved fortuitous for Nagano.

In the last twenty-five years of the twentieth century Rupert Murdoch secured his status as a global media mogul through major acquisitions or by establishing new companies in the United States (*New York Post,* Twentieth Century FOX, the Los Angeles Dodgers Baseball Club, FOX TV), Britain (British Sky Broadcasting [BskyB]), Asia (Star TV), and China (Phoenix TV). In his native Australia Murdoch's Channel 7 owns the Olympic television rights through 2008. With respect to his television properties Murdoch employs sport programming as a "battering ram" to establish a company's presence in a new market or to promote existing networks. His efforts to establish FOX as a U.S. Olympic broadcaster fell short in the 1990s, as did his controversial 1998 bid (through BskyB) to purchase Manchester United, one of the world's leading soccer clubs. Through ownership interest in a number of U.S. professional sport franchises (New York Knicks, New York Rangers, and Los Angeles Lakers) and FOX's aggressive purchase of a number of sport television rights properties (National Hockey League, World Series, Super Bowl), however, Murdoch established himself as a major player in the North American sport scene in the 1990s.[32]

One week before all parties convened in New York for final deliberations the negotiating environment changed markedly. Pound sent a hurried message to Kobayashi requesting a prompt reply. NBC withdrew from negotiations, realizing that its maximum bid was not competitive. Meanwhile ABC executives—still suffering the residual effect of the $75 million loss on the Calgary Olympics, noted Pound—were unlikely to challenge CBS, which wanted to enhance its reputation as the U.S. Winter Olympic broadcaster. Rupert Murdoch, who was anxious to elevate the status of FOX in the United States through the acquisition of the rights to an Olympic festival, represented the wild card. Murdoch's overture to Pound, which was known to representatives of the other networks, increased the expected sale price of the Nagano rights. Neither CBS nor ABC, however, understood the extent of Pound's concern relative to FOX's fitness to assume the role of Olympic broadcaster. With approval from Samaranch and Frank, Pound suggested that the IOC negotiate directly with CBS for a $375 million contract. If CBS agreed, Pound would approach ABC looking for a better bid; however, he doubted ABC's degree of interest at that price. Pound planned to call FOX to advise officials of the IOC's decision to pursue a contract with an experienced Olympic broadcaster. Success, he noted, hinged on keeping this proposal confidential.[33] On 19 January 1994 the IOC announced the award of the U.S. rights for the Nagano Games to CBS for $375 million.

Within three weeks of the Nagano announcement Pound pressured his IOC colleague Un Yong Kim to push Japanese television executives to increase their offer for the 1996 Atlanta Centennial Games. "It would be important to have a good result from the Japan negotiations," he observed during a meeting of the Executive Board in Lillehammer; "otherwise [the IOC] would face serious difficulties in relation to the U.S. television rights in all of the future Games" because "[t]he U.S. could easily move into a protectionist mode." U.S. television executives, said Pound, resented that "other countries, Japan in particular, were not paying their fair share."[34] Kim dismissed Pound's overture. He noted that the IOC needed to maintain an ongoing relationship with broadcasters, including their Japanese partners, and that it had to accept certain market realities. "The value of the Japanese rights," replied Kim, "would have no bearing on the success or failure of the [Atlanta] Games."[35] He concluded negotiations with representatives of the Japanese Olympic Pool in 1995 for $99.5 million. Even though the contract exceeded the $62.5 million paid by the Japanese for the rights to the Barcelona Olympics, the change in the value of the yen versus the U.S. dollar meant that its value was lower than the Barcelona contract.[36]

EBU, JAPAN, AND THE NAGANO OLYMPIC WINTER GAMES

In his report to the IOC Executive Board in June 1994 Pound noted the discrepancy in payments made by U.S. television networks in comparison to EBU and the Japanese pool. CBS's $375 million contract for Nagano translated into a $3.98 payment per U.S. TV household, whereas EBU and the Japanese pool negotiated contracts for the 1994 Lillehammer Olympic Winter Games for $0.17 and $0.31 per household in their respective territories. Such data, emphasized Pound, necessitated an aggressive approach on the part of the IOC to improve the value of the European and Japanese contracts for Nagano.[37]

Samaranch and Hodler received three offers for European television rights. EBU offered a maximum of $72 million, a noticeable increase on the $24 million contract for the Lillehammer Games; but this sum was linked to a demand, which was later dropped, that EBU receive the right to match a better bid for the 2000 Sydney Olympics. A consortium of private networks, César Walther Lüthi Telesport (CWL Telesport), offered $140 million, although this sum included the cost of technical support from the host broadcaster normally paid by individual broadcasters in addition to the rights fee. With guaranteed coverage to only 80% of Europe, even Pound exhibited anxiety about CWL Telesport's proposal. Finally, UFA offered a hefty $100 million for the Nagano rights, but with a stipulation that it had to be accepted within five days. Samaranch appreciated EBU's solid offer, and its level of expertise required consideration. If FOX had been excluded as a potential U.S. broadcaster for Nagano because of its lack of experience in Olympic broadcasting, he opposed awarding the rights to an inexperienced network in Europe.[38] Pound's silence reflected his resignation that EBU's offer was likely the best attainable. Hodler concluded a deal with EBU for $72 million in early 1995.

With respect to the Japanese market, domestic broadcasters paid a premium in light of Nagano's host city status. Un Yong Kim negotiated a $37.5 million deal with the Japanese pool for rights to the Nagano Olympic Winter Games. It was a noticeable and expected increase on the $9 million and $12.7 million contracts he had consummated on behalf of the 1992 Albertville and 1994 Lillehammer OCOGs. The Nagano negotiations established a benchmark in the Japanese region. During the flurry of post–Sunset Project negotiations Kim negotiated $36 million and $38.5 million agreements with the Japanese pool for the 2002 Salt Lake City and 2006 (Turin) Olympic Winter Games, respectively.[39]

IOC/USOC DIALOGUE ON THE USOC'S SHARE OF U.S. TELEVISION MONEY

The USOC perceived the IOC's decision to grant it 10% of the U.S. Olympic television contracts beginning with the Albertville and Barcelona contracts as an entering wedge to pursue its financial aspirations. In 1989 and 1990, in the months preceding the introduction of the McMillen bill, the USOC lobbied the IOC for an increase in its share of future U.S. Olympic television contracts.[40] The USOC then used the McMillen bill as a means of squeezing the IOC for further concessions, but without immediate dividends.

Discussions concerning the USOC's share of U.S. Olympic television revenue continued through 1991 and 1992. A meeting between Michael Payne and USOC deputy secretary-general John Krimsky in February 1991 failed to bring the parties to an agreement.[41] Discussions percolated for another eighteen months. Pound believed that the two sides were close to a reasonable solution; but Harvey Schiller, USOC executive director, balked. The USOC desired that any new agreement include increases in the USOC's share of the U.S. television contracts for the 1998 Nagano Olympic Winter Games and the 2000 Summer Olympics. Schiller's demand for a 20% share of U.S. television revenue beginning in 2004 also aroused Pound's anxieties. He responded that the IOC might be willing to consider a shift to 15%.[42]

Schiller believed that the key to any USOC/IOC deal remained an increase in the USOC's share of television revenue in 1998 and 2000. Further discussions with Pound resulted in Schiller's second proposal. The USOC wanted 10% of the U.S. television contracts (1998 and 2000) plus "an amount, unspecified, to be negotiated by the IOC and USOC," if the IOC selected Salt Lake City as the host city for the 2002 Olympic Winter Games. Otherwise the USOC required a minimum of 12.5%. This minimum percentage shifted to 15% of the U.S. contract for the 2004 Summer Olympics.[43]

While Pound did not dismiss Schiller's proposal out of hand, he indicated that finding additional revenue for the USOC for 1998 and 2000 was a stumbling block. Nagano had signed its host city agreement, and bid cities for the 2000 Olympics based their budget projections on the preexisting terms of the IOC's financial arrangements with the USOC. It was not possible to deduct money from the OCOGs, ISFs, NOCs, or IOC. Schiller suggested that the extra money could be compensation for the USOC acting as the IOC's adviser in U.S. negotiations, a role normally fulfilled by professional consultants. Pound responded: "While you are, no doubt, every bit as good at television negotiations as you are at golf, with the greatest respect in the world, the U.S. television market in these troubled times is such that we *both* need the very best of professional advice if we are to maximize the revenues and maintain the preeminent position of the Olympic Games as a television property." He believed it might be possible to pull some of the money from the TOP revenues because it was difficult for the IOC to retain the current formula, which granted the USOC more sponsorship money than received by all of the other NOCs combined.[44] Pound's response could be interpreted as his method of tweaking the noses of Schiller and his colleagues.

Not satisfied with Pound's rejection of the USOC's terms, Schiller bypassed him and directed the USOC's proposal to Samaranch. Schiller's note to Samaranch ignored Pound's earlier comments on the matter. Upon learning of Schiller's overture to his boss, Pound sent a blistering memorandum to Schiller, taking him to task for going over his head. The memorandum leaves little to the imagination with respect to the growing enmity between the two men. "Your action in resorting to the IOC President when you know perfectly well that the matter has been delegated to me has been interpreted as suggesting that the IOC may not determine who shall represent it in this matter, which is not acceptable behavior on the part of the USOC," wrote Pound. "No doubt you would feel the same if the IOC were to go over your head to the President of the USOC, suggesting that someone other than you deal with the matter on behalf of the USOC." Schiller claimed that Pound had refused to discuss the issue with him at the April 1993 meeting of the Atlanta Coordination Commission meeting and was not "taking the matter seriously." The agenda of the Coordination Commission's meeting involved Atlanta's needs, replied Pound, and not IOC/USOC issues. He could not help but note, however, that when an opportunity had presented itself during a lunch meeting to discuss the television question, "you [Schiller] left the room in a snit" when the discussion was momentarily interrupted by a member of the Coordination Commission who required some information. "Any time someone demands millions of the IOC's dollars, I assure you I take the matter seriously indeed," he wrote.[45]

Pound elaborated on why the USOC's demand for a larger share of U.S. television revenue troubled him. The IOC and USOC first reached an agreement on providing 10% of the U.S. television contract to the USOC in 1986. At that time the IOC accepted the USOC's claim that the U.S. network's ability to sublicense the use of the IOC-approved composite logo to Olympic broadcast advertisers adversely affected its sponsorship program. "You persuaded us," Pound wrote Schiller, "that the broadcasters were, in effect, thus able to offer 'competing' sponsorships and that there was a diversion of sponsorship funds which might otherwise go to the USOC." This formed the sole basis of the USOC's claim, he noted. Now the IOC was willing to accept the USOC's request that third-party use of the composite logo be prohibited. "In the circumstances," Pound wrote, "I am sure you can appreciate the difficulty which I have in understanding why the USOC should have *any* share of U.S. television revenues, when the only basis for requesting a share has now been removed as a problem for the USOC in its sponsorship efforts."[46] Pound's entrenched position remained the unlimited shelf life of the 1986 Broadcast Marketing Agreement concerning the USOC's 10% share. He and Schiller did not find a solution.

The crux of the problem remained the IOC's refusal to grant 20% of U.S. television revenue to the USOC and the USOC's insistence that this percentage be established as the future benchmark in any agreement. Talks ground to a halt as the working relationship between the IOC Marketing Department and the USOC deteriorated further in 1993, 1994, and 1995. While Samaranch and USOC president LeRoy Walker enjoyed a good relationship, marketing issues embroiled Pound, Payne, and USOC officials Schiller and Krimsky in bitter confrontation. The next flash point regarding the television issue occurred in the wake of the IOC's decision to push forward with the Sunset Project.

THE SUNSET PROJECT

Some Olympic observers regard NBC's deal for Sydney ($705 million) and Salt Lake City ($545 million) for a combined sum of $1.25 billion, signed early in 1995, as the first long-term television rights contract signed by the IOC.[47] It is important to keep in mind three points concerning provenance of multi-Games television rights agreements, however. First, Pound considered selling the 1996 Atlanta and 1998 Nagano rights for the U.S. territory as a package. Second, EBU approached the IOC about the prospect of purchasing the 1992 Albertville and 1994 Lillehammer Olympic Winter Games rights as a package. Third, Rupert Murdoch's Channel 7 acquired the Australian television rights for the 1996 Atlanta ($30 million) and 2000 Sydney ($45 million) festivals for $75 million in early 1995.[48] The NBC/Salt Lake City/Sydney negotiations process neither represented the first time that the IOC considered signing a multi-Games television rights agreement nor in fact resulted in the first such agreement consummated.

It is nonetheless accurate to state that the Sydney/Salt Lake contract was pivotal in terms of acting as a springboard for the Sunset Project. Following the negotiations in Lausanne concerning the Sydney and Salt Lake City contract, Pound and Dick Ebersol, president of NBC Sports, pondered the possibility of establishing a U.S. television contract covering the 2004, 2006, and 2008 festivals. In their discussions they assumed that all festivals would take place in non-U.S. sites. Pound and Ebersol agreed to draft a document that would address pertinent issues. This task was labeled the "Sunset Project." Pound suggested that they prepare independent lists outlining issues to be assessed. Subsequent discussions could refine their approach.[49] Their efforts resulted in the signing of a $2.3 billion contract for U.S. television rights for the 2004 Athens Summer Games ($793 million), 2006 Turin Olympic Winter Games ($613 million), and 2008 Summer Olympics ($894 million) two months after their initial talks on the subject. The NBC deal touched off a spate of similar contract signings for other markets in 1996 and 1997. How did all of this come to pass?

U.S. TELEVISION RIGHTS AND THE 2000 SYDNEY OLYMPICS

In April 1995 Richard Pound believed that the U.S. market might yield as much as $600 million for the Sydney Olympic Organizing Committee and the Olympic Movement. Even though CBS was not projected as a serious bidder, Rupert Murdoch and the FOX Network stepped up their pursuit of U.S. Olympic television rights, pushing executives and accountants at NBC and ABC to keep pace. Murdoch held informal discussions with SOCOG concerning the prospect of purchasing the worldwide television rights for Sydney.[50] The IOC did not approve this arrangement. Pound and Samaranch agreed that "we should be very careful before placing ourselves (and the Games) in the hands of a single business entity."[51] Nonetheless, Pound believed that FOX had demonstrated the capacity to provide high-quality sport programming and deserved a level playing field with the "big three" U.S. networks.[52]

In late June Pound and Samaranch discussed the possibility of awarding U.S. television rights for Sydney jointly to NBC and ABC.[53] Such an arrangement, thought Pound, might result in more revenue and increase the total number of hours of coverage. Even though he did not question FOX's ability to deliver quality sport programming, Pound believed that its territorial "reach" could not match the results of a collaborative effort by ABC and NBC.[54] Maximizing the amount of coverage concerned the IOC in light of NBC's decision to restrict coverage of the Atlanta Games to its main network, thereby limiting the total number of hours of coverage.[55] Dick Ebersol, Dennis Swanson (president, ABC Sports), Pound, and Frank met in New York on 10 July. Ebersol and Swanson "professed to be bullish" on the proposal.[56] The networks hoped to prevent FOX from raiding the Olympic market in similar fashion to the manner in which it had successfully entered the arena for professional baseball and football television rights. Also, a collaborative effort promised a reduction in the rights fees that each network would have to pay if it was the sole Olympic rights holder.

As Swanson and Ebersol's dialogue continued during the summer months it became clear to them, and to Richard Pound, that the plan was not workable. Insurmountable difficulties in coordinating the sales of advertising and marketing efforts appeared. While the networks reached a tentative agreement for one to cover the opening ceremony and the other to televise the closing ceremony, dividing up the event coverage proved troublesome.[57] Possibly fearing that the Disney Corporation's recent purchase of ABC might alter the network's long-term approach to the purchase of Olympic television rights and responding to recent sport property acquisitions completed by ABC and CBS, NBC made a preemptive bid of $1.25 billion for the U.S. television rights for Sydney and Salt Lake City. It did this without ABC's or FOX's knowledge.[58] NBC tendered its offer less than a week after Murdoch had discussed with the IOC the prospect of purchasing the U.S. rights for $700 million. The IOC accepted the NBC offer, and Pound subsequently determined the distribution of the total sum to the respective festivals.[59] The IOC announced the deal in early August.

NBC's offer satisfied the IOC's major concerns for the sale of the Sydney rights and provided the network with promising opportunities to recoup its expenditure. From a revenue standpoint the contract pleased the IOC, especially when one considers that Pound only three months earlier had believed a sale price of $600 million might be possible. Also, NBC pledged to cover the Games on the main network and two cable channels, CNBC (Consumer News and Business Channel) and MSNBC (Microsoft National Broadcasting Company), thereby expanding the total number of hours of Olympic coverage in the United States.[60] This programming strategy satisfied the IOC, whose pursuit of the NBC/ABC deal in part reflected its desire to increase the hours of coverage beyond the number available to American viewers of the upcoming Centennial Games. For its part, NBC could (1) package its advertising sales and coordinate its promotional efforts for the two festivals, (2) offset the travel and production costs for Sydney through the reduced bill for producing an Olympic telecast from a domestic site in 2002, (3) rely on an experienced team of producers and announcers, and (4) expect that inflation over the course of the six-year deal would reduce its expense in "real" dollars. In Pound's words, "NBC thought that what it might lose on the swings (Sydney) it would make up on the roundabouts (Salt Lake City)."[61]

CHARTING THE FUTURE:
TV REVENUE AND THE IOC'S FINANCIAL SECURITY

At the IOC Executive Board meeting in Lausanne in September 1995 Pound returned to the idea of negotiating long-term television deals for Olympic festivals for which the site had not yet been determined. He supported pursuing such a plan because of the opportunity to secure the Olympic Movement's financial position and its fiscal health in the medium term. In addition, bid committees benefited from a firm grasp on the amount of money available from the sale of television rights before structuring their final budget plans. The IOC, added Pound, "would be spared the haggling with which OCOGs tended to trammel TV rights negotiations."[62] Samaranch, Kim, and India's Ashwini Kumar advocated listening to approaches from the networks for long-term deals. Hodler predicted fruitful negotiations with EBU on multi-Games contracts. Anita DeFrantz, playing the devil's advocate, posed the idea that long-term deals might lead the public to believe that the networks could influence the site selection process. Australia's Kevan Gosper also expressed reservations. He considered that selling the rights closer to the event offered the safest means of maximizing revenue and obtaining the best offers.[63] Still, Samaranch and Pound interpreted the tenor of the discussion as a green light for Pound to explore the possibility of a long-term U.S. deal.

Samaranch's proposal to reduce the share of Olympic television revenue distributed to future OCOGs (beginning with the 2004 Summer Olympics) from 60% to 49%, thereby increasing the Olympic Movement's portion of the available money from 40% to 51%, also stirred much debate.[64] Samaranch wanted to tighten the language in future host city agreements concerning the role of the OCOGs in television negotiations. Ambiguities existed, he felt, that left serious doubt about the responsibility and authority of the IOC for concluding television deals. Pound lobbied against excluding the OCOGs from discussions concerning television, especially because of their mandate to provide the technical infrastructure for the broadcasters. For two reasons he did not agree with altering the distribution of the television revenue in favor of the IOC. First, he doubted a favorable verdict in the court of public opinion. Second, a move to increase the IOC's share would stimulate the USOC to renew its demand for an increase in its 10% share of the U.S. television contract. "An important contribution to public sympathy for the Games," noted Pound, "lay in the IOC's ability to say that most of the revenue went towards organizing the Games." The IOC needed to ensure a well-organized festival and, in the event that Samaranch's proposed formula deprived an OCOG of revenue necessary to guarantee this eventuality, "it would reflect badly on the IOC."[65] Samaranch rebutted Pound's points by proclaiming that the "IOC was putting on the show, and it had to have the majority of the rights." DeFrantz labeled the plan to reduce the OCOGs' share of future revenue a "punitive gesture."[66] Though Gosper sided with Pound and DeFrantz, their positions formed a minority view.

Ashwini Kumar, Pal Schmitt, and Alexandre de Merode expressed support for Samaranch's proposals. De Merode believed that the IOC might have to deal with future entreaties from the athletes for the money. Schmitt and Kumar envisioned this distribution plan as a means of increasing the amount of revenue channeled to the NOCs and ISFs. When discussion closed, Samaranch called for a vote on the two proposals. On the first the Executive Board (by a vote of 7–3) agreed to amend the Host City Agreement for the 2004 Summer Olympics with respect to language concerning the IOC's television negotiating authority. Samaranch's second initiative, the proposal to lower the OCOG split of television revenue to 49%, was accepted by a narrow margin (5–4, with one abstention).[67]

THE NBC/IOC PARTNERSHIP

Throughout October and November 1995 Pound and Ebersol attempted to build on the momentum of the announcement of the Sydney/Salt Lake City contract. Samaranch, Pound, and François Carrard, the IOC's director-general, were the only IOC officials involved in the process. By the end of November the basic elements of the long-term contract had been established. The Sydney/Salt Lake City contract provided the foundation for the financial components of the Sunset contract. For 2004 Ebersol and Pound agreed to apply a 3% year-over-year increase to the figure contracted for the Sydney Olympics ($705 million), resulting in a sum of $793 million. This inflation formula was extended through 2008, establishing a sale price of $894 million. They employed the same principle with respect to the 2006 Olympic Winter Games, with the Salt Lake City element of the first contract ($545 million) serving as the base figure, thereby producing a figure of $613 million. A 50-50 revenue-sharing agreement between NBC and the IOC for each festival where NBC advertising revenue exceeded the sum of its rights fee and production costs supplemented the $2.3 billion agreement.[68]

When the IOC Executive Board convened in early December in Nagano Pound and Samaranch sought their colleagues' approval of the contract. Pound reviewed the financial terms of the proposed deal. NBC, he noted, was averse to linking the increase in the value of the contract to the rate of inflation but supported the 3% year-over-year clause. The IOC sacrificed the opportunity to take advantage of the market, conceded Pound, but the deal offered financial security to the IOC and an opportunity to complete long-term financial planning. He also considered the timing propitious because the USOC was still locked into a 10% share of U.S. television revenue. "This percentage would certainly not decrease, and there was a chance that they would ask for more," Pound observed.[69]

The Executive Board supported the NBC Sunset contract. DeFrantz judged the results of Pound's negotiations "an extraordinary opportunity" but harbored some reservations about the impact of the contract on the IOC's relationships with NBC's competitors, ABC and CBS. Schmitt believed that the "IOC should strike while the iron was hot." A pleasantly startled Ashwini Kumar exclaimed: "It [is] unbelievable, that hard-headed businessmen should wish to guarantee the future of the Olympic Movement for at least a decade." De Merode and Gosper also spoke in favor of the deal.[70] The Executive Board granted its approval of the NBC contract. On 12 December Pound held a press conference with Ebersol and other NBC officials in New York to announce the terms of the U.S. Olympic television rights agreement for the 2004, 2006, and 2008 festivals.

In early 2001, as the U.S. networks prepared to jockey for negotiating television rights to the 2010 Olympic Winter Games and the 2012 Olympics, DeFrantz's reservations bore further consideration. Sean McManus, president of CBS Sports, predicted a decline in U.S. television revenue unless the IOC repaired its relationship with CBS, ABC, and FOX. For public consumption the networks expressed lukewarm interest in re-entering the negotiating fray. "We didn't feel we were dealt with fairly last time. It wasn't even a negotiation. The IOC seems to have forgotten there are three other networks in the United States," commented McManus. "Dick Pound's address book for U.S. networks," he concluded, "only seems to have the letter n."[71] McManus's tough talk seemed designed to ensure an open negotiation process for upcoming festivals.

The IOC/NBC agreement served as a template for IOC officials in negotiations with broadcasters from other regions. In January 1996 the IOC reached a long-term agreement (2002 to 2008) with Australia's Channel 7 for $140,825,000.[72] When the Executive Board convened in March, members reviewed the results of negotiations with EBU. The EBU deal covered the Sydney ($350 million), 2004 ($394 million), and 2008 ($443 million) Summer Games and the Salt Lake City ($120 million) and 2006 ($135 million) Winter festivals, for a combined sum of $1.442 billion.[73] The new format for negotiations with representatives of the world's television networks was firmly established.[74]

USOC/IOC FIREWORKS

Though privately the USOC may have felt grudging admiration for Pound's negotiating efforts, in public arenas of discourse representatives expressed indignation. The USOC resented being "kept out of the loop" on Pound's discussions with Ebersol concerning the follow-up agreement signed in December. For a number of years the USOC had aggressively lobbied the IOC for a greater degree of involvement in U.S. television negotiations. And on occasion Pound had consulted the USOC concerning the U.S. television market in the 1990s. The USOC viewed the long-term deal, negotiated without its input, as a setback to its domestic authority.[75]

The USOC soon issued a claim for an increased share of U.S. Olympic television revenue for the 2004, 2006, and 2008 festivals. Schultz envisioned a change in the USOC's share from 10% to 20%, with the possibility of a further increase post-2008.[76] In order to pressure the IOC the USOC refused to approve the second NBC contract. Powers granted to the USOC by virtue of the Amateur Sports Act (ASA) underscored the USOC's obstinacy. The USOC sought to squeeze Pound, who was cool toward changing the USOC's share. The USOC, he reasoned, received a guaranteed $230 million. That was sufficient. Pound realized that the situation required some form of accommodation; however, his unflinching resolve was chiefly intended for the consumption of his fellow IOC officials who might be inclined to acquiesce to the demand for 20%. While the IOC/USOC agreement signed in 1986 was legally binding and was of unlimited duration, the USOC remained adamant that it deserved more money.[77]

Anxious to settle the issue with the USOC and bring a degree of stability to USOC/IOC relations, Samaranch engaged in preliminary discussions with Dick Schultz. In advance of the Atlanta Games Schultz amended the USOC's position and indicated that his organization viewed a shift to 15% as satisfactory.[78] Without the knowledge of Pound or Samaranch, however, Schultz and his USOC colleagues also pursued their own agenda on Capitol Hill.

An alert NBC staff member in Washington discovered an attempt by the USOC, in Pound's words, "to sneak through some very important changes to the [ASA] during the last days of the legislative season, without a hearing and attached as an amendment to a completely unrelated bill."[79] The amendments removed the authority to conduct television negotiations in the United States from the IOC. When notified of the USOC's activities, "we went bananas," recalled Pound. Samaranch, Pound, and Carrard confronted Schultz at Atlanta's Olympic Stadium during the course of the Centennial Games. Schultz denied any knowledge of the legislation. When presented with a memo sent to him by the USOC's Washington lobbyist concerning the bill, Schultz retreated and stated that "the amendments were housekeeping amendments." Pound read aloud pertinent sections of the bill that were prejudicial to the IOC's interests.[80] Samaranch strongly advised Schultz to remove the amendment from the bill under consideration in the Senate. Grudgingly, Schultz complied.

The IOC scheduled a summit meeting for October 1996 to deal with the soured relationship between the USOC and the IOC. Pound, long frustrated by the USOC's attitude with respect to the IOC's television and marketing policies, recognized the long-term importance of the results of this meeting. The USOC efforts in Washington represented one element of a prolonged attempt to consolidate the administration of all Olympic matters in the United States in its headquarters in Colorado Springs, especially those involving finance. Pound, for his part, maintained the IOC's right to "do business" in the United States. In a pre-meeting brief Pound counseled Samaranch and his colleagues that the challenge to the IOC's position in the United States was serious. Samaranch must not yield: "The basic position of the USOC is that, in the United States, the IOC has no role and that it is the USOC which controls and run all things Olympic . . . The fundamental attitude of the USOC toward the IOC is that the IOC knows nothing about the Olympic Movement in the United States and that the IOC should not be carrying on any activity in the United States, including the sale of television rights." He pressed the point further: "The IOC is tolerated [by the USOC], barely, because it has the power to award the Games to U.S. cities on occasion. In all other respects, it is denigrated by officials and staff members of the USOC at virtually every possible opportunity to try to undermine the role of the IOC. To give some flavor to this attitude, the IOC is often referred to by some USOC officials as 'Eurotrash.'" Pound warned that it "would be unwise to underestimate the degree of antipathy to the IOC which exists within the USOC."[81]

Prior to the Executive Board meeting in October USOC officials (Walker, Schultz, Krimsky, and Alfredo LaMont) met with their IOC counterparts Samaranch, Pound, DeFrantz, Gosper, Thomas Bach, Carrard, and Payne and the IOC's director of legal affairs, Howard Stupp.[82] Samaranch delivered a rather blunt message to the USOC. He compared the Olympic Movement to a club. "Being a member was not compulsory," he added, "but members had to abide by the rules."[83] Samaranch told the USOC representatives that the IOC "could get along without the USOC and was prepared to do so."[84] DeFrantz believed Samaranch's message that the USOC "could be in the club or out of it" had set the tone for the meeting.[85] Still, IOC officials recognized the unique nature of the U.S. market and the benefit of successful U.S. Olympic teams in terms of driving the IOC's revenue generation program. The IOC agreed to elevate the USOC's share of U.S. television contracts to 12.75% starting in 2004.[86]

Richard Pound's successful effort to convince his IOC colleagues of the need for redress concerning the share of Olympic television revenue shouldered by the U.S. networks and his pursuit of long-term television contracts confirm his central role in IOC activities in the area of revenue generation. The successful implementation of the Sunset Project provided the IOC and OCOGs with a measure of financial security. No doubt Salt Lake City officials, caught in the maelstrom of controversy in early 1999, were relieved that all major television contracts were in place.

Television policy changes in the late 1980s and 1990s gradually reduced conflict with OCOGs, but the intensification of battles with the USOC offset this gain. These skirmishes concerned the USOC's concept of its role in television negotiations in the United States and its desire for more money. Driven by an ambition to increase its revenue base, the USOC played off its face-to-face negotiations with Pound and Michael Payne against its legislative agenda in Washington. The McMillen bill serves as one example of this tactic.

The USOC's effort to modify the Amateur Sports Act prior to the Centennial Olympic Games was a gamble. If the USOC succeeded in pushing through the changes without the IOC's knowledge, the IOC would have been drawn into a public confrontation with the USOC. This process was fraught with trouble for the IOC, which would have been portrayed for American public consumption as the "bad guy" by the USOC. The USOC could claim that too much U.S. money flowed out of the country.[87] Even though the IOC could argue that the USOC had usurped its intellectual property rights, the reaction of the U.S. Congress was difficult to predict. Schultz's decision to pursue changes to the ASA without informing Samaranch during discussions concerning the USOC's share of U.S. television revenue backfired when an NBC employee discovered the proposed amendments to the Senate bill. When a disappointed and angered Samaranch delivered a stern message to Schultz and his colleagues in October 1996, he placed the USOC on the defensive. Any hope for 15% of the U.S. television contract or control of future negotiations had been dashed. The two sides reached agreement on the USOC's share (12.75%), but the process reflected the massive fissure between the IOC and USOC in terms of interorganizational trust.[88]

CHAPTER 12

PROTECTING AMERICAN DOLLARS

Mr. Samaranch Goes to Washington

The most contemporary drama of dislocation between the IOC and the USOC burst onto the stage of public awareness in late November 1998. A Salt Lake City newspaper reporter alleged that officials of the committee charged with the responsibility of securing the 2002 Winter Olympic Games had committed serious improprieties. The original allegation focused on the "gift" of a college scholarship for an IOC member's daughter in exchange for his vote to help send the Games to Salt Lake City.[1] Other allegations of improper conduct on the part of bid committee leaders and IOC members rapidly surfaced.

The circle of alleged corruption widened beyond simply the Salt Lake City bid committee and certain IOC members. USOC representatives came under fire for their roles in the corruption scenario, as did officials of the bid committee for Sydney's successful quest to host the 2000 Games. A severe public outcry arose as the unfolding story captured world media attention for some three months. In alarmed crisis management Olympic organizations implicated in the scandal formed commissions to investigate the facts and pinpoint wrongdoing.[2] With the possibility that a violation of federal laws might have occurred, the United States Justice Department directed the FBI to launch an investigation. The general result of all this was much finger pointing. The USOC's investigative commission—created by its president, Bill Hybl, and chaired by former U.S. senator George Mitchell—denounced the IOC as a closed, unaccountable, and ethically culpable body perpetuating a compromising gift-giving/receiving culture.[3] Well before the USOC's action the IOC had formed its own investigative commission headed by the ubiquitous Richard Pound. By the time Pound's commission submitted its final report, four IOC members had resigned, six had been expelled, ten had received severe warnings, and Cameroon's René Essomba, whose name was linked to the very first disclosures of alleged corruption, had died. The USOC did not escape entirely from the IOC's findings either. Wrote Pound in the report: "It is possible that many of the excesses which occurred on this occasion might have been avoided had the USOC been more active in discharging its responsibilities, including the bringing of any violations of rules to the attention of the IOC. Bidding cities are entitled to expect more guidance in these matters from their National Olympic Committees."[4]

A large measure of public reaction called for the immediate resignation of Samaranch. Less reactionary but deeply disturbed by the events precipitated by the Salt Lake City disclosures, Olympic-related groups offered abundant recommendations for change, a sweeping majority of which aimed squarely at alterations in the structure of the IOC and its manner of doing business. The IOC reacted quickly in the wake of the Salt Lake City disclosures. Scores of meetings, study and debate, written depositions from sports groups, and input from independent individuals, of which Henry Kissinger was perhaps the most noted, culminated in numerous changes to the *Olympic Charter.* Some fifty reform measures were adopted, including a new Ethics Commission and a drastic change in the IOC terms of membership. Beginning with the selection of the 2006 Winter Olympic Games host city, the IOC banned visits by individual IOC members to candidate cities bidding for the right to host the great international sports festival.[5] Instead a special IOC Commission, at IOC expense, now visits host city candidates.

No postscandal investigation was more virulent than that recorded in America, punctuated by the fiery comments of some members of the U.S. Congress. This reflected the fact that the first and ultimately most flagrant examples of bribery and corruption involved an American city. The United States was the only country in the world to demand the IOC president's appearance before a federal government investigative committee.

Throughout the spring and summer of 1999 the U.S. Congress tried several times without success to get Samaranch to appear before one of its subcommittees for questioning on issues related to the Salt Lake City disclosures. On the advice of the Executive Board Samaranch delayed a Washington visit until the IOC had announced its reform measures. By early December this had been accomplished. The time was right to travel to Washington. A mid-December visit might be lost among the public issues that captured media attention at the time. Focus on Y2K (Year 2000), presidential candidates, upcoming primaries, and Hillary Clinton's possible run for a Senate seat lowered media interest in a 79-year-old Spanish aristocrat's visit to the American capital.

Juan Antonio Samaranch does not exemplify a man whose demeanor is relaxed and confident in front of the media, particularly when the discourse is carried out completely in English. Spanish and Catalan are his "first" languages; French, his "second." Readers may recall Samaranch's disastrous interview with Bob Simon of CBS's popular investigative news program *60 Minutes* aired during the Nagano Olympic Winter Games. Simon's aggressive questioning concerning Samaranch's past affiliation with Francisco Franco's regime in Spain as well as funding issues pertinent to the Nagano festival left a startled Samaranch in an acute state of discomfiture, fumbling for responses. Appearing before an aroused congressional subcommittee with an agenda to lower the IOC's influence in the United States, while at the same time raising that of the USOC, posed an intimidating challenge for the IOC president. Be that as it may, there was simply too much at stake in the way of future dollars for the Modern Olympic Movement worldwide from American business enterprise for Samaranch to continue to ignore Congress. In mid-December 1999, as most people faced the last stages of pre-Christmas shopping, he flew to Washington. François Carrard accompanied him. Richard Pound flew from Montréal to meet them in the U.S. capital.

On Wednesday, 15 December, speaking and being spoken to in Spanish through an interpreter (a condition of his appearance), Samaranch appeared before members of the House Committee of Commerce Subcommittee on Oversights and Investigations. The gallery was packed with spectators; a formidable gaggle of media people wielded cameras, pencils, laptop computers, and tape recorders. Seven representatives formed the "hearing panel," chaired by Fred Upton from Michigan. They sat behind a long table adorned with a battery of microphones. Facing them sat a somber Juan Antonio Samaranch, flanked on either side by a translator: one to translate questions addressed to him into Spanish, the other to translate his answers into English. Pound and Carrard sat behind their president. To begin the proceedings Samaranch was sworn in; then he read a prepared opening statement (9,640 words) in English.[6] The committee then opened its questioning. Chairman Upton fired the first salvo, declaring that "we are here because the Olympic Games are too important to allow a culture of corruption to be whitewashed and perpetuated by a paper called reforms."[7] One after the other, the charges flew across the committee room: the IOC reforms were simply an exercise in "window-dressing . . . a whitewash"; the newly created IOC ethics panel "lacks teeth"; anticorruption rules won't even apply "to the IOC president or his successor."[8] At times the dialogue got nasty and personal, even a bit theatrical. Congressman Joe Barton of Texas ridiculed Samaranch's desire to be addressed as "His Excellency" and, following reference to the alleged luxury of his living expenses in Lausanne, called for his immediate resignation.[9] Congressman Henry Waxman belabored a point that really underpinned the entire proceedings—one on which the USOC and IOC had previously drawn swords: "a long term extension of Olympic television rights granted without competition to the NBC television network."[10]

Through it all Samaranch sat unruffled, at times even serene, resolved in his conviction that the IOC had met the challenges imposed and reformed its house. Pound and Carrard had prepared their boss well. Both were experienced masters in the art of dealing with aroused adversaries. In the end, after six hours of testimony (two hours by Samaranch), the subcommittee vowed close monitoring of the IOC's pledge to change and threatened to "implement legislation that would ban American companies from financially supporting the Olympics" if officials failed to follow through.[11] The crux of the matter—the real motivation behind Congress's desire to confront Samaranch in the nation's capital—was revealed. United States government officials appeared less concerned with the Salt Lake City scandal and more interested in the leverage that the scandal afforded them, the opportunity to interrogate Samaranch on their turf with respect to Olympic finance issues.

Major U.S. newspaper accounts of the hearing judged Samaranch's performance before the committee as generally effective. If "His Excellency" had been moderately persuasive in defusing the subcommittee's charges, the testimony of three important American allies took the political wind out of Upton's sails. Testifying on behalf of the IOC were Henry Kissinger, former U.S. secretary of state; Howard Baker, former senator from Tennessee; and former White House chief of staff Kenneth Duberstein. All were highly respected in the halls of Congress. There would be no bullying of them. Kissinger and Baker served as members of the IOC 2000 Reform Commission. Kissinger told the committee that the IOC had "come as close to achieving [reforms] as possible, replacing corrupt members with enthusiastic athletes."[12] Baker pleaded for the lawmakers "to be patient . . . Samaranch is well meaning . . . fully dedicated to reform." Duberstein announced that "Samaranch is living reform every day."[13] Following the questions and answers, a weary but relieved Samaranch and his colleagues retired from the proceedings, confident that if given a chance to work IOC reforms would satisfy congressional USOC "protectionists." A certain amount of self-assurance, if not a measure of euphoria, gripped the aging IOC president. "If they ask me to come again, I will come again," he said with a confident air.[14]

REFLECTIONS

It is no great secret that the financial health of both the IOC and its most flamboyant offspring, the USOC, is fundamentally embedded in the competitive zeal of U.S. television networks and corporate business giants bent on linking their endeavors with the world's most illustrious sports spectacle—the Olympic Games. The ability of the IOC to generate billions of dollars through the marketing of television rights and corporate sponsorship affiliations is matched by the USOC's impressive revenue production from roughly the same sources. The IOC's financial endeavors are aimed to a large extent at helping to underwrite the activities of the Olympic Movement across the world. Conversely, the USOC is equally driven to enhance the fortunes of U.S. Olympic athletes in competition with Olympic athletes from other countries. Thus the "two hands in the same pot" syndrome produced a reactionary and often fiery relationship between the two giants of Olympic commercialism. A smoldering relationship between the two evolved in the 1980s when the modest transfers of U.S. dollars to the Olympic Movement from commercial forces mushroomed into an avalanche that far exceeded even the most optimistic predictions. During the 1990s the negative relationship between the two organizations magnified, prodded by their parallel efforts to exploit the American Olympic money marketplace.

The difference in the European and American style of doing business is a fundamental cause for the fracture and unrest that has existed and may continue to exist between the IOC and the USOC. The USOC reflects the quintessential American approach: an energetic, aggressive, confrontational, "in your face" style of performance. This, of course, is a trait that has been engendered in Americans since colonial times. To Europeans, however, the American style is hostile, repugnant, and certainly to be eschewed. Finesse, polite discourse, tacit action, guile, and craftiness are embedded in European tradition. For decades such a tradition has been part of the IOC's manner of doing business. But in the face of rapid developments in Olympic commercialism in the 1980s Juan Antonio Samaranch, a personification of the European approach, appointed a hard-nosed, nononsense Canadian, Richard Pound, to deal with the Americans. He viewed Pound's appointment as the best means available to protect IOC interests and counter the USOC's hard tactics. Clearly, Madame Monique Berlioux was not the person to guide IOC financial fortunes in their juxtaposition with U.S. Olympic interests. When negotiations involving millions and millions of dollars are at stake one can imagine the rancor that can arise, even between family members, when one feels manipulated by the other. Given the presence of these basic philosophical and practical dichotomies, it is not surprising to witness family discussions degenerating into bona-fide family feuding.

For the time being the IOC's huge financial interests in the United

States remain secure.[15] USOC leaders failed to gain what they treasured most and tried to obtain on more than one occasion—absolute authority over the disposition of revenues generated from American business and television firms. As the dollar value of U.S. business and television enterprises linked to Olympic endeavors spiraled to dizzying heights in the 1990s, so, too, did the troubled relations between the IOC and its most difficult child, the USOC. When, and in what form, the next challenge to parental authority might come is anyone's guess. If and when it arrives Juan Antonio Samaranch will not be party to such proceedings. He stood down as IOC president in July 2001. The Washington episode marked his final challenge as head of an Olympic Movement in confrontation with its most rambunctious constituents.

Recently the two organizations have signaled a desire for better interorganizational relations. It appears that the IOC and the USOC have at least in part resolved some differences and are reaching toward mutual understanding and an improved relationship. Part of this new atmosphere can be attributed to the absence from the USOC scene of certain officials who enjoyed confrontation. The most outstanding example of this type was John Krimsky Jr. Krimsky and Richard Pound, fund-raising point-men for the USOC and IOC, respectively, clashed repeatedly on financial negotiation issues. Each represented his organization with zeal, skill, and determination. The constant buffeting of their self-interests, however, did little to promote understanding and goodwill. For thirteen years (1986 to 1999) Krimsky, the USOC's deputy secretary-general and managing director of business affairs, buckled on his armor time and time again to battle the IOC for a larger share of American Olympic television rights fees and TOP monies from the U.S. corporate world. He also raised the framework for the USOC's own domestic marketing initiatives. The result was staggering. He generated more than $2 billion, a goodly portion of it through hard-nosed negotiation with the IOC for an off-the-top 10% share of American television rights fees and 20% of TOP revenues.[16] In the summer of 1999 Krimsky left the USOC to become president and chief executive officer of Relationship Management Programs, Inc., some of whose clients are linked to USOC sponsorship endeavors.[17] With the departure of Krimsky the often-embattled circumstances surrounding IOC and USOC negotiations on financial matters showed promise of abating.

In Brazil in May 2000 IOC president Samaranch sat down with U.S. Olympic officials, including Norm Blake, the USOC's new chief executive officer. The meeting's agenda focused on the USOC's explanation to Samaranch of the entirely new and massive restructuring of the American NOC, a process that had been completed by Blake only three months earlier. Clearly, detente was in the air. Old spats were pushed to the background, at least for the time being. The meeting proceeded in a congenial manner. Samaranch listened to Blake, then offered advice—"fatherly, I might add," noted Blake. Said Samaranch: "Whether you know it or not, you're going to be judged on the medal count" (in Atlanta the United States had won 101 medals, including 44 gold). Blake found Samaranch "engaging and very personable." "He's very anxious for me to succeed," added Blake.[18]

Blake's tenure as the USOC's chief executive officer was short-lived, however. Employees chafed under his management approach and opposed his "money for medals" scheme that compromised support for "minor" sports. The USOC spent much of 2000 embroiled in its own problems. Blake's interim replacement, Scott Blackmun, and the USOC's new president, Sandra Baldwin, were dedicated to bringing stability back to the USOC's operation in Colorado Springs. So, too, is the newly appointed permanent CEO, Lloyd Ward, former CEO of the Maytag Corporation. Indeed, Samaranch's successor must place the USOC's health and IOC/USOC relations at the top of his agenda. Given the percentage of dollars from U.S. business and television sources, it is in the best interests of the IOC to maintain a healthy American Olympic body that functions in harmonious partnership rather than in sometimes confrontational and acrimonious rivalry.

CHAPTER 13

REFLECTIONS

Commercial Revenue, the Samaranch Presidency, and Challenges for Jacques Rogge

Thirty years ago an aging Avery Brundage bemoaned the infusion of commercial revenue into Olympic affairs. When he stepped down as IOC president in 1972, he warned that the internecine arguments concerning "who received what" threatened to fracture the Olympic Movement. Persistent infighting among the IOC, OCOGs, ISFs, and NOCs left him disillusioned. Lord Killanin challenged Brundage's disillusionment, claiming that the money was more likely to act as the "glue" that would keep the Olympic Movement together. Killanin was right. The IOC, a transnational organization that brings together people from different cultures representing the interests of different constituencies (sports/countries), is often subject to internal bickering and conflict and at times more than a little intrigue. The success of the IOC's Olympic marketing program during the Samaranch presidency, however, provided security and the possibility of administrative growth for the IOC, NOCs, and ISFs around the world.

In the preceding pages we have charted the IOC's path from a financially challenged sport organization to its current status as a commercial leviathan. We also have explored why this transformation occurred and its obvious results. The scenario unfolded as a result of a philosophical shift in the IOC's approach to commercial revenue necessitated by fiscal realities. A business strategy pondered by Lord Killanin and constructed and zealously championed by his successor, Juan Antonio Samaranch, and his right hand in marketing matters, Richard Pound, buried Avery Brundage's vision of the IOC and its "amateur ideal."

When Samaranch moved into his new residence in Lausanne in 1980, his top priority focused on forming a secure foundation for the IOC's revenue-generation program. With the uncertainty of world geopolitics, the repeated threats of Olympic boycotts in the 1960s and 1970s, and their actuality in the 1980s, Samaranch pursued financial stability for the IOC as a means of protecting the Olympic Movement's interests worldwide. Television money, the vast majority of which was tied to the competitive U.S. market, provided over 90% of the IOC's budget when Samaranch assumed his presidential duties. This fact disturbed him greatly. Peter Ueberroth, fiscal architect of the 1984 Los Angeles Olympic Games, revolutionized the manner in which Organizing Committees funded the staging of Olympic festivals by capitalizing on the private sector. In Lausanne, in great measure induced by the sports business acumen and persuasion of Horst Dassler, Samaranch pursued the corporate sector as a major partner in financing the IOC and the Olympic Movement. The power of the Olympic rings and the "Olympic mystique" as the central elements of a comprehensive marketing program exceeded all expectations.

Though the IOC's managerial efforts with respect to revenue generation during the Samaranch presidency reflect a significant degree of achievement, the massive transformation of the IOC's financial operation prompts reflection. How has the infusion of corporate capital altered the Olympic Movement and its parent figure, the IOC, during the last twenty years?

DIVERSIFYING THE IOC'S REVENUE BASE: SAMARANCH'S STRATEGY AND ITS RESULTS

A financial windfall for the Olympic Movement, determined Samaranch, depended on raising the status of the Olympics as the world's grandest and most important sport festival. How might such a lofty standard be secured and maintained? Through a deliberate strategy Samaranch opened the Olympics to professional athletes. The entry of professional athletes into the Olympic precinct stimulated renewed interest in the IOC's most treasured marketplace, the United States, enabling it to trade the "Olympic mystique" and the powerful five-ring logo for the combination to the vault of U.S. corporate dollars. Under Samaranch the IOC continued Killanin's policy of extracting maximum television rights revenue from the U.S. market. Television networks continued to exchange money for profit potential, image enhancement, and the use of Olympic telecasts to attract new viewers and promote upcoming programming. Corporate executives recognized the worldwide popularity of the Olympics as a promising vehicle for the promotion of a company's image and products. The Olympic Games became the world's hottest sport commodity.

In 1986 the IOC made the decision to stagger the Summer and Winter festivals on a biennial basis, beginning with the 1994 Olympic Winter Games. This plan provided a steady flow of revenue into IOC coffers, eliminated the four-year lull between Olympic telecasts, and kept the Olympics a prominent feature of media reports as bidding cities scrambled for the right to host the Games. The Games became an everyday news item in the world media.

Even though the IOC's alliance with multinational companies in gathering sponsorship revenues rendered badly needed resources for the Olympic treasury, the newly acquired benefit rested largely on a single dimension—the American corporate marketplace. It is important to note that when the IOC fell under intense scrutiny in the wake of the Salt Lake City revelations Richard Pound and IOC marketing director Michael Payne spent hours in meetings with executives from major American Olympic sponsors and NBC (the IOC's U.S. television partner network) in an effort to shore up continued support for the tarnished Olympic enterprise. Preservation of financial security was fundamental beyond all other considerations. A loss of American support threatened the ability of the IOC and host cities to stage the Olympic festivals on the scale to which the enterprise had grown. Without its commercial partners the IOC's financial house might well collapse and visions of the Olympics becoming a UNESCO entity draw closer to reality. Happily for the IOC, NBC and the corporate sponsors held firm.

The IOC is a much larger organization today, having grown from an operation with a handful of employees under Killanin in the 1970s to a staff that now numbers well over 200 (including Olympic Museum staff). In increasing numbers marketing, licensing, and legal experts occupy administrative offices in Lausanne. The showpiece of the IOC's presence in Lausanne is the Olympic Museum, which opened in July 1993. Its formidable construction cost (almost $85 million) was largely underwritten by the assistance of the corporate sector. While critics characterize the IOC's facilities as "palatial" or "grand," this criticism seems overstated considering that the IOC manages a worldwide network of 199 National Olympic Committees and has a relationship with more than 40 international sports federations. Its precincts are not unlike many of the headquarters buildings and grounds of some of the world's major business corporations.

The IOC differs little from professional sport enterprises whose existence depends on the corporate sector. Without stadium-naming rights, commercial advertising, the sale of corporate luxury boxes as well as the corporate sector's season ticket base, and television rights sales there would be fewer professional sport franchises, fewer multimillionaire athletes and agents, and even fewer opportunities for the public to witness sports events without paying sky-high admission prices. Similarly, without the infusion of corporate sector support and the careful nurturing of the Olympic brand, there would be fewer athletes at Olympic festivals, fewer events on the Olympic program, fewer bid cities, and greater public debt in cities staging the Games. As reflected in Sydney, as well as other host cities since the 1984 Los Angeles Games, public debt for putting on the Games would have doubled or in some cases even tripled without the gathering of commercial revenue from television and corporate sponsorship sources. "With the sheer size and complexity of today's Olympic Games," concedes Michael Payne, "it has reached the point where if there were no sponsors, there would be no Games."[1]

The biennial avalanche of Olympic advertising and aggressive marketing of the Olympic rings evokes criticism from some journalists, social commentators, and academics who decry Olympic festivals as "made for television spectacles" staged against a backdrop of enveloping commercialism. These spectacles, they argue, diminish the focus on the sport experience of the individual athlete and result in a series of massive sport festivals (over 10,600 athletes competed in Sydney) that mainly serve the interests of the corporate sector. Jacques Rogge, a three-time Olympian (yachting) and Belgian orthopedic surgeon, whose recent successful campaign for the IOC presidency rested on his European heritage, squeaky clean image, Samaranch's support, and his stewardship of the Coordination Commission for the Sydney Olympics, did little to dissuade such talk when he observed: "We need spectators at the Games, but the IOC does not insist on 100,000-seat stadiums. The Olympics are primarily put on for television."[2]

Certainly the scheduling of Olympic events is influenced by the needs of television. North American television viewers often bemoan the intrusion of commercial advertising in the sports events of Olympic telecasts. Discussion concerning the addition of new sports to the Olympic program inevitably involves the prospect for each sport to generate additional television viewers and consumers for products sold by major Olympic sponsors and television advertisers. But while some grouse about the transformation of Olympic festivals in recent years, Richard Pound states succinctly that television networks and corporate sponsors serve and will continue to serve a critical role in the production of Olympic festivals: "Take away sponsorship and commercialism from sport today and what is left? A large, sophisticated, finely tuned engine developed over a period of 100 years—with no fuel."[3]

Despite all criticism the Olympic Games remain immensely popular. A record audience of 3.7 billion people watched Olympic television coverage from Sydney. Almost 20,000 accredited media personnel conveyed Olympic news to the world's population via television, radio, newspaper, and the Internet. No one has threatened (seriously) to jump from the Olympic ship; in fact the IOC fends off proposals for the admission of many new sports.

There simply is no better way to promote a particular sport than through membership in the Olympic program. New member nations in the global community are quick to establish National Olympic Committees and seek membership in the Olympic Movement. The cost of doing that is cheap; the benefits, in a relative sense, are enormous.

While the burgeoning and increasingly unwieldy size of the Summer Games festivals predates the IOC's marriage with the corporate sector in the 1980s, the IOC/corporate sector relationship exacerbated the problem of gigantism. How can the organizational undertaking be pared down while at the same time promoting gender equity and exercising restraint against enlarging the already dominant place on the Olympic program of sports primarily practiced in the Western world?

Jacques Rogge's early musings on this subject reflect a measure of naïveté. Rather than engaging the ISFs in constructive dialogue to establish a new Olympic program, he believes that the necessary changes can be realized by "cutting down on accreditations, technology and construction costs."[4] With the same numbers of athletes and sports on the Olympic program, there is little possibility for change in the quantity of competitive venues required, and little hope for an appreciable dent in construction costs incurred by Olympic organizers. Rogge's ruminations fail to address the heart of the matter—the numbers of athletes and sports—unless, of course, he seeks to reduce the size of the competitive venues and hence their seating capacities and cost of construction. Such an approach would likely result in a greater percentage of event seats being allocated to IOC guests and sponsors.

In addition to gigantism, the doping crisis poses a second dilemma. The "commercial" profile of medal winners in premier Olympic events provided the prospect of riches for some successful athletes. In almost all regions of the world NOCs and/or national governments provide tidy sums for Olympic medal winners, believing that the success of a country's athletes projects positive messages of the nation's health and social vitality. When mixed with the desire to excel, an inherent urge in the makeup of Olympians, this has led to a proliferation of incidents of drug-enhanced performances. As the lowering of competition times in the pool or on the track continued, eyebrows arched. Was the performance legitimate? The question is an all too common refrain in the press box at Olympic venues as well as in living rooms around the world. The victim, of course, is the truly special athlete, who transcends the boundaries of achievement with performance generated by nothing more than determination, skill, solid coaching, and countless hours of training. Rogge considers the doping problem to be his most serious challenge in the years ahead. "If tomorrow, mothers do not want to send their young children to sports clubs because they are afraid of drugs," commented Rogge on the heels of his election, "it could be the end of sport."[5]

The doping problem preceded the arrival of the corporate sector in Olympic affairs; but the inherent increase in the marketability of Olympic winners, together with the prospect of riches from the state and sponsorship endorsement, provided more temptation for athletes to use performance-enhancing drugs. The IOC lost the "drug war" in the 1980s and 1990s, and it is fair to state that Lausanne officials hardly mustered for the conflict. The Olympic Movement lacked the will to tackle the designer-drug manufacturers who provided the foundation of success for Olympic athlete "cheats." The possible legal morass for the IOC resulting from an athlete's challenge of a positive drug test also acted as a deterrent. A number of prominent NOCs, including the USOC, did little to assist in building a consensus in favor of comprehensive drug testing. "Olympic officials have found it much easier to denounce such practices than to ban them," observes Alfred Senn, author of *Power, Politics and the Olympic Games.*[6] Whether the IOC's effort to combat the problem through the establishment of the World Anti-Doping Agency (WADA) will prove effective or simply represents a worthy initiative arrived at too late to have an impact remains to be seen.

Many readers of the *Sydney Morning Herald* probably smiled over their morning coffee when they turned to the *Olympics* section on 28 September 2000, day 13 of the Sydney Olympics. Under the headline "Now Eric cuts a dash at Bondi . . . with a little help from his friends," the front-page photo shows a smiling Eric Moussambani, the toast of Sydney, enjoying a surf outing on Bondi's famous waves.[7] Eric the Eel, as he was rapidly nicknamed, traveled to Sydney from his native Equatorial Guinea to represent his country in the 100 meters freestyle swimming event. He swam the distance in 1 minute 52.78 seconds, almost a full minute slower than the qualifying time, and 7.4 seconds slower than Dutchman Pieter van den Hoogenband's world record swim at the Games in an event twice the distance, the 200 meters freestyle. That Moussambani was even in Sydney is a testament to the money available to the world's NOCs through the IOC's Solidarity fund. To help with infrastructure costs associated with participating in the Sydney Games, each NOC received $40,000, plus $400 per competing athlete. Moussambani's appearance in Sydney points to a Solidarity shortcoming. The sideshow, carnivalesque quality of Moussambani's Olympic performance raised questions about whether the Eel, whose scant competitive record encompassed training limited to a mere nine-month period before the Sydney Games opened, should have been allowed to compete. Among those embarrassed by his performance were some of the Eel's fellow Equatorial Guinea citizens. When Moussambani returned home, managers of the hotel where he trained before the Games banned his future use of the pool. To them, his performance had been a national mortification.

There is still much currency in Coubertin's words comparing the value of "winning" to the "struggle," and it is vital that the Olympics remain open to athletes from developing nations. Moussambani's desperate swim of two lengths of Sydney's pristine, state-of-the-art Olympic pool, however, underscored the existence of many Olympians whose competitive experience is compromised due to their country of birth. The next generation of Olympic swimmers representing Equatorial Guinea must be better equipped to compete. With respect to athlete development in emerging or underprivileged nations, the IOC can and should do more. Its Olympic Aid Program (championed by Johann Olav Koss), which resembles a "Sports Peace Corps," should be expanded greatly, particularly in those global areas like Moussambani's homeland.

Samaranch's decisions to marry the Olympic Movement to corporate sponsors and open the Games to professional athletes yielded the desired result. The Olympic Games retained their status as the preeminent sports event in the world despite recent challenges from the World Cup (Soccer), the World Track and Field Championships, and pretenders such as the Goodwill Games. Even though it represents an intimidating challenge, an Olympic festival is a television producer's dream assignment. The production possibilities inherent in athletic dramas like the U.S. hockey triumph over the Soviet Union (Lake Placid, 1980); the outstanding talents of German figure skater Katarina Witt (Calgary, 1988); the Herculean performance of Norway's speed-skating phenom Johann Olav Koss (Lillehammer, 1994); the Franz Klammer–like hair-raising downhill ski runs of Austria's Hermann Maier (Nagano, 1998); the formidable athleticism of gymnast Nadia Comaneci (Montréal, 1976); the steely resolve of Muhammad Ali to light the Olympic flame in Atlanta (1996); and the poise, determination, and class of Australia's Aboriginal track sensation Cathy Freeman (Sydney, 2000) are scarcely matched in the sporting world.

Despite concerns about the prevalence of commercialism, Olympic festivals, which bring together the world's best athletes from different sporting disciplines, remain celebrations of human possibility in terms of athletic achievement, technological progress, and community building. Civic leaders in many of the world's major cities vie for the right to host Olympic festivals. They cherish the prestige and opportunity to promote their respective communities on the world's stage, the short- and medium-term tourism possibilities, and the legacy of athletic facilities and other infrastructure improvements.

One cannot argue the fact that the rise of Olympic commercialism resulted in a loss of innocence for Coubertin's brainchild. We need only look to Berlin (1936), Melbourne (1956), Mexico City (1968), Munich (1972), and the boycotts of the Moscow (1980) and Los Angeles (1984) festivals to explore that story. Still, Samaranch's agenda, labeled "revolutionary" by his biographer David Miller, is subject to current and future debate. Critics lament the intrusion of global commerce into the Olympic Movement and the commodification (a reduction "in the value of any act or object to only its monetary exchange value, ignoring historical, artistic or relational added values") of the Olympic Games.[8] Supporters, however, point to the ability of television networks to transmit Olympic images around the world to an ever-increasing audience and the critical roles played by corporate sponsors in delivering the technological support required to stage these mega-events. Collectively, their financial support also ensures the participation of hundreds of athletes from developing nations who otherwise would not experience such opportunities.

Nonetheless, Samaranch's invitation to the corporate sector to become a major financial partner of the IOC contributed greatly to what will remain a lasting black mark in his presidency—the prostituting of the bidding process for Olympic festivals. The stakes involved in the Olympic bid process mushroomed exponentially under his leadership. With the added security of corporate backing should their efforts bear fruit, bid committees applied the "full court press" in their attempts to land the Games for their respective communities. The Olympic Movement's new wealth challenged the integrity of the Olympic enterprise and exposed the embarrassing conduct of some IOC members. In an effort to cull favor bid committees lavished gifts, college scholarships for dependents, expense-paid trips, even hard cash on IOC members in return for their votes. Tales of Olympic "agents" who sold the votes of some IOC members reached the public. The questionable undertakings of bid committees received wide press coverage as well. While many resisted, a few IOC members attached a sense of entitlement to their position. The IOC's effort to monitor its members' conduct lacked vigor. Too late, IOC leaders conceded their error in not pursuing evidence of such wayward conduct on the part of some members.[9] For Samaranch, 1999 was a year of trials. But he bears much of the blame because these events accelerated under his stewardship. Television reports and newspaper articles scored the IOC for its management of the bid process and lax enforcement of its rules. The reform measures introduced in late 1999 appeased some but not all.

In the aftermath of the Salt Lake City scandal, sport leaders, social commentators, journalists, academics, politicians, and others from diverse walks of life offered their two cents' worth of wisdom to the IOC on ways to reconstitute itself for the future. The IOC listened, accepted some advice, and dismissed other suggestions, subsequently pursuing its reform agenda. Individuals at the center of the IOC's power structure believe that they have charted a new path for the IOC that will enhance accountability, athlete input, and public confidence. Time will tell if their optimism is well founded. One thing is certain: the Salt Lake City scandal and its fallout placed the IOC on a shorter leash with the public and the media for the foreseeable future. The work of Jacques Rogge and other Olympic officials in the new millennium will be subject to much greater scrutiny.

OBSERVATIONS ON OLYMPIC MARKETING AND THE FUTURE

As we close this history, a number of observations seem pertinent to the future success of the IOC's marketing initiatives:

1. *The continued success of the IOC's Marketing Program depends on the ability of the IOC to guarantee exclusivity for its primary sponsors.* The IOC understands this imperative, judging by its effort to monitor the Internet (and take swift action against websites "streaming" events from Sydney) during the Sydney Olympics as a means of protecting the rights of its television network partners. This campaign parallels an ongoing attempt to tackle ambush marketers who threaten the rights of the TOP sponsors. The energies and resources required to protect the exclusive rights of the television partners and corporate sponsors will only grow as the number (and popularity) of viable transmission media for Olympic events increases (broad band, etc.).

2. *It is imperative that the IOC continue to avoid the lure of Pay-TV and maintain its policy of keeping competition venues free of commercial advertising.* The world's population must have access to Olympic coverage, which should focus on the athletes and their performances to the greatest extent possible. Most viewers and followers of the Olympics understand the need for commercial sponsors and accept their participation, but the public's continued goodwill in this area depends on the IOC's resolve.

3. *The sale of television contracts and TOP sponsorships must occur on a basis that benefits cities bidding for the right to host an Olympic festival.* Public and corporate support for an Olympic bid can only be generated if a city's population and business leaders are fully aware of

the definitive revenue available from corporate sponsors and television networks. Television contracts must be concluded in advance of the awarding of an Olympic festival to a city through the use of the Sunset Project model, and the same timetable for corporate sponsorship agreements merits serious consideration. From a financial perspective, bidding for (and successful acquisition of) the right to host an Olympic festival is a calculated risk. It is incumbent upon the IOC to reduce that risk to the lowest possible level, since host cities are responsible for assuming accrued debt (unless, of course, the host city works out an arrangement with regional or national governments, as was the case in Sydney).

4. *The IOC's ability to "manage its message" concerning its spending practices can be improved.* Admittedly, the media often show less interest in "feel good" stories than in scandal, but too many people around the world lack an understanding of the IOC's spending practices as well as its share of television and corporate sponsorship revenue. Can commercial contract goals established by the IOC's marketing officials be linked with long-term projects (requiring expenditures beyond those involved in the production of an Olympic site complex) whose nature becomes part of the public domain? Greater synergy among the individuals negotiating television and corporate sponsorship deals, the parties determining IOC spending priorities (Executive Board members and administrators of the Solidarity program), and the IOC's media representatives offers the opportunity to demonstrate the "good" to the public and skeptical members of the Fifth Estate.

MOSCOW MACHINATIONS AND THE MAN
WHO COULDN'T SAY GOOD-BYE

In July 2001 IOC members convened in Moscow for one of the most historic, highly anticipated, and media-frenzied sessions in the organization's history. Eschewing concerns expressed in some quarters of the world concerning China's record on human rights, IOC delegates overwhelmingly supported Beijing's bid for the 2008 Summer Olympics. IOC members were also charged with the responsibility of selecting Juan Antonio Samaranch's successor. Belgium's Jacques Rogge emerged from the pool of five candidates who coveted the most powerful position in world sport. Both decisions stirred debate and controversy.

With respect to Beijing, IOC members determined that the time had come to deliver the Games to China, the world's most populous nation.

Beijing's bid benefited from the unequivocal support of the IOC's outgoing president, Juan Antonio Samaranch. Despite a strong bid encompassing an athlete-centered focus, Toronto's candidature suffered from the fact that Canada, a comparatively small Olympic nation, has hosted the Olympics on two previous occasions (Montréal, 1976; and Calgary, 1988). Despite the cachet of Paris and the city's historical link with the Olympic Movement's founder, Pierre de Coubertin, the Paris bid committee faced a similar hurdle. Olympic athletes have competed on French soil on five occasions (Paris, 1900 and 1924; Chamonix, 1924; Grenoble, 1968; and Albertville, 1992).

To their critics, IOC members offered hope that reaching out to the Chinese in this fashion would foster change in China's human rights record. The heightened scrutiny of the world community and media in the following seven years, argued IOC members, would act as a lever for change. Former U.S. president Jimmy Carter's national security adviser Zbigniew Brzezinski agreed. When comparing the Beijing award to the IOC's granting of the 1980 Summer Olympics to Moscow and the Soviets' goal of exploiting the achievement as a political victory, Brzezinski concluded that "the Olympics may be a triumph for China, but by intensifying the pressures for change the Games are quite unlikely to be a triumph for China's waning Communism. In fact, the Games may accelerate its fading."[10]

In the past twenty years many Chinese citizens have witnessed startling change in personal wealth, discretionary income, and availability of consumer goods. In the eyes of the world community, however, China's albatross remains its human rights record. The award of the Games to Beijing, based on optimism that Chinese leaders would effect change in this area, might very well lead to positive initiatives in the ensuing decade. The true test rests in whether these changes will endure.

While IOC delegates considered China's domestic policies in the decision-making process, the role played by economic realities must not be lost in a review of Beijing's success. The CEOs of the Olympic Movement's TOP corporate sponsors were delighted by the prospect of carving a sizable niche in the massive Chinese marketplace of some 1.4 billion people. In light of Beijing's win, a North American site for the 2012 Summer Olympics becomes a distinct possibility. Such a prospect leaves the IOC with an attractive rights package (combined with the rights to the 2010 Olympic Winter Games) to entice U.S. television executives in the next few years.

The election of Jacques Rogge as Juan Antonio Samaranch's successor similarly captivated a world audience. While Beijing's victory gives evidence of the IOC's belief in the ambulatory nature of the Olympic Games, Rogge's triumph further confirms that the same concept does not apply to the IOC presidency. Europe's grip on this office remains firm. The end of Rogge's first presidential term in 2009 will mark 95 years of European presidential leadership in the IOC's 115-year history. In fact, the striking centralization of political power and decision-making authority in Europe poses a potential problem for Rogge. For a "Movement" that purports to be "international," this is not a particularly healthy administrative circumstance. Europeans hold approximately 45% of all seats on the IOC. Two-thirds of the members of the IOC's powerful Executive Board are European. Rogge's management of the USOC file will also be tested. In the wake of the Moscow session, the United States, the financial engine of the Olympic Movement, enjoys no representation on the Executive Board and has fewer IOC members (four) than countries such as Switzerland (five) and Italy (five).

Despite Canadian Richard Pound's work on a number of critical portfolios (marketing, WADA, the USOC, and the IOC's internal investigation of improprieties concerning the Salt Lake City bid process) during Samaranch's presidency and twenty-three years of service to the IOC, the Spaniard sabotaged Pound's campaign to succeed him. First, he supported Rogge; his public expression of neutrality with respect to the presidential election was a façade. Second, mere minutes before the presidential vote he publicly censured Pound for what he considered to be the bungling of the IOC's effort to facilitate the execution of WADA's mandate.[11] This criticism came from the same individual who awarded the Olympic Order to Erich Honecker, former president of East Germany, a nation notorious for one of the most drug-ridden sport programs in Olympic history. Did Samaranch bear a grudge for Pound's opposition to raising the IOC's mandatory retirement age for members to eighty in 1995? IOC members' support for this initiative permitted Samaranch to serve through 2001.

Surprisingly, Pound finished third in the race behind South Korea's Un Yong Kim. Drawing support from the Asian bloc, Kim waged a serious campaign for the presidency. By capitalizing on his connections to the ISFs through his presidency of the General Assembly of International Sports Federations he tried to surmount lingering concerns about the severe warning received from Pound's investigative commission that dealt with the Salt Lake City bid process. Kim's campaign also suffered eleventh-hour troubles in Moscow when the IOC Ethics Commission launched an investigation of his pledge, if elected, to provide IOC members with a yearly stipend.

During reflections on his presidential tenure shortly before the vote to succeed him Samaranch declared that "the IOC I am leaving my successor has nothing to do with the IOC I received in 1980."[12] He is correct in this assertion. The financial foundation of the IOC and its place on the world stage have changed significantly in the past twenty-one years. With Jacques Rogge's election, however, many observers question whether Samaranch has left the IOC to anyone. Early indications are that in retirement Samaranch will retain his suite at Lausanne's Palace Hotel, manage the affairs of the Olympic Museum, now named in his honor, and attend IOC Executive Committee meetings, at which he will have a voice but no vote by virtue of his new title as honorary president. In a final act of shocking nepotism, the aging Spaniard manipulated his son's appointment to IOC membership. Rogge was Samaranch's choice for the presidency. Despite Rogge's success with the Sydney Coordination Commission and his likable personality, with a mere three years of service on the IOC's powerful Executive Board the best that can be said about his presidential qualifications is that he is untested. One Olympic insider ventured that Samaranch's influence over Rogge by virtue of his seat at Executive Board meetings might resemble "a ventriloquist and his doll."[13] Samaranch's lingering health problems in the wake of the Moscow session might relieve Rogge of the prospect of having to deal with Samaranch's shadow. Still, Rogge's first critical challenge is assertively to demonstrate his independence and that Richard Pound's view will prevail—that Rogge will distance himself from his mentor. "I've been in business long enough," deadpanned a disappointed Pound following his election defeat, "to learn that there is nothing as ex- as an ex-president."[14]

What will historians write about Samaranch's presidency thirty years from now? "For sure, one finds warts and areas to be praised," concluded Olympic historian John Lucas.[15] His decisions to open the Games to professional athletes and launch TOP spurred the popularity of the Games and their potential to generate revenue, especially in the U.S. market. He strengthened ties among the IOC, ISFs, and NOCs. And he will be lauded for his handling of the negotiations with South and North Korean officials prior to the Seoul Olympics that ensured a successful festival in 1988. He will also be remembered for his diplomatic acumen, which enabled him to establish a relationship with the world's political leaders.

The negative aspects of Samaranch's presidential leadership, however, will also provide grist for historians. While he has been praised by some for his efforts to increase the number of female athletes in Olympic competition, women enjoy scarcely any more power in the halls of IOC decision-making than they did in 1980. For an individual who demonstrated time and time again a unique ability to move people toward supporting his goals and agenda, he failed to generate consensus within the Olympic Movement concerning the need to "root out" drug cheats aggressively. Was that a priority for him? The frequent addition of new sports to the Olympic program offered an increasing number of the world's athletes an opportunity to participate in the Olympic Games. But this development came with a price tag. The immense organizational, logistical, and financial challenges inherent in hosting a Summer Olympics, due to the unbridled growth of the Olympic program during his presidency, prevented major cities in emerging nations from launching a serious bid to host an Olympic festival. The accelerating commodification of the Olympic Games has led many to question whom the Games are for—the athletes or the world of business? Finally, Juan Antonio Samaranch must bear full responsibility for the IOC's recent image crisis. Until confronted by the Salt Lake City nightmare, he demonstrated neither the will nor the courage to curb the excesses of bid committees and the IOC's pronounced gift culture.

Despite the fallout from the Salt Lake City scandal and the public's enhanced reservations regarding the ethics and image of the Olympic Movement, the popularity of the Olympic Games has survived largely intact. The public's continuing goodwill depends on Jacques Rogge. Will he demonstrate that he is not Samaranch's marionette? Will he confront the doping problem effectively? Will he limit the growth and/or reduce the size of the Games? Will he ensure equity for women in Olympic decision-making? Will he give due regard to environmental concerns at prospective Olympic sites, ensuring that the rights of those who feel threatened by the staging of Olympic festivals in their communities (homeless and low-income individuals as well as skeptical taxpayers) are protected? The IOC's financial foundation is secure. What will Rogge establish as his goals for the constructive use of the IOC treasury? And how will the IOC, under his leadership, address heightened security concerns at future Olympic sites stemming from the tragic events of 11 September 2001 in New York City, Washington, D.C., and southern Pennsylvania? Rogge's success in dealing with this matrix of issues will inform the judgment of historians who assess his leadership.

NOTES

PREFACE

1. John Kenneth Galbraith, *The Affluent Society*, 4th ed. (Boston: Houghton Mifflin Company, 1984). Galbraith instructs us that most goods produced are not of urgent importance for carrying out our lives. But "if production is to increase, wants must be effectively contrived" (p. 132). An "elaborate myth" (p. 114) surrounds demand for goods, much of it perpetrated by advertising.

2. See *Marketing Matters* (Lausanne: IOC, September 2000): 10.

3. Marc Bloch, *The Historian's Craft* (New York: Alfred A. Knopf, 1953), pp. 138–39.

AN EPILOGUE AS PROLOGUE:
SYDNEY 2000, "THE GREATEST GAMES EVER"

1. For the exact text of Samaranch's closing remarks, see "And the Winner Is . . . the Whole World," *Sydney Daily Telegraph*, 2 October 2000. The phrase "whole world" was used by the *Daily Telegraph* writer to describe Samaranch's long list of thank-yous to people who "made this fantastic success possible." Samaranch's beaming countenance accompanied the article. Clearly, he had much to be relieved and thankful for relative to his last public Olympic moment.

2. For Samaranch's remarks on this occasion, see "Winners the People of Sydney," *Sydney Daily Telegraph*, 20 October 2000.

3. The feeling that "all was well" in the Olympic world resonated across the five Olympic continents. For example, in England the *London Daily Mirror* trumpeted, "Good on ya, sport!—Wizards of Oz gave Olympics back its heart." The *London Daily Mail*'s Ian Woolridge pontificated: "Forty years of covering the Olympic Games convinces me that never again will they be celebrated on such a scale as in Sydney . . . No city on Earth will outshine what we have experienced here." The Madrid daily *El País* announced: "The Games were a perfect answer to the Olympic crisis following corruption . . . the best medication for the disease." The *Washington Post* told American readers: "The Sydney Games were an organizational marvel, an aesthetic wonder, a smashing success. . . ." The *Johannesburg Citizen* in South Africa enthused: "The Australians were simply brilliant." Cited in David Hein, "World Sings Our Praises," *Sydney Daily Telegraph*, 4 October 2000.

4. The three medals (two silver, one bronze) led to a nation in despair.

5. For instance, the federal government spent approximately $500 million on facilitating elite athlete performance (coaching, training, and competition, not infrastructure) during the four years prior to the 2000 Games. See, for example, Adele

Horin, "Counting the Cost, at $40m Per Gold Medal," *Sydney Morning Herald,* 30 September 2000. Following the Games the AOC announced a total collective award of $1.7 million to its medal-winning athletes. These awards ranged from a high of $60,000 paid to swimmer Ian Thorpe (who won five medals, two of them gold) to an award of $15,000 to taekwondo gold medalist Lauren Burns. For more on this, see Tom Salom, "Million-Dollar Club: Top Olympians Claim Lion's Share of Bonuses," *Sydney Daily Telegraph,* 25 November 2000.

6. Cited by Horin, "Counting the Cost." Sydney's Olympic Games appear to have had a pronounced effect on a general turn by youth toward fitness and sport, especially Olympic sport. The Australian Sports Commission, surveying some sixty sporting clubs and organizations around Australia, reported "big membership increases across all Olympic sports, including obscure ones." Deborah Cameron, "Post-Games, It's the Groupies' Time to Play," *Sydney Morning Herald,* 2 December 2000. The New South Wales government launched an energetic campaign to change lifestyles of young Australians. In response to Premier Bob Carr's lament that "[t]he physical activity that was a part of our way of life has evaporated . . . You can see it in our obese kids," a task force was established and a Gold Medal Fitness program was instituted, involving the nation's Olympians and Paralympians (Nathan Vass, "Game Plan: Olympic Champions to Promote Exercise," *Sydney Sunday Telegraph,* 8 October 2000).

7. In particular the expected horde of Olympic spectators produced endless pre-Games pontification on the perceived inadequacies of Sydney's transit system. On the contrary, transportation proved to be a major triumph. The "system" (bus, train, and ferry) carried almost 5 million people to Olympic Park alone over nineteen days (sixteen days of events, including the closing ceremonies, and the opening ceremonies with two dress rehearsals). Additionally, 1.5 million traveled on the system to venues located outside Olympic Park. See "IOC, SOCOG, It's O.V.E.R, O.K.?" *Sydney Morning Herald,* 4 November 2000. During the Games, approximately 38 million journeys were make to and from Olympic venues. See "Transport Effort Worthy of Medal," *Sydney Daily Telegraph,* 4 October 2000.

8. A barrage of criticism, some of it justified, surfaced in the local Sydney press during the months and weeks prior to the opening of the Games. Within SOCOG itself vacations taken at critical periods by senior administrators, breakdown in vertical communication from senior management to lower levels, problems in the relationship with the OCA, ticket allocation and distribution policy, and confusion and anxiety prompted by the question "Will it work?" (transportation systems, weather, crisis control, security) conspired to lead many to conclude that the Games had come off in outstanding fashion in spite of, not because of, the moguls at the top and middle levels of the great endeavor's administration. The most virulent criticism was leveled at the allocation and distribution of event tickets. "In every Games, you have a black file for something that didn't work," said Michael Payne, IOC marketing director. "In Atlanta it was the technology and problems with commercialism. The black file here was the managing of the ticket process." Bruce Horovitz, "Irked UPS Mulls Whether to Abandon Sponsorship," *USA Today,* 28 September 2000.

9. See "Sydney, Learning Lessons in Atlanta," *Sydney Morning Herald*, 3 August 1996.

10. The term "ambush marketing" was created to describe the activities of companies that sought to associate themselves with an event such as the Olympic Games without paying for the privilege.

11. For more on Sydney's control of "commercial awareness," see "In Sydney, No Cover for Ambush Ads," *International Herald Tribune*, Saturday–Sunday, 30 September–1 October 2000.

12. See *Marketing Matters* (Lausanne: IOC, May 2001): 1.

13. See, for instance, "Viewing Record Topples," *Sydney Sunday Telegraph*, 17 September 2000. Despite the fact that 72% of all Sydney households watched the opening ceremonies, two events of British royal history commanded even larger percentages of the Sydney television audience: the 1997 funeral of Princess Diana (79%) and the 1981 wedding of Prince Charles and Diana (75%). See David Dale, "The Ratings Were on the Wall," *Sydney Morning Herald*, 7 October 2000.

14. Shortly before the Games began, the Australian dollar had dipped below 55 cents against its U.S. counterpart. By the end of the Games the Aussie dollar had weakened even further, dropping to 51.8 cents. The roman numeral IV refers to the fourth cycle of TOP since its inception in 1985 (from 1 January 1997 through 31 December 2000).

15. See *Marketing Matters* (Lausanne: IOC, May 2001): 3. An interesting sidelight of Sydney's record-breaking ticket sales was the effect that it had on advance ticket sales for the next Olympic Games, in Salt Lake City in February 2002. The first opportunity to buy Salt Lake City Olympic tickets was timed to mesh with the end of the Sydney Games. Salt Lake organizers, noting the disappointing Nielsen viewer rating figures for NBC's delayed coverage of the Sydney Games, feared the worst. Ticket sales opened on 10 October; tickets worth $45 million were sold on the first day. Within two weeks tickets worth another $35 million had been sold, 90% of them through the Internet—all this with the opening of the Games 472 days away. See "Success Gives Utah Boost," *Sydney Daily Telegraph*, 24 October 2000.

16. Obviously, a commercial marketplace with some 270 million individuals would normally present a better prospect for gross sales than one with 19 million people.

17. From 15 September to 26 September official Olympic merchandise outlets at Games competition venues alone recorded sales grossing $30 million. By the time the Games closed on the evening of 1 October, the Olympic Superstore in Olympic Park had achieved sales totaling almost $20 million. For more on this, see "Merchandise Sales Reach $30m Early," *Sydney Daily Telegraph*, 27 September 2000.

18. See *Marketing Matters* (Lausanne: IOC, May 2001): 5.

19. For a post-Games report on this, see "Coins Turn into Gold," *Sydney Sunday Telegraph*, 8 October 2000. See also *Sydney Daily Telegraph*, 25 September 2000, which confirmed that Sydney had eclipsed coin sales of all previous Olympics, and "Games Makes a Mint," *Sydney Daily Telegraph*, 6 December 2000.

20. "Olympics Reap $1bn for Trade," *Sydney Daily Telegraph*, 13 October 2000.

21. "Small Business Getting to Woo World Markets," *Sydney Daily Telegraph*, 13 October 2000.

22. "It's Time to Cash In on Sydney's 'Sexy' Image," *Sydney Daily Telegraph*, 9 December 2000.

23. "Carr on a China Visit," *Sydney Sunday Telegraph*, 5 November 2000. The fact that Beijing was a favorite to capture the bid for the 2008 Olympic Games obviously made the Australians, "who had done it well," and the Chinese, "who needed to do it well" if they won the bid (to be announced in July 2001), natural trading partners: Australians as sellers of Olympic expertise and the Chinese as buyers. An embarrassing sequel to Carr's China visit took place a month after his return. In response to his invitation a 100-member Chinese delegation bearing a rare and unique Chinese antique gold vase valued at $850,000 Australian visited Australia in early December to begin negotiations with New South Wales government officials. A mix-up in protocol resulted in the absence of an Australian official to greet the party. A spokesperson for the Australian International Trade Organization expressed "disappointment." The state opposition in Parliament went further. With tongue in cheek, deputy leader Berry O'Farrell exclaimed: "The Premier and his government need the political equivalent of Viagra to maintain interest in running the state." "Chinese Visitors Snubbed," *Sydney Daily Telegraph*, 7 December 2000.

24. See David Humphries, "NSW Forges School Ties with China," *Sydney Morning Herald*, 6 November 2000. One of the federal government's largest contributions to the Games was an approximately $500 million Australian expenditure for Olympic security. The only major security incidents during the entire period of the Games were two bomb scares—"expected explosive devices left around Sydney"—handled by bomb search personnel. "Two Bomb Scares at Games," *Sydney Daily Telegraph*, 24 November 2000.

25. David Humphries, "China Wooed as Athens Shuns Olympic Builders," *Sydney Morning Herald*, 8 November 2000.

26. "Carr Chasing US Business," *Sydney Daily Telegraph*, 2 December 2000.

27. "Dollar Hits Tourism Adds," *Sydney Sunday Telegraph*, 26 November 2000.

28. Cited by Lisa Southgate, "Olympics Pays Off with Tourism Boom," *Weekend Australian*, 11–12 November 2000.

29. Michael Millett, "Shortage of Space Casts Tourism Pall," *Sydney Morning Herald*, 2 December 2000.

30. "Games Lifts Tourism Bar," *Sydney Daily Telegraph*, 6 December 2000.

31. "Tourism Jobs Set to Boom," *Sydney Daily Telegraph*, 7 December 2000.

32. Phillip McCarthy, "Sydney Dancers Reap Olympic Dividend," *Sydney Morning Herald*, 28 November 2000.

33. See Rick Westwood, "Thorpedo Chases US Cash," *Sydney Daily Telegraph*, 27 September 2000.

34. The market life of a successful Olympian is generally much shorter than that of other "professional" athletes, whose images are far more sustained on a day to day, season to season, year to year basis. According to *Business Review Weekly's* survey of the gross earnings of Australian sports stars for the year 2000, Thorpe, the top-rated Olympic athlete, ranked twenty-second on the list ($1.2 million Aus-

tralian). The disparity between Thorpe and golfer Greg Norman (first on the list) was some $46 million. Cited by *Sydney Daily Telegraph,* 9 December 2000.

35. Sophie Tedmanson, "Making Money from Memories," *Sydney Daily Telegraph,* 27 September 2000.

36. See Lucy Clark, "Annual Earning Up to $10m," *Sydney Daily Telegraph,* 27 September 2000.

37. Anna Cook, "Tatiana Wants to Cash In on Success," *Sydney Daily Telegraph,* 27 September 2000. See also Philippa Walsh and Ben English, "Gold Opportunity: Marketing Fortune Awaits Games Stars," *Sydney Daily Telegraph,* 27 September 2000.

38. Australia's states are New South Wales, Queensland, Victoria, South Australia, Western Australia, and off-shore Tasmania. Its territories are Australian Capital Territory (Canberra) and Northern Australia.

39. Philippa Walsh, "AMP Torch Ignites Emotion and Profit," *Sydney Daily Telegraph,* 15 September 2000.

40. Philippa Walsh, citing BHP chief executive officer Paul Anderson, in "BHP Shines in Global Coming Out Party," *Sydney Daily Telegraph,* 30 September 2000.

41. Ibid.

42. See Jane Counsel, "BHP to Remain Flexible on HBI Deadline," *Sydney Morning Herald,* 3 November 2000.

43. "Lifting the Lindemans Brand Value," unpublished Lindemans Report document, 31 August 2000, p. 7. The authors are grateful to Clare Madden, Lindemans marketing manager, and Michelle Lawlor, Lindemans public relations official, for their knowledge and insight on Lindemans' Olympic sponsorship involvement.

44. As the sole sponsor in the alcohol class, Lindemans' total Olympic investment can be counted in the tens of millions of dollars, including cash payments (to the Olympic teams of Australia, Canada, and Great Britain), large-scale print advertisement (particularly in the United States and Great Britain), exclusive value-in-kind wine products at IOC, AOC, and SOCOG functions as well as all Olympic venues before and during the Games, constructing and operating Lindemans Wine Bar at Olympic Park throughout the period of the Games (at least 260,000 people visited the wine bar during the Games, buying 105,615 glasses of wine), administering a special hospitality center for some 800 distributor clients in Australia and overseas, and organizing a formidable breakfast reception at the Lindemans winery in the Hunter Valley for Olympic officials of all types, during which an Olympic torch relay exchange occurred. Although Lindemans is reluctant to reveal "the bottom line cost" for all this, competitors in the Hunter Valley estimate a total investment of at least $100 million Australian.

45. Michelle Lawlor to the authors, 12 December 2000.

46. See *Marketing Matters* (Lausanne: IOC, May 2001): 5. See also "Lifting the Lindemans Brand Value," p. 8.

47. See "Wine Exports Sparkle," *Sydney Daily Telegraph,* 7 December 2000.

48. "Lifting the Lindemans Brand Value," p. 8.

49. See Kathy Lipari, "Ads, Fanfare and Corporate Kudos," *Sydney Daily Telegraph,* 6 October 2000. For Westpac's figures, Lipari cites "a Westpac spokesman."

50. Anthony Hughes, "Westpac Record Merger Talks Off," *Sydney Morning Herald*, 4 November 2000.

51. Lipari, "Ads, Fanfare and Corporate Kudos." Here Lipari quotes Tom Shepard, VISA's senior vice-president for international marketing.

52. "In Sydney, No Cover for Ambush Ads," *Paris International Herald Tribune*, 30 September–1 October 2000.

53. Darling Harbor, a trendy "gathering place" during the Games, hosted the competitions in boxing, weightlifting, fencing, judo, freestyle and Greco-Roman wrestling, and volleyball. The precinct also served as the central marshaling point for thousands of partying Olympic tourists, day after day, sometimes all night, reminiscent of Plaza España beneath Montjuic hill during the Barcelona Games in 1992.

54. Peter Lalor, "Olympic Flame Ignited Market," *Sydney Daily Telegraph*, 21 October 2000.

55. See "Visitors to Games Missed Home Fare," *Sydney Daily Telegraph*, 13 December 2000.

56. Peter Trute, "Games Cheats Ten Earnings," *Sydney Daily Telegraph*, 6 December 2000.

57. Bruce Horovitz, "Irked UPS Mulls Whether to Abandon Sponsorship," *USA Today*, 28 September 2000.

58. See, for instance, "UPS Won't Deliver Renewal of IOC Deal," *London (Ontario) Free Press*, 22 December 2000.

59. Cited by the New South Wales Parliament opposition treasury spokesperson in David Penworthy's "Revealed: Our 2.1 bn Games Bill," *Sydney Daily Telegraph*, 13 October 2000.

60. The authors are grateful to Ray Moore, OCA's chief consulting accountant in Michael Knight's office, for providing a copy of OCA's "Interim Report."

61. For more on this, see "Trade Wins Gold, But $A Dives," *Sydney Morning Herald*, 1 November 2000. The effect of the Games boosted exports by $1.4 billion Australian, pushing the trade balance in September to a $677 million surplus, compared with a deficit of $1.3 billion in August.

62. See Catriona Dixon, "Burning Success Strikes Home: What Did Australians Really Think of the Sydney Olympic Games?" *Sydney Daily Telegraph*, 2 December 2000.

63. In macroeconomic terms this statement is given credence by the complex research of Holger Preuss. See his *Economics of the Olympic Games: Hosting the Games, 1972–2000* (Sydney: Walla Walla Press, 2000). For an equally assertive but more isolated study, see F. Brunet, *Economy of the 1992 Barcelona Olympic Games* (Lausanne: International Olympic Committee, 1994). Despite the arguments of Preuss and Brunet regarding the enduring value of Olympic sports facilities to the host city, a Sydney assessment one year after the 2000 Games gives reason for concern. For instance, the giant Olympic stadium, envisioned to host forty football matches during the year 20001, has had only a half-dozen thus far. One of the stadium's biggest investors has asked the NSW government for more than $10 million to help with operating costs. The use and operating costs of other Sydney Olympic facilities (Aquatic Center, Tennis Center, and Basketball Super Dome) also present a generally dismal picture. As one disenchanted Sydneyite groused: "I predict our grandchildren will be paying off these facilities" (Dennis Passa, "No More Fun and

Games: Sydney Still Trying to Figure Out What to Do with Olympic Facilities," *Toronto Sunday Sun,* 16 September 2001).

64. Stephen Brunt, "Olympics Find Their Saving Grace," *Toronto Globe and Mail,* 2 October 2000.

65. Bob Carr, "Why Sydney Needs to Celebrate and Pay for the Privilege," *Sydney Morning Herald,* 3 November 2000.

1. ESTABLISHING A PROSPECTIVE GOLD MINE: THE EARLY YEARS

1. For some specific examples, see G. Redmond, *The Caledonian Games in Nineteenth Century America* (Rutherford: Farleigh-Dickinson University Press, 1971), and *The Sporting Scots in Nineteenth Century Canada* (Toronto: Associated University Press, 1982); J. Ruhl, "The Olympic Games of Robert Dover, 1612–1984," in *Sport History: Official Report 1984 Olympic Scientific Congress* (Niederhausen: Schors-Verlag, 1985); and Robert K. Barney, " 'For Such Olympic Games': German-American Turnfests as Preludes to the Modern Olympic Games," in Fernand Landry, Marc Landry, and Magdeleine Yerlès, eds., *Sport: The Third Millennium* (Saint-Foy: University of Laval Press, 1991), pp. 697–705. For a general survey, see G. Redmond, "Towards Modern Revival of the Olympic Games: The Various 'Pseudo-Olympics' of the 19th Century," in Jeffrey O. Segrave and Donald Chu, eds., *The Olympic Games in Transition* (Champaign: Human Kinetics Press, 1988), pp. 71–87.

2. By far the best English-language account of Brookes's Much Wenlock Games and the so-called Zappian Olympics is found in David C. Young, *The Modern Olympics: A Struggle for Revival* (Baltimore: Johns Hopkins University Press, 1996).

3. For an excellent account of the most successful of Zappas's Olympic Games (the 1870 spectacle) as well as the failure of subsequent Games, see ibid., pp. 42–52.

4. Several biographies of Coubertin focus largely on his "Olympic quest." See, for instance, John J. MacAloon, *This Great Symbol: Pierre de Coubertin and the Origin of the Modern Olympic Games* (Chicago: University of Chicago Press, 1981); Marie-Thérèse Eyquem, *Pierre de Coubertin: L'épopée olympique* (Paris: Calmann-Lévy, 1966); and Yves-Pierre Boulongne, *La vie et l'oeuvre pédagogique de Pierre de Coubertin* (Ottawa: Leméac, 1975).

5. The vexing issue of "amateurism" continued to be debated for almost a century longer. It was not fully resolved until the 1970s and 1980s, with the emergence of IOC president Lord Killanin's trust fund system followed by his successor Juan Antonio Samaranch's decision to grant authority on the issue to each ISF.

6. The authors are grateful to Dionysios Tritaris, Ph.D. candidate at Aristotle University–Thessaloniki, for these data. See his unpublished paper "Power, Politics and Private Purse: An Introduction to the Organizational Challenges of the 1896 Olympic Games" (December 2000).

7. Greek Independence Day, 25 March, marked the date of the opening of the Games according to the Greek calendar (the Julian calendar). On the calendar that Europe and most of the rest of the world followed (the Gregorian calendar) the date was 5 April.

8. Four English-language treatments of the first Modern Olympic Games rise

above all others: Bill Mallon and Ture Widlund, *The 1896 Games: Results for All Competitors in All Events, with Commentary* (Jefferson, N.C.: McFarland & Company, 1998); John J. MacAloon, *This Great Symbol: Pierre de Coubertin and the Origins of the Modern Olympic Games* (Chicago: University of Chicago Press, 1981); and Richard Mandell, *The First Modern Olympics* (Berkeley: University of California Press, 1976). In particular, see Young, *The Modern Olympics: A Struggle for Survival.*

9. The most complete and authoritative work in any language on what passed for the 1900 Olympic Games is Bill Mallon, *The 1900 Olympic Games: Results for All Competitors in All Events, with Commentary* (Jefferson, N.C.: McFarland & Company, 1998).

10. For an explanation of the complicated award and transfer of the 1904 Games, see Robert Knight Barney, "Born from Dilemma: America Awakens to Olympic Games," *Olympika* 1 (1992): 92–135.

11. For the best description of participation statistics for the St. Louis Olympic Games, see Bill Mallon, *The 1904 Olympic Games: Results for All Competitors in All Events, with Commentary* (Jefferson, N.C.: McFarland & Company, 1999).

12. See *Olympic Games, London, 1908—Marathon Race* (London: Vail & Co. Printers, 1908), Special Collections, D. B. Weldon Library, University of Western Ontario, London, Ontario, Canada.

13. The most comprehensive overview of the American-British controversies that occurred during the 1908 Olympic Games, sometimes referred to as "The Battle of Shepherd's Bush," is given by Bill Mallon and Ian Buchanan in *The 1908 Olympic Games: Results for All Competitors in All Events, with Commentary* (Jefferson, N.C.: McFarland & Company, 2000), pp. 327–405.

14. Several writers have focused on the disharmony that prevailed between the Americans and the British during the 1908 Games, but the analysis offered by F. A. M. Webster is perhaps the most precise and unbiased. See his *Olympic Cavalcade* (London: Hutchinson & Co., Publishers, 1948), pp. 59–85.

15. See IOC Marketing Department, "The History of Olympic Marketing," *Olympic Marketing: 1999 Fact File* (Winter 1999): 33.

16. For more on the grand scale of the congress, as well as its agenda business, see Arnd Krüger, "Forgotten Decisions: The IOC on the Eve of World War I," *Olympika* 6 (1997): 85–98.

17. Actually, Coubertin's "new" Olympic flag made an unofficial appearance before the public on 5 April 1914 in Chatby Stadium in Alexandria, Egypt, on the dual occasion of celebrating the Pan-Egyptian Games and the twentieth anniversary of the birth of the Modern Olympic Movement.

18. For a discussion on the development of the Olympic symbol, see Robert Knight Barney, "This Great Symbol," *Olympic Review* 301 (November 1992): 627–31 and 641. The baron's original pronouncement clearly enunciated "five parts of the world," not five continents. Fifteen years later, reflecting on the creation of the symbol, Coubertin substituted the word "continents" for "parts." Despite his original explanation, since 1929 the *Olympic Charter* has stated that the five rings represent the five continents of the world, meaning, from a European perspective, Asia, Africa, Oceania, Europe, and the Americas.

19. Though Coubertin named Swiss IOC member Godefroy de Blonay to act as president of the IOC during his military service, the record indicates that Blonay did little to carry on the affairs of office. There is abundant evidence to support the fact that Coubertin, even when serving in the military, energetically engaged in correspondence and media intervention concerning Olympic business. Blonay's "custodianship" of the IOC presidency has never received scholarly attention, perhaps because there is little that can be reported.

20. Nine IOC members convened in Lausanne in April 1919 to decide on the first postwar Olympic Games host. Yielding to the influence of Belgium's Count Henri Baillet-Latour, they selected the city of Antwerp over four other candidates in "a unanimous tribute to Belgium." Karl Lennartz, "The Presidency of Henri de Baillet-Latour (1925–1942)," in *The International Olympic Committee—One Hundred Years: The Idea—the Presidents—the Achievements,* vol. 1 (Lausanne: IOC, 1994), pp. 105–7.

21. The best scholarly account of the organization of the Antwerp Games is by the Belgian researcher Roland Renson: *La VII Olympiade—Anvers 1920: Les jeux ressuscités* (Antwerp: Comité Olympique et Interfédéral Belge, 1995).

22. For more on the financial and commercial implications of the Antwerp Games, see Roland Renson, "Sport and Business in the City: The Antwerp Olympic Games of 1920 and the Urban Elite," *Olympika* 6 (1997): 73–84.

23. *Rapport officiel des jeux de la VII Olympiade, Anvers 1920* (Leuven, Belgium: Sportsmuseum Flanders, 1921), p. 52.

24. See *Guide des Jeux Olympiques: VIIIe Olympiade—Paris 1924* (Paris: Games of the VIIIth Olympiad Organizing Committee, 1924).

25. See Lennartz, "The Presidency of Henri de Baillet-Latour," p. 180.

26. For the best analysis of the organization and financial affairs of the Chamonix Winter Games of 1928, see Pierre Arnaud and Tierry Terret, *Le rêve blanc, Olympisme et sport d'hiver en France: Chamonix 1924, Grenoble 1968* (Bordeaux: Presses Universitaires de Bordeaux, 1993). See also Johannes Pallière, "Les primiers jeux d'hiver de 1924: La grande bataille de Chamonix," *L'Histoire en Savoie* 26, no. 103 (September 1991).

27. Several scholars have attempted to unravel the complex set of circumstances surrounding women's entry into track and field at the Olympic Games. For the most thorough discussion, see Guy Schultz, "The I.A.A.F. and the I.O.C.: Their Relationship and Its Impact on Women's Participation in Track and Field at the Olympic Games, 1912–1932" (unpublished M.A. thesis, University of Western Ontario, 2000). For less detailed but still useful treatments, see G. Pallett, *Women's Athletics* (Dulwich, England: Normal Press, 1955); Mary Leigh and Térèse Bonin, "The Pioneering Role of Madame Alice Milliat and the FSFI in Establishing International Trade [*sic*] and Field for Women," *Journal of Sport History* 4, no. 1 (Spring 1977); and Gertrud Pfister, "The Struggle for Olympia: The Women's World Games and Participation of Women in Olympic Games," *Journal of the International Council for Health, Physical Education, Recreation, and Dance* 32, no. 4 (Summer 1996).

28. See Mark Pendergrast, *For God, Country and Coca-Cola* (New York:

Charles Scribner's Sons, 1993), p. 173; for succeeding Olympic Games, see ibid., pp. 222–23, 247, 283, 318–27.

29. In 1959 an aspiring Olympic historian, John Lucas, was granted a short interview with Coubertin's widow, the Baroness de Coubertin, then ninety-eight. Lucas asked the baroness to reminisce about her husband and the Olympic Games. He was struck by one of her responses: "He spent all his money on the Olympics, and most of mine too, and I had more than he did." This anecdote was reported to the authors by Lucas, arguably the doyen of Olympic historians.

30. "Minutes, 12th IOC Session, Luxemburg—1910," in Wolf Lyberg, ed., *The IOC Sessions, 1894–1955* (Lausanne: IOC, 1994), p. 58.

31. "Minutes, 20th IOC Session, Lausanne—1921," ibid., p. 102.

32. "Minutes, 21st IOC Session, Paris—1922," ibid., p. 107.

33. "Minutes, 25th IOC Session, Lisbon—1926," ibid., p. 133.

2. AVERY BRUNDAGE AND THE GREAT BREAD WAR: AN OLYMPIAN PRECEDENT

1. Frederick W. Rubien, ed., *Report on the American Olympic Committee: Games of the Xth Olympiad* (New York: American Olympic Committee), pp. 63–64. See also Robert K. Barney, "Resistance, Persistence, Providence: The 1932 Los Angeles Olympic Games in Perspective," *Research Quarterly for Exercise and Sport* 67, no. 2 (June 1996): 148.

2. See Barney, "Resistance, Persistence, Providence," p. 156. Knowing that California's "athletic carnival" would cost in excess of $2 million, Hoover was sensitive about being associated with the project. He reportedly told friends: "It's a crazy thing. And it takes some gall to expect me to be part of it." Cited in A. J. Stump, "The Games That Almost Weren't," *American Heritage* 33 (1982): 67.

3. Barney, "Resistance, Persistence, Providence," p. 155.

4. Built for $400,000, the village was designed so that when it was dismantled and sold for salvage following the Games the Baldwin Hills site would be restored to its original state as an undeveloped future real estate site. A chain-link fence enclosed the village precinct. An elaborate landscaping plan was developed—25,000 geraniums, 5,000 shrubs, and 800 six-foot palms were planted. Forty thousand linear feet of welded steel pipe conveyed water to the village; ten miles of drainage pipes carried waste away. Refrigeration was provided by ice; cooking fuel arrived in the form of bottled propane gas. See "The Olympic Village Idea," in *Official Report: The Games of the Tenth Olympiad—Los Angeles 1932* (Los Angeles: Tenth Olympiad Committee, 1933).

5. See John Kieran and Arthur Daley, *The Story of the Olympic Games: 776 B.C. to 1972* (Philadelphia: J. B. Lippincott Company, 1973), pp. 129–51.

6. *Los Angeles Sunday Times* advertisement for Helms Olympic Bread, 14 August 1932, Avery Brundage Collection, 1908–75 (hereafter cited as ABC), Box 225, Reel 131, International Centre for Olympic Studies Archives (hereafter cited as ICOSA).

7. For biographical information on Paul Helms, see ABC, Box 225, Reel 131,

ICOSA. See also *Who Was Who in America,* vol. 3, *1951–1960* (Chicago: Marquis Company, 1963).

8. Although Helms applied for registration of the marks and words in 1932, his official application (#360,431) was not approved by the United States Trade-Mark Registration Office until 20 September 1938. See "Draft of Proposed Agreement between Paul H. Helms and Counsellors for the United States Olympic Committee," appended to letter from Arthur M. Smith (counselor) to Avery Brundage, 30 December 1949, ABC, Box 225, Reel 131, ICOSA.

9. It is a curious fact that the idea of duly registering the Olympic marks in the United States had in fact occurred to the USOA in advance of the Olympic Games of 1932. In an exchange of correspondence between Frederick W. Rubien, secretary of the USOA, and Col. A. G. Berdez, secretary of the IOC, the question rose as to exactly how the different-colored rings in the Olympic symbol should be arranged. Rubien and his USOA colleagues, including Brundage, had been uncertain. Berdez finally resolved the matter to Rubien's satisfaction. In his final letter to Berdez on the subject he wrote: "We have taken up the matter of having the IOC emblem registered with a patent firm here in New York City but I doubt very much if it is possible to arrange this. I will forward to you the official opinion as soon as it is announced." Indeed, such registration never occurred. See Frederick Rubien to A. G. Berdez, 16 May 1932, International Olympic Committee Archives, Lausanne, Switzerland (hereafter cited as IOCA).

10. The information pertinent to Helms's arrival in Los Angeles, the subsequent establishment of his bakery business there, and his machinations in becoming the official bakery product supplier for the Olympic Village are described in a letter to Avery Brundage written by USOA counsel John Terry McGovern in October 1949, giving a chronological review of the entire Olympic Bread scenario as painstakingly recounted to him by Helms himself. See John Terry McGovern to Avery Brundage, 18 October 1949, ABC, Box 225, Reel 131, ICOSA.

11. Ibid.

12. See *Los Angeles Times,* 30 July through 30 August 1932.

13. Weber's Bakery published its advertisements under the slogan: "Have you changed yet?"—an obvious reference to Helms Olympic Bread. Weber's, a larger bakery operation than Helms Bakeries, used an early form of an "ambush marketing" link to the Olympic Games by displaying the "Olympic shield," the IOC's five-ring logo, and the Latinized version of the Olympic motto in its advertising. Its advertising did not allude to being "official Olympic baker," which is how Helms consistently portrayed his firm.

14. Ibid.

15. Ibid.

16. *Los Angeles Sunday Times* advertisement for Helms Olympic Bread, 14 August 1932, ABC, Box 225, Reel 131, ICOSA (emphasis in original).

17. Brundage's letter to Schroeder has not survived, but Brundage sent a copy of it to IOC member and Los Angeles resident William May Garland. Garland acknowledged having received it. See William May Garland to Avery Brundage, 14 October 1938, ABC, Box 225, Reel 131, ICOSA.

18. For the most comprehensive treatment of Brundage, see Allen Guttmann,

The Games Must Go On: Avery Brundage and the Olympic Movement (New York: Columbia University Press, 1984).

19. Ibid. Garland was incorrect in referring to the shield on Helms's advertisement as an IOC mark. In effect the red and white striped shield had been an unregistered American NOC mark since the Interim Greek Games of 1906 in Athens.

20. Avery Brundage to William May Garland, 19 October 1938, ABC, Box 225, Reel 131, ICOSA.

21. This scenario was related to Brundage in McGovern's letter to him in mid-October 1948. See John T. McGovern to Avery Brundage, 18 October 1949, IOCA.

22. In the letter written by McGovern on 18 October 1949, in which he outlined to Brundage his conversations with Helms at the New York meetings, he presented information on Helms's 1948 Olympic Games Bread contract. McGovern described it as one "let to the highest bidder with no suggestion even that advertising be forbidden, although it was known at that time that Helms had been using advertising matter and a package covered with the emblem; and the bread was accepted in packages containing all the advertising matter." John T. McGovern to Avery Brundage, 18 October 1949, ABC, Box 225, Reel 131, ICOSA.

23. Avery Brundage to John Jewett Garland, 18 December 1948, ABC, Box 225, Reel 131, ICOSA. Garland replaced his father, William May Garland, as an IOC member from the United States of America on 28 June 1948. See "Minutes, 43rd IOC Session, London—1948," in Wolf Lyberg, ed., *The IOC Sessions, 1894–1955* (Lausanne: IOC, 1994), p. 250.

24. Avery Brundage to John Jewett Garland, 18 December 1948, ABC, Box 225, Reel 131, ICOSA. In his letter to Garland, Brundage indicated that the USOA had always "relied on the cooperation of the public and of the advertising fraternity instead of resorting to law" when conflicts had developed, such as the one with Paul Helms.

25. John T. McGovern to Avery Brundage, 13 June 1949, ABC, Box 225, Reel 131, ICOSA.

26. J. Lyman Bingham to Avery Brundage, 6 July 1949, ABC, Box 225, Reel 131, ICOSA.

27. Ibid.

28. John McGovern to Avery Brundage, 7 July 1949, ABC, Box 225, Reel 131, ICOSA (emphasis in original).

29. Avery Brundage to Daniel J. Ferris (USOA Executive Board member-at-large), 27 September 1949, ABC, Box 225, Reel 131, ICOSA.

30. Avery Brundage to W. R. Schroeder, 20 July 1949, ABC, Box 225, Reel 131, ICOSA.

31. International Olympic Committee, "Protection of the Olympic Words and Rings: Notice for the National Olympic Committees," *IOC Bulletin* 16 (July 1949): 20.

32. Ibid. (emphasis ours).

33. This bit of information is contained in the document "Outline of Circumstances Leading to Present Activities of United States Olympic Association's Legislation Sub-Committee in Negotiation with Paul Helms," ABC, Box 225, Reel 131, ICOSA.

34. Ibid.

35. International Olympic Committee, "About the Protection of Olympic Words, Emblems and Rings," *IOC Bulletin* 18 (November 1949): 20.

36. Sigfrid Edström to John J. Garland, 9 September 1949, ABC, Box 225, Reel 131, ICOSA.

37. John J. Garland to J. Sigfrid Edström, 14 October 1949, ABC, Box 225, Reel 131, ICOSA.

38. Richard E. Cross to John T. McGovern, 13 September 1949, ABC, Box 225, Reel 131, ICOSA.

39. See Paul Helms to Avery Brundage, 30 September 1949, ABC, Box 225, Reel 131, ICOSA.

40. Paul H. Helms to Avery Brundage, 30 September 1949, ABC, Box 225, Reel 131, ICOSA. Brundage made several handwritten comments on Helms's letter of 30 September, most of them notes challenging the bakery owner's statements and listing possible actions such as a boycott of Los Angeles track and field meets by American athletes. Brundage's impression of Helms is perhaps captured in his afterthought jotted on Helms's letter: "has money, wants respect and esteem."

41. Ibid.

42. McGovern's report forms the essence of his letter to Avery Brundage, 18 October 1949, ABC, Box 225, Reel 131, ICOSA.

43. Before traveling to Los Angeles for the confrontation with Helms, Brundage entertained Cross and Smith as house guests at his palatial home overlooking the Pacific Ocean in Santa Barbara. There they discussed the strategies to be employed in the meeting with Helms. See Arthur M. Smith to Avery Brundage, 30 December 1949, ABC, Box 225, Reel 132, ICOSA.

44. The agreement in principle was appended to the personal letter written to Brundage by Arthur M. Smith. See Arthur M. Smith to Avery Brundage, 30 December 1949, ABC, Box 225, Reel 132, ICOSA.

45. Avery Brundage to Paul Helms, 28 December 1949, ABC, Box 225, Reel 131, ICOSA.

46. Avery Brundage to Otto Mayer, 22 February 1950, ABC, Box 225, Reel 132, ICOSA.

47. The so-called American shield logo (in the USOA's case, "Olympic shield")—a shield with vertical red and white stripes set off at the top by a blue horizontal band, referred to by trademark officials as an escutcheon—had been used by more than one American organization or business, the most recognizable being the Union Pacific Railroad Company.

48. Arthur M. Smith to C. E. McDowell (attorney for Helms Bakeries), 24 February 1950, ABC, Box 225, Reel 132, ICOSA.

49. John T. McGovern to Avery Brundage, 21 March 1950, ABC, Box 225, Reel 131, ICOSA.

50. John T. McGovern to Avery Brundage, 15 June 1950, ABC, Box 225, Reel 131, ICOSA.

51. John T. McGovern to Avery Brundage, 27 June 1950, ABC, Box 225, Reel 131, ICOSA.

52. John T. McGovern to Avery Brundage, 27 June 1950, ABC, Box 225, Reel 131, ICOSA.

53. John T. McGovern to Avery Brundage, 3 July 1950, ABC, Box 225, Reel 131, ICOSA.

54. John T. McGovern to Avery Brundage, 2 October 1950, ABC, Box 225, Reel 131, ICOSA (emphasis in original).

55. John T. McGovern to Avery Brundage, Gustavus Kirby, USOA Officers, Members of the Executive Board, Associate Counsel Judge Mahoney, Richard Cross, Arthur Smith, and Esquire Pincus Sober and Fred Steers, 5 July 1950, ABC, Box 225, Reel 131, ICOSA. The "U.S.O.C." mentioned in McGovern's letter was a subcommittee of the USOA; its chief responsibility was to organize and administer the means for getting American athletes to the Olympic Games.

56. Avery Brundage to John T. McGovern, 6 July 1950, ABC, Box 225, Reel 131, ICOSA.

57. John T. McGovern to Avery Brundage, 7 July 1950, ABC, Box 225, Reel 131, ICOSA.

58. Arthur Smith to John T. McGovern, 24 February 1950, ABC, Box 225, Reel 131, ICOSA.

59. *United States Statutes at Large, 1950–1951,* vol. 64, *Part I: Public Laws and Reorganization Plans* (Washington, D.C.: United States Government Printing Office, 1952), p. 901.

60. Ibid., p. 902.

61. John T. McGovern to United States Olympic Association, 5 July 1950, ABC, Box 225, Reel 131, ICOSA.

62. Avery Brundage to Fred C. Matthei, 4 October 1950, ABC, Box 225, Reel 131, ICOSA.

63. Cited in McGovern to United States Olympic Association, 5 July 1950, ABC, Box 225, Reel 131, ICOSA.

64. Ibid.

3. SHOWDOWN IN MELBOURNE, 1956: EVOLUTION OF THE OLYMPIC TELEVISION RIGHTS CONCEPT

1. S. W. Head and C. H. Sterling, *Broadcasting in America* (Boston: Houghton Mifflin, 1987), p. 53.

2. For an interesting account of the early history of radio sport programming in Great Britain and Australia, see John McCoy, "Radio Sports Broadcasting in the United States, Britain and Australia, 1920–1956 and Its Influence on the Olympic Games," *Journal of Olympic History* 5, no. 1 (Spring 1997): 20–25.

3. Ibid., p. 20.

4. See Robert K. Barney, "Resistance, Persistence, Providence: The 1932 Olympic Games in Perspective," *Research Quarterly for Exercise and Sport* 67, no. 2 (June 1996): 159n44.

5. *Listener* 16, no. 394 (July 1936): 199. As cited by McCoy, "Radio Sports Broadcasting," p. 23.

6. For historical background on the development of television, see, for instance, *The Golden Web: A History of Broadcasting in the United States, Volume II, 1933–1955* (New York: Oxford University Press, 1968); Asa Briggs, *The BBC: The*

First Fifty Years (New York: Oxford University Press, 1985); and Monika Elsner, Thomas Müller, and Peter Spangenberg, "The Early History of German Television: The Slow Development of a Fast Medium," *Historical Journal of Film, Radio and Television* 10, no. 2 (1990): 193–219.

7. Briggs, *The BBC: The First Fifty Years,* pp. 161, 206.

8. Heinz-Dietrich Fischer, "From Cooperation to Quasi-Congruency—Interdependence between the Olympic Games and Television," in Heinz-Dietrich Fischer and Stefan Reinhard Melnik, eds., *Entertainment: A Cross-Cultural Examination* (New York: Hastings House Publishers, 1979), p. 211.

9. *The XIth Olympic Games, Berlin, 1936, Volume I* (official report) (Berlin: Wilhelm Limpert, ca. 1936), pp. 342–43.

10. *London Times,* 3 August 1936.

11. Finnish Organizing Committee, Report of the General Secretary, IOC Session in London, England, June 1939, ABC, Box 156, Reel 88, ICOSA.

12. For an overview of "Olympic affairs" carried on during the early phases of World War II, see Karl Lennartz, "Difficult Times: Baillet-Latour and Germany, 1931–1942," *Olympika* 7 (1994): 99–105.

13. J. Sigfrid Edström to all IOC members, 1 September 1945, IOCA.

14. See Karl Lennartz, "The Presidency of Sigfrid Edström (1942–1952)," in *The International Olympic Committee—One Hundred Years: The Idea—the Presidents—the Achievements,* vol. 2 (Lausanne: IOC, 1995), p. 24. Lord Aberdare, having survived the Battle of Britain, voiced his concern over resuming the Olympic Games so soon after the conclusion of World War II. In response Edström and Brundage said that they felt that the Games were more necessary now than at any other time in the Olympic Movement's history. For a further treatment of the events surrounding the Executive Committee's first postwar meeting in London, see Allen Guttmann, *The Olympics: The History of the Modern Games* (Urbana: University of Illinois Press, 1992), pp. 75–76.

15. Guttmann, *The Olympics,* p. 75.

16. See Lennartz, "The Presidency of Sigfrid Edström," p. 25.

17. Larry Siddons, *The Olympics at 100: A Celebration in Pictures* (Indianapolis: Macmillan Publishing, 1995), p. 56.

18. Lord David George Burghley became a British IOC member in 1933 and remained a member until his death in 1981. He was an Executive Board member from 1951 to 1970 and IOC vice-president from 1954 to 1966.

19. See Stephen R. Wenn, "A History of the International Olympic Committee and Television, 1936–1980" (Ph.D. dissertation, Pennsylvania State University, 1993), p. 21.

20. See International Olympic Committee Marketing Department, *1999 Olympic Marketing Fact File* (Lausanne: IOC, 1999), p. 34. Reports at the time stated that the "BBC later pleaded desperate poverty, but, as they were all gentlemen, when the BBC paid, the organizers never cashed the check."

21. *The Official Report of the Organising Committee for the XIVth Olympiad* (London: Organising Committee for the XIVth Olympiad, 1948), pp. 121–22.

22. "Minutes of the 41st Session of the International Olympic Committee," Stockholm, 18–21 June 1947, IOCA.

23. Lennartz, "The Presidency of Sigfrid Edström," pp. 66–67.

24. International Olympic Committee Marketing Department, *1999 Olympic Marketing Fact File*, p. 34.

25. Lennartz, "The Presidency of Sigfrid Edström," p. 67.

26. See Guttmann, *The Olympics*, p. 84. Guttmann cites John Jewett Garland, IOC member in the United States, as recalling that Brundage and Burghley were tied after sixteen rounds. On the twenty-fifth round Brundage finally gained a majority, winning by a vote of 30–17, with 2 abstentions.

27. It is assumed that Killanin made this overture in written form, but the document is not extant. Brundage refers to Killanin's entreaty in his letter to the members of the IOC Executive Board dated 3 August 1955. See Avery Brundage to Lord Killanin, 3 August 1955, ABC, Box 58, Reel 35, ICOSA.

28. IOC chancellor Otto Mayer reminded Brundage of Ahearne's statements on television at that time in Otto Mayer to Avery Brundage, 31 July 1957, ABC, Box 114, Reel 62, ICOSA. Ahearne desired to divide future television revenue among the IOC, ISFs, and OCOGs.

29. Lord Killanin to Avery Brundage, 24 August 1955, ABC, Box 58, Reel 35, ICOSA.

30. Benjamin G. Rader, *In Its Own Image: How Television Has Transformed Sports* (New York: Free Press, 1984), pp. 18–19.

31. See Jeffrey Neal-Lunsford, "Sport in the Land of Television: The Use of Sport in Network Prime-Time Schedules, 1946–1950," *Journal of Sport History* 19 (Spring 1992): 56–76.

32. Leo Bogart, "Television's Effect on Spectator Sports," in M. Marie Hart, ed., *Sport in the Socio-Cultural Process* (Dubuque: Wm. C. Brown Co., 1976), p. 396. The rights for the 1947 World Series had been sold for $65,000. See also Rader, *In Its Own Image*, p. 55.

33. *The National Collegiate Athletic Association Yearbook—1948* (New York: NCAA, 1949), p. 121; and Robert A. Kintner (president, American Broadcasting Company) to Harold Stassen (president, University of Pennsylvania), 23 August 1950, Papers of the Office of the President 1950–1955, Box 54, "I-C Ath. TV—I" Folder, University of Pennsylvania Archives.

34. For these events and further information on Brundage's early thoughts on television's revenue potential, see Wenn, "A History of the International Olympic Committee and Television," pp. 12–41.

35. Avery Brundage to Members of the Executive Board, 3 August 1955, ABC Box 114, Reel 62, ICOSA.

36. Ibid.

37. David Lord Burghley to Avery Brundage, 23 September 1955, ABC, Box 57, Reel 34, ICOSA.

38. Lord Killanin to Avery Brundage, 24 August 1955, ABC, Box 58, Reel 35, ICOSA.

39. Guttmann, *The Games Must Go On*, p. 218.

40. Lewis Luxton (deputy chairman, Melbourne Organizing Committee) to Avery Brundage (president, International Olympic Committee), 13 May 1957, ABC, Box 114, Reel 62, ICOSA.

41. Brundage's thoughts on these matters are summarized in Avery Brundage to Members of the IOC Executive Board, 3 August 1955, ABC, Box 114, Reel 62, ICOSA.

42. *Chicago Daily News,* 27 January 1956, ABC, Box 161, Reel 92, ICOSA. These countries were Belgium, Denmark, France, Holland, Italy, Switzerland, the United Kingdom, and West Germany. RAI was granted exclusive radio and television rights to the Cortina Games in exchange for its agreement to handle all technical arrangements for the foreign radio and television companies. The Organizing Committee provided RAI with a contribution of 10,000,000 lire ($16,000). See *VII Olympic Winter Games* (Cortina D'Ampezzo: Comitato Olimpico Nazionale Italiano, 1956), p. 421, IOCA. A second source indicates that the Organizing Committee's investment was much larger ($64,000). See "Procès-verbal de la réunion de la Commission Exécutive," Cortina D'Ampezzo, 22 January 1956, p. 1, IOCA.

43. For an enlightening description of dealings between Kent-Hughes and his organizing colleagues and government officials, see Shane Cahill, " 'A Very Hard Crowd to Have Dealings With': International and Australian Television Networks' Resistance to the Demands of the 1956 Melbourne Olympic Games Organizing Committee for a Fee for Television Coverage, 1955–1956," in *On-line Proceedings: Forty Years of Television Conference* (Published by the National Centre for Australian Studies, Monash University, 1996), available on the Internet from http://www.arts.edu.au/ncas/resources/40years/Cahill.shtml.

44. The views of the Melbourne organizers are summarized in two documents located in ABC, Box 114, Reel 62, ICOSA. See W. S. Kent-Hughes, "Report on Television and Films—Olympic Games 1956," 25 March 1957; and Lewis Luxton to Avery Brundage, 13 May 1957.

45. Peter Whitchurch to Avery Brundage, 15 September 1959, ABC, Box 114, Reel 62, ICOSA.

46. Lewis Luxton to Avery Brundage, 13 May 1957, ABC, Box 114, Reel 62, ICOSA.

47. W. S. Kent-Hughes, "Report on Television and Films—Olympic Games 1956," 25 March 1957, ABC, Box 114, Reel 62, ICOSA.

48. See, for instance, John Day (director of news, Columbia Broadcasting System) to Avery Brundage, 23 January 1956; Roger Tatarian (European news manager, United Press Associations) to Avery Brundage, 23 January 1956; Jack E. Muth (European news manager, Movietone News, Inc.) to Avery Brundage, 24 January 1956; Henry Lawrenson (managing editor, Australian Movietone News) and Ken Hall (managing editor, Cinesound Newsreel) to Avery Brundage, 5 April 1956; and William R. McAndrew (director of news, National Broadcasting Company) to Avery Brundage, 6 April 1956, ABC, Box 114, Reel 62, ICOSA.

49. W. S. Kent-Hughes, "Report on Television and Films—Olympic Games 1956," 25 March 1957, ABC, Box 114, Reel 62, ICOSA.

50. Jack E. Muth to Avery Brundage, 24 January 1956; and Frank Donghi (assignment editor, CBS News) to Avery Brundage, 31 March 1956, ABC, Box 114, Reel 62, ICOSA.

51. Roger Tatarian to Avery Brundage, 23 January 1956, Box 114, Reel 62, ICOSA.

52. Henry Lawrenson and Ken Hall to Avery Brundage, 5 April 1956, Box 114, Reel 62, ICOSA.

53. See Cahill, "'A Very Hard Crowd to Have Dealings With,'" p. 17.

54. William R. McAndrew to Avery Brundage, 6 April 1956, Box 114, Reel 62, ICOSA.

55. Avery Brundage to William R. McAndrew, 28 April 1956, ABC, Box 114, Reel 62, ICOSA.

56. William R. McAndrew to Avery Brundage, 3 May 1956, ABC, Box 114, Reel 62, ICOSA.

57. W. S. Kent-Hughes, "Report on Television and Films—Olympic Games 1956," 25 March 1957, ABC, Box 114, Reel 62, ICOSA.

58. Ibid.; and *The Official Report of the Organizing Committee for the Games of the XVI Olympiad Melbourne 1956* (Melbourne: Organizing Committee for the Games, ca. 1957), p. 157.

59. J. P. Meroz to Otto Mayer (chancellor, IOC), 29 October 1956, ABC, Box 114, Reel 62, ICOSA.

60. George Griffith Jr. to Avery Brundage, 6 December 1956, ABC, Box 114, Reel 62, ICOSA; and "Nobody Was First," *New York Times,* 9 December 1956.

61. W. S. Kent-Hughes, "Report on Television and Films—Olympic Games 1956," 25 March 1957, ABC, Box 114, Reel 62, ICOSA.

62. Ibid.; "Nobody Was First," *New York Times,* 9 December 1956; and Robert Joseph Lucas, "A Descriptive History of the Interdependence of Television and Sports in the Summer Olympic Games, 1956–1984" (M.A. thesis, San Diego State University, 1984), pp. 11–13. See also Cahill, "'A Very Hard Crowd to Have Dealings With,'" p. 12. Further, Cahill records that Ampol paid Channel 9 £8,000 to advertise on its Olympic broadcasts.

63. Lewis Luxton to Avery Brundage, 13 May 1957, Box 114, Reel 62, ICOSA.

64. "Nobody Was First," *New York Times,* 9 December 1956.

65. George Griffith Jr. to Avery Brundage, 6 December 1956, ABC, Box 114, Reel 62, ICOSA.

66. Harry Robert, Frank F. Donghi, and Leonard Allen to Avery Brundage, 13 February 1957, ABC, Box 114, Reel 62, ICOSA.

67. "Minutes of the 51st Session of the International Olympic Committee," Cortina D'Ampezzo, 24–25 January 1956, p. 20, IOCA.

68. Ibid., pp. 18–19.

69. Ibid., pp. 19–20.

70. Avery Brundage to Harry Robert, 11 April 1957; Harry Robert to Avery Brundage, 25 April 1957; Avery Brundage to Harry Robert, 15 May 1957; Harry Robert to Avery Brundage, 24 May 1957; and Otto Mayer to Avery Brundage, 21 December 1957, ABC, Box 114, Reel 62, ICOSA.

71. *Olympic Charter 1958* (Lausanne: IOC, 1958), pp. 29–30, IOCA.

72. Garroni's suggestion is discussed in Avery Brundage to Marcello Garroni, 18 July 1958, ABC, Box 168, Reel 96, ICOSA.

73. Ibid.; and Avery Brundage to Giulio Onesti (president, Rome Organizing Committee), 19 August 1958, ABC, Box 168, Reel 96, ICOSA.

74. Exeter to Avery Brundage, 2 April 1957, ABC, Box 54, Reel 32, ICOSA.

75. Avery Brundage to Harry Robert (sports editor, Hearst Metrotone News, Inc.), 31 December 1957, ABC, Box 114, Reel 62, ICOSA.

76. Harry Robert to Avery Brundage, 24 May 1957, ABC, Box 114, Reel 62, ICOSA.

77. "Minutes of the 54th Session of the International Olympic Committee," Sofia, 23–28 September 1957, p. 7, IOCA.

78. "Athletics in the Modern World and the Olympic Games" (an analysis and extracts from a lecture by Coubertin to the Parnassus Club, Athens, 1894), in Pierre de Coubertin, *The Olympic Idea—Discourses and Essays* (Schorndorf: Verlag Karl Hoffman, 1967), p. 83.

79. See, for instance, Alan E. Bartholemy (general secretary, VIIIth Olympic Winter Games Organizing Committee) to Otto Mayer, 10 July 1957, ABC, Box 165, Reel 94, ICOSA; and Giulio Onesti (president, Rome Organizing Committee) to Avery Brundage, 6 May 1960, ABC, Box 168, Reel 96, ICOSA.

80. Avery Brundage to Kenneth (Tug) Wilson (president, United States Olympic Association), 20 August 1955, ABC, Box 165, Reel 94, ICOSA. His reference to the term "picnic ground" is found in Avery Brundage to Cortlandt T. Hill, 12 November 1955, ABC, Box 165, Reel 94, ICOSA.

81. Avery Brundage to Alexander Cushing (president, VIIIth Olympic Games Organizing Committee), 16 September 1955, ABC, Box 165, Reel 94, ICOSA.

82. Avery Brundage to Kenneth (Tug) Wilson, 20 August 1955, ABC, Box 165, Reel 94, ICOSA.

83. Alexander Cushing to Avery Brundage, 15 October 1955; and Alexander Cushing to Avery Brundage, 30 November 1955, ABC, Box 165, Reel 94, ICOSA.

84. Avery Brundage to Alexander Cushing, 16 September 1955, ABC, Box 165, Reel 94, ICOSA.

85. Alexander Cushing to Avery Brundage, 30 November 1955, ABC, Box 165, Reel 94, ICOSA.

86. Goodwin J. Knight (governor of California) to the IOC, 17 January 1956, ABC, Box 165, Reel 94, ICOSA.

87. Avery Brundage to Albert E. Sigal, 19 November 1955; Alexander Cushing to Otto Mayer, 26 February 1956, ABC, Box 165, Reel 94, ICOSA.

88. Alan E. Bartholemy to Otto Mayer, 10 July 1957, ABC, Box 165, Reel 94, ICOSA.

89. Ibid.

90. John M. Peirce (director of finance, State of California) to Avery Brundage, 7 May 1956, ABC, Box 165, Reel 94, ICOSA.

91. Avery Brundage to Members of the IOC Executive Board, 3 August 1955, ABC Box 114, Reel 62, ICOSA.

92. Alexander Cushing to Avery Brundage, 9 September 1955, ABC, Box 165, Reel 94, ICOSA.

93. Avery Brundage to Alexander Cushing, 16 September 1955, ABC, Box 165, Reel 94, ICOSA.

94. Otto Mayer to the Rome Organizing Committee, 14 September 1955, ABC, Box 168, Reel 95, ICOSA.

95. Otto Mayer to Alan E. Bartholemy, 17 June 1957, ABC, Box 165, Reel 94, ICOSA.

96. Otto Schantz, "The Presidency of Avery Brundage (1952–1972)," in *The International Olympic Committee—One Hundred Years: The Idea—the Presidents—the Achievements*, vol. 2 (Lausanne: IOC, 1995), p. 177.

97. Alan E. Bartholemy to Otto Mayer, 10 July 1957, ABC, Box 165, Reel 94, ICOSA.

98. Avery Brundage to the Olympic Winter Games Organizing Committee, 7 August 1957, ABC, Box 165, Reel 94, ICOSA.

99. Prentis C. Hale (president, VIIIth Olympic Winter Games Organizing Committee) to Avery Brundage, 9 July 1957, ABC, Box 165, Reel 94, ICOSA.

100. Otto Mayer to Avery Brundage, 31 July 1957, ABC, Box 114, Reel 62, ICOSA.

101. "Minutes of the 54th Session of the International Olympic Committee," Sofia, 22–27 September 1957, p. 8, IOCA.

102. Avery Brundage to Otto Mayer, 4 August 1959, ABC, Box 168, Reel 95, ICOSA.

103. Giulio Onesti to Avery Brundage, 6 May 1960, ABC, Box 168, Reel 96, ICOSA.

104. Ibid.; "Minutes of the Meeting of the 56th Session of the International Olympic Committee," San Francisco, 15–16 February 1960, pp. 7–8, IOCA; Otto Mayer to Giulio Onesti, 18 September 1961; and Giulio Onesti to Avery Brundage, 19 October, ABC, Box 61, Reel 36, ICOSA.

105. Guttmann, *The Olympics*, p. 104.

106. Despite the government subsidies, the bobsled events were called off because the OCOG had refused to spend $750,000 on the construction of the bob run for only a handful of participating nations. For an extended discussion, see "Minutes of the 54th Session of the International Olympic Committee," 22–27 September 1957, Sofia, p. 6, IOCA.

107. Alfred E. Senn, *Power, Politics, and the Olympic Games* (Champaign, Ill.: Human Kinetics, 1999), p. 121.

108. See Lennartz, *The International Olympic Committee*, vol. 2, p. 178.

109. Guttmann, *The Olympics*, p. 105. Guttmann attributes the quote to German journalist Heinz Maegerlein.

110. International Olympic Committee Marketing Department, *1999 Olympic Marketing Fact File*, p. 35.

111. Wenn, "A History of the International Olympic Committee and Television," pp. 88, 93. CBS televised twenty hours of the events in Rome (five of them in prime-time using tape delays), while the British sent home approximately forty hours of live telecasts. See Senn, *Power, Politics, and the Olympic Games*, p. 121.

112. International Olympic Committee Marketing Department, *1999 Olympic Marketing Fact File*, p. 35.

113. "Droits de télévision versés par les organismes de télévision pour les Jeux d'Olympiade (en dollars US)," 1986, IOCA.

114. Otto Mayer to Giulio Onesti, 18 September 1961; Giulio Onesti to Avery Brundage, 19 October 1961, ABC, Box 61, Reel 36, ICOSA. In the 19 October let-

ter Onesti stated that the final transfer of funds, which brought the total channeled to the IOC to $53,521, provided closure for the IOC/OCOG arrangement.

115. "Minutes of the Meeting of the IOC Executive Board," Rome, 19 and 24 August 1960, p. 6, IOCA.

4. CONFLICT IN THE OLYMPIC MOVEMENT: AVERY BRUNDAGE, TELEVISION MONEY, AND THE ROME FORMULA IN THE 1960S

1. See Karl Lennartz, "The Presidency of Sigfrid Edström (1942–1952)," in *The International Olympic Committee—One Hundred Years: The Idea—the Presidents—the Achievements*, vol. 2 (Lausanne: IOC, 1995), p. 180.

2. Ibid. Innsbruck won the election to host the 1964 Winter Games with a clear lead (49 votes) over Calgary (9 votes) and Lahti (0 votes). The poor performance by Lahti was due to a lack of mountains, which made it impossible to hold the alpine ski competitions in Finland.

3. "Summary of Olympic Television Rights: Olympic Winter Games," 27 July 1998, Personal Files of Richard Pound (hereafter cited as PFRP), p. 1.

4. Dorling Kindersley Limited, *Chronicle of the Olympics* (London: Dorling Kindersley Limited, 1998), p. 107.

5. The Ninth Olympic Winter Games attracted 986 male and 200 female athletes to Innsbruck. This was the first time that the number of competitors at an Olympic Winter Games exceeded 1,000. The schedule included a record thirty-four events, including luge and tobogganing, which made its Olympic debut.

6. Quoted in Lord Killanin and John Rodda, eds., *The Olympic Games: Eighty Years of People, Events and Records* (New York: Macmillan Publishing, 1976), p. 182.

7. "Minutes of the 34th Session of the International Olympic Committee," Oslo, 26, 28 February–1 March 1935, Oslo, IOCA.

8. The vote came out clearly in favor of the Japanese capital, with thirty-four votes. Its rivals—Detroit, Vienna, and Brussels—received ten, nine, and five votes, respectively. See "Minutes of the 56th Session of the International Olympic Committee," Munich, 25–28 May 1959, p. 7, IOCA.

9. According to Guttmann, the Japanese invested a total of two billion dollars and "incalculable psychic energy" in the hosting of the Games of the Eighteenth Olympiad. Allen Guttmann, *The Olympics: A History of the Modern Games* (Urbana: University of Illinois Press, 1992), p. 110.

10. Quoted in Dorling Kindersley Limited, *Chronicle of the Olympics*, p. 111. The architecture was so impressive that its designer, Kenzo Tange, received a number of international prizes. The IOC also honored him with the Olympic diploma. See *The Official Report of the Organizing Committee for the XVIIIth Olympiad*, vol. 1 (Tokyo: Organizing Committee for the XVIIIth Olympiad, 1964), pp. 529–30.

11. "Olympics Costing Tokyo 186 Million: 62 Million Going for Games, Rest for City Spruce-up," *New York Times*, 5 July 1964.

12. See International Olympic Committee Marketing Department, *1999 Olympic Marketing Fact File* (Lausanne: IOC, 1999), p. 35.

13. These cigarettes were marketed with the collaboration of various government departments and agencies. The Tokyo organizers stated that each pack of

Peace cigarettes "is sold with a numbered premium ticket. Those who draw the winning number will receive a prize of 365 packs—the Olympic emblem is printed on a cobalt blue background on all packs" (*XVIII Olympiad Official Bulletin* 4: 11, IOCA). "Olympia" cigarettes were "made with a mild, pleasant mixture of Turkish and Greek tobacco . . . on sale since April 1, 1963, for the purpose of obtaining funds for the 1964 Olympic Games in Tokyo" (*XVII Olympiad Official Bulletin* 10: 8, IOCA).

14. International Olympic Committee Marketing Department, *1999 Olympic Marketing Fact File*, p. 35. Later the IOC universally banned the tobacco category from a commercial sponsorship link to the Olympic Games.

15. See Larry Siddons, *The Olympics at 100: A Celebration in Pictures* (Indianapolis: Macmillan Publishing, 1995), p. 70.

16. The 1964 Tokyo Organizing Committee received $1,577,778 for the television rights to the Olympic Games. See "Summary of Olympic Television Rights: Olympic Winter Games," 27 July 1998, PFRP, p. 1.

17. See Fernand Landry and Magdeleine Yerlès, "The Presidencies of Lord Killanin (1972–1980) and Juan Antonio Samaranch (1980–)," in *The International Olympic Committee—One Hundred Years: The Idea—the Presidents—the Achievements*, vol. 3 (Lausanne: IOC, 1996), p. 173; and Stephen R. Wenn, "A History of the International Olympic Committee and Television, 1936–1980" (Ph.D. diss., Pennsylvania State University, 1993), pp. 117–23.

18. Avery Brundage to Kurt Beyer, 11 December 1964, ABC, Box 171, Reel 98, ICOSA; "Minutes of the Meeting of the IOC Executive Board," Paris, 9–10 July 1965, p. 2, IOCA.

19. IOC, *Olympic Charter* (Lausanne: IOC, 1966), p. 33. The ban on this type of sponsorship was temporary and not included in 1967: see IOC, *Olympic Charter* (Lausanne: IOC, 1967), p. 39.

20. See Lennartz, "The Presidency of Sigfrid Edström," p. 182.

21. "Minutes of the 62nd Session of the International Olympic Committee," Innsbruck, 26–28 January 1964, p. 10, IOCA.

22. Nestled in the French Alps, Grenoble is 200 meters above sea level.

23. As the Tenth Olympic Winter Games opened, a total of seven satellite Olympic Villages had been established. See Dorling Kindersley Limited, *Chronicle of the Olympics*, p. 117.

24. Lennartz, "The Presidency of Sigfrid Edström," p. 182 (quotation); Dorling Kindersley Limited, *Chronicle of the Olympics*, p. 117.

25. Quoted in Guttmann, *The Olympics*, p. 128.

26. Ibid.

27. See David S. Aikman, "Presentation to the International Olympic Academy," in IOC and International Olympic Academy, eds., *Proceedings: Thirty-eighth Session of the International Olympic Academy* (hereafter cited as IOA) (Lausanne: IOC/IOA, 1999), p. 73.

28. Quoted in Guttmann, *The Olympics*, p. 128.

29. The American Broadcasting Corporation provided the U.S. market with 27 and 40 hours of coverage of the Grenoble and Mexico City Olympic Games, respectively. See Richard K. Alaszkiewicz and Thomas L. McPhail, "Olympic Televi-

sion Rights," *International Review for Sociology of Sport* 21 (1986): 212. The European Broadcasting Union and Intervision networks had access to 150 hours of coverage of the 1968 Olympic Winter Games in Grenoble. See *Rapport officiel: Comité d'organisation des Xèmes Jeux Olympiques d'hiver* (Grenoble: Organizing Committee for the Xth Winter Olympic Games, 1968), p. 149.

30. "Summary of Olympic Television Rights: Olympic Winter Games," 27 July 1998, p. 1, PFRP.

31. Mexico City won with thirty votes, ahead of Detroit (fourteen), Lyon (twelve), and Buenos Aires (two). See "Minutes of the 61st Session of the International Olympic Committee," Baden-Baden, 16–20 October 1963, p. 6, IOCA.

32. See Guttmann, *The Olympics*, p. 129.

33. "Minutes of the Meeting of the IOC Executive Board," Lausanne, 20–21 April 1968, p. 7, IOCA; see also "Notes on the Executive Board Meeting," 21 April 1968, ABC, Box 179, Reel 102, ICOSA.

34. David Wallechinsky, *The Complete Book of the Olympics* (Boston: Little, Brown & Company, 1991), p. xxi.

35. Siddons, *The Olympics at 100*, pp. 76–77. With Mexico's economy in disarray and poverty endemic, many saw the hundreds of millions of dollars spent on Olympic facilities for the 1968 Olympic Games as an appalling waste of money.

36. Quoted ibid., pp. 129–30. Although the Olympic Games opened without incident, a cloud of tension surrounded the event. To ensure that the Games continued, Mexican troops and tanks patrolled the streets and surrounding region of Mexico City.

37. Ibid., p. 130.

38. See *The Official Report of the Organizing Committee for the XIXth Olympiad*, vol. 2 (Mexico City: Organizing Committee for the XIXth Olympiad, 1969), pp. 23–26.

39. "Olympic Games Television Rights Summary: Summer Games," 27 July 1998, p. 1, PFRP.

40. International Olympic Committee Marketing Department, *1999 Olympic Marketing Fact File*, p. 35.

41. Avery Brundage to Giulio Onesti (IOC member, Italy), 25 January 1966, ABC, Box 101, Reel 55, ICOSA.

42. "Minutes of the Meeting of the IOC Executive Board," Rome, 22–24 April 1966, pp. 8–9, IOCA.

43. "Minutes of the 65th Session of the International Olympic Committee," Rome, 25–29 April 1966, pp. 4–5, ABC, Box 93, Reel 51, ICOSA.

44. Giulio Onesti to Avery Brundage, 19 October 1961, ABC, Box 61, Reel 37, ICOSA.

45. Avery Brundage to Otto Mayer, 4 August 1959, ABC, Box 168, Reel 96, ICOSA.

46. As outlined by Otto Mayer to Avery Brundage, 31 July 1957, ABC, Box 114, Reel 62, ICOSA.

47. Exeter to Brundage, 24 January 1960; Exeter to Brundage, 26 March 1961; and Exeter to Brundage, 7 April 1961, ABC, Box 54, Reel 32, ICOSA.

48. Avery Brundage to Albert Mayer, 19 May 1966, ABC, Box 60, Reel 35,

ICOSA; and Avery Brundage to Roger Coulon (Fédération Internationale de Lutte Amateur), 11 September 1967, ABC, Box 207, Reel 119, ICOSA.

49. Armand Massard to Avery Brundage, 23 September 1960, ABC, Box 60, Reel 35, ICOSA.

50. Avery Brundage to Armand Massard, 14 October 1960, ABC, Box 60, Reel 35, ICOSA.

51. "Minutes of the 59th Session of the International Olympic Committee," Athens, 19–21 June 1961, pp. 2–3, IOCA.

52. Guru Dutt Sondhi to Avery Brundage, 17 June 1965, ABC, Box 63, Reel 37, ICOSA.

53. Giulio Onesti to Avery Brundage, 24 June 1965, ABC, Box 61, Reel 36, ICOSA.

54. Exeter to Avery Brundage, 10 June 1965, ABC, Box 55, Reel 33, ICOSA.

55. "Minutes of the Meeting of the IOC Executive Board," Rome, 19 and 24 August 1960, pp. 3–4, 6, IOCA; and "Minutes of the Meeting of the 58th Session of the International Olympic Committee," Rome, 20 and 22–23 August 1960, p. 3, IOCA.

56. *Olympic Charter 1962* (Lausanne: IOC, 1962), p. 27.

57. Avery Brundage to Exeter, 31 March 1961; and Exeter to Avery Brundage, 7 April 1961, ABC, Box 54, Reel 32, ICOSA.

58. Exeter to Avery Brundage, 26 March 1961, ABC, Box 54, Reel 32, ICOSA.

59. Exeter to Avery Brundage, 26 March 1961; Exeter to Avery Brundage, 7 April 1961; and Exeter to Avery Brundage, 31 May 1961, ABC, Box 54, Reel 32, ICOSA.

60. "Minutes of the Meeting of the IOC Executive Board," Athens, 15 June 1961, pp. 1–2, IOCA.

61. "Minutes of the 59th Session of the International Olympic Committee," Athens, 19–21 June 1961, pp. 2–3, IOCA.

62. Circular Letter to the International Federations [#182], July 1961, ABC, Box 70, Reel 39, ICOSA.

63. Otto Mayer to Friedl Wolfgang, 23 March 1961, ABC, Box 169, Reel 96, ICOSA.

64. Avery Brundage to Armand Massard, 1 April 1963, ABC, Box 60, Reel 35, ICOSA.

65. Exeter to Rudyard H. Russell, 8 March 1967, ABC, Box 101, Reel 55, ICOSA.

66. "Europeans Beam First Television to Screens in U.S.," *New York Times*, 12 July 1962.

67. "State Dept. Reports Telstar May Be Used," *New York Times*, 28 August 1962.

68. "Japan Hopes US Telstar Communications Satellite Can Be USed for Global Telecasts," *New York Times*, 12 July 1962.

69. "Live TV of Tokyo Olympics Being Explored," *New York Times*, 26 January 1964.

70. "Syncom II Satellite Tested by NASA and NBC for Live Coverage of Games," *New York Times*, 24 April 1964.

71. Robert Joseph Lucas, "A Descriptive History of the Interdependence of Television and Sports in the Summer Olympic Games, 1956–1984" (M.A. thesis, San Diego State University, 1984), pp. 20–21; James L. McClain, "Cultural Chauvinism and the Olympiads of East Asia," *International Journal of History of Sport* 7 (December 1990): 389.

72. "Syncom II Satellite Tested by NASA and NBC for Live Coverage of Games."

73. Guttmann, *The Olympics,* p. 110.

74. "Memorandum of Conversation, 8 June 1964," Department of State, Bureau of Educational and Cultural Affairs Collection, Cabinet #4, Box 16, Special Collections Department, University of Arkansas Library. The authors would like to express their appreciation to Geoff Davison for alerting us to the contents of this document; "Live TV of Tokyo Olympics Being Explored."

75. "Syncom III to Be Tested in October in an Attempt to Relay Pictures to US and Canada," *New York Times,* 23 July 1964.

76. "Japan Irked by 3 Hr. Delay," *New York Times,* 11 October 1964.

77. "J. Gould on Dispute over Syncom Telecasts," *New York Times,* 18 October 1964.

78. "Seduta delle Federazoni Internazionali Sportive" (Minutes of the Meeting of the International Sport Federations), Rome, 22 April 1966, p. 2/9, ABC, Box 81, Reel 45, ICOSA.

79. Ibid., pp. 2/13–14.

80. Avery Brundage to Ivar Vind, 13 September 1965, ABC Box 64, Reel 38, ICOSA.

81. "Seduta delle Federazoni Internazionali Sportive" (Minutes of the Meeting of the International Sport Federations), Rome, 22 April 1966, p. 2/10, ABC, Box 81, Reel 45, ICOSA.

82. Avery Brundage to Ivar Vind, 13 September 1965, ABC, Box 64, Reel 38, ICOSA.

83. Avery Brundage to Guru Dutt Sondhi, 3 July 1965, ABC, Box 63, Reel 37, ICOSA.

84. Guru Dutt Sondhi to Avery Brundage, 17 June 1965, ABC, Box 63, Reel 37, ICOSA.

85. Avery Brundage to Guru Dutt Sondhi, 3 July 1965, ABC, Box 63, Reel 37, ICOSA.

86. "Minutes of the Meeting of the IOC Executive Board with the Delegates of the National Olympic Committees," Madrid, 4 October 1965, pp. 5–6, IOCA; Ivar Vind to Giulio Onesti, 24 August 1965, ABC, Box 61, Reel 36, ICOSA. While Vind and Clark Flores supported directing money to the NOCs, they opposed Onesti's plan for an umbrella organization. See Guttmann, *The Olympics,* p. 117.

87. Giulio Onesti to Ivar Vind, 8 September 1965, ABC, Box 61, Reel 36, ICOSA.

88. Giulio Onesti to Avery Brundage, 24 June 1965, ABC, Box 61, Reel 36, ICOSA.

89. "Minutes of the Meeting of the IOC Executive Board with the Delegates of the National Olympic Committees," Madrid, 4 October 1965, p. 5, IOCA.

90. Exeter to Avery Brundage, 10 June 1965, ABC, Box 55, Reel 33, ICOSA.

91. Guttmann, *The Olympics,* pp. 115–17.

92. Ibid., p. 115.

93. Avery Brundage to Giulio Onesti, 25 January 1966, ABC, Box 101, Reel 55, ICOSA.

94. Avery Brundage to Giulio Onesti, 12 February 1966, ABC, Box 101, Reel 54, ICOSA; and Exeter to Avery Brundage, 23 February 1966, ABC, Box 55, Reel 33, ICOSA.

95. Avery Brundage to Giulio Onesti, 25 January 1966; and Giulio Onesti to Avery Brundage, 9 February 1966, ABC, Box 101, Reel 54, ICOSA.

96. "Preliminary Report to the Executive Board of the IOC on Television Policy," ABC, Box 101, Reel 54, ICOSA.

97. Exeter to Giulio Onesti, 31 March 1966, ABC, Box 55, Reel 33, ICOSA.

98. Giulio Onesti to Exeter, 7 April 1966, ABC, Box 55, Reel 33, ICOSA.

99. "Preliminary Report to the Executive Board of the IOC on Television Policy," ABC, Box 101, Reel 54, ICOSA.

100. "Seduta delle Federazoni Internazionali Sportive" (Minutes of the Meeting of the International Sport Federations), Rome, 22 April 1966, p. 2/15, ABC, Box 81, Reel 45, ICOSA.

101. Ibid., pp. 2/15–19.

102. "Minutes of the Meeting of the IOC Executive Board," Rome, 22–24 April 1966, pp. 8–9, IOCA.

103. "Minutes of the 65th Session of the International Olympic Committee," Rome, 25–29 April 1966, pp. 4–5, ABC, Box 93, Reel 51, ICOSA.

104. "Minutes of the Meeting of the IOC Executive Board," Rome, 22–24 April 1966, p. 3, IOCA.

105. Avery Brundage to Albert Mayer, 19 May 1966, ABC, Box 60, Reel 35, ICOSA.

106. Avery Brundage to Exeter, 19 May 1966, ABC, Box 55, Reel 33, ICOSA. Exeter understood that Brundage was suggesting the use of television money as a lever to obtain greater cooperation from the ISFs in the enforcement of amateur regulations. Exeter thought that this might be possible but believed that telling the ISFs how they could spend the money would "cause the most terrific row and also be impractical." Exeter to Avery Brundage, 31 May 1966, ABC, Box 55, Reel 33, ICOSA.

107. "Meeting of the IOC Executive Board with the International Sport Federations," Lausanne, 27–28 January 1968, p. 5, ABC, Box 93, Reel 51, ICOSA.

108. "Minutes of the Meeting of the General Assembly of International Federations," Lausanne, 21–23 April 1967, ABC, Box 207, Reel 120, ICOSA.

109. Exeter to Avery Brundage, 16 January 1967, ABC, Box 55, Reel 33, ICOSA.

110. "Meeting of the IOC Executive Board with the International Sport Federations," Lausanne, 27–28 January 1968, p. 5, IOCA.

111. Exeter to Avery Brundage, 16 January 1967, ABC, Box 55, Reel 33, ICOSA.

112. V. C. Sugahadasa (president, National Olympic Committee of Ceylon) to

the president of the National Olympic Committee of Ireland, 25 March 1968, ABC Box 61. Exeter attributed the text of this letter, which attempted to recruit Ireland's support for the PGA, to Onesti and referred to Onesti's claim that his agitation had prompted the move to grant television money to the NOCs as "impudent." Exeter to Avery Brundage, 27 May 1968, ABC, Box 55, Reel 33, ICOSA.

113. Exeter to Avery Brundage, 12 January 1967; Exeter to Avery Brundage, 16 January 1967; Exeter to Avery Brundage, 23 January 1967; Exeter to Avery Brundage, 12 June 1967; Exeter to Avery Brundage, 27 August 1967, ABC, Box 55, Reel 33, ICOSA.

114. Roger Coulon to Avery Brundage, 10 March 1967, ABC, Box 207, Reel 120, ICOSA.

115. "Report of the Commission No. 3—Finances," GAIF, Lausanne, 22 April 1967, p. 3, ABC, Box 207, Reel 120, ICOSA.

116. Exeter to Avery Brundage, 27 August 1967, ABC, Box 55, Reel 33, ICOSA.

117. Avery Brundage to Roger Coulon, 11 September 1967, ABC, Box 207, Reel 119, ICOSA.

118. "Summarised Minutes of the Meeting of the Finance Commission of the IOC and Representatives of the International Federations' Commission and the Federations of Judo, Shooting, and Athletics," Mexico City, 6 October 1968, pp. 1–3, IOCA.

119. "Minutes of the Meeting of the IOC Executive Board," Amsterdam, 8–16 May 1970, p. 15, IOCA.

120. "Meeting between the Three IOC Vice-Presidents and the Representatives of the International Federations," in "Minutes of the Meeting of the IOC Finance Commission," Munich, 17 and 28 August and 1 September 1972, p. 7, IOCA.

121. "Minutes of the Meeting of the IOC Finance Commission," Munich, 17 and 28 August and 1 September 1972, p. 4, IOCA.

122. The inaugural meeting of the Finance Commission was held in September 1967. "Minutes of the Meeting of the IOC Finance Commission," Lausanne, 24–25 September 1967, IOCA; Avery Brundage to Reginald Alexander, 24 October 1967; and Avery Brundage to Lord Luke, 24 October 1967, ABC, Box 98, Reel 53, ICOSA.

123. "Minutes of the Meeting of the IOC Finance Commission," Lausanne, 21 March 1969, Annex #2, pp. 1–2, IOCA.

124. "Minutes of the Meeting of the IOC Finance Commission," Lausanne, 8 October 1974, Annex #6, "Commission des Finances/Finance Commission," p. 27, IOCA.

125. Avery Brundage to Exeter, 18 January 1967, ABC, Box 55, Reel 33, ICOSA.

126. Avery Brundage to Reginald Alexander, 24 October 1967, ABC, Box 98, Reel 53, ICOSA; Avery Brundage to Jean de Beaumont, 9 April 1968; and Avery Brundage to Jean de Beaumont, 23 May 1969, ABC, Box 51, Reel 30, ICOSA.

127. Avery Brundage to Jean de Beaumont, 19 November 1969, ABC, Box 51, Reel 30, ICOSA; Lord Luke to Jean de Beaumont, 20 November 1969; Monique Berlioux to Lord Luke, 25 November 1969; Monique Berlioux to Reginald Alexan-

der, 25 November 1969; and Monique Berlioux to Avery Brundage, 24 November 1969, ABC, Box 98, Reel 53, ICOSA.

128. "Minutes of the Meeting of the IOC Finance Commission," Warsaw, 4 and 6–8 June 1969, pp. 4–6, IOCA; and "Memorandum Submitted to the Finance Commission of the IOC on the Present Position Regarding License Fees in Respect of Television Rights at the Games of the XXth Olympiad Munich 1972," in "Minutes of the Meeting of the IOC Finance Commission," Munich, 28 January 1971, Annex #3, pp. 9–14, IOCA.

129. Reginald Alexander to Avery Brundage, 12 March 1969, ABC, Box 98, Reel 53, ICOSA.

130. Allen Guttmann, *The Games Must Go On: Avery Brundage and the Olympic Movement* (New York: Columbia University Press, 1984), p. 219.

131. "Minutes of the Meeting of the IOC Executive Board," Lausanne, 27–30 May 1972, p. 7, IOCA.

132. "Répartition des droits de télévision versés aux fédérations internationales 1964–1976 (en U.S. dollars)," 1986, IOCA.

133. *Olympic Marketing: 1998 Fact File* (Lausanne: IOC, 1998), p. 35.

134. Lord Killanin, *My Olympic Years* (London: Secker & Warburg, 1983), p. 9.

135. Jean de Beaumont to Avery Brundage, 4 November 1971, ABC, Box 51, Reel 30, ICOSA.

136. "Minutes of the Meeting of the IOC Executive Board," Lausanne, 27–30 May 1972, p. 7. IOCA.

137. Stephen R. Wenn, "Growing Pains: The Olympic Movement and Television, 1966–1972," *Olympika* 4 (1995): 14–15.

138. Killanin, *My Olympic Years,* pp. 21–22.

5. TELEVISION AND THE 1970S: MUNICH AND MONTRÉAL

1. Herbert Kunze to Avery Brundage, 11 April 1969; Lord Luke to Herbert Kunze, 3 November 1969; Willi Daume to Lord Luke, 20 November 1970, ABC, Box 98, Reel 53, ICOSA; Exeter to Avery Brundage, 17 November 1969; Avery Brundage to Exeter, 20 November, 1969; and Exeter to Avery Brundage, 15 January 1970, ABC, Box 55, Reel 33, ICOSA.

2. Tomoo Sato to Lord Luke, 2 October 1969; and Tomoo Sato to Lord Luke, 6 October 1969, "Droits de TV Sapporo 1972" Binder, IOCA.

3. Lord Luke to Herbert Kunze, 3 November 1969, ABC, Box 98, Reel 53, ICOSA; and Lord Luke to Shohei Sasaka, 3 March 1970, "Droits de TV Sapporo 1972" Binder, IOCA.

4. Exeter to Avery Brundage, 17 November 1969; and Exeter to Avery Brundage, 15 January 1970, ABC, Box 55, Reel 33, ICOSA.

5. "Minutes of the Meeting of the IOC Finance Commission," Warsaw, 4 and 6–8 June 1969, pp. 1–10, IOCA; "Minutes of the Meeting of the IOC Executive Board," Dubrovnik, 23–27 October 1969, p. 10, IOCA; and Avery Brundage to Lord Luke, 7 January 1970, ABC, Box 98, Reel 53, ICOSA.

6. Tomoo Sato to Lord Luke, 4 September 1970, "Droits de TV Sapporo 1972" Binder, IOCA.

7. Willi Daume to Lord Luke, 20 November 1970, ABC, Box 98, Reel 53, ICOSA.

8. "Memorandum Pertaining to the Distribution of Proceeds from Television between the International Olympic Committee and the Organizing Committee for the Games of the XXth Olympiad Munich 1972," in "Minutes of the Meeting of the Finance Commission," Lausanne, 20 February 1970, Annex #1, p. 8, IOCA.

9. Exeter to Avery Brundage, 17 November 1969, ABC, Box 55, Reel 33, ICOSA.

10. "Minutes of the Meeting of the IOC Finance Commission," Lausanne, 20 February 1970, Annex #3, p. 29, IOCA. It appears that the Executive Board approved the contract but subsequently rescinded that approval. "Minutes of the Meeting of the IOC Executive Board," Lausanne, 21–23 February 1970, Annex #10, p. 73, IOCA; and Lord Luke to Willi Daume, 28 July 1970, "Minutes of the Meeting of the IOC Finance Commission," Lausanne, 1 October 1970, Annex #2, p. 8, IOCA.

11. "Minutes of the Meeting of the IOC Finance Commission," Munich, 28 January 1971, p. 4; and "Minutes of the Meeting of the IOC Executive Board," Lausanne, 13–14 March 1971, p. 20, IOCA.

12. "Minutes of the 65th Session of the International Olympic Committee," Rome, 25–28 April 1966, p. 9, IOCA.

13. The broadcast rights for the Sapporo Olympic Winter Games sold for $8,475,269, more than three times the $2,612,822 generated by the organizers of the 1968 Grenoble Games. See "Summary of Olympic Television Rights: Olympic Winter Games," 27 July 1998, pp. 1–2, PFRP.

14. International Olympic Committee Marketing Department, *1999 Olympic Marketing Fact File,* (Lausanne: IOC, 1999), p. 35.

15. Quoted in Allen Guttmann, *The Olympics: A History of the Modern Games* (Urbana and Chicago: University of Illinois Press, 1992), p. 134.

16. Dorling Kindersley Limited, *Chronicle of the Olympics* (London: Dorling Kindersley Limited, 1998), p. 127.

17. "Minutes of the 65th Session of the International Olympic Committee," Rome, 25–28 April 1966, p. 8, IOCA. Willi Daume, who died in 1996 at the age of eighty-two, was an IOC member and president of the German NOC (1961–92).

18. Larry Siddons, *The Olympics at 100: A Celebration in Pictures* (Indianapolis: Macmillan Publishing, 1995), p. 82.

19. Guttmann, *The Olympics,* p. 135.

20. Siddons, *The Olympics at 100,* p. 82.

21. International Olympic Committee Marketing Department, *1999 Olympic Marketing Fact File,* p. 35.

22. Fernand Landry and Magdeleine Yerlès, "The Presidencies of Lord Killanin (1972–1980) and Juan Antonio Samaranch (1980–)," in *The International Olympic Committee—One Hundred Years: The Idea—the Presidents—the Achievements,* vol. 3 (Lausanne: IOC, 1996), p. 187.

23. Willi Daume, "Organizing the Games," in Lord Killanin and John Rodda, eds., *The Olympic Games: Eighty Years of People, Events and Records* (New York: Macmillan Publishing, 1976), p. 155.

24. Siddons, *The Olympics at 100,* p. 86.

25. Ibid. With the Olympic flag at half-staff, the memorial service in the Olympic Stadium began with the orchestra from the Munich Opera House playing Ludwig van Beethoven's *Egmont Overture*. Willi Daume spoke first, followed by Shmuel Lalkin, the Israeli team manager. Finally, in one of his final acts as IOC president, Avery Brundage addressed those who had gathered. In his speech he mourned the loss of the slain athletes and coaches, calling the murder one of "two savage attacks" on the Olympics, the other being the threat by various African nations to boycott the Games if Rhodesia had been allowed to compete because of its apartheid policies. His coupling of the two events aroused much criticism within the Olympic and international community, resulting in a formal apology regretting "any misinterpretation" of his words. Following the memorial service, teams from Norway and the Netherlands as well as several individual athletes returned home.

26. Richard D. Mandell, *Sport: A Cultural History* (New York: Columbia University Press, 1984), p. 155.

27. "Minutes of the Meeting of the IOC Finance Commission," Varna, 4 and 7 October 1973, p. 5, IOCA; Lord Killanin to Karl-Keinz Klee, 7 October 1973, "N.1 Droits de TV Innsbruck du 1.2.73" Binder, IOCA; and "Meeting of Monday 5th November 1973," "N.1 Droits de TV Innsbruck du 1.2.73" Binder, IOCA.

28. "Minutes of the Meeting of the IOC Executive Board," Lausanne, 2–5 February 1973, p. 9, IOCA; and Lord Killanin to Monique Berlioux, 21 March 1973, "N.1 Droits de TV Montreal du 4.12.69 au 30.6.76" Binder, IOCA.

29. Monique Berlioux to Lord Luke, 2 May 1973, "N.1 Droits de TV Montreal du 4.12.69 au 30.6.73" Binder, IOCA.

30. "Minutes of the Meeting of the IOC Executive Board," Lausanne, 2–5 February 1973, p. 9, IOCA.

31. "Droits de télévision versés par les organismes de télévision pour les Jeux d'Olympiade (en dollars U.S.)," IOCA. The original price for the rights and technical services package for the Moscow Games had been $5.95 million, but in light of the absence of the U.S. team and representatives of other nations the IOC and EBU agreed to a reduction of $297,500. The IOC thought this settlement preferable to potential court proceedings.

32. Charles Curran to Lord Killanin, undated, ca. December 1973, "N.2 Droits TV Dossier General Innsbruck ABC/UER 1972/1976" Binder, IOCA; "Olympics Black-out in Europe?" *Irish Press,* 17 January 1975, clipping, "N.4 Droits de TV Montreal du 1.1.75 au 31.8.75" Binder, IOCA; and Lord Killanin to Roger Rousseau, 26 March 1975, "N.4 Droits de TV Montreal du 1.1.75 au 31.8.75" Binder, IOCA.

33. "Correspondence by Telex," Lord Killanin to Roger Rousseau, 14 August 1975, "N.4 Droits de TV Montreal du 1.1.75 au 31.8.75" Binder, IOCA; "Aide-Memoire—Lord Killanin—Montreal—TV," 5 September 1975; and Lord Killanin to Jim Worrall, 9 September 1975, "N.5 Droits de TV Montreal du 1.9.75 au 30.4.76" Binder, IOCA.

34. "Extract—President's Visit to Montreal 3rd/7th November 1972," 10 November 1972, "N.1 Droits de TV Montreal du 4.12.69 au 30.6.73" Binder, IOCA.

35. Ibid.; and Lord Killanin to Roger Rousseau, 8 December 1972, "N.1 Droits de TV Montreal du 4.12.69 au 30.6.73" Binder, IOCA.

36. "Meeting of the IOC Finance Commission with the Representatives of the Organising Committee of the Games of the XXIst Olympiad, London, 28 November 1972," "N.1 Droits de TV Montreal du 4.12.69 au 30.6.73" Binder, pp. 4–7, IOCA.

37. Lord Killanin to Monique Berlioux, 5 December 1972; and Lord Killanin to Roger Rousseau, "N.1 Droits de TV Montreal du 4.12.69 au 30.6.73" Binder, IOCA.

38. "Telex Addressed to Lord Killanin from NBC," ca. 20 December 1972, "N.1 Droits de TV Montreal du 4.12.69 au 30.6.73" Binder, IOCA.

39. Monique Berlioux to Roger Rousseau, 21 December 1972, "N.1 Droits de TV Montreal du 4.12.69 au 30.6.73" Binder, IOCA.

40. "ABC Will Spend $25 Million for Summer Olympic Rights," *New York Times,* 4 January 1973.

41. "ABC Warns NBC on '76 Olympics," *New York Times,* 21 December 1972.

42. "ABC Is Accused on '76 Olympics," *New York Times,* 16 January 1974.

43. "Minutes of the Meeting of the IOC Finance Commission," Lausanne, 1 and 3 February 1973, p. 8, IOCA.

44. Lord Killanin to the IOC Finance Committee, 31 January 1973, "N.1 Droits de TV Montreal du 4.12.69 au 30.6.73" Binder, IOCA.

45. "Minutes of the Meeting of the IOC Finance Commission," Lausanne, 1 and 3 February 1973, Lausanne, p. 8, IOCA.

46. Ibid., p. 2.

47. "Minutes of the Meeting of the IOC Executive Board," Lausanne, 2–5 February 1973, pp. 7–9, IOCA.

48. Roger Rousseau to Lord Killanin, 15 February 1973, "N.1 Droits de TV Montreal du 4.12.69 au 30.6.73" Binder, IOCA.

49. Lord Killanin to Roger Rousseau, 27 February 1973, "N.1 Droits de TV Montreal du 4.12.69 au 30.6.73" Binder, IOCA.

50. "Meeting of the IOC Finance Commission with the Representatives of the Organising Committee of the Games of the XXIst Olympiad, London, 28 November 1972," "N.1 Droits de TV Montreal du 4.12.69 au 30.6.73" Binder, pp. 1–3.

51. J. W. Rengelink to Lord Killanin, 25 January 1973, "N.1 Droits de TV Montreal du 4.12.69 au 30.6.73" Binder, IOCA.

52. Lord Killanin to Monique Berlioux, 14 May 1973, "N.1 Droits de TV Montreal du 4.12.69 au 30.6.73" Binder, IOCA.

53. "Minutes of the Meeting of the IOC Finance Commission," Paris, 12 June 1973, p. 2, IOCA.

54. "Minutes of the Meeting of the IOC Finance Commission," Varna, 4 and 7 October 1973, pp. 2–3, IOCA.

55. Ibid., p. 3.

56. Ibid., p. 5.

57. For information on Berlioux, see Paul Levesque, "A Case Study of the Rise and Demise of Power: Monique Berlioux, IOC Director, 1969–1985" (unpublished paper, University of Western Ontario, 1993); and Morley Myers, "IOC's Berlioux: Diffident, Powerful, Indispensable," *International Herald-Tribune,* 22 December 1983.

58. "Minutes of the Meeting of the IOC Finance Commission," Varna, 4 and 7 October 1973, pp. 4, IOCA.

59. "Minutes of the Meeting of the IOC Executive Board," Lausanne, 9–11 February 1974, p. 12, IOCA; and "Minutes of the Meeting of the IOC Finance Commission," Paris, 28 January 1974, p. 4, IOCA.

60. "Minutes of the Meeting of the IOC Executive Board," Lausanne, 9–11 February 1974, p. 12, IOCA.

61. "Notes on the Work of the Television Sub-Committee," 23 June 1974, "TV/Divers 1974–1985" Binder, "1974–1979" Folder, p. 1, IOCA.

62. Charles Curran to Lord Killanin, 12 December 1973, "N.2 Droits TV Dossier General Innsbruck ABC/UER 1972/1976" Binder, IOCA.

63. Charles Curran to Lord Killanin, undated, ca. December 1973, "N.2 Droits TV Dossier General Innsbruck ABC/UER 1972/1976" Binder, IOCA.

64. Lord Killanin to Count Jean de Beaumont, Lord Luke, Marc Hodler, Herman van Karnebeek, and Willi Daume, 18 April 1974, "N.2 Droits TV Dossier General Innsbruck ABC/UER 1972/1976" Binder, IOCA. Killanin provided the members of the Finance Commission with an excerpt from a speech given by Curran in November 1973.

65. Charles Curran to Lord Killanin, 26 February 1974, "N.2 Droits TV Dossier General Innsbruck ABC/UER 1972/1976" Binder, IOCA.

66. Lord Luke to Lord Killanin, 26 March 1974, "N.2 Droits TV Dossier General Innsbruck ABC/UER 1972/1976" Binder, IOCA.

67. Lord Killanin to Count Jean de Beaumont, Lord Luke, Marc Hodler, Herman van Karnebeek, and Willi Daume, 18 April 1974, "N.2 Droits TV Dossier General Innsbruck ABC/UER 1972/1976" Binder, IOCA.

68. "Notes on the Work of the Television Sub-Committee," 23 June 1974, "TV/Divers 1974–1985" Binder, "1974–1979" Folder, p. 1, IOCA.

69. "Memorandum on the Television Rights," "TV/Divers 1974–1985" Binder, "1974–1979" Folder, p. 4, IOCA.

70. "Role and Function of the Expert," "TV/Divers 1974–1985" Binder, "1974–1979" Folder, p. 3, IOCA.

71. "Memorandum on the Television Rights," "TV/Divers 1974–1985" Binder, "1974–1979" Folder, p. 4, IOCA.

72. Ibid., p. 1.

73. "Minutes of the Meeting of the Television Sub-Committee," Lausanne, 4 October 1974, p. 2, IOCA.

74. "Minutes of the Meeting of the IOC Executive Board," Lausanne, 1–3 June 1974, p. 26, IOCA.

75. "Memorandum on the Television Rights," "TV/Divers 1974–1985" Binder, "1974–1979" Folder, p. 1, IOCA.

76. Lord Killanin, *My Olympic Years* (London: Secker & Warburg, 1983), p. 120.

77. "Minutes of the Meeting of the IOC Finance Commission," Lausanne, 8 October 1974, pp. 2–4, IOCA.

78. "Minutes of the IOC Finance Commission," Vienna, 18 October 1974, p. 4, IOCA.

79. "Report of Dr. Schätz on the Television Broadcasting Rights for the Games

of the XXIst Olympiad—Montreal 1976," in "Minutes of the Meeting of the IOC Finance Commission," Lausanne, 8 October 1974, Annex #2, p. 15, IOCA.

80. "Minutes of the Meeting of the IOC Executive Board," Vienna, 18–24 October 1974, pp. 3, 9, IOCA.

81. "Report of Dr. Schätz on the Television Broadcasting Rights for the Games of the XXIst Olympiad—Montreal 1976," in "Minutes of the Meeting of the IOC Finance Commission," Lausanne, 8 October 1974, Annex #2, p. 17, IOCA.

82. "Minutes of the Meeting of the IOC Finance Commission," Vienna, 18 October 1974, p. 3, IOCA.

83. "Minutes of the Meeting of the IOC Executive Board," Vienna, 18–24 October 1974, p. 6, IOCA.

84. Ibid., p. 3.

85. Ibid., pp. 8–15.

86. "Meeting of the 14th October 1974—Montreal Television," "N.3 Droits de TV Montreal du 1.9.74/31.12.74" Binder, pp. 1–9, IOCA.

87. "Report of Dr. Schätz on the Television Broadcasting Rights for the Games of the XXIst Olympiad—Montreal 1976," in "Minutes of the Meeting of the IOC Finance Commission," Lausanne, 8 October 1974, Annex #2, p. 16, IOCA.

88. Lord Killanin to Roger Rousseau, 13 December 1974, "N.3 Droits de TV Montreal du 1.9.74/31.12.74" Binder, IOCA.

89. "Europe Balks at Olympic Coverage," *New York Times,* 15 December 1974, section 5; "Olympics May Not Be on TV," *Dublin Evening Press,* clipping, "N.3 Droits de TV Montreal du 1.9.74/31.12.74" Binder, IOCA; and "Olympics Blackout in Europe?" *Irish Press,* 17 January 1975, clipping, "N.4 Droits de TV Montreal du 1.1.75 au 31.8.75" Binder, IOCA.

90. Georges Straschnov to Monique Berlioux, 9 January 1975, "N.4 Droits de TV Montreal du 1.1.75 au 31.8.75" Binder, IOCA.

91. "Confidential Report on the Meeting of 29th January 1975 at Lausanne: Montreal COJO/EBU Negotiations concerning Television Rights," 6 February 1975, "N.4 Droits de TV Montreal du 1.1.75 au 31.8.75" Binder, p. 2, IOCA.

92. "Joint EBU/OIRT Communiqué," "N.4 Droits de TV Montreal du 1.1.75 au 31.8.75" Binder, IOCA.

93. "Confidential Report on the Meeting of 29th January 1975, at Lausanne: Montreal COJO/EBU Negotiations concerning Television Rights," 6 February 1975, "N.4 Droits de TV Montreal du 1.1.75 au 31.8.75" Binder, pp. 1–2, IOCA.

94. "Joint EBU/OIRT Communiqué," "N.4 Droits de TV Montreal du 1.1.75 au 31.8.75" Binder, IOCA.

95. "COJO Television Rights Statement," press release, "N.4 Droits de TV Montreal du 1.1.75 au 31.8.75" Binder, IOCA.

96. Lord Killanin to Roger Rousseau, 26 March 1975, "N.4 Droits de TV Montreal du 1.1.75 au 31.8.75" Binder, IOCA.

97. Jean de Beaumont to Lord Killanin, 6 May 1975, "N.4 Droits de TV Montreal du 1.1.75 au 31.8.75" Binder, IOCA; "Minutes of the Meeting of the IOC Finance Commission," Lausanne, 19, 22 May 1975, p. 2, IOCA; and "Minutes of the Meeting of the IOC Executive Board," Rome, 14–16 May 1975, and Lausanne, 23 May 1975, p. 10, IOCA.

98. Lord Killanin to Roger Rousseau, 29 May 1975, "N.4 Droits de TV Montreal du 1.1.75 au 31.8.75" Binder, IOCA.

99. David McKenzie to Monique Berlioux, 1 August 1975, "N.4 Droits de TV Montreal du 1.1.75 au 31.8.75" Binder, IOCA.

100. "Transcript of Letter from Dr. Walter Schätz, dated Montreal 12th August 1975," "N.4 Droits de TV Montreal du 1.1.75 au 31.8.75" Binder, IOCA.

101. Ibid.

102. "Olympians Reject $9.3 Million TV Bid," *New York Times,* 13 August 1975; Lord Killanin to Roger Rousseau, 14 August 1975, "N.4 Droits de TV Montreal du 1.1.75 au 31.8.75" Binder, IOCA.

103. Charles Curran to Lord Killanin, 20 August 1975, "N.4 Droits de TV Montreal du 1.1.75 au 31.8.75" Binder, IOCA.

104. IOC, Lausanne to Charles Curran, 25 August 1975; Antony Dean (EBU) to IOC, Lausanne, 25 August 1975, "N.4 Droits de TV Montreal du 1.1.75 au 31.8.75" Binder, IOCA; "Aide Memoire—Lord Killanin—Montreal—TV," 5 September 1975, "N.5 Droits de TV Montreal du 1.9.75 au 30.4.76" Binder, IOCA.

105. Ibid.; "Killanin, Drapeau Discuss TV Snag," *New York Times,* 8 September 1975; Lord Killanin to Jim Worrall, 9 September 1975; and Roger Rousseau to IOC, Lausanne, 11 September 1975, "N.5 Droits de TV Montreal du 1.9.75 au 30.4.76" Binder, IOCA.

106. Lord Killanin to Charles Curran, 15 September 1975, "N.5 Droits de TV Montreal du 1.9.75 au 30.4.76" Binder, IOCA.

107. "BBC Will Pay £500,000 for Olympic Television," Lord Luke Personal File, 1969–78, "1975–1978" Folder, IOCA; and "Olympic TV Coverage Deal Agreed," *London Times,* 13 September 1975.

108. See "Candidate Cities/Olympic Winter Games," 27 July 1998, p. 2, PFRP.

109. See "Minutes of the Meeting of the IOC Executive Board," Munich, 18–22 August 1972, 6–8 and 10–11 September 1972, pp. 17–20, IOCA; and "Minutes of the Meeting of the IOC Executive Board," Lausanne, 2–5 February 1973, pp. 19–29, IOCA.

110. See "Candidate Cities/Olympic Winter Games," 27 July 1998, p. 3, PFRP.

111. Dorling Kindersley Limited, *Chronicle of the Olympics,* p. 139.

112. The Innsbruck OCOG had originally concluded a $10 million agreement with ABC, with $2.2 million designated as a technical service payment. Upon learning of the agreement, an irritated IOC pressed for a reduction of the technical services fee to $2 million and written confirmation that no further money would be deducted for technical services in future television contracts. Karl-Heinz Klee, secretary-general, Organisation-Committee der XII Olympischen Winterspiele Innsbruck 1976, agreed to the IOC's terms. See "Minutes of the Meeting of the IOC Finance Commission," Varna, 4 and 7 October 1973, pp. 2–5, IOCA.

113. Siddons, *The Olympics at 100,* p. 89.

114. Ibid., p. 88.

115. See Bill Henry, *An Approved History of the Olympic Games,* ed. Patricia Henry Yeomans (Sherman Oaks, Calif.: Alfred Publishing Co., 1984), p. 404. According to J. Wilton Littlechild, a leader among indigenous peoples throughout Canada, the Indians identified by Henry were all actors of non-Native ancestry dressed to resemble Indians.

116. Jack Ludwig, *Five Ring Circus: The Montréal Olympics* (Toronto: Doubleday Canada Limited, 1976), p. 164. The live satellite pictures of Moscow were actually images previously recorded by the Montréal Organizing Committee. This deception was discovered when it was realized that the images displayed on the scoreboards did not account for the time differential between Moscow and Montréal.

117. Killanin also believed that geopolitics also threatened the IOC's financial security. The cancellation of an Olympic festival would paralyze its operations because of the effect on television contracts and the IOC's cash flow. Killanin proposed establishing a 10% reserve from television money for the IOC, ISFs, and NOCs. Following a three-year dialogue, the IOC decided to adopt the following approach to distributing television money from the Lake Placid and Moscow Games: (1) one-third of the global sum of the IOC/ISF/NOC share was allocated to the IOC; (2) 10% of the remaining money was placed in a general reserve fund; (3) a second deduction of 10% was dedicated to a fund to offset some of the expense required to provide judges and referees at Olympic sites; and (4) the remaining money was divided equally between the ISFs and NOCs. "Minutes of the 81st Session of the International Olympic Committee," Montevideo, 5–7 April 1979, pp. 13–14; and "Report by Comte de Beaumont, Chairman of the Finance Commission," Annex #10, pp. 67–70, IOCA.

118. Lord Luke to the mayors of Denver and Montréal, 15 May 1970, "Minutes of the Meeting of the IOC Finance Commission," 1 and 3 February 1970, Annex #5, p. 33; Lord Killanin to Roger Rousseau, 8 December 1972, "N.1 Droits de TV Montreal du 4.12.69 au 30.6.73" Binder; and "Notes on the Work of the Television Sub-Committee," 23 June 1974, "TV/Divers 1974–1985" Binder, "1974–1979" Folder, p. 1, IOCA.

119. Reginald S. Alexander to Avery Brundage, 12 March 1969, ABC, Box 98, Reel 53, ICOSA.

6. CONFRONTATIONS GALORE: LAKE PLACID, MOSCOW, AND THE 1980 OLYMPIC FESTIVALS

1. "Minutes of the Meeting of the IOC Finance Commission," Lausanne, 21 January 1975, pp. 6–7, IOCA.

2. "Minutes of the Meeting of the IOC Executive Board," Lausanne 20–22 February 1975, p. 7, IOCA; Monique Berlioux to Ronald McKenzie (president, LPOC), 26 February 1975, "Lake Placid 1980/TV-General 1976" Binder, IOCA; Lord Killanin to Monique Berlioux, 4/3/75, "Lake Placid '80 TV Dossier General" Binder, IOCA; and Norman L. Hess to Monique Berlioux, 5 March 1975, "Lake Placid 1980/TV-General 1976" Binder, IOCA.

3. Monique Berlioux to Norman Hess, 17 March 1975, "Lake Placid 1980/TV-General 1976" Binder, IOCA.

4. Monique Berlioux to Lord Killanin, 15 March 1973, "N.1 Droits de TV Montreal du 4.12.69 au 30.6.73" Binder, IOCA.

5. John M. Wilkins to Monique Berlioux, 15 March 1976, "Lake Placid '80 TV Dossier General" Binder, IOCA.

6. Norman Hess to Lord Killanin, 1 October 1975; and Monique Berlioux to

Norman Hess, 6 November 1975, "Lake Placid '80 TV Dossier General" Binder, IOCA.

7. Lord Killanin to Charles Curran, 5 January 1976, "Lake Placid '80 TV Dossier General" Binder, IOCA.

8. "Television Rights Lake Placid," Annex #3, "Lake Placid (Meeting in Innsbruck [Hotel Tyrol] on 1st February 1976)," pp. 4–5, "Lake Placid 1980/TV-General 1976" Binder, IOCA.

9. Ibid., p. 4.

10. ABC Sports Inc. (Roone Arledge) to the Organizing Committee for the 13th Olympic Winter Games—Lake Placid 1980, "Lake Placid 1980/TV-General 1976" Binder, IOCA.

11. Jean de Beaumont to Lord Killanin, 3 March 1976, "Lake Placid '80 TV Rights ABC I" Binder, IOCA.

12. Lord Killanin to Jean de Beaumont, 15 March 1976, "Lake Placid '80 TV Dossier General" Binder, IOCA.

13. James R. Spence, Jr. (ABC) to Ronald McKenzie, 1 March 1976, "Lake Placid '80 TV Rights ABC I" Binder, IOCA; John M. Wilkins to Monique Berlioux, 15 March 1976, "Lake Placid '80 TV Dossier General" Binder, IOCA.

14. John M. Wilkins to Monique Berlioux, 15 February 1976, "Television Rights Lake Placid," Annex #3, pp. 2–3, "Lake Placid 1980/TV-General 1976" Binder, IOCA.

15. Anonymous to Monique Berlioux, 28 February 1976, "Lake Placid '80 TV Dossier General" Binder, IOCA.

16. Monique Berlioux to Ronald McKenzie, 4 March 1976, "Television Rights Lake Placid," Annex #3, p. 2, "Lake Placid 1980/TV-General 1976" Binder, IOCA.

17. John M. Wilkins to Monique Berlioux, 6 March 1976; and Monique Berlioux to John M. Wilkins, 8 March 1976, "Lake Placid '80 TV Dossier General" Binder, IOCA.

18. Norman L. Hess to Robert Wussler, 21 February 1976, "Lake Placid '80 TV Dossier General" Binder, IOCA.

19. John Wilkins to Robert Wussler, 27 February 1976, "Lake Placid '80 TV Dossier General" Binder, IOCA.

20. "Two Networks Protest on 1980 Olympics," *New York Times*, 13 March 1976.

21. John Wilkins to Monique Berlioux, 15 March 1976, "Lake Placid '80 TV Dossier General" Binder, IOCA.

22. Corydon B. Dunham to Lord Killanin, 12 March 1976, "Lake Placid '80 TV Dossier General" Binder, IOCA.

23. Robert T. Howard to Lord Killanin, 25 March 1976, "Lake Placid '80 TV Dossier General" Binder, IOCA.

24. John Schneider to IOC, 25 March 1976, "Lake Placid '80 TV Dossier General" Binder, IOCA.

25. Robert Wood to Ronald McKenzie, 16 March 1976, "Lake Placid '80 TV Dossier General" Binder, IOCA.

26. Roone Arledge to Monique Berlioux, 12 March 1976, "Lake Placid '80 TV Dossier General" Binder, IOCA.

27. Marvin Josephson to Monique Berlioux, 29 March 1976, "Lake Placid '80 TV Dossier General" Binder, IOCA.

28. "Report on Visit to Lake Placid—6th, 7th, 8th April 1976," 5 May 1976, "Lake Placid '80 TV Dossier General" Binder, IOCA.

29. Roone Arledge to Monique Berlioux, 21 May 1976; and John M. Wilkins to Monique Berlioux, 21 May 1976, "Lake Placid '80 TV Rights ABC I" Binder, IOCA.

30. Fred B. Rooney to Monique Berlioux, 21 May 1976, "Television Rights Lake Placid," Annex #4, p. 1, "Lake Placid 1980/TV-General 1976" Binder, IOCA.

31. Val Adams, "CBS Bids 14 M for 1980 Winter Olympic Rights," *New York Daily News,* 29 May 1976. See also "Lake Placid '80 TV Dossier General" Binder, IOCA.

32. "Director's Resume of Meetings Held in Paris, May 1976," "Television Rights Lake Placid," "Lake Placid 1980/TV-General 1976" Binder, IOCA.

33. Adams, "CBS Bids 14 M for 1980 Winter Olympic Rights," 29 May 1976, "Lake Placid '80 TV Dossier General" Binder, IOCA.

34. Roone Arledge to Jean de Beaumont, 3 June 1976, "Lake Placid '80 TV Rights ABC I" Binder, IOCA. Beaumont strongly denied leaking the rival bids to ABC. Jean de Beaumont to Barry Frank, 10 June 1976, "Lake Placid '80 TV Dossier General" Binder, IOCA.

35. John M. Wilkins to Monique Berlioux, 23 August 1976, "Lake Placid 1980/TV-General 1976" Binder, IOCA.

36. Lord Killanin to Jean de Beaumont, 3 June 1976; and Monique Berlioux to Lord Killanin, 10 June 1976, "Lake Placid '80 TV Dossier General" Binder, IOCA.

37. John M. Wilkins to Monique Berlioux, 23 August 1976, "Lake Placid 1980/TV-General 1976" Binder, IOCA.

38. Monique Berlioux to John Wilkins, 16 September 1976, "Lake Placid 1980/TV-General 1976" Binder, IOCA.

39. John M. Wilkins to Monique Berlioux, 23 August 1976, "Lake Placid 1980/TV-General 1976" Binder, IOCA. In this letter Wilkins referred to a letter from Berlioux dated 30 July in which the IOC's terms were outlined. See "Press Release," 11 June 1976, "Lake Placid '80 TV Dossier General" Binder, IOCA.

40. "Meeting to Discuss the Lake Placid Organising Committee/ABC Television Contract for the 1980 Games," Barcelona, 10–13 October 1976, "Lake Placid 1980/TV-General 1976" Binder, IOCA.

41. "Report of Visit to the USA by the IOC Director and Advisers," "Minutes of the Meeting of the IOC Finance Commission," Paris, 5 January 1977, Annex #2, p. 9, IOCA.

42. Ibid., pp. 8–10.

43. Julian K. Roosevelt to Jean de Beaumont, 8 December 1976, "Minutes of the Meeting of the IOC Finance Commission," Paris, 5 January 1977, Annex #3, p. 15, IOCA.

44. Jean de Beaumont to Lord Killanin, 15 December 1976, "Minutes of the Meeting of the IOC Finance Commission," Paris, 5 January 1977, Annex #3, pp. 15–17, IOCA.

45. Lord Killanin to Julian K. Roosevelt, 29 December 1976, "Minutes of the

Meeting of the IOC Finance Commission," Paris, 5 January 1977, Annex #3, pp. 18–19.

46. "Minutes of the Meeting of the IOC Finance Commission," Paris, 5 January 1977, p. 2, IOCA.

47. "Report of Visit to the USA by the IOC Director and Advisers," "Minutes of the Meeting of the IOC Finance Commission," Paris, 5 January 1977, Annex #2, p. 9, IOCA.

48. The Executive Board approved the original plan. See "Minutes of the Meeting of the IOC Executive Board," Abidjan, 29–30 March 1977, p. 9, IOCA. The Finance Commission received legal advice in April 1977. "Legal Comments on the Draft Regulation for Candidate Cities and Their Obligations with Regard to Television Rights," "Minutes of the Meeting of the IOC Finance Commission," Lausanne, 27 April 1977, Annex #4, p. 11, IOCA.

49. "Minutes of the 79th Session of the International Olympic Committee," Prague, 15–18 June 1977, p. 35; and Annex #33, pp. 98–102, IOCA.

50. William Oscar Johnson, "A Contract with the Kremlin," *Sports Illustrated* 46 (21 February 1977): 16–17.

51. Ibid., p. 14.

52. Ibid., p. 17.

53. Ibid., p. 16.

54. Harry F. Waters (with Susan Malsch), "Olympic Race," *Newsweek* 88 (13 December 1976): 66. David A. Klatell and Norman Marcus, *Sports for Sale: Television, Money and the Fans* (New York: Oxford University Press, 1988), p. 169, report that NBC, after having obtained the agreement, decided not to air the program.

55. Johnson, "A Contract with the Kremlin," p. 16; and Waters (with Malsch), "Olympic Race," p. 66.

56. Klatell and Marcus, *Sports for Sale*, p. 169.

57. Robert Joseph Lucas, "A Descriptive History of the Interdependence of Television and Sports in the Summer Olympic Games, 1956–1984" (M.A. thesis, San Diego State University, 1984), pp. 44–54; Benjamin G. Rader, *In Its Own Image: How Television Has Transformed Sports* (New York: Free Press, 1984), p. 117; and Waters (with Malsch), "Olympic Race," p. 66.

58. Klatell and Marcus, *Sports for Sale*, p. 168.

59. Johnson, "A Contract with the Kremlin," p. 16.

60. Stephen R. Wenn, "A Turning Point for IOC Television Policy: U.S. Television Rights Negotiations and the 1980 Lake Placid and Moscow Olympic Festivals," *Journal of Sport History* 25 (Spring 1998): 91. For an overview, see Stephen J. Whitfield, *The Culture of the Cold War* (Baltimore: Johns Hopkins University Press, 1991), pp. 127–28; and Karl W. Ryavec, *United States Soviet Relations* (New York: Longman, 1989), pp. 241–99.

61. Lord Killanin to Ignati Novikov, 23 September 1976, "Moscou 80 Television, Film, Cassette etc. Audio-Visuel Radio 1976–1980" Binder, IOCA.

62. Lord Killanin to Monique Berlioux, 22 October 1976, "Moscou 80 Television, Film, Cassette etc. Audio-Visuel Radio 1976–1980" Binder, IOCA.

63. Lord Killanin to Ignati Novikov, 23 September 1976, "Moscou 80 Television, Film, Cassette etc. Audio-Visuel Radio 1976–1980" Binder, IOCA.

64. Vitaly Smirnov to Lord Killanin, "Moscou 80 Television, Film, Cassette etc. Audio-Visuel Radio 1976–1980" Binder, IOCA.

65. "Minutes of the Meeting of the IOC Executive Board," Barcelona, 13–17 October 1976, p. 20, IOCA.

66. "Meeting between the Chairman of the Finance Commission, the Director of the IOC, Mr. Daniel Mortureux and Mr. Vladimir Koval, Executive Vice-President of the Organising Committee for the Games of the XXIInd Olympiad (Moscow, 1980)," in "Minutes of the Meeting of the IOC Finance Commission," Paris, 5 November 1976, Annex #4, p. 45, IOCA.

67. "Message Dictated by the President to the Director—Moscow, November 1976," 22 November 1976, "Moscou 80 Television, Film, Cassette etc. Audio-Visuel Radio 1976–1980" Binder, IOCA.

68. "Resume of the Mission of Messrs. D. Mortureux and G. Straschnov to Moscow, 1–3 December 1976," p. 1, "Moscou 80 Television, Film, Cassette etc. Audio-Visuel Radio 1976–1980" Binder, IOCA.

69. Ibid., pp. 1–2.

70. Lord Killanin to Vitaly Smirnov, 9 December 1976, "Moscou 80 Television, Film, Cassette etc. Audio-Visuel Radio 1976–1980" Binder, IOCA. For background information on SATRA, see "ABC's Exclusive Olympic Rights Apparently Over," *New York Times,* 18 December 1976; and "SATRA Corp. Says It Has No Backers for Olympic TV," *New York Times,* 25 December 1976.

71. Val Adams, "Soviet Stand Angers Nets," *New York Daily News,* 13 December 1976, clipping, "Moscou 80 Television, Film, Cassette etc. Audio-Visuel Radio 1976–1980" Binder, IOCA.

72. Johnson, "A Contract with the Kremlin," p. 18.

73. Ryavec, *United States Soviet Relations,* p. 241.

74. Johnson, "A Contract with the Kremlin," p. 15.

75. Ibid., p. 18.

76. Ibid.

77. Jim Spence (with Dave Diles), *Up Close and Personal: The Inside Story of Network Television Sports* (New York: Atheneum Publishers, 1988), p. 296.

78. Johnson, "A Contract with the Kremlin," p. 19.

79. "U.S. Networks Lose Soviet Olympic Deal," *New York Times,* 22 December 1976.

80. "Satra Corp. Says It Has No Backers for Olympic TV," *New York Times,* 25 December 1976.

81. "Minutes of the Meeting of the IOC Finance Commission," Paris, 5 January 1977, pp. 1–2, IOCA.

82. "Soviet Opens Olympic Door to 3 Networks," *New York Times,* 19 January 1977.

83. Johnson, "A Contract with the Kremlin," p. 19; Roone Arledge to Monique Berlioux, 25 January 1977, "Moscou 80 Television, Film, Cassette etc. Audio-Visuel Radio 1976–1980" Binder, IOCA; and "CBS Out of Talks on Games," *New York Times,* 26 January 1977.

84. Johnson, "A Contract with the Kremlin," p. 19.

85. "Report regarding Final Negotiations with the Television Companies for

the Moscow Television Rights," 8 February 1977, p. 1, "Moscou 80 Television, Film, Cassette etc. Audio-Visuel Radio 1976–1980" Binder, IOCA.

86. "The Sporting Life," *New York Times*, 3 February 1977.

87. Johnson, "A Contract with the Kremlin," p. 19.

88. "NBC Is Sued for $275 Million over Broadcasting Rights to Olympics," *New York Times*, 11 February 1977.

89. "Minutes of the Meeting of the IOC Finance Commission," Paris, 6 October 1977, p. 3, IOCA; "Minutes of the Meeting of the IOC Executive Board," Lausanne, 19–20 October 1977, p. 15, IOCA; and "Minutes of the Meeting of the IOC Executive Board," Tunis, 25–26 January 1978, pp. 10–12, IOCA.

90. "Minutes of the Meeting of the IOC Executive Board," Tunis, 25–26 January 1978, p. 10, IOCA.

91. "Minutes of the Meeting of the IOC Finance Commission," Paris, 23 May 1978, p. 4; and "Minutes of the Meeting of the IOC Executive Board," Athens, 13–14, 16, and 18 May 1978, p. 10, IOCA.

92. "Minutes of the Meeting of the IOC Executive Board," Lausanne, 30–31 August 1978, pp. 8–10, IOCA.

93. "Minutes of the Meeting of the IOC Executive Board," Lausanne, 9–10 March 1979, p. 5, IOCA.

94. Jimmy Carter, *Keeping Faith: Memoirs of a President* (London: Harper-Collins, 1982), pp. 475–76; "Soviet Afghanistan Invasion Ends Detente," in *Congress and the Nation 1977–1980: A Review of Government and Politics*, vol. 5 (Washington, D.C.: Congressional Quarterly, Inc., 1981), p. 82; and Derick L. Hulme Jr., *The Political Olympics: Moscow, Afghanistan, and the 1980 U.S. Boycott* (New York: Praeger Publishers, 1990), p. 17.

95. Samuel Pisar (Law Offices of Samuel Pisar) to Monique Berlioux, 17 February 1981; J. I. Huhs (Huhs and Pisar) to Monique Berlioux, 14 August 1981; J. I. Huhs to Monique Berlioux, 26 August 1981; John I. Huhs to Monique Berlioux, 2 July 1980; Monique Berlioux to Lord Killanin, 22 January 1980; and "Report of the Meeting with Representatives of the Moscow OCOG regarding Disputes Concerning Television Contracts," 24 September 1980, p. 3, "Moscou 80 Television, Film, Cassette etc. Audio-Visuel Radio 1976–1980" Binder, IOCA; and "Droits de télévision par les organismes de télévision pour les Jeux d'Olympiade (en dollars U.S.)," IOCA.

96. Larry Siddons, *The Olympics at 100: A Celebration in Pictures* (Indianapolis: Macmillan Publishing, 1995), p. 94.

97. Allen Guttmann, *The Olympics: A History of the Modern Games* (Urbana and Chicago: University of Illinois Press, 1992), p. 149.

98. See Siddons, *The Olympics at 100*, p. 94.

99. The first Soviet troops were airlifted into Afghanistan on 26 December 1979, and their numbers mounted steadily. This was the first deployment of Soviet infantry outside the Eastern bloc since World War II. At its height, the Soviet government committed 100,000 soldiers in the remote, mountainous country of Afghanistan.

100. After seizing power in a palace coup in 1978, Afghanistan's first Marxist president, Noor Muhammad Taraki, attempted to build a centralized Communist

state in a land where local autonomy had prevailed for centuries. Taraki succeeded only in provoking a holy war by fundamentalist Muslims. Before the year was out he was ousted and killed by his deputy, Hafizullah Amin. Amin was even less successful in consolidating his power, losing control of seventy-five percent of Afghanistan's twenty-eight provinces to guerrilla forces. The rebel advances concerned the Soviet government, as Afghanistan was originally considered a buffer from the hostile subcontinent. The Kremlin was also offended by Amin's maverick communism.

101. Guttmann, *The Olympics,* p. 150.

102. "Minutes of the Meeting of the IOC Executive Board," Lausanne, 21–23 April 1980, pp. 53–57, IOCA.

103. Fernand Landry and Magdeleine Yerlès, "The Presidencies of Lord Killanin (1972–1980) and Juan Antonio Samaranch (1980–)," in *The International Olympic Committee—One Hundred Years: The Idea—the Presidents—the Achievements,* vol. 3 (Lausanne: IOC, 1996), p. 161.

104. See *The Official Report of the Organizing Committee for the XIIIth Winter Games, Lake Placid: Final Report* (Lake Placid: Organizing Committee for the XIIIth Winter Games, n.d.), pp. 219–22. The Organizing Committee's efforts to solicit the assistance of the federal government to offset the $8.5 million deficit and close the financial files of the 1980 Olympic Winter Games were rebuffed. In July 1981, however, the governor of New York signed a bill resulting in the absorption of the remaining debts of the Lake Placid OCOG.

105. Sixty-five countries did not participate in the Moscow Olympic Games, including the USA, Canada, the Federal Republic of Germany, Japan, China, Kenya, and Norway. See IOC, *Brief History of the Games of the Olympiad* (Lausanne: IOC, 1997), p. 10.

106. See *The Official Report of the Organizing Committee for the Games of the XXIInd Olympiad,* vol. 2 (Moscow: Organizing Committee for the XXIInd Olympiad, 1981), pp. 496–501. Of all the products produced for the Moscow Olympic Games, none equaled the range and number of Misha, the official mascot of the Games of the Twenty-second Olympiad. Approximately 145 companies produced 250 different products utilizing the mascot's image. By the conclusion of the 1980 Olympic Games, manufacturers had produced a total of 10.9 million units.

107. Dorling Kindersley Limited, *Chronicle of the Olympics* (London: Dorling Kindersley Limited, 1998), p. 153.

108. Ibid., p. 524 (approximate conversion rate for the period: 0.661 ruble = $1 U.S.).

109. Siddons, *The Olympics at 100,* p. 94.

110. See Bill Henry, *An Approved History of the Olympic Games,* ed. Patricia Henry Yeomans (Sherman Oaks, Calif.: Alfred Publishing Co., 1984), p. 431.

7. PROTECTING AND EXPLOITING THE OLYMPIC MYSTIQUE: THE EMERGENCE OF TOP

1. Richard E. Cross to John T. McGovern, 13 September 1949, ABC, Box 225, Reel 132, ICOSA.

2. For extended discussion of the Canadian Olympic Association's efforts to protect Olympic insignia that might be unlawfully used, see Mans Posthuma, ed., "Olympic Words and Symbols: Who Do They Belong To?" *Olympinfo* 7, no. 5 (November 1991): 1.

3. Pierre de Coubertin, *Olympic Memoirs,* trans. Geoffrey de Navacelle (Lausanne: Comité International Olympique, 1989), pp. 87–92. For a discussion on the Olympic five-ring symbol and colors, see Robert K. Barney, "This Great Symbol: Tricks of History," *Olympic Review* 301 (9 November 1992): 627–31, 641.

4. "Minutes of the 79th Session of the International Olympic Committee," Prague, 15–18 June 1977, pp. 76–77, IOCA. The specific by-law to Rule 6 referred to reads: "The IOC is the responsible authority for the protection of the Olympic flag, Olympic symbol and Olympic motto that are its exclusive property. It shall take every appropriate step possible to obtain their legal protection on a national and international basis. It shall also lend its support to efforts the NOCs must make to obtain the protection of the Olympic flag, symbol and motto for the IOC within their country."

5. *Acts of the Parliament of Canada,* 1973, 21–22 Elizabeth 2, c. 31.

6. *Acts of the Parliament of Canada,* 1975, 23–24 Elizabeth 2, c. 68.

7. *Acts of the Parliament of Canada,* 1973, 21–22 Elizabeth 2, c. 31. In this act the term "Olympic Corporation" means the OCOG of the 1976 Olympic Games, a body incorporated under the laws of the Province of Quebec.

8. Kenneth McKay, telephone interview by authors, Toronto, Ontario, 8 March 1995.

9. *The Official Report of the Organizing Committee for the XXIst Olympiad,* vol. 1 (Montréal: Organizing Committee for the 1976 Olympic Games, 1978), pp. 61–64.

10. For an extended discussion of McKay's registration attempts, see Hughes G. Richard, ed., *Robic-Leger Canadian Trade-Marks Act Annotated,* no. 1 (Toronto: Carswell Publishers, 1995).

11. Ibid., pp. 9-8B–9-9.

12. *Register of Trade Marks v. Canadian Olympic Assoc.,* 67 C.P.R. (2d) 59 (1982), p. 53.

13. See *Register of Trade Marks v. Canadian Olympic Assoc.,* 67 C.P.R. (2d) 59 (1982).

14. "Minutes of the 79th Session of the International Olympic Committee," Prague, 15–18 June 1977, IOCA.

15. In 1873, as Vienna undertook preparations for the first International Exhibition of Inventions, organizers were alarmed by the fact that many foreign exhibitors refused to attend due to fears that their ideas would be "stolen" and exploited commercially in other countries. In an effort to dispel such fears a number of states joined together to implement procedures by which an international convention charged with the protection of intellectual creations might be established (the term "convention" here signifies an agreement between sovereigns or states made at a formal assembly of persons for some common object).

After nearly a decade of negotiation between various states, the foundations of what is now known as WIPO began to emerge. Described as the first major international treaty devised to help inventors and designers of one country obtain protection in other countries for their intellectual creations, the Paris Convention for the Protection of Industrial Property (Paris Convention), with fourteen member states, was established in 1884 and quickly organized an International Bureau to carry out its mandate.

With the Paris Convention all but concluded, the concept of copyright emerged with the adoption of the Berne Convention for the Protection of Literary and Artistic Works. The objective of this convention was to help "nationals" of its member states obtain international protection of their right to control and receive payment for the use of their creative works. Like the Paris Convention, the Berne Convention set up an International Bureau to administer its affairs. In 1893 the two bureaus were united to form an international organization called the United International Bureau for the Protection of Intellectual Property (best known by the French acronym BIRPI). With its international headquarters in Berne, Switzerland, and a small staff of seven, this organization was the predecessor of WIPO.

As the importance of intellectual property grew, the structure and form of the new "united" organization began to change. BIRPI relocated its headquarters from Berne to Geneva in 1960 in an effort to be closer to other international organizations with offices in Geneva. A decade later, following the "entry into force" of the Convention Establishing the World Intellectual Property Organization, signed at Stockholm on 14 July 1967, BIRPI was renamed WIPO. The resulting structural and administrative reforms, combined with expanding responsibilities, have resulted in a rapid increase in the membership of the organization as well as the intellectual property unions administered by WIPO. This history was compiled through the use of a number of sources from the World Intellectual Property Organization (hereafter cited as WIPO) Website (Geneva, Switzerland, June 1998 [cited 1 May 1999]); available from http://www.wipo.int/, including "World Intellectual Property Organization: The Beginning," p. 3; "Paris Convention for the Protection of Industrial Property of March 20, 1883"; "World Intellectual Property Organization: The Beginning," p. 3; "Convention Establishing the World Intellectual Property Organization"; and "Members of the WIPO Governing Bodies and Committees."

16. See "General Information," in WIPO Website (Geneva, Switzerland, 1999 [cited 1 March 2000]), p. 5; available from http://www.wipo.int/.

17. The World Trade Organization was established with the successful conclusion of the Uruguay Round General Agreement on Tariffs and Trade (GATT) Multilateral Trade Negotiations on 15 April 1994. Ibid., p. 12.

18. See "World Intellectual Property Organization History," in WIPO Website (Geneva, Switzerland, 1998 [cited 1 May 1999]); available from http://www.wipo.int/.

19. Ibid.

20. WIPO now administers twenty-one treaties, two of which are with other international organizations. See "General Information," in WIPO Website (Geneva, Switzerland, 1999 [cited 1 March 2000]); available from http://www.wipo.int/.

21. "Message from Dr. Kamil Idris, Director General of WIPO," in WIPO Website (Geneva, Switzerland, 1998 [cited 23 April 1998]); available from http://www.wipo.int/.

22. See "Madrid Agreement concerning the International Registration of Marks of April 14, 1891," in WIPO Website (Geneva, Switzerland, 1998 [cited 1 May 1999]); available from http://www.wipo.int/. The countries linked to this agreement may, within a period of one year of registration, notify the WIPO that they do not accept the registration of the Olympic symbol for their territory.

23. As of 17 January 2000 the Madrid Agreement concerning the International Registration of Marks had sixty-four member states. For further information on the Madrid Agreement, see "Texts of Madrid Agreement, Protocol Relating to the Madrid Agreement and Common Regulations," in WIPO Website (Geneva, Switzerland, 1999 [cited 1 March 2000]); available from http://www.wipo.int/.

24. For an extended discussion on the International Committee of the Red Cross dealing primarily with the period 1945–75, see David P. Forsythe, *Humanitarian Politics: The International Committee of the Red Cross* (Baltimore: Johns Hopkins University Press, 1977).

25. "Minutes of the Meeting of the IOC Executive Board," Tunis, 25–26 January 1978, p. 5, IOCA.

26. "Minutes of the 79th Session of the International Olympic Committee," Prague, 15–18 June 1977, IOCA. The specific section of point 6 of the by-law to Rule 6 reads: "The design of an Olympic emblem must be submitted to the IOC Executive Board for approval. Such approval is subject to the fact that there is no risk of confusion between that emblem and the Olympic symbol (the five rings alone)."

27. "Minutes of the Meeting of the IOC Executive Board," Tunis, 25–26 January 1978, p. 58, IOCA.

28. Howard Stupp, "The Evolution of the Legal Status of the International Olympic Committee in the Twentieth Century," in *Proceedings: Twenty-eighth Session of the International Olympic Academy* (Lausanne: IOC/IOA, 1988), pp. 151–57. "Other non-governmental institutions" refers to organizations with headquarters based in Switzerland.

29. Alexander was coopted at the IOC Session in Rome in 1960 and remained active until his death in 1990 at the age of seventy-six. See "Minutes of the 58th Session of the International Olympic Committee," Rome, 20 and 22–23 August 1960, p. 4, IOCA.

30. "Minutes of the 84th Session of the International Olympic Committee," Baden-Baden, 23 and 29 September–2 October 1981, p. 292, IOCA.

31. For an extended discussion on Public Law 95-606 (the Amateur Sports Act), see Frank Zang, ed., *1992 United States Olympic Committee Fact Book* (Colorado Springs: United States Olympic Committee, 1992), pp. 9–11. This law, designed in the 1970s to quell the animosity between the National College Athletic Association (NCAA) and AAU over control of amateur athletics in the United States, made the USOC the controlling body with respect to American Olympic competition. It also provided a reaffirmation and extension of the 21 September 1950 congressional Act to Incorporate the United States Olympic Association, which gave it absolute jurisdiction over the use of Olympic emblems, logos, and words within the United States and its territories. The treaty, entitled Nairobi Treaty on the Protection of the Olympic Symbol, is open to membership by any

member state of WIPO, the Paris Union, the United Nations, or any of the specialized agencies brought into relationship with the United Nations. The treaty entered into force on 25 October 1982, one month after the "third instrument of ratification, acceptance, approval or accession" had been submitted by a state to the director-general of WIPO. All countries that are party to the treaty are under the obligation to prevent registration of the mark and to take appropriate measures against the use of the mark or other signs for commercial purposes except when an Olympic symbol was registered in that state before the treaty entered into force with respect to that state. Whenever a license fee is paid to the IOC for its authorization to use the Olympic symbol for commercial purposes part of the revenue accrued is awarded to the NOCs located in the countries that are party to the treaty. See "Contracting Parties of Treaties Administered by WIPO: Nairobi Treaty on the Protection of the Olympic Symbol," in WIPO Website (Geneva, Switzerland, 1998 [cited 15 April 1999]); available from http://www.wipo.int/. The first states to deposit their instruments of ratification on 25 September 1982 were Equatorial Guinea, Ethiopia, and Kenya.

32. Klaus Hempel to Juan Antonio Samaranch, n.d., ISL Marketing File, IOCA.

33. International Sports Leisure Marketing AG, *A Presentation to the International Olympic Committee* (New Delhi: International Olympic Committee Executive Board, 1983). The Olympic Programme has been renamed The Olympic Partners.

34. See "Candidate Cities/Olympic Winter Games," 27 July 1998, p. 3, Personal Files of Richard Pound (hereafter cited as PFRP).

35. *The Official Report of the Organizing Committee of the XIVth Winter Olympic Games, Final Report* (Sarajevo: Organizing Committee of the XIVth Winter Olympic Games, 1984), p. 183 (approximate conversion rate for the period: 239.5 dinars = $1 U.S.).

36. IOC president Juan Antonio Samaranch quoted in Michael R. Payne, "Myths of Olympic Marketing," paper presented at the USOC Olympic Congress, New York, 29 October 1993, p. 4, IOCA.

37. International Olympic Committee Marketing Department, *1999 Olympic Marketing Fact File* (Lausanne: IOC, 1999), p. 36. Unlike Montréal, Los Angeles commissioned a limited number of firms holding licenses as well as the range of Olympic products produced. At the beginning of 1984 Los Angeles received and processed over eight thousand applications for marketing licenses, covering over three hundred product categories. Fernand Landry and Magdeleine Yerlès, "The Presidencies of Lord Killanin (1972–1980) and Juan Antonio Samaranch (1980–)," in *The International Olympic Committee—One Hundred Years: The Idea—the Presidents—the Achievements*, vol. 3 (Lausanne: IOC, 1996), p. 188.

38. Richard B. Perelman, ed., *Olympic Retrospective: The Games of Los Angeles* (Los Angeles: Los Angeles Olympic Organizing Committee, 1985), pp. 118–19.

39. Dorling Kindersley Limited, *Chronicle of the Olympics* (London: Dorling Kindersley Limited, 1998), p. 163.

40. "Olympic Games Television Rights Summary: Summer Games," 27 July 1998, p. 5, PFRP.

41. International Olympic Committee Marketing Department, *1999 Olympic Marketing Fact File*, p. 36.

42. Landry and Yerlès, "The Presidencies of Lord Killanin (1972–1980) and Juan Antonio Samaranch (1980–)," pp. 188–89.

43. See "Minutes of the IOC/ISL Meeting," 6 December 1984, ISL Union with IOC File, p. 6, IOCA.

44. Copyright protection is limited in time. Many countries have adopted as a general rule a term of protection that starts at the time of the creation of the work and ends fifty years (in some countries seventy years) after the death of the author. In some countries, however, there are exceptions for certain kinds of works (e.g., photographs, audiovisual works) or for certain uses (e.g., translations).

45. "Minutes of the IOC/ISL Meeting," 6 December 1984, ISL Union with IOC File, p. 6, IOCA.

46. "Minutes of the Meeting of the IOC Executive Board," Calgary, 25–28 February 1985, p. 167, IOCA.

47. "Minutes of the Meeting of the IOC Executive Board," Berlin, 31 May, 1–3 and 6 June 1985, p. 34, IOCA.

48. Ibid., p. 35.

49. "Minutes of the Meeting of the IOC Executive Board," Lausanne, 28 May 1985, p. 202, IOCA.

50. "Minutes of the Meeting of the IOC Executive Board," Lisbon, 15 and 18 October 1985, p. 76, IOCA. The first study was submitted to the IOC on 13 December 1984 by Professor Alois Troller and lawyer Jacqueline Schwarz. The second study, requested by François Carrard, was written on 21 February 1985 by Professor François Dessemontet, who had the advantage of reading the first study prior to drafting his own.

51. "Minutes of the Meeting of the IOC Executive Board," Lausanne, 10–12 February 1986, p. 44, IOCA.

52. "Minutes of the Meeting of the IOC Executive Board," Seoul, 22–24 April 1986, p. 154, IOCA.

53. Ibid., p. 42.

54. Ibid., p. 43. François Carrard insisted that if a new symbol was to be designed it would be extremely important to commission an artist of "world renown," warning that even a person as famous as Hans Erni might not command sufficient "prestige" worldwide for the purpose. Without providing a suitable candidate, Carrard suggested "an artist of absolute worldwide reputation, such as Miro or Picasso if they were alive," to design the new emblem. This, he felt, would add additional protection to the symbol in the future. He further argued that if this step could not be taken the IOC's position would remain "somewhat weaker."

55. At the IOC Executive Board meeting in Lausanne in December 1986 Pound indicated that following the previous Executive Board meeting in Seoul he had met with representatives of Coca-Cola, Federal Express, and VISA to discuss the protection of the Olympic symbol. According to Pound, the "sponsors had been unanimously in favour of retaining the rings which were immediately identifiable to all as the symbol of the Olympic Games and Movement." "Minutes of the Meeting of the IOC Executive Board," Lausanne, 10–11 October 1986, p. 50, IOCA.

56. Ibid., p. 51.

57. "Minutes of the Meeting of the IOC Executive Board," Lausanne, 1987, p. 3, IOCA.

58. The utilization of national legislation relating to the protection of the Olympic rings was seen as a viable alternative to the international ratification of the Nairobi Treaty on the Protection of the Olympic Symbol.

59. "Minutes of the Meeting of the IOC Executive Board," Lausanne, 24–26 June 1988, p. 125, IOCA. François Carrard also suggested that it would be in the best interest of the IOC to implement a "restrictive and prudent policy . . . when adopting emblems or other authorized logos, in order to see to it that the image of the Olympic symbol itself be neither weakened nor diluted."

60. A majority of the world's Western industrialized countries have already protected the Olympic symbol for the benefit of their NOC.

61. The Latin phrase *post mortem auctoris* translates as "after the death of the originator."

62. See *The Official Report of the Organizing Committee for the XXIst Olympiad,* vol. 1 (Montréal: Organizing Committee of the 1976 Olympic Games, 1978), pp. 58–59. The total cost of the 1976 Olympic Games was calculated at $1.596 billion (CDN) and the revenues at $606 million.

63. Ibid., p. 58.

64. As of 31 October 1994 the remaining debt from the Montréal Olympic Games amounted to $420 million (CDN) dollars. Given the predicted interest rates at the time, the U.S. dollar exchange rates, and the tobacco tax allocated to the "Olympic" debt, it was forecast that the deficit would be repaid in the year 2013. See Landry and Yerlès, "The Presidencies of Lord Killanin (1972–1980) and Juan Antonio Samaranch (1980–)," p. 163.

65. See *The Official Report of the Organizing Committee for the XXIst Olympiad* (Montréal: Organizing Committee of the 1976 Olympic Games, 1978).

66. Monique Berlioux, to Whom It May Concern, 19 November 1979, ISL Marketing File, IOCA; see also Monique Berlioux, to Whom It May Concern, 7 December 1979, ISL Marketing File, IOCA.

67. Ems Magnus (marketing manager, ISL Marketing AG) to Horst Dassler, 8 September 1983, ISL Marketing File, IOCA.

68. Ibid. To correct the situation, the IOC noted that it would have to sue LEVI's because it cannot sue the NOC. In hopes of avoiding another court case, the IOC asked the USOC to create a new emblem. The resulting design included the five interlocking rings and the letters "USA."

69. ISL, created shortly after the finals of the 1982 Soccer World Cup, had approached the IOC in hopes of developing a worldwide sponsorship marketing program involving various multinational corporations that would generate income for the Olympic Movement and, of course, enhance its own company.

70. Ems Magnus (marketing manager, ISL Marketing AG) to Horst Dassler, 8 September 1983, ISL Marketing File, IOCA. The first session of the Intelicense-IOC court case was on 30 August 1983.

71. See "Minutes of the Meeting of the IOC Executive Board," Mexico City, 7–8 November 1984, p. 78, IOCA.

72. See "Minutes of the Meeting of the IOC Executive Board," Berlin, 31 May, 1–3, 6 June 1985, p. 127, IOCA. The award in favor of the USOC included $50,000 damages against ISM, $80,000 damages against Intelicense, subject to an accounting, $74,000 in attorneys' fees against ISM and Intelicense jointly, and $8,000 in attorneys' fees against Intelicense alone.

73. Ibid., p. 76.

74. See "Minutes of the Meeting of the IOC Executive Board," Lisbon, 15 and 18 October 1985, p. 18, IOCA.

75. See "Minutes of the Meeting of the IOC Executive Board," Lausanne, 10–12 February 1986, p. 122, IOCA.

76. Ibid., p. 123.

77. See "Minutes of the Meeting of the IOC Executive Board," Seoul, 22–24 April 1986, p. 47, IOCA. Curiously, the new Intelicense claim was dated 16 August 1985 but was not served until late January 1986.

78. Ibid., p. 162, IOCA. The IOC's attorneys characterized the damages sought by Intelicense as extravagant.

79. Ibid., p. 163.

80. Following a closed-door session at the IOC Executive Board meetings in Berlin in 1985, the Executive Committee unanimously decided to bring to a conclusion the service of Monique Berlioux as IOC director. With the position of director vacated, the Executive Committee appointed, for an unspecified period, as administrator ad interim Raymond Gafner, IOC member in Switzerland. Pursuant to the Executive Board's decision, Gafner began his duties on 7 June 1985 with the same means at his disposal as the former director. At the same Executive Board meetings the Executive Committee decided to undertake without delay all necessary steps toward the recruitment of a new director of the IOC. See "Minutes of the Meeting of the IOC Executive Board," Berlin, 31 May, 1–3 and 6 June 1985, pp. 8–10, IOCA. At the IOC Executive Board meetings in Barcelona in April 1989 the Executive Committee unanimously decided to appoint IOC legal adviser François Carrard director general of the IOC, effective 1 September 1989. See "Minutes of the Meeting of the IOC Executive Board," Barcelona, 4–6 June 1989, pp. 19–21, IOCA.

81. See "Minutes of the Meeting of the IOC Executive Board," Seoul, 22–24 April 1986, p. 47, IOCA. Samaranch commented that "a rather small and insignificant affair had grown out of proportion relative to its importance."

82. Ibid., p. 166

83. See "Minutes of the Meeting of the IOC Executive Board," Stockholm, 25 and 27–28 April 1988, p. 19, IOCA.

84. See "Minutes of the Meeting of the IOC Executive Board," Lausanne, 24–26 July 1988, p. 27, IOCA.

85. "Minutes of the Meeting of the IOC Executive Board, Barcelona," 24–26 April 1989, pp. 19–21, IOCA. By April 1989 the Intelicense-IOC legal dispute had lasted more than six years.

86. "Minutes of the Meeting of the IOC Executive Board," Belgrade, 24–26 April 1990, pp. 30–32, IOCA.

87. "Minutes of the Meeting of the IOC Executive Board," Barcelona, 4–6 June 1990, p. 6, IOCA.

88. "Minutes of the Meeting of the IOC Executive Board," Tokyo, 13–16 September 1990, pp. 5–6, IOCA.

89. Klaus Jürgen Hempel to Juan Antonio Samaranch, November 1982, ISL Marketing File, IOCA.

90. Juan Antonio Samaranch to Klaus Hempel, 17 December 1982, ISL Marketing File, IOCA.

91. Klaus Jürgen Hempel to Juan Antonio Samaranch, November 1982, ISL Marketing File, IOCA.

92. ISL, "A Presentation to the International Olympic Committee," New Delhi, 1983, p. 1, IOCA.

93. See "Minutes of the Meeting of the Commission of New Sources of Financing," Lausanne, 9 October 1986, p. 5, IOCA. Samaranch had been concerned about this IOC budgetary fact as early as 1982, when it became apparent that approximately 95% of IOC revenue was derived from the sale of television rights.

94. See "Minutes of the Meeting of the Commission of New Sources of Financing," Seoul, 10 September 1988, p. 10, IOCA. Of particular concern to the IOC was the enormous dependency on revenues generated through the sale of television rights to U.S. broadcasters, which by 1982 accounted for an overwhelming share of total world sales for television rights.

95. At the fourth meeting of the Commission of New Sources of Financing convened in Berlin on 1 June 1985, Guirandou-N'Diaye provided members with a brief overview of the commission's history, including an account of the "IOC's activities in the field of commercialism" that focused on the impact of the worldwide sponsorship program approved by the commission in New Delhi in late March 1983. See "Minutes of the Meeting of the Commission of New Sources of Financing," Berlin, 1 June 1985, p. 1, IOCA.

96. Muriel Cohen to Monique Berlioux, 25 March 1983, ISL Marketing File, IOCA.

97. Monique Berlioux to Muriel Cohen, 19 April 1983, ISL Marketing File, IOCA.

98. Walter Tröger to Monique Berlioux, 9 May 1983, ISL Marketing File, IOCA.

99. Monique Berlioux to Walter Tröger, 19 May 1983, ISL Marketing File, IOCA.

100. Monique Berlioux to members of the International Olympic Committee, 18 May 1983, ISL Marketing File, IOCA. In November 1983 Berlioux dispatched a letter addressed to all National Olympic Committees containing additional information on the IOC/ISL agreement. In the letter she stated that the agreement was "based on commercialising the Olympic emblem under the overall control of the IOC." Monique Berlioux to all NOCs, 30 November 1983, ISL Marketing File, IOCA.

101. See "Minutes of the Meeting of the Commission of New Sources of Financing," Lausanne, 9 October 1986, p. 5, IOCA.

102. *IOC Commercialisation—Report No. 10* (Zurich: IOC, 1983).

103. Lord Luke (vice-chairman, IOC Finance Commission) to Juan Antonio Samaranch, 22 February 1984, ISL Marketing File, IOCA.

104. See "Résumé de la réunion de contact avec I.S.L. tenue," in "C.I.O. Commercialisation—Rapport," no. 10, 1 May 1983, ISL Marketing File, IOCA. In attendance were representatives of the ISL, Dentsu, McCann, USOC, BOA, and IOC.

105. François Carrard to Monique Berlioux, Daniel Russell, International Olympic Committee Members, 20 May 1983, ISL Marketing File, IOCA.

106. Monique Berlioux to Horst Dassler, and Francis Craighill (counsel to ISL), 25 May 1983, ISL Marketing File, IOCA (emphasis ours).

107. "Preliminary Agreement between: The International Olympic Committee (IOC) and ISL Licensing AG (ISL)," 2 June 1983, Lausanne, p. 1, IOCA.

108. Ems Magnus to Monique Berlioux, 3 June 1983, ISL Marketing File, IOCA.

109. Klaus Jürgen Hempel and Jürgen Lenz to Juan Antonio Samaranch, 24 November 1983, ISL Marketing File, IOCA.

110. Jürgen Lenz to Don Miller, 23 February 1984, ISL Marketing File, IOCA. Despite numerous attempts to contact Miller by telephone, Lenz was forced to send a "follow-up" letter echoing his request for a rapid decision on a presentation date and conclusion of an agreement between USOC/ISL. See Jürgen Lenz to Don Miller, 14 June 1984, ISL Marketing File, IOCA.

111. See Don Miller to Jürgen Lenz, 14 June 1984, ISL Marketing File, IOCA. Miller wasted little time responding to Lenz's letter, received earlier that same day. Although the USOC was taking a favorable attitude toward the ISL project, Miller noted that due to the boycott situation no immediate decision could be expected. For a copy of Jürgen Lenz's letter, see Jürgen Lenz to Don Miller, 14 June 1984, ISL Marketing File, IOCA.

112. Tae Woo Roh to William E. Simon, 22 June 1984, ISL Marketing File, IOCA.

113. Bill Wardle to Jürgen Lenz, 3 July 1984, ISL Marketing File, IOCA.

114. Jürgen Lenz to Bill Wardle, 5 July 1984, ISL Marketing File, IOCA.

115. Juan Antonio Samaranch to William E. Simon, 14 June 1984, ISL Marketing File, IOCA.

116. ISL, "SPONSORSHIP: A Proposal to the National Olympic Committee" (Lucerne: ISL Marketing File, 1984), IOCA. The Executive Board of the USOC was presented with the proposal on 9 July 1984.

117. Jürgen Lenz to Don Miller, 5 August 1984, ISL/TOP I General File, IOCA.

118. Jürgen Lenz to Juan Antonio Samaranch, 5 August 1984, ISL/TOP I General File, IOCA.

119. Walter Meier to Juan Antonio Samaranch, 12 September 1984, ISL/TOP I General File, IOCA.

120. Juan Antonio Samaranch to Walter Meier, 20 September 1984, ISL Marketing File, IOCA.

121. Don Miller to Jürgen Lenz, 7 September 1984, ISL Marketing File, IOCA.

122. IOC/ISL Meeting, 14 May 1985, Lausanne, ISL Union With IOC File, IOCA.

123. "Minutes of the Meeting of the IOC Executive Board," Lausanne, 28 May 1985, pp. 177–78, IOCA.

124. George D. Miller to Jürgen Lenz, 17 September 1986, ISL/TOP I General File, IOCA.

125. George Miller to Juan Antonio Samaranch, 21 January 1987, ISL/TOP I General File, IOCA.

126. George Miller to Jürgen Lenz, 17 September 1986, ISL/TOP I General File, IOCA.

127. Juan Antonio Samaranch to George Miller, 22 December 1986, ISL/TOP I General File, IOCA.

128. ISL, *Sponsor Handbook: The Olympic Programme—Action* (Lucerne: ISL, n.d.), p. 21.

129. Andrew Craig to John Krimsky, 5 February 1987, ISL/TOP I General File, IOCA.

130. John Krimsky to Andrew Craig, 10 February 1987, ISL/TOP I General File, IOCA.

131. Richard Pound to Andrew Craig, 16 March 1987, ISL/TOP I General File, IOCA. In his communication Pound notes that he spoke with George Miller by telephone from his Montréal law office.

132. For a short portrait of Krimsky's career with Pan-Am, see *1990 U.S. Olympic Committee Fact Book* (Colorado Springs: U.S. Olympic Committee, 1990), p. 26.

133. See "John Krimsky Leaves USOC, Hockey's Dave Ogrean Takes Marketing Helm," *Olympian* (July–August 1999): 42.

134. Ibid. Pound's counsel on this point aimed at reminding Craig not to become too immersed in affairs from which a relatively negligible number of dollars were generated. In the greater scheme of things royalty payments were minuscule when compared to sponsorship payments received from a business being associated with TOP.

135. Michael Payne (ISL) to B. I. Kim (director, Business Dept. II, SLOOC) and Bill Wardle, 15 September 1987, ISL/TOP I General File, IOCA.

136. Baaron Pittenger to Richard Pound, 7 December 1987, ISL/TOP II General File, IOCA.

137. Baaron Pittenger to Klaus Hempel, 13 February 1988, ISL/TOP II General File, IOCA.

138. Baaron Pittenger to Juan Antonio Samaranch, 5 March 1988, ISL/TOP II General File, IOCA.

139. "Minutes of the Meeting of the Commission of New Sources of Financing," Seoul, 10 September 1988, p. 2, IOCA.

140. Howard Stupp to Juan Antonio Samaranch, 9 March 1988, ISL/TOP II General File, IOCA.

141. Howard Stupp to Juan Antonio Samaranch, 14 March 1988, ISL/TOP II General File, IOCA.

142. Andrew Craig to Baaron Pittenger, 25 May 1988, ISL/TOP II General File, IOCA.

143. Andrew Craig to John Krimsky, 7 June 1988, ISL/TOP II General File, IOCA.

144. Andrew Craig to Howard Stupp, 13 June 1988, ISL/TOP II General File, IOCA.

145. Guy P. Radius (ISL counsel) to Richard Kline (USOC counsel), 29 June 1988, ISL/TOP II General File, IOCA.

146. "Minutes of the Meeting of the Commission of New Sources of Financing," Seoul, 10 September 1988, p. 2, IOCA. Pound noted that the problem arose because of internal political problems but warned that the OCOG's problems were likely to become those of the IOC should it be unable to resolve the situation.

147. Michael Payne to John Krimsky, 13 April 1989, ISL/TOP I General File, IOCA.

148. John Krimsky to Michael Payne, 14 April 1989, ISL/TOP I General File, IOCA.

149. Michael Payne to John Krimsky, 18 April 1989, ISL/TOP I General File, IOCA.

150. John Krimsky to Michael Payne, 18 April 1989, ISL/TOP I General File, IOCA.

151. Michael Payne to John Krimsky, 21 April 1989, ISL/TOP I General File, IOCA.

152. John Krimsky to Michael Payne, 18 April 1989, ISL/TOP I General File, IOCA. In his letter to Payne Krimsky's phrase "the learned Pound" refers to Richard W. Pound.

153. John Krimsky to Michael Payne, 14 April 1989, ISL/TOP I General File, IOCA.

154. John Krimsky to Guy Radius, 4 May 1989, ISL/TOP I General File, IOCA.

155. "Minutes of the Meeting of the IOC Executive Board," Puerto Rico, 27–29 August 1989, p. 31, IOCA.

156. Andrew Craig to Howard Stupp, 30 April 1990, ISL/TOP II General File, IOCA.

157. Howard Stupp to Andrew Craig, 7 May 1990, ISL/TOP II General File, IOCA.

8. MONIQUE BERLIOUX'S ZENITH:
SARAJEVO AND LOS ANGELES TELEVISION NEGOTIATIONS

1. David Miller, *Olympic Revolution: The Biography of Juan Antonio Samaranch* (London: Pavilion Books, 1992), p. 252.

2. Berlioux's workaholic tendencies and her demands for a similar degree of commitment from IOC employees alienated some staff members and resulted in a high degree of turnover in personnel.

3. For Berlioux's influence, see Allen Guttmann, *The Olympics: A History of the Modern Games* (Urbana and Chicago: University of Illinois Press, 1992), pp. 114–15, 142; Lord Killanin, *My Olympic Years* (London: Secker & Warburg, 1983), pp. 79–80; Miller, *Olympic Revolution*, pp. 33–35; and Peter Ueberroth (with Richard Levin and Amy Quinn), *Made in America: His Own Story* (New York: William Morrow and Company, 1985), p. 68. With respect to Berlioux's involvement in Olympic television rights negotiations in the 1970s, see Stephen R. Wenn, "Television Rights Negotiations and the 1976 Montréal Olympics," *Sport History*

Review 27 (November 1996): 111–38; and Stephen R. Wenn, "A Turning Point for IOC Television Policy: U.S. Television Rights Negotiations and the 1980 Lake Placid and Moscow Olympic Festivals," *Journal of Sport History* 25 (Spring 1998): 87–118.

4. "Notes on the Work of the Television Sub-Committee," 23 June 1974, "TV Divers 1974–1985" Binder, "1974–1979" Folder, IOCA. At this time the IOC drew 98% of its operating revenue from its share of television rights money.

5. Stephen R. Wenn, "Growing Pains: The Olympic Movement and Television, 1966–1972," *Olympika* 4 (1995): 1–22; Wenn, "Television Rights Negotiations and the 1976 Montréal Olympics"; and Wenn, "A Turning Point for IOC Television Policy."

6. For events leading to the establishment of the Rome Formula (at the IOC's Rome Session in 1966), see Stephen R. Wenn, "An Olympian Squabble: The Distribution of Olympic Television Revenue, 1960–1966," *Olympika* 3 (1994): 27–47.

7. The Munich Olympic Organizing Committee, led by Daume, signed a $13.5 million (U.S.) contract with ABC. While $7.5 million was identified as the rights payment subject to the Rome Formula, Daume reserved the remaining $6 million as a technical services fee payable to the Organizing Committee. The IOC successfully discouraged Sapporo organizers from adopting the same policy, but Innsbruck and Montréal officials proved eager to capitalize on this precedent. See Wenn, "Growing Pains," pp. 8–10; and Wenn, "Television Rights Negotiations and the 1976 Montréal Olympics," pp. 114–17, 134. Through some sleight-of-hand tactics with documentation Montréal officials obtained IOC approval to include a technical services payment in all television contracts.

8. Wenn, "Television Rights Negotiations and the 1976 Montréal Olympics," pp. 114–17; and Wenn, "A Turning Point for IOC Television Policy," pp. 93–99.

9. The IOC Session passed a legislative change to Rule 49 in the *Olympic Charter* mandating this new approach. "Minutes of the 79th Session of the International Olympic Committee," Prague, 15–18 June 1977, pp. 35, 99–103, IOCA.

10. Miller, *Olympic Revolution*, p. 252. Miller cites Pound as stating: "[Samaranch] asked me to handle television in 1983, partly because he knew this would irritate Monique Berlioux, who was then still the Director [of the IOC] and [who] had negotiated previous deals."

11. Los Angeles organizers and the IOC encountered some difficulties in establishing a contract between the two parties concerning their respective responsibilities. During the early stages of discussion Los Angeles officials sought complete control of the television negotiations process. The following excerpt details the opinion of Georges Straschnov, the IOC's television adviser, expressed after he had read the first draft of the IOC/Los Angeles contract proposed by Los Angeles: "In the first draft, the television broadcasting and distribution rights were assigned completely to the Organising Committee world-wide with the equivalent radio rights assigned only within the United States, though in the second draft these too were accorded throughout the world. This permitted the Organising Committee to negotiate all contracts freely, with the IOC allowed to attend negotiations and approve the contracts, though such approval could not be withheld 'unreasonably.' This meant that the IOC would be relinquishing all rights to the Organising

Committee without any control and supervision over negotiations, which was extremely dangerous and infringed Rule 49." "Minutes of the Meeting of the IOC Executive Board," Athens, 13–14, 16, and 18 May 1978, p. 17, IOCA. The eventual resolution of this issue involved granting Los Angeles some latitude in negotiations, but the IOC was to be informed completely and retained the right to approve contracts. Berlioux stated that "the Organising Committee for Los Angeles had signed an agreement with the IOC wherein it had agreed to inform the IOC of all negotiations." "Minutes of the Meeting of the IOC Executive Board," Puerto Rico, 26–29 June 1979, p. 8, IOCA. Concerned about media reports detailing Los Angeles's early discussions with television networks interested in acquiring U.S. television rights, Berlioux reminded Peter Ueberroth of the IOC's rights. Los Angeles had solicited a $500,000 deposit from interested networks in order to guarantee them an opportunity to bid for the television rights. In her letter of 30 April Berlioux wrote: "Under an agreement concluded with the IOC the Organising Committee has undertaken to observe the IOC rules and regulations. These prescribe among other things that no television contract will be negotiated without the IOC (Rule 49)." Monique Berlioux to Peter Ueberroth, 30 April 1979, "Los Angeles TV-General 1984 1978–1979–1980" File, IOCA. Killanin's correspondence also indicates that Los Angeles possessed more authority than Sarajevo in negotiations. A few days later Killanin asked Los Angeles's Paul Ziffren to "keep us advised when you have any negotiating meeting in case we want to send an observer as provided in our contract." Lord Killanin to Paul Ziffren, 4 May 1979, "Los Angeles TV-General 1984 1978–1979–1980" File, IOCA.

12. Ahmed Karabegovic to Monique Berlioux, 11 December 1979, "Sarajevo TV-General 1978–1979" File, IOCA.

13. Monique Berlioux to Ahmed Karabegovic, 13 December 1979, "Sarajevo TV-General 1978–1979" File, IOCA.

14. The best support for Berlioux's version of discussions on this matter is found in Monique Berlioux to Ahmed Karabegovic, 7 January 1980, "Sarajevo TV-General Janvier/Mai 1980" File, IOCA.

15. Monique Berlioux to Ahmed Karabegovic, 7 December 1979, "Sarajevo TV-General 1978–1979" File, IOCA: "The agreement above mentioned will be recommended by the President of the IOC, Lord Killanin, and the President of the Finance Commission, Count de Beaumont, to the Executive Board for ratification at its next meeting."

16. Ahmed Karabegovic to Monique Berlioux, 7 January 1980, "Sarajevo TV-General Janvier/Mai 1980" File, IOCA.

17. Monique Berlioux to Ahmed Karabegovic, 7 January 1980, "Sarajevo TV-General Janvier/Mai 1980" File, IOCA.

18. Ahmed Karabegovic to Monique Berlioux, 8 January 1980, "Sarajevo TV-General Janvier/Mai 1980" File, IOCA.

19. MW (vice-president, programs, CBS Sports) to Monique Berlioux, 10 January 1980; and Monique Berlioux to Vice-President, Programs, CBS Sports, 14 January 1980, "Sarajevo TV-General Janvier/Mai 1980" File, IOCA.

20. Arthur A. Watson (president, NBC Sports) to Monique Berlioux, 18 January 1980, "Sarajevo TV-General Janvier/Mai 1980" File, IOCA; and "Report by the IOC Representatives on Their Visit to Sarajevo regarding Television Negotiations

with the American Broadcasting Companies 21st–24th January 1980," p. 2, "Sarajevo TV-General Janvier/Mai 1980" File, IOCA (hereafter cited as "Mortureux/Coupat Report").

21. "Statement Given on January 23, 1980, at 9 A.M. by the NBC Representatives, according to the Priory [sic] Established Order," "Sarajevo TV-General Janvier/Mai 1980" File, IOCA.

22. "Mortureux/Coupat Report," p. 2.

23. "Tentative Programme of American TV Companies' Visit to Sarajevo, January 19–25 1980," p. 4, "Sarajevo TV-General Janvier/Mai 1980" File, IOCA.

24. "Mortureux/Coupat Report," p. 2.

25. Ibid., pp. 2–3.

26. Ibid., p. 3.

27. Ibid., p. 4.

28. This information was relayed to the authors during Zecevic's reaction to a paper presented at the Fourth International Symposium for Olympic Research at the International Centre for Olympic Studies, London, Ontario, in October, 1998. The published paper in question was Stephen R. Wenn, "Conflicting Agendas: Monique Berlioux, Ahmed Karabegovic and U.S. Television Rights Negotiations for the 1984 Sarajevo Olympic Winter Games," in Robert K. Barney, Kevin B. Wamsley, Scott G. Martyn, and Gordon H. MacDonald, eds., *Global and Cultural Critique: Problematizing the Olympic Games—Proceedings of the Fourth International Symposium for Olympic Research* (London, Ontario: International Centre for Olympic Studies, 1998), pp. 115–27.

29. "Mortureux/Coupat Report," p. 4.

30. This description was provided by Richard Pound during commentary at a session at the 1998 North American Society for Sport History Conference at the University of Windsor, May 1998.

31. "Mortureux/Coupat Report," p. 5.

32. Monique Berlioux to Lord Killanin, 24 January 1980, "Sarajevo TV-General Janvier/Mai 1980" File, IOCA.

33. Lord Killanin to Monique Berlioux, 24 January 1980, "Sarajevo TV-General Janvier/Mai 1980" File, IOCA.

34. "Telephone Conversation between Lord Killanin and Monique Berlioux," 24 January 1980, "Sarajevo TV-General Janvier/Mai 1980" File, IOCA.

35. John Martin (vice-president, programming, ABC Sports) to Ahmed Karabegovic, 24 January 1980; and Frank Smith (CBS Sports) to SOOC, 24 January 1980, "Sarajevo TV-General Janvier/Mai 1980" File, IOCA.

36. Lord Killanin to Monique Berlioux, 25 January 1980, "Sarajevo TV-General Janvier/Mai 1980" File, IOCA. Killanin supplied Berlioux with a verbatim copy of Sucic's telex in this communication.

37. "Mortureux/Coupat Report," p. 6.

38. "Discussion on TV Rights with the Sarajevo OCOG," 15 February 1980, in "Minutes of the Meeting of the Finance Commission," Lake Placid, 11, 14, and 16 February 1980, p. 3, IOCA.

39. "Minutes of the Meeting of the Finance Commission," Lake Placid, 11, 14, and 16 February 1980, pp. 5–6, IOCA.

40. Ibid., p. 6; and "Discussion on Television Rights with the Sarajevo

OCOG," 20 February 1980, in "Minutes of the Meeting of the Finance Commission," Lake Placid, 11, 14, and 16 February 1980, p. 7, IOCA.

41. "Minutes of the Meeting of the Finance Commission," Lake Placid, 11, 14, and 16 February 1980, p. 6, IOCA.

42. "Discussion on Television Rights with the Sarajevo OCOG," 20 February 1980, in "Minutes of the Meeting of the Finance Commission," Lake Placid, 11, 14, and 16 February 1980, p. 7, IOCA.

43. Monique Berlioux to Members of the Finance Commission, 23 February 1980, "Sarajevo TV-General Janvier/Mai 1980" File, IOCA.

44. "Discussion on Television Rights with the Sarajevo OCOG," 20 February 1980, in "Minutes of the Meeting of the Finance Commission," Lake Placid, 11, 14, and 16 February 1980, p. 7, IOCA.

45. Monique Berlioux to Members of the Finance Commission, 23 February 1980, "Sarajevo TV-General Janvier/Mai 1980" File, IOCA.

46. Monique Berlioux to CTV Network (Canada), 28 March 1980; and, for Karabegovic's reaction, Ahmed Karabegovic to Monique Berlioux, 2 April 1980, "Sarajevo TV-General Janvier/Mai 1980" File, IOCA. Karabegovic confirmed his intent to "jointly conduct [future] commercial discussions." Ahmed Karabegovic to Monique Berlioux, 21 March 1980, located in the same file.

47. Ahmed Karabegovic to Monique Berlioux, 2 April 1980, "Sarajevo TV-General Janvier/Mai 1980" File, IOCA.

48. Monique Berlioux to Ahmed Karabegovic, 16 April 1980, "Sarajevo TV-General Janvier/Mai 1980" File, IOCA.

49. Ahmed Karabegovic to Monique Berlioux, 2 April 1980, "Sarajevo TV-General Janvier/Mai 1980" File, IOCA.

50. "Report on the Meeting between the IOC and the Representatives of the Sarajevo OCOG, Lausanne, 20th May 1980," p. 5, "Sarajevo TV-General Juin/Décembre 1980" File, IOCA.

51. Ibid., p. 7.

52. Ibid., pp. 9–13.

53. "Minutes of the Meeting of the Finance Commission," Essen, 6 June 1980, pp. 2–3, IOCA.

54. Ahmed Karabegovic to Monique Berlioux, 9 June 1980, "Sarajevo TV-General Juin/Décembre 1980" File, IOCA.

55. Monique Berlioux to Ahmed Karabegovic, 9 June 1980, "Sarajevo TV-General Juin/Décembre 1980" File, IOCA. For the Executive Board's decision, see "Minutes of the Meeting of the IOC Executive Board," Lausanne, 9–10 June 1980, p. 12, IOCA.

56. "Minutes of a Meeting of the IOC, Sarajevo OCOG and the ABC Television Network Held at the Château de Vidy on Thursday, 12th June 1980," p. 2, "Sarajevo TV-General Juin/Décembre 1980" File, IOCA.

57. Ibid., pp. 3–4.

58. Ibid., p. 5.

59. "Minutes of a Meeting of the IOC, Sarajevo OCOG and the ABC Television Network Held at the Château de Vidy on Wednesday, 18th June 1980," pp. 1–2, "Sarajevo TV-General Juin/Décembre 1980" File, IOCA.

60. Key documents in support of this conclusion are "Television Negotiations with the Australian Broadcasting Companies for the XIVth Winter Games in Sarajevo 1984—Lausanne, 17th June 1981," "Sarajevo TV-General Juin/Décembre 1981" File, IOCA; Johnny Esaw to CTV Television Network (Canada), Internal Memo, 16 March 1982, "Sarajevo TV-General Janvier/Juillet 1982" File, IOCA; "Report of the Meeting IOC/OCOG-Sarajevo/EBU Friday June 18 1982," "Sarajevo TV-General Janvier/Juillet 1982" File, IOCA; "Summary of the Meeting IOC/Sarajevo/NHK-Japan, Lausanne 11.08.82," "Sarajevo TV-General Août/Décembre 1982" File, IOCA; Monique Berlioux to Masaji Kiyokawa (IOC member, Japan), 12 August 1982, "Sarajevo TV-General Août/Décembre 1982" File, IOCA; and "Summary of the Meeting IOC/Sarajevo/OIRT, Lausanne 23.09.82," "Sarajevo TV-General Août/Décembre 1982" File, IOCA.

61. "Mortureux/Coupat Report," p. 6.

62. The authors have not reviewed the final contracts; however, confirmation of this change appears in "Minutes of the Meeting of the IOC Executive Board," Sarajevo, 2 and 4 December 1981, pp. 20–21. During a keynote address to the North American Society for Sport History (May 1998), Richard Pound also noted the timing of this change to the host city contract.

63. William Pratt (president, Calgary Olympic Organizing Committee) to Juan Antonio Samaranch, 23 July 1983; William Pratt to Monique Berlioux, 3 August 1983; and "Text of the Agreement regarding Television Concluded between the IOC and the SLOOC," 26 September 1983, in "Minutes of the Meeting of the Finance Commission," Lausanne, 16 November 1983, pp. 37–41, IOCA.

64. Ahmed Karabegovic to Monique Berlioux, 29 September 1980, "Sarajevo TV-General Juin/Decembre 1980," File, IOCA.

65. In his letter to Berlioux Karabegovic wrote: "Since we have not yet definied [*sic*] in written form, the IOC/OCOG agreement on the finacial [*sic*] transaction of US dol 10 mil of loan, where accordingly the IOC should assign to the OCOG on October 15, 1980 US dol 3 mil., we kindly ask you to determine as soon as possible the date and mode of realization of this agreement." The minutes of a meeting of the Executive Board in late October, however, lead to a different conclusion. "The Sarajevo OCOG were now requesting an immediate loan of US$ 10 million, but the Comte de Beaumont pointed out that it was dangerous to lend large sums of money to an organisation facing financial difficulties." "Minutes of the Meeting of the IOC Executive Board," Lausanne, 30–31 October 1980, p. 10, IOCA.

66. "Minutes of the Meeting of the IOC Executive Board," Lausanne, 9 April 1981, p. 1, IOCA.

67. Ibid., p. 2.

68. "Minutes of the Meeting of the IOC Executive Board," Lausanne, 24–25 November 1983, pp. 36–37, IOCA.

69. "Minutes of the Meeting of the Finance Commission," Paris, 24 March 1981, p. 2; "Minutes of the Meeting of the IOC Executive Board," Lausanne, 9 April 1981, pp. 1, 7–8; "Minutes of the Meeting of the Finance Commission," Lausanne, 3 June 1981, pp. 1–3; "Minutes of the Meeting of the IOC Executive Board," Lausanne, 4 June 1981, p. 67; "Minutes of the Meeting of the Finance Commission," Lausanne, 16 December 1981, pp. 3–4, IOCA.

70. "Minutes of the Meeting of the IOC Executive Board," Sarajevo, 2 and 4 December 1981, p. 21, IOCA.

71. Ueberroth, *Made in America,* p. 28.

72. Ibid., pp. 26–27.

73. Ibid., pp. 60–61.

74. "Official Report of the Los Angeles Olympics Organizing Committee," p. 304. An excerpt from the report dealing with finances was supplied to the authors by members of the IOC's Documentation Services Department.

75. Ueberroth, *Made in America,* p. 52; and Paul Ziffren (chairman, Board of Directors, LAOOC) and Rodney W. Rood (secretary, Board of Directors, LAOOC) to ABC Sports Inc. (c/o Charles Stanford, director, legal and business affairs), 9 April 1979, "Los Angeles TV-General 1984 1978–1979–1980" File, IOCA.

76. Monique Berlioux to Peter Ueberroth, 30 April 1979; and Lord Killanin to Paul Ziffren, 4 May 1979, "Los Angeles TV-General 1984 1978–1979–1980" File, IOCA.

77. Peter Ueberroth to Monique Berlioux, 10 May 1979, "Los Angeles TV-General 1984 1978–1979–1980" File, IOCA.

78. Lord Killanin to Paul Ziffren, 11 May 1979, "Los Angeles TV-General 1984 1978–1979–1980" File, IOCA.

79. Monique Berlioux to Peter Ueberroth, 11 May 1979, "Los Angeles TV-General 1984 1978–1979–1980" File, IOCA.

80. Ibid.

81. Monique Berlioux to Peter Ueberroth, 21 May 1979; and Peter Ueberroth to Monique Berlioux, 8 June 1979, "Los Angeles TV-General 1984 1978–1979–1980" File, IOCA.

82. "Report on the Meeting between Mr. Wolper, Chairman of Los Angeles Television Committee and the Director and Financial Adviser of the IOC 11th June 1979," p. 2, "Los Angeles TV-General 1984 1978–1979–1980" File, IOCA.

83. Ibid., pp. 2–3.

84. Ueberroth, *Made in America,* p. 66; and "$175 Million Olympics TV Bid Predicted," *Los Angeles Times,* 12 September 1979, "Los Angeles TV-General 1984 1978–1979–1980" File, IOCA.

85. Ueberroth, *Made in America,* pp. 66–68.

86. Ibid., p. 68.

87. Ibid., p. 69; "Official Report of the Los Angeles Olympics Organizing Committee," p. 305.

88. "Minutes of the EBU/LAOOC/IOC Meeting, 11 May 1981," pp. 1–2, "Los Angeles TV-General 1984 1981" File, IOCA. The document was untitled. It accompanied a letter sent by Peck Prior (executive director, media, LAOOC) to Monique Berlioux dated 21 May 1981.

89. Ibid., p. 2.

90. Ibid.

91. Ibid., pp. 2–3.

92. Ibid., p. 4.

93. Regis de Kalbermatten to Peter Ueberroth, 10 June 1981, "Los Angeles TV-General 1984 1981" File, IOCA. Kalbermatten also sent Ueberroth a typed translation of the *Stuttgarter Zeitung* article dated 29 May 1981.

94. Peter Ueberroth to Regis de Kalbermatten, 17 June 1981, "Los Angeles TV-General 1984 1981" File, IOCA.

95. "Minutes of the Meeting of the 84th IOC Session," Baden-Baden, 29 September–2 October 1981, p. 4, IOCA.

96. Ibid., p. 5.

97. Peter Ueberroth to Juan Antonio Samaranch, 11 November 1981, "Los Angeles TV-General 1984 1981" File, IOCA.

98. Juan Antonio Samaranch to Peter Ueberroth, 12 November 1981, "Los Angeles TV-General 1984 1981" File, IOCA.

99. Peter Ueberroth to Juan Antonio Samaranch, 27 November 1981, "Los Angeles TV-General 1984 1981" File, IOCA; "Minutes of the Meeting of the IOC Executive Board," Sarajevo, 2 and 4 December 1981, p. 6, IOCA; and Regis de Kalbermatten to Peter Ueberroth, 26 November 1981, "Los Angeles TV-General 1984 1981" File, IOCA.

100. Peter Ueberroth to Juan Antonio Samaranch, 27 November 1981, "Los Angeles TV-General 1984 1981" File, IOCA.

101. "Minutes of the Meeting of the IOC Executive Board," Sarajevo, 2 and 4 December 1981, pp. 6–7, IOCA.

102. Ibid., p. 7.

103. Peter Ueberroth to Juan Antonio Samaranch, 2 December 1981; and Juan Antonio Samaranch to Peter Ueberroth, 3 December 1981, "Los Angeles TV-General 1984 1981" File, IOCA.

104. Jim Spence (with Dave Diles), *Up Close and Personal: The Inside Story of Network Television Sports* (New York: Atheneum Publishers, 1988), p. 36. Spence confirmed that ABC was aware of CBS's $90 million bid for television rights for the Sarajevo Olympic Winter Games. He also noted that ABC had a source in Lausanne during the Calgary negotiations. Arledge's privileged position in negotiations with the Montréal and Lake Placid Olympic Organizing Committees had been protested by NBC and CBS executives.

105. R. Kevan Gosper to Monique Berlioux, 20 January 1982, "Los Angeles 1984 TV-General Janv.–Mars 1982" File, IOCA.

106. "Australia's Network 10 Wins Exclusive Television Rights for 1984 Olympic Games," news release, 1 February 1982, "Los Angeles 1984 TV General Janv.–Mars 1982" File, IOCA; and "Minutes of the Meeting of the IOC Executive Board," Los Angeles, 3 and 5 February 1982, p. 8, IOCA.

107. Monique Berlioux to Peter Ueberroth, 22 April 1982; Peter Ueberroth to Monique Berlioux, 22 April 1982; Monique Berlioux to Roku Ito (secretary-general, ABU), 26 April 1982; and Monique Berlioux to Michael O'Hara, 26 April 1982, "Los Angeles 1984 TV-General Avril–Déc. 1982" File, IOCA.

108. Sumadi (president, ABU) to Juan Antonio Samaranch, 28 July 1982, "Los Angeles TV-General 1984 Avril–Déc. 1982" File, IOCA.

109. Juan Antonio Samaranch to Mr. Sumadi, 30 July 1982, "Los Angeles TV-General 1984 Avril–Déc. 1982" File, IOCA. The IOC accepted Los Angeles's position in part because ABU had failed to honor its contract for the 1980 Moscow Olympics. Even though a settlement had been reached, ABU's financial commitment would not be resolved before the deadline for technical equipment requests set down by LAOOC. Roku Ito to Monique Berlioux, 8 June 1982; and Monique

Berlioux to Michael O'Hara, 22 April 1982, "Los Angeles TV-General 1984 Avril–Déc. 1982" File, IOCA.

110. Miller, *Olympic Revolution,* p. 252.

111. "1984 Summer Olympics Africa/Caribbean Rate Card," "Los Angeles TV-General 1984 Janv.–Mars 1983" File, IOCA.

112. European rights for the Barcelona Games split between EBU, TVE (Spain), and OIRT (Eastern Europe) totaled $94.5 million.

113. Discussion with Richard Pound, Montréal, 26 November 1998.

114. "Minutes of the Meeting of the IOC Executive Board," Lausanne, 4–6 December 1991, pp. 43–44, IOCA; and Skip Rozin, "Empowering the Olympic Movement: A Look at the Business Dynamics behind the Olympics," special advertising section reprint, *Fortune 500,* Time Inc. USA (undated), p. 7.

115. For documentation dealing with the Japanese negotiations, see Takeshi Tanaka (managing director, NHK) to Monique Berlioux, 24 February 1982; and Monique Berlioux to Takeshi Tanaka, 25 February 1982, "Los Angeles 1984 TV-General Janv.–Mars 1982" File, IOCA; Peter Ueberroth to Monique Berlioux, 6 April 1982; Monique Berlioux to Peter Ueberroth, 7 April 1982; Katsuji Shibata (president, Japanese Olympic Committee) to Juan Antonio Samaranch, 12 June 1982; Michael O'Hara to Takeshi Tanaka and Taiji Kawate (director, National Association of Commercial Broadcasters in Japan), 15 June 1982; Monique Berlioux to Masaji Kiyokawa (IOC member, Japan), 12 August 1982; Monique Berlioux to Peter Ueberroth, 9 November 1982; Monique Berlioux to Masaji Kiyokawa, 10 November 1982; Daniel Russell (IOC secretariat) to Monique Berlioux, 24 November 1982, "Los Angeles TV-General 1984 Avril–Déc. 1982" File, IOCA. When the deal was reached, Los Angeles made a unilateral decision to sign a deal with the Japanese executives for $19 million. The rights fee, however, was $16.5 million—only $5 million was payable to the IOC. Berlioux was disturbed that the deal was reached after she had left the meeting. The Japanese would not sign a deal for the contracted terms. Berlioux indicated before her departure that the IOC would accept $5 million from the Japan deal but only in the event that Los Angeles reduced its demands. Samaranch also expressed his displeasure with LAOOC's action. He maintained that more favorable terms could have been reached if the negotiations had been held earlier in accordance with his wishes. Michael O'Hara to Monique Berlioux, 26 January 1983; Danny Russell to Monique Berlioux, 27 January 1983; Monique Berlioux to Peter Ueberroth, 1 February 1983; Peter Ueberroth to Monique Berlioux, 2 February 1983; Juan Antonio Samaranch to Peter Ueberroth, 9 February 1983, "Los Angeles TV-General 1984 Janv.–Mars 1983" File, IOCA.

116. "Droits de télévision versés par les organismes de télévision pour les Jeux d'Olympiade (en dollars US)," IOC, 1986, IOCA.

9. THE GUARD CHANGES IN LAUSANNE: RICHARD POUND, TELEVISION NEGOTIATIONS, AND THE 1988 OLYMPIC FESTIVALS

1. David Miller, *Olympic Revolution: The Biography of Juan Antonio Samaranch* (London: Pavilion Books, 1992), pp. 33–35.

2. Ibid., p. 35; "Minutes of the Meeting of the IOC Executive Board," Berlin, 31 May, 1–3, 6 June 1985, pp. 69–71; and "Minutes of the 90th Session of the International Olympic Committee," Berlin, 4–6 June 1985, pp. 42–44, IOCA. Berlioux was permitted to provide a statement to the Session: "Rumours. Press reports. My departure from the IOC has been announced. I owe you a full explanation. For many years, I have devoted myself to the service of sport and in particular to the Olympic Movement as an athlete, as an official, as your main assistant, as Director of the IOC. I have held this position for 18 years. Of course, I may occasionally have found myself in disagreement with some of you on particular issues. But this is only normal in an organisation like ours which gathers so many eminent members of such rich and varied character. My only rule of conduct has always been the interests of the Movement and its ideals. As time progressed, differing opinions with the Executive Board have led me—like a journalist evoking a conscience clause—to decide to bring my functions as Director to an end. I will continue however to fulfil my duties until the end of this Session. I should like to thank you for the confidence you have placed in me and for your help which have enabled me to develop an administration that I believe to be efficient and healthy. I shall always be proud of the level it has reached. I shall say no more. A Director has moved on. Long live Olympism as its founder, my fellow countryman Pierre de Coubertin, would have wanted."

3. This conclusion is drawn from a number of discussions with Richard Pound as well as his comments appearing in *Olympic Marketing Fact File* (Lausanne: IOC, 1998), p. 7. It is a major argument appearing in publications distributed by the IOC Marketing Department, such as *Supporting the Dream: Financing the Olympic Movement* (Lausanne: IOC, 1998); and *Olympic Market Research Analysis Report* (Lausanne: IOC, 1997).

4. OCO'88 and SLOOC hired Frank as a consultant. See "TransWorld International Appointed Exclusive Representative for 1988 Calgary Winter Olympics," TWI press release, 30 September 1983, "Calgary 1988 TV-General 1984" File, IOCA; and Tae Woo Roh (president, SLOOC) to Juan Antonio Samaranch, 27 January 1984, "Seoul '88 TV General 1981, 1982, 1983, 1984 Jusqu'à Mai 1984" File, IOCA. For Pound's receptivity to some of Frank's advice, see "Minutes of the Meeting of the IOC Executive Board," Mexico City, 7–8 November 1984, p. 24, IOCA.

5. Richard Pound to Juan Antonio Samaranch, 26 September 1985; and Richard Pound to Juan Antonio Samaranch, 30 September 1985, "Seoul 1988 TV-General 1985 II" File, IOCA.

6. "Minutes of the Meeting of the IOC Executive Board," Calgary, 25–28 February 1985, pp. 53–56; and "Minutes of the Meeting of the IOC Executive Board," Lisbon, 15 and 18 October 1985, p. 42, IOCA.

7. Bill Abrams, "Olympic Gold: How Networks Vied in Gruelling Bidding For '88 Winter Games," *Wall Street Journal,* 22 February 1984, "Calgary 1988 TV-General 1984" File, IOCA.

8. Jim Spence (with Dave Diles), *Up Close and Personal: The Inside Story of Network Television Sports* (New York: Atheneum Publishers, 1988), pp. 41–42.

9. "Olympics Didn't Give Big Boost to Ratings for ABC: Audience Slips 15%

from 1980," *Wall Street Journal,* 22 February 1984, "Calgary 1988 TV-General 1984" File, IOCA.

10. Abrams, "Olympic Gold," p. 29.

11. Spence, *Up Close and Personal,* p. 33.

12. William Pratt to Juan Antonio Samaranch, 23 July 1983; and Monique Berlioux to William Pratt, 5 August 1983, "Calgary 1988 TV-General 1981–1982, Janvier/Octobre 1983" File, IOCA.

13. William Pratt to Monique Berlioux, 6 November 1983; Richard Pound to Monique Berlioux, 11 November 1983; and Monique Berlioux to Richard Pound, 14 November 1983, "Calgary 1988 TV-General Novembre/Décembre 1983" File, IOCA.

14. "Minutes of the Meeting of the IOC Executive Board," Lausanne, 24 and 25 November 1983, pp. 7–8, IOCA; "Minutes of the Meeting of the IOC Executive Board," Los Angeles, 21–23, 30 July, 2, 4, 6, and 11–13 August 1984, p. 6, IOCA; Richard Pound to Monique Berlioux, 31 August 1983; Richard Pound to Juan Antonio Samaranch, 13 September 1983, "Calgary 1988 TV-General 1981–1982, Janvier/Octobre 1983" File, IOCA.

15. Monique Berlioux to Richard Pound, 16 September 1983; Richard Pound to Monique Berlioux, 19 September 1983; Monique Berlioux to Richard Pound, 3 October 1983; and Richard Pound to Monique Berlioux, 4 October 1983, "Calgary 1988 TV-General 1981–1982, Janvier/Octobre 1983" File, IOCA.

16. Richard Pound to Juan Antonio Samaranch, 29 December 1983, "Calgary '88 TV-General Novembre/Décembre 1983" File, IOCA; Richard Pound to Monique Berlioux, 6 January 1984, "Calgary 1988 TV-General 1984" File, IOCA. The clause in question is crossed out and the word "delete" appears in the margin of the Pound to Berlioux missive.

17. Richard Pound to Arthur Watson, 9 January 1984, "Calgary 1988 TV-General 1984" File, IOCA.

18. Spence, *Up Close and Personal,* pp. 35–43.

19. Richard Pound to Arthur Watson, 9 January 1984, "Calgary 1988 TV-General 1984" File, IOCA.

20. Spence, *Up Close and Personal,* pp. 37–39.

21. Ibid., pp. 36–38.

22. Ibid., p. 39.

23. Ibid., p. 40.

24. Juan Antonio Samaranch to Frank King, 11 July 1986, "Calgary 1988 TV-General 1986" File, IOCA.

25. This thinking was relayed to the authors during a discussion with Richard Pound at his Montréal law office on 26 November 1998. For a sample of Pound's written concerns on the low fees paid by EBU, see "Minutes of the Meeting of the IOC Executive Board," Seoul, 22–24 April 1986, Annex #10, "Report to IOC Executive Board Re: Television Rights," p. 81, IOCA.

26. "Minutes of the Meeting of the IOC Executive Board," Seoul, 22–24 April 1986, "Report to the IOC Executive Board Re: Television Rights," Annex #10, p. 81, IOCA.

27. Ibid., p. 15.

28. "Draft Co-operation Agreement (IOC-EBU)," 12 March 1986, "Calgary 1988 TV-General 1986" File, IOCA; Richard Pound to Howard Stupp, 19 June 1986, "RWP/IOC 7398-026 Seoul TV" File, Personal Files of Richard Pound, Montréal, Canada (hereafter cited as PFRP).

29. "Minutes of the Meeting of the IOC Executive Board," Lausanne, 11–13 February 1987, p. 20, IOCA.

30. Richard Pound to Juan Antonio Samaranch, 26 September 1985, "Seoul 1988 TV-General II" File, IOCA.

31. Ibid.

32. Richard Pound to Juan Antonio Samaranch, 30 September 1985, "Seoul 1988 TV-General 1985 II" File, IOCA. For a statement of the USOC position, see George D. Miller (secretary-general, USOC) to Roone Arledge, 29 October 1985, "Calgary 1988 TV-General 1985" File, IOCA.

33. Howard Stupp to Juan Antonio Samaranch, 2 October 1985, "Seoul 1988 TV-General 1985 II" File, IOCA.

34. "Minutes of the Meeting of the IOC Executive Board," Calgary, 25–28 February 1985, pp. 53–56, IOCA. There was little progress by October. "Minutes of the Meeting of the IOC Executive Board," Lisbon, 15 and 18 October 1985, p. 42, IOCA.

35. Juan Antonio Samaranch to Richard Pound, 1 October 1985, "Seoul 1988 TV-General 1985 II" File, IOCA.

36. "Signature of the Contract for the US Television Rights—Games of the XXIVth Olympiad in Seoul 1988," 26 March 1986, Appendix 1, "Seoul 1988/TV-General Janvier–Juillet 1986" File, IOCA.

37. "Minutes of the Meeting of the IOC Executive Board," Lausanne, 10–11 October 1986, p. 40, IOCA. The contract with the 1992 candidate cities presented in December 1985 included the provision that the IOC would negotiate television agreements in consultation with the OCOGs.

38. Richard Pound to Juan Antonio Samaranch, 11 October 1983; "Allocation of Television Revenue—Seoul—1988: Study by Mr. Richard W. Pound—Lausanne 24th November 1983," "Seoul '88 TV-General 1981, 1982, 1983, 1984 Jusqu'à Mai 1984" File, IOCA.

39. Richard Pound to Juan Antonio Samaranch, 11 October 1983, "Seoul '88 TV General 1981, 1982, 1983, 1984 Jusqu'à Mai 1984" File, IOCA.

40. Juan Antonio Samaranch to Tae-Woo Roh, 25 November 1983, "Seoul '88 TV General 1981, 1982, 1983, 1984 Jusqu'à Mai 1984" File, IOCA; "Agreement," 29 December 1983, "Seoul '88 TV-General 1981, 1982, 1983, 1984 Jusqu'à Mai 1984" File, IOCA.

41. Richard Pound to Monique Berlioux, 20 February 1984, "Seoul '88 TV-General 1981, 1982, 1983, 1984 Jusqu'à Mai 1984" File, IOCA.

42. Ashwini Kumar to Juan Antonio Samaranch, 8 April 1984; Monique Berlioux to Richard Pound, 17 April 1984, "Seoul '88 TV-General 1981, 1982, 1983, 1984 Jusqu'à Mai 1984" File, IOCA; "IOC/SLOOC Meeting, 5 April 1984"; "Record of Discussion: CBS Presentation Meeting, 6 April 1984"; "Record of Discussion: ABC Presentation Meeting, 6 April 1984"; and "Record of Discussion: NBC Presentation Meeting, 7 April 1984," "RWP/IOC 7398-026 Seoul TV 1988" File, PFRP.

43. Ashwini Kumar to Juan Antonio Samaranch, 8 April 1984, "Seoul '88 TV-General 1981, 1982, 1983, 1984 Jusqu'à Mai 1984" File, IOCA.

44. Ibid.; and Monique Berlioux to Richard Pound, 17 April 1984, "Seoul '88 TV-General 1981, 1982, 1983, 1984 Jusqu'à Mai 1984" File, IOCA.

45. Monique Berlioux to Richard Pound, 17 April 1984, "Seoul '88 TV-General 1981, 1982, 1983, 1984 Jusqu'à Mai 1984" File, IOCA.

46. This comment is found in a supplementary note to Samaranch. Ashwini Kumar to Juan Antonio Samaranch, 9 April 1984, "Seoul '88 TV-General 1981, 1982, 1983, 1984 Jusqu'à Mai 1984" File, IOCA.

47. Ashwini Kumar to Juan Antonio Samaranch, 8 April 1984, "Seoul '88 TV-General 1981, 1982, 1983, 1984 Jusqu'à Mai 1984" File, IOCA.

48. Richard Pound to Monique Berlioux, 18 April 1984, "Seoul '88 TV-General 1981, 1982, 1983, 1984 Jusqu'à Mai 1984" File, IOCA.

49. Ashwini Kumar to Juan Antonio Samaranch, 8 April 1984; and Monique Berlioux to Richard Pound, 17 April 1984, "Seoul '88 TV-General 1981, 1982, 1983, 1984 Jusqu'à Mai 1984" File, IOCA.

50. Roone Arledge to Juan Antonio Samaranch, 18 March 1985; Alex Gilady (vice-president, international program planning and development, NBC) to Juan Antonio Samaranch, 16 August 1985, "Seoul 1988 TV-General 1985 I" File, IOCA; and Ashwini Kumar to Juan Antonio Samaranch, 8 April 1984, "Seoul '88 TV-General 1981, 1982, 1983, 1984 Jusqu'à Mai 1984" File, IOCA.

51. "Report to the Finance Commission Paris 6th June 1986," in "Seoul 1988 TV-General Août–Décembre 1986" File, IOCA.

52. "Minutes of the Meeting of the IOC Executive Board," Los Angeles, 21–23 and 30 July, 2, 4, 6, and 11–13 August 1984, pp. 6, 28, IOCA; "Minutes of the Meeting of the Finance Commission," Los Angeles, 24 July 1984, pp. 1–2, IOCA.

53. Michael O'Hara to Robert H. Helmick, 7 September 1984, "RWP/IOC 7398-026 Seoul TV 1988" File, PFRP.

54. "Report on Previous Events Relating to TV Rights Negotiations: July, 1984," p. 5, "RWP/IOC 7398-026 Seoul TV 1988" File, PFRP. This document was produced by SLOOC.

55. "Minutes of the Meeting of the IOC Executive Board," Los Angeles, 21–23 and 30 July, 2, 4, 6, and 11–13 August 1984, pp. 7, 18, IOCA.

56. When Walter Tröger, IOC sports director, raised concerns about placing so much emphasis on the needs of U.S. television, Samaranch did not disagree with his sentiments. Samaranch noted, however, that realistically it had to be remembered that the United States paid a significantly greater amount for the rights than all other territories combined. "Minutes of the Meeting of the IOC Executive Board," Mexico City, 7–8 November 1984, p. 24, IOCA.

57. Kenneth Reich, "Olympic Events Won't Be Changed to Suit TV, Officials Decide," 26 November 1984, *Los Angeles Times,* "Seoul 1988 TV-General Juin–Décembre 1984" File, IOCA.

58. "Minutes of the 89th IOC General Session," Lausanne, 1–2 December 1984, p. 24, IOCA.

59. Barry Frank to Richard Pound, ? October 1984, "RWP/IOC 7398-026

Seoul TV 1988" File, PFRP. It is not possible to provide complete information concerning the date of this missive. Pound's response is dated 4 October.

60. Richard Pound to Barry Frank, 4 October 1984, "RWP/IOC 7398-026 Seoul TV 1988" File, PFRP.

61. Barry Frank to Richard Pound, ? October 1984, "RWP/IOC 7398-026 Seoul TV 1988" File, PFRP. Again, the date on this document was clipped off when it was filed. It is clear that the letter represents Frank's response to Pound's communication dated 4 October.

62. "Minutes of the Meeting of the IOC Executive Board," Mexico City, 7–8 November 1984, p. 24, IOCA.

63. Miller, *Olympic Revolution,* p. 30.

64. Ibid., p. 31.

65. Ibid.

66. "Minutes of the Meeting of the IOC Executive Board," Los Angeles, 21–23 and 30 July, 2, 4, 6, and 11–13 August 1984, p. 18, IOCA.

67. Ibid.

68. Ibid., pp. 18–19.

69. Ibid., p. 19.

70. Ibid., p. 49.

71. Miller, *Olympic Revolution,* p. 31.

72. Richard Pound to Sei Young Park (deputy secretary-general, SLOOC), 2 August 1985, "Seoul 1988 TV-General 1985 I" File, IOCA.

73. William Taaffe, "The Big Three Aren't Sold on Seoul," *Sports Illustrated* 63 (23 September 1985): 47, 50. In 1984 Frank informed SLOOC that a combined TV/cable package might reap $850 million. See Barry Frank to Sei Young Park, 28 February 1984, "RWP/IOC 7398-026 Seoul TV 1988" File, PFRP. Pound noted that Seoul expected $750 million. "Minutes of the Meeting of the IOC Executive Board," Lisbon, 15 and 18 October 1985, p. 53, IOCA.

74. "Minutes of the Meeting of the IOC Executive Board," Lisbon, 15 and 18 October 1985, p. 53, IOCA.

75. Richard Pound to Sei Young Park, 2 August 1985, "Seoul 1988 TV-General 1985 I" File, IOCA.

76. Taaffe, "The Big Three Aren't Sold on Seoul," p. 50.

77. "Meeting between the IOC and the SLOOC regarding Television Rights Negotiations for the Games of the XXIVth Olympiad," 11 September 1985, p. 1, "Seoul 1988 TV-General 1985 II" File, IOCA.

78. Taaffe, "The Big Three Aren't Sold on Seoul," p. 47.

79. Richard Pound to Arthur Watson, 28 January 1985, "Seoul 1988 TV-General 1985 I" File, IOCA.

80. Richard W. Pound, *Five Rings over Korea: The Secret Negotiations behind the 1988 Olympic Games in Seoul* (Boston: Little, Brown & Company, 1994), pp. 126–27.

81. Taaffe, "The Big Three Aren't Sold on Seoul," p. 55.

82. "Report to the Finance Commission Paris, 6th June 1986," p. 4, "Seoul 1988 TV General Août–Décembre 1986" File, IOCA.

83. Richard Pound to Sei Young Park, 2 August 1985, "Seoul 1988 TV-General 1985 I" File, IOCA.

84. Taaffe, "The Big Three Aren't Sold on Seoul," p. 55.

85. "Report to the Finance Commission Paris 6th June 1986," p. 4, "Seoul 1988 TV-General Août–Décembre 1986" File, IOCA; Taaffe, "The Big Three Aren't Sold on Seoul," p. 50. Samaranch broached the prospect of lost revenue if an agreement was not signed at the preliminary meeting between the IOC and SLOOC. "Meeting between the IOC and SLOOC regarding Television Rights Negotiations for the Games of the XXIVth Olympiad," 11 September 1985, p. 1, "Seoul 1988 TV-General 1985 II" File, IOCA.

86. "Report to the Finance Commission Paris, 6th June 1986," p. 4, "Seoul 1988 TV-General Août–Décembre 1986" File, IOCA.

87. Roone Arledge to Richard Pound, 23 September 1985; Neal Pilson to Richard Pound, 23 September 1985; and Arthur Watson to Richard Pound, 20 September 1985, "Seoul 1988 TV-General 1985 II" File, IOCA.

88. Richard Pound to Sei Young Park, 24 September 1985, "Seoul 1988 TV-General 1985 II" File, IOCA.

89. Richard Pound to Juan Antonio Samaranch, 24 September 1985, "Seoul 1988 TV-General 1985 II" File, IOCA.

90. Spence, *Up Close and Personal,* pp. 46–49; William Taaffe, "Seoul Pins Its Hopes on NBC," *Sports Illustrated* 63 (14 October 1985): 96, "Seoul 1988/TV-General Janvier–Juillet 1986" File, IOCA.

91. "Report to the Finance Commission Paris 6th June 1986," p. 6, "Seoul 1988 TV General Août–Décembre 1986" File, IOCA.

92. Un Yong Kim to Richard Pound, 2 December 1985; Richard Pound to Un Yong Kim, 3 December 1985; and Un Yong Kim to Richard Pound, 4 December 1985, "Seoul 1988 TV-General 1985 II" File, IOCA.

93. Juan Antonio Samaranch to Tae Woo Roh, 5 December 1985, "Seoul 1988 TV-General 1985 II" File, IOCA.

94. Ibid.

95. Tae Woo Roh to Juan Antonio Samaranch, 6 December 1985, "Seoul 1988 TV-General 1985 II" File, IOCA.

96. "Report to the IOC Executive Board—Re: Television Rights," 4 April 1986, pp. 4–5, "Seoul 1988/TV-General Janvier–Juillet 1986" File, IOCA. For instance, the IOC's share of the television contract was placed in escrow until the Games were closed. The IOC could, however, gain access to the interest payments. Further, if four or more of the top ten medal-winning countries from the 1976 Montréal Olympics did not attend, NBC could obtain a reduction in the rights fee if it proved damages. If the USOC chose not to participate, NBC was entitled to cancel the contract and claim a refund of the rights money previously transferred plus production expenses plus interest earned. Thus if Seoul failed to stage the Games or Samaranch was unable to guarantee the participation of the Eastern bloc nations the price of such failure was high.

97. "Report to the Finance Commission Paris, 6th June 1986," p. 4, "Seoul 1988 TV-General Août–Décembre 1986" File, IOCA.

98. "Minutes of the Meeting of the IOC Executive Board," Lausanne, 11–12 February 1986, p. 5, IOCA.

99. Ibid., p. 7; and "Minutes of the Meeting of the IOC Executive Board," Seoul, 22–24 April 1986, p. 4, IOCA.

100. Juan Antonio Samaranch to Young Ho Lee, 21 November 1985; and Young Ho Lee to Juan Antonio Samaranch, 27 November 1985, "Seoul 1988 TV-General 1985 II" File, IOCA.

101. Un Yong Kim to Richard Pound, 1 September 1986 (postmark), "RWP/IOC 7398-026 Seoul TV 1988" File, PFRP.

102. Ibid.

103. "Minutes of the Meeting of the IOC Executive Board," Lausanne, 11–12 February 1986, p. 7, IOCA.

104. "Minutes of the Meeting of the IOC Executive Board," Seoul, 22–24 April 1986, p. 15, IOCA; and "Excerpt from EBU TV Agreement," "Seoul 1988/TV-General Janvier–Juillet 1986" File, IOCA.

105. See "Note Card to File/22 July 1986," "RWP/IOC 7398-026 Seoul TV 1988" File, PFRP. In Pound's handwriting on the note card the following notation appeared: "Budget of 1MM for the project (c/b paid to me anywhere in the world). First attempt to bribe!!"

106. The three newspaper reporters were Karlo Berkovich, Joel Rubinoff (*Kitchener Waterloo Record*), and Randy Starkman (*Toronto Star*). For a record of Berkovich's published reaction, see "Olympics Now Bare to Examine," *Kitchener-Waterloo Record,* 20 January 1999. For Starkman's published response, see "Pound Vows Cleanup," *Toronto Star,* 20 January 1999.

107. See "Note Card to File/22 July 1986," "RWP/IOC 7398-026 Seoul TV 1988" File, PFRP.

108. Barry Frank to Richard Pound, 6 June 1986, "RWP/IOC 7398-026 Seoul TV 1998" File, PFRP.

109. Discussion with Richard Pound, Montréal, 26 November 1998; and Dean D. S. Song to Richard Pound, 20 August 1986, "RWP/IOC 7398-026 Seoul TV 1988" File, PFRP.

110. "Press Release," 19 March 1987, "Seoul 1988 TV-General Janvier–Mai 1987" File, IOCA.

111. "Report on Meeting Held between the IOC and Representatives from the Japanese Television Pool: Lausanne, 15th January 1987," p. 1, "Seoul 1988 TV-General Janvier–Mai 1987" File, IOCA.

112. Ibid., p. 2.

113. "Minutes of the Meeting of the IOC Executive Board," Lausanne, 22–23 April 1987, p. 28, IOCA.

114. Richard Pound to Juan Antonio Samaranch, 26 March 1987, "RWP/IOC 7398-026 Seoul TV 1988" File, PFRP.

115. Robert H. C. Chan (general-manager, TVB Hong Kong) to Juan Antonio Samaranch, 11 May 1987; and Robert H. C. Chan to Deacon Chiu (chairman, ATV Hong Kong), 18 May 1987, "Seoul 1988 TV-General Janvier–Mai 1987" File, IOCA.

116. Jermyn Lynn (manager, international affairs, TVB Hong Kong) to Juan Antonio Samaranch, 25 March 1988, "Seoul 1988 TV-General Avril–Mai 1988" File, IOCA.

117. Howard Stupp to Sung Min Cho (SLOOC), 24 August 1988, "Seoul 1988 TV-General Juin–Août 1988" File, IOCA. The rights fee moved from $900,000 to $1 million in consideration of the existence of two rights holders.

10. THE IOC'S NEW CORPORATE FACE:
THE RISE OF MERIDIAN MANAGEMENT

1. At the IOC Executive Board meeting in Lillehammer in December 1990 Richard Pound submitted a confidential report indicating that the twelfth, and final, TOP-II sponsor had been signed (Bausch and Lomb). "Minutes of the Meeting of the IOC Executive Board," Lillehammer, 9–11 December 1990, p. 100, IOCA.

2. "Minutes of the Meeting of the IOC Executive Board," Barcelona, 14–16 April 1991, p. 123, IOCA.

3. The resignation of Klaus Hempel and Jürgen Lenz marked the beginning of the end for ISL's involvement in TOP.

4. Ibid. See also "Minutes of the Meeting of the New Sources of Finance Commission," Birmingham, 14 June 1991, p. 54, IOCA.

5. Ibid., p. 127. An IOC-ISF marketing meeting was scheduled for 15 April 1991 in Barcelona to discuss the ISFs' participation in TOP. At the meeting a proposal was presented that focused on the development of a special sports-specific mark centered on the pictograms as well as event hospitality opportunities. The IOC/ISF package, if approved, would be offered to all TOP III sponsors as an optional supplement to the main program.

6. "Minutes of the Meeting of the IOC Executive Board," Birmingham, 10–11 June 1991, p. 109, IOCA. The five sponsor headquarters that Samaranch visited included Kodak, Bausch and Lomb, and Coca-Cola in the United States and Brother and Matsushita in Japan.

7. "Minutes of the Meeting of the IOC Executive Board," Monaco and Seville, 5 and 8–9 May 1992, p. 109, IOCA.

8. Ibid., p. 46.

9. Ibid., p. 109.

10. "Minutes of the Meeting of the IOC Executive Board," Barcelona, 17–19 July 1992, p. 153, IOCA.

11. "Minutes of the Meeting of the IOC Executive Board," Lausanne, 7–8 December 1992, p. 50, IOCA; and "IOC Executive Board Minutes," Atlanta, 15–17 March 1993, p. 76, IOCA.

12. "Minutes of the Meeting of the IOC Executive Board," Monaco, 17–20 September 1993, p. 187, IOCA.

13. At a meeting of the Commission of New Sources of Financing in July 1992 Richard Pound indicated that the Sponsor Advisory Group was "a scheme to benefit from TOP sponsors as resources for the IOC." He stated that it would be "offered as a right under the TOP III program, and should be mutually beneficial." As such, the group would "function as a sub-commission advising the Commission of New Sources of Financing" and would be composed of "senior marketing executives from TOP sponsors." "Minutes of the Meeting of the New Sources of Finance Commission," Barcelona, 16 July 1992, p. 17, IOCA.

14. "Minutes of the Meeting of the IOC Executive Board," Lausanne, 19–22 June 1993, p. 116, IOCA. For an agenda of the meeting, see "Minutes of the Meeting of the IOC Executive Board," Lausanne, 19–22 June 1993, p. 122, IOCA.

15. "Minutes of the Meeting of the New Sources of Finance Commission," Lausanne, 25 June 1993, p. 35, IOCA.

16. "Minutes of the Meeting of the IOC Executive Board," Lausanne, 24–26 June 1994, p. 115, IOCA.

17. "Minutes of the Meeting of the New Sources of Finance Commission," Lausanne, 27 June 1994, p. 26, IOCA.

18. "Minutes of the Meeting of the IOC Executive Board," Lausanne, 24–26 June 1994, p. 115, IOCA.

19. Ibid., p. 51; and "Minutes of the Meeting of the New Sources of Finance Commission," Lausanne, 27 June 1994, p. 26, IOCA.

20. Ibid., p. 115. Another of the changes in the management of ISL was the departure of Andrew Craig, who was replaced by Bo Seifert, managing director, marketing services and international business development, ISL. The ISL Lausanne office opened in July 1994, under the direction of Laurent Scharapan.

21. IBM was excluded from this calculation because of its commitment to a long-term contract with the IOC (through the year 2000).

22. "Minutes of the Meeting of the New Sources of Finance Commission," Lausanne, 27 June 1994, p. 26, IOCA.

23. The Games were awarded to Lillehammer at the Ninety-fourth IOC Session in Seoul on 15 September 1988. See Candidate Cities/Olympic Winter Games, 27 July 1998, Personal Files of Richard Pound, Montréal, Canada (hereafter cited as PFRP), p. 4.

24. Dorling Kindersley Limited, *Chronicle of the Olympics* (London: Dorling Kindersley Limited, 1998), p. 201.

25. Ibid.

26. See Fernand Landry and Magdeleine Yerlès, "The Presidencies of Lord Killanin (1972–1980) and Juan Antonio Samaranch (1980–)," in *The International Olympic Committee—One Hundred Years: The Idea—the Presidents—the Achievements*, vol. 3 (Lausanne: IOC, 1996), p. 195.

27. See International Olympic Committee Marketing Department, *1999 Olympic Marketing Fact File* (Lausanne: IOC, 1999), p. 36.

28. Lars Elton, *Norsk Olympisk design: Design og arkitektur til de XVII Olympiske winterleker* (Oslo: Norsk Form, 1995), p. 6.

29. Quoted ibid.

30. See International Olympic Committee Marketing Department, *1994 Olympic Marketing Fact File* (Lausanne: IOC, 1994), p. 24. Only thirty-six of the original one thousand companies that approached the Lillehammer OCOG were approved as official licensees of the 1994 Olympic Winter Games.

31. Ibid. More than 120 countries and territories viewed television coverage of the 1994 Olympic Winter Games, compared to the 86 countries broadcasting the Albertville Games in 1992. For the first time in Olympic broadcasting history the Olympic Winter Games were officially broadcast on the African continent by the M-Net (South and Central Africa) and ART (Arab Radio and Television; North Africa and the Middle East) satellites.

32. At the height of ambush marketing the IOC began using the term "parasite" rather than "ambush" to describe the practice. The IOC Marketing

Department, however, decided that the "word 'ambush' actually got the message across more effectively." "Minutes of the Meeting of the New Sources of Finance Commission," Lausanne, 25 June 1993, p. 36, IOCA.

33. During the Calgary Olympic Winter Games in 1988 the public observed numerous instances of ambush marketing, including but not limited to Wendy's "ambushing" McDonald's, American Express "ambushing" VISA, and Quality Inns "ambushing" Hilton.

34. "Minutes of the Meeting of the IOC Executive Board," Monaco and Seville, 5 and 8–9 May 1992, p. 108, IOCA.

35. See International Olympic Committee Marketing Department, *1994 Olympic Marketing Fact File,* p. 47.

36. See "Minutes of the Meeting of the New Sources of Finance Commission," Barcelona, 16 July 1992, p. 23, IOCA. As a proactive measure the Barcelona OCOG retained "specialist lawyers" who could immediately "deal with infringements" and took steps with the chief justice of the Barcelona civil court to ensure the availability of a judge during the Olympic Games.

37. During the "run-up" to the Games of the Twenty-sixth Olympiad in Atlanta, the USOC was spending $1 million a year to stop illegal use of the Olympic marks. "Minutes of the Meeting of the New Sources of Finance Commission," Lausanne, 25 June 1994, p. 37, IOCA.

38. We use the term "below-the-line" to represent the traditional view that "ambush marketing" is an immoral activity. In contrast, the term "above-the-line" is used to connote the ethical form of marketing communications. This area of research remains an underexamined aspect of marketing communications. For an extended discussion of "ambush marketing," see Tony Meenaghan, "Point of View: Ambush Marketing—Immoral or Imaginative Practice?" *Journal of Advertising Research* 34, no. 5 (September/October 1994): 77–88.

39. "Minutes of the Meeting of the IOC Executive Board," Atlanta, 15–17 March 1993, p. 94, IOCA.

40. Ibid., pp. 84–85.

41. Ibid., p. 92.

42. Ibid., p. 95.

43. Ibid., p. 92.

44. Ibid., p. 93.

45. "Minutes of the Meeting of the IOC Executive Board," Lausanne, 25 January 1995, p. 15, IOCA.

46. Richard W. Pound to Christoph Malms, 5 May 1994, IOC/ISL Relationship: TOP-IV File, IOCA.

47. Ibid. In this memorandum to Christoph Malms Pound admitted that "the TOP Program cannot, realistically, exist without the participation of the USOC" and that any future plan must take this fact into account.

48. "Minutes of the Meeting of the IOC Executive Board," Lausanne, 25 January 1995, p. 85, IOCA. Among other companies expressing a strong interest in joining TOP was the U.S.-based restaurant company McDonald's. The corporation would soon join the other TOP-IV sponsors, with exclusive global Olympic marketing rights in the branded restaurant category.

49. Richard W. Pound to Christoph Malms, 5 May 1994, IOC/ISL Relationship: TOP-IV File, IOCA.

50. IOC, "Minutes of the Marketing Liaison Committee for TOP IV," Karuizawa, 1995, p. 1, IOCA. Attending the meeting were Richard W. Pound, chairman MCM; Michael R. Payne, IOC marketing director; Howard M. Stupp, IOC director of legal affairs; Mark R. Dzenick, IOC marketing manager, business development; John Moore, marketing director, Sydney OCOG; Terumasa Aoki, deputy director, general marketing, Nagano OCOG; Takeshi Yoshizawa, senior staff, Marketing Section 1, Nagano OCOG; Mr. Nihonmatsu, Marketing Section 1, Nagano OCOG; Tomohiro Tohyama, legal counsel, Nagano OCOG; Richard D. Schultz, executive director, USOC; John Krimsky Jr., deputy secretary-general, managing director, business affairs, USOC; and Wendy Reymond, secretary to the IOC marketing director.

51. Ibid., p. 2.

52. Laurent Scharapan was senior vice-president of ISL. See Richard W. Pound to members of the IOC Commission of New Sources of Financing, 5 January 1996, IOC/ISL Relationship: TOP-IV File, p. 2, IOCA.

53. Sponsor Advisory Group to Richard W. Pound, 20 November 1995, IOC/ISL Relationship: TOP-IV File, IOCA.

54. "Minutes of the Marketing Liaison Committee for TOP IV," Karuizawa, 1995, p. 2, IOCA.

55. Ibid.

56. Ibid.

57. These events marked the conclusion of TOP-III (1993–1996) relative to the Games of the Twenty-sixth Olympiad in Atlanta (19 July 1996–4 August 1996) and the beginning of TOP-IV (1997–2000). See "Minutes of the Marketing Liaison Committee for TOP IV," Karuizawa, 1995, p. 2, IOCA.

58. Ibid.

59. Ibid., p. 3.

60. Ibid.

61. This figure took into account that in the past sales, NOC-liaison, and sponsor service had been roughly divided on a one-third/one-third/one-third basis, representing approximately $10 million per third.

62. "Minutes of the Marketing Liaison Committee for TOP IV," Karuizawa, 1995, p. 2, IOCA.

63. Ibid., p. 4.

64. Dentsu has led the Japanese communications industry for almost one hundred years. Founded in 1901 by Hoshiro Mitsunaga, Dentsu began as a news telegraphic service and advertising firm. The agency's activities have expanded beyond traditional mass-media services to involve nearly every aspect of creative communications. Dentsu is a privately operated company, with its headquarters in Tokyo employing nearly 6,000 workers. It maintains thirty-one offices in Japan, including the head office, six overseas offices, and subsidiaries and affiliates in forty-seven cities in thirty-four countries around the globe. See "Corporate Philosophy," in Dentsu Website (Tokyo, Japan, 1999 [cited 24 March 2000]); available from http://www.dentsu.co.jp/ENG/.

65. "Minutes of the Marketing Liaison Committee for TOP IV," Karuizawa, 1995, p. 3, IOCA.

66. Jean-Marie Weber to Richard W. Pound, 20 December 1995, IOC/ISL Relationship: TOP-IV File, IOCA; see also Jean-Marie Weber to Richard W. Pound, 12 December 1995, IOC/ISL Relationship: TOP-IV File, IOCA.

67. Richard W. Pound to Michael R. Payne, 20 December 1995, IOC/ISL Relationship: TOP-IV File, IOCA.

68. Richard W. Pound to Jean-Marie Weber, 20 December 1995, IOC/ISL Relationship: TOP-IV File, IOCA. Pound also put ISL on notice that the existing IOC proposal would be withdrawn if it did not provide confirmation of its acceptance by the close of business on 22 December 1995.

69. Brigitte Baenkler-Dassler to Juan Antonio Samaranch, 21 December 1995, IOC/ISL Relationship: TOP-IV File, IOCA. The Dassler name is synonymous with the Adidas athletic shoe and apparel company, founded by Adi Dassler in 1920. Eventually Adi's son, Horst Dassler, took over the company. Following his death in 1987, his sisters, who had inherited all of the family holdings, sold Adidas to Bernard Tapie, a French financier. The Dassler sisters maintained ownership of its other holdings, including ISL.

70. Ibid.

71. Richard W. Pound to NOC presidents, NOC secretaries-general, NOC marketing contacts, 5 January 1996, IOC/ISL Relationship: TOP-IV File, IOCA.

72. Richard W. Pound to members of the IOC Commission of New Sources of Financing, 5 January 1996, IOC/ISL Relationship: TOP-IV File, p. 2, IOCA.

73. Michael R. Payne to Jean-Marie Weber, 13 September 1996, IOC/ISL Relationship: TOP-IV File, IOCA.

74. Richard W. Pound to Michael R. Payne, 24 June 1998, IOC/ISL Relationship: TOP-IV File, IOCA.

75. Christopher C. Welton to Michael Payne, 25 March 1996, IOC/ISL Relationship: TOP-IV File, IOCA. In consultation with George Hirthler of Copeland/Hirthler Design in Atlanta, Georgia, and the IOC, Scharapan and Welton selected "Meridian Management SA" as the name of the new company. According to Welton, the name conveyed the "global nature" of the firm's business and had the added advantage of being "similar in most major European languages." A variety of alternative names had been considered, including "Signature TOP SA," "Axis TOP SA," and "Meridian TOP SA." See Michael Payne to Juan Antonio Samaranch, 6 March 1996, IOC/ISL Relationship: TOP-IV File, IOCA; Christopher C. Welton to Michael R. Payne, 20 March 1996, IOC/ISL Relationship: TOP-IV File, IOCA; Christopher C. Welton to Michael Payne, 25 March 1996, IOC/ISL Relationship: TOP-IV File, IOCA.

76. Ibid. The "business relationship" between the IOC and MM was difficult for some within the IOC Executive Board to understand. At the IOC Executive Board meeting in Lausanne in 1997 Anita DeFrantz, IOC member in the United States, asked if the IOC would benefit if MM "made a profit." In response Pound indicated that "as a shareholder with a 25% economic share in Meridian, it would receive 25% of any profit the firm made." "Minutes of the Meeting of the IOC Executive Board," Lausanne, 30–31 August, 1–2 September 1997, p. 35, IOCA.

77. Ibid. According to Pound, the IOC was particularly concerned about the USOC attempting to acquire a shareholding position in Meridian Management SA.

78. "Minutes of the Meeting of the IOC Executive Board," Atlanta, 11–13 July 1996, p. 97, IOCA.

79. Christopher C. Welton to Michael Payne, 25 March 1996, IOC/ISL Relationship: TOP-IV File, IOCA.

80. As of 9 September 1996 the IOC and MM assumed the lead in closing all remaining TOP agreements. Michael R. Payne to Jean-Marie Weber, 13 September 1996, IOC/ISL Relationship: TOP-IV File, IOCA.

81. See IOC: Marketing Department, "TOP Programme: TOP IV Revenue Distribution," *Marketing Matters* 15 (1999): 9.

82. Meridian Management SA, " 'Double-Nickels': The Theory of TOP V Pricing," TOP-V Programme File, 1997, p. 1, IOCA. The proposed TOP-V sponsorship fee of $55 million was established by adding a "ten percent premium or multiplier" to the "benchmark" fee of $45 million charged during TOP-IV. The adjusted figure ($49.5 million) was then increased by a "three percent inflation factor from the start of TOP-IV until the start of TOP-V (4 years)." The final number was "then rounded to arrive at a suggested price of $55 million."

83. "Minutes of the Meeting of the IOC Executive Board," Lausanne, 30–31 August, 1–2 September 1997, p. 27, IOCA. The impetus for the establishment of long-term television contracts, originally labeled "The Sunset Project," came from discussions between Richard Pound and NBC's president of sports, Dick Ebersol. See Richard Pound to Dick Ebersol, 2 October 1995, IOC Sunset File, Personal Computer Files of Richard Pound, Stikeman Elliott Law Offices, Montréal, Canada (hereafter cited as PCFRP); and "Minutes of the Meeting of the IOC Executive Board," Lausanne, 24–26 September 1995, pp. 3–4, IOCA.

84. The SEMA Group is one of the world's leading information technology and business services companies, with 20,200 employees in over 140 locations worldwide. In 1999 its turnover reached $1.41 billion, an increase of 23% over 1998. SEMA Group's main activities are business and technology consulting, systems integration and development, specialist software products, IT and business services outsourcing, and business recovery. See "SEMA Group Profile," in SEMA Group Website (London, Great Britain, 1999 [cited 24 March 2000]); available from http://www.semagroup.com/.

85. See "IOC Highlights: Week 32, 10 August–16 August 1998," in IOC Website (Lausanne, Switzerland, 1999 [cited 24 March 2000]); available from http://www.olympic.org/. The departure of IBM, and the addition of SEMA Group, further diminishes the IOC's sole dependence on the financial support of U.S.-based corporations.

11. TURF WAR: THE USOC, IOC,
AND OLYMPIC TELEVISION IN THE 1990S

1. "Minutes of the Meeting of the IOC Executive Board," Lausanne, 4–6 December 1991, pp. 43–44, IOCA.

2. "Olympic Games Television Rights Summary—Summer Games," IOC TV

Data File, Personal Computer Files of Richard Pound, Stikeman Elliott Law Offices, Montréal, Canada (hereafter cited as PCFRP). Prior to the 1994 Lillehammer Olympic Winter Games, OIRT (the Eastern Europe government-sponsored network) collapsed. Since then EBU has negotiated the rights for West and East Europe.

3. "Minutes of the Meeting of the IOC Executive Board," Lausanne, 24–26 July 1988, p. 23, IOCA.

4. "Minutes of the 92nd Session of the IOC," Istanbul, 9–12 May 1987, p. 45, IOCA.

5. "Minutes of the IOC Executive Board," Lausanne, 24–26 July 1988, p. 23, IOCA.

6. "Minutes of the Meeting of the IOC Executive Board," Stockholm, 25 April 1988, p. 37, IOCA.

7. "Minutes of the Meeting of the IOC Executive Board," Lausanne, 24–26 July 1988, p. 23, IOCA.

8. Ibid., pp. 23–25.

9. Ibid., p. 26.

10. "Minutes of the Meeting of the IOC Executive Board," Vienna, 7–8 December 1988, p. 29, IOCA.

11. "Minutes of the Meeting of the IOC Executive Board," Courcheval, 22–24 January 1989, p. 37, IOCA.

12. Personal communication, Richard Pound to the authors, 23 June 1999.

13. *Congressional Record—Extension of Remarks,* 101st Congress, 2nd Session (136 Cong. Rec. E 3452), vol. 136, no. 148, Thursday, October 25, 1990.

14. "Minutes of the Meeting of the IOC Executive Board," Puerto Rico, 27–29 August 1989, p. 31, IOCA; and "Minutes of the Meeting of the IOC Executive Board," Belgrade, 24–26 April 1990, p. 49, IOCA.

15. "Notes of Meeting with Congressman Tom McMillen, Washington D.C.," 17 January 1991, IOC-USOC File, PCFRP.

16. Richard Pound to Edward J. Markey (chairman, Committee on Energy and Commerce Subcommittee on Telecommunications and Finance), 30 September 1991 (draft), IOC-USOC File, PCFRP.

17. "Notes of Meeting with Congressman Tom McMillen, Washington D.C.," 17 January 1991, PCFRP.

18. Ibid.

19. "Minutes of the Meeting of the IOC Executive Board," Birmingham, 10–11 June 1991, p. 43, IOCA.

20. "Marketing Report to the Executive Board, June 1991," in "Minutes of the Meeting of the IOC Executive Board," Birmingham, 10–11 June 1991, Annex #12, p. 108, IOCA.

21. "Minutes of the Meeting of the IOC Executive Board," Birmingham, 10–11 June 1991, p. 6, IOCA.

22. "Minutes of the Meeting of the IOC Executive Board," Berlin, 17–19 September 1991, pp. 41–42, IOCA.

23. Ibid., p. 42.

24. "Minutes of the Meeting of the IOC Finance Commission," Lausanne, 25 November 1991, p. 12; and "Minutes of the Meeting of the IOC Executive Board," Lausanne, 4–6 December 1991, p. 43, IOCA.

25. Richard Pound to Un Yong Kim and François Carrard, 4 June 1993, IOC 1996 TV File, PCFRP.

26. Pound believed that if ACOG had been able to delay negotiations for a number of months an improved offer would have been forthcoming from one of the U.S. networks. He notes that two years later NBC paid in excess of $700 million for the 2000 Sydney Olympics. The discrepancy between the U.S. contracts for Atlanta and Sydney is even more glaring when one considers the favorable telecasting situation for Atlanta's broadcaster in terms of production costs, travel, and time zones. Pound estimated that the offer for Atlanta might have been improved by $50 or perhaps even $100 million. Personal communication, Richard Pound to the authors, 30 April 1999. ACOG needed to push forward with negotiations in order to obtain the collateral to borrow the money necessary to construct facilities. Richard Pound to Un Yong Kim and François Carrard, 4 June 1993, IOC 1996 TV File, PCFRP.

27. "Memorandum regarding Possible Strategy to Maximize U.S. Television Rights for Both the 1996 and 1998 Olympics," IOC 1996 TV File, PCFRP.

28. It is interesting to note that in considering Frank's proposal Pound believed that an $800 million contract for the two festivals was achievable. On the basis of the value of past Winter Games rights in comparison to Summer Games rights, Atlanta would have received approximately $500 million, with Nagano obtaining the remaining $300 million. "Memorandum regarding Possible Strategy to Maximize U.S. Television Rights for Both the 1996 and 1998 Olympics," IOC 1996 TV File, PCFRP. While Atlanta was forced to settle for $456 million in July 1993, Nagano received $375 million from negotiations staged in early 1994. Of the "big three" U.S. networks, CBS was the only serious bidder for the Nagano rights, but the emergence of FOX as a bidder provided Pound with a lever to maximize the sale price.

29. "Marketing Report to the IOC Executive Board, Monaco, 15–20 September 1993," in "Minutes of the Meeting of the IOC Executive Board," Monaco, 17–20 September 1993, Annex #19, p. 175, IOCA.

30. "Minutes of the Meeting of the IOC Executive Board," Lausanne, 6–8 December 1993, p. 58, IOCA.

31. Richard Pound to Un Yong Kim and François Carrard, 14 December 1993, IOC 1998 TV File, PCFRP.

32. Maurice Roche, *Mega-Events and Modernity: Olympics and Expos in the Growth of Global Culture* (London/New York: Routledge, 2000), pp. 170–81. Roche notes that the "battering ram" comment was Murdoch's.

33. Richard Pound to Makoto Kobayashi, 12 January 1994, IOC 1998 TV File, PCFRP.

34. "Minutes of the Meeting of the IOC Executive Board," Lillehammer, 4–6 February 1994, p. 34, IOCA.

35. Ibid., p. 35.

36. "Marketing Report to the IOC Executive Board, Budapest, June 12–14,

1995," in "Minutes of the Meeting of the IOC Executive Board," Budapest, 12–14 June 1995, Annex #12, p. 119, IOCA. The figures provided for the two contracts were 9,572,409,896 yen (Barcelona) and 8,308,250,000 yen (Atlanta).

37. Ibid.

38. "Minutes of the Meeting of the IOC Executive Board," Paris, 14–16 December 1994, pp. 32–36, IOCA.

39. NHK was the Japanese rights holder for the Albertville and Lillehammer festivals. For Japanese contract figures, see "Olympic Television Rights Summary—Winter Games," IOC TV Data File, PCFRP. For reference to the Japanese contract for the Nagano Games, see "Marketing Report to the IOC Executive Board," in "Minutes of the Meeting of the IOC Executive Board," Lausanne, 4–6 March 1996, Annex #6, p. 92, IOCA.

40. "Minutes of the Meeting of the IOC Executive Board," Puerto Rico, 27–29 August 1989, p. 31, IOCA"; "Minutes of the Meeting of the IOC Executive Board," Belgrade, 24–26 April 1990, p. 49, IOCA.

41. "Marketing Report to the IOC Executive Board, 14–16 April 1991, Barcelona," in "Minutes of the Meeting of the IOC Executive Board," Barcelona, 14–16 April 1991, p. 127, IOCA.

42. Richard Pound to Harvey Schiller (draft), 11 November 1992, IOC-USOC File, PCFRP.

43. Richard Pound to Harvey Schiller (draft), 3 December 1992, IOC-USOC File, PCFRP.

44. Ibid. (emphasis in original).

45. Richard Pound to Harvey Schiller, 12 April 1993, IOC-USOC File, PCFRP.

46. Ibid. (emphasis in original).

47. Each contract included an additional $10 million in advertising on NBC's Olympic broadcasts or in the form of pre-event promotion. Therefore, the total value of the contracts was $715 million (Sydney) and $555 million (Salt Lake City).

48. "Marketing Report to the IOC Executive Board, Monaco, 2–4 April 1995," in "Minutes of the Meeting of the IOC Executive Board," Monaco, 2–4 April 1995, Annex #6, p. 71, IOCA.

49. Richard Pound to Dick Ebersol, 2 October 1995, IOC Sunset File, PCFRP.

50. Richard Pound to Juan Antonio Samaranch, 13 April 1995, IOC 2000 TV File, PCFRP.

51. Richard Pound to Juan Antonio Samaranch, 29 April 1995, IOC 2000 TV File, PCFRP.

52. Richard Pound to Juan Antonio Samaranch, 13 April 1995, IOC 2000 TV File, PCFRP.

53. Richard Pound to Juan Antonio Samaranch, 26 June 1995, IOC Sunset File, PCFRP.

54. Richard Pound to Dick Ebersol and Dennis Swanson, 27 June 1995, IOC Sunset File, PCFRP.

55. Personal communication, Richard Pound to the authors, 12 May 1999.

56. Richard Pound to File, 10 July 1995, IOC Sunset File, PCFRP.

57. Personal communication, Richard Pound to the authors, 12 May 1999.

There were a number of issues to consider, including (1) whether or not the two networks would establish a joint unit for the project, (2) the number of composite logos, (3) copyright ownership of the Olympic film, (4) the arbitration processes in the case of disputes between ABC and NBC, and (5) event scheduling. Richard Pound to Dick Ebersol, Dennis Swanson and Barry Frank, 10 July 1995, IOC Sunset File, PCFRP.

58. Alan Abrahamson and Randy Harvey of the *Los Angeles Times* have spun the tale (uncorroborated by documentation) that Ebersol's preemptive bid was made directly to Samaranch in the secretive surroundings of a hotel room in Göteberg, Sweden, in August 1995 during the IAAF's World Track and Field Championships. See Alan Abrahamson and Randy Harvey, "How NBC Got the Gold," *Los Angeles Times,* 13 August 2000.

59. "Minutes of the Meeting of the IOC Executive Board," Lausanne, 24–26 September 1995, pp. 3, 20, IOCA; and personal communication, Richard Pound to the authors, 12 May 1999.

60. National Broadcasting Company Inc. to International Olympic Committee, 4 August 1995, IOC Sunset File, PCFRP. In June 1999 NBC announced that American viewers would be provided with 330 hours of coverage across the three channels. This figure represents a substantial increase on NBC's 169 hours of coverage from Atlanta. "Olympics: NBC Has Big Plans," *Toronto Sun,* 23 June 1999, p. 112; *Marketing Matters: The Olympic Marketing Newsletter* 10 (Winter 1996–97): 5. Practically on the eve of the 2000 Games NBC announced an additional increase in hours of planned coverage from the planned 330 figure to 437.5. See *Marketing Matters: The Olympic Marketing Newsletter* 16 (May 2000): 11.

61. Personal communication, Richard Pound to the authors, 12 May 1999.

62. "Minutes of the Meeting of the IOC Executive Board," Lausanne, 24–26 September 1995, p. 3, IOCA.

63. Ibid., pp. 3–4.

64. The 60/40 split had been first used for the Atlanta Olympic Games, replacing the 66.6/33.3 traditional formula. "Minutes of the Meeting of the IOC Executive Board," Puerto Rico, 30 August–1 September 1989, p. 29, IOCA.

65. "Minutes of the Meeting of the IOC Executive Board," Lausanne, 24–26 September 1995, p. 45, IOCA.

66. Ibid., p. 46.

67. Ibid.

68. "Notes for Remarks by Richard W. Pound: Olympic Television Announcement re 2004, 2006, 2008: New York, December 12, 1995," IOC Sunset File, PCFRP.

69. "Minutes of the Meeting of the IOC Executive Board," Nagano, 4–6 December 1995, pp. 63–65, IOCA.

70. Ibid.

71. James Christie, "IOC Won't Play Games, Pound Says," *Toronto Globe and Mail* (Section S), 24 February 2001.

72. "Draft Press Release: Australian Television Rights," 17 January 1996, Lausanne, IOC Sunset File, PCFRP.

73. "Marketing Report to the IOC Executive Board, Lausanne, 4–6 March

1996," in "Minutes of the Meeting of the IOC Executive Board," Lausanne, 4–6 March 1996, Annex #6, p. 93, IOCA.

74. Un Yong Kim closed a long-term deal with Japan before the end of the year that covered the Sydney ($135 million U.S.), 2004 ($155 million), and 2008 ($180 million) Summer Games and Salt Lake City ($37 million) and 2006 Winter Games ($38.5 million). "Minutes of the Meeting of the IOC Executive Board," Cancún, 14–16 November 1996, p. 5, IOCA.

75. "Briefing Memorandum: IOC-USOC Meeting October 8, 1996," IOC-USOC File, PCFRP.

76. "Minutes of the Meeting of the IOC Executive Board," Lausanne, 4–6 March 1996, p. 33; "Marketing Report to the IOC Executive Board, Atlanta, July 11–13 1996," in "Minutes of the Meeting of the IOC Executive Board," 11–13 July 1996, Atlanta, Annex #9, p. 106, IOCA.

77. "Minutes of the Meeting of the IOC Executive Board," Lausanne, 4–6 March 1996, p. 33, IOCA.

78. "Briefing Memorandum: IOC-USOC Meeting October 8, 1996," IOC-USOC File, PCFRP.

79. Ibid.

80. Personal communication, Richard Pound to the authors, 12 May 1999.

81. "Briefing Memorandum, IOC-USOC Meeting October 8, 1996," IOC-USOC File, PCFRP.

82. "Minutes of the Meeting of the IOC Executive Board," Lausanne, 8–10 October 1996, p. 15, IOCA.

83. Ibid., p. 16.

84. Personal communication, Richard Pound to the authors, 12 May 1999.

85. "Minutes of the Meeting of the IOC Executive Board," Lausanne, 8–10 October 1996, p. 16, IOCA.

86. Ibid., pp. 15–16. The financial impact on the IOC and members of the Olympic Movement was softened by the fact that the IOC would receive 51% of the Olympic television revenue as opposed to 40% beginning in 2004.

87. "Briefing Memorandum: IOC-USOC Meeting October 8, 1996," IOC-USOC File, PCFRP.

88. In April 1998 Pound, Payne, and Carrard met with Schultz and Krimsky because of the IOC's suspicion that the USOC was renewing its efforts to amend the Amateur Sports Act with respect to television negotiations. "Minutes of the Meeting of the IOC Executive Board," Sydney, 27–29 April 1998, pp. 7–8, IOCA.

12. PROTECTING AMERICAN DOLLARS:
MR. SAMARANCH GOES TO WASHINGTON

1. The specific allegations were that living expenses and college tuition payments at a university in Washington, D.C., had been authorized by Salt Lake City bid committee officials on behalf of the daughter of the late René Essomba, IOC member in Cameroon.

2. Investigative commissions were formed by the OCOGs of the Sydney (Australia) and Salt Lake City Games as well as the USOC, IOC, and the U.S. Depart-

ment of Justice. For Sydney, see "Examiner for SOCOG Report," T. A. Sheridan, Independent Examiner, 12 March 1999, ICOSA. For the USOC, see "Report of the Special Bid Oversight Commission," 1 March 1999, ICOSA. For the IOC, see "Report of the IOC Ad Hoc Commission to Investigate the Conduct of Certain IOC Members and to Consider Possible Changes to the Procedures for the Allocation of the Games of the Olympiad and Olympic Winter Games," 24 January 1999; and "Second Report of the IOC Ad Hoc Commission to Investigate the Conduct of Certain IOC Members and to Consider Possible Changes to the Procedures for the Allocation of the Games of the Olympiad and Olympic Winter Games," 11 March 1999, ICOSA. For Salt Lake City, see "Report to the Board of Trustees," 8 February 1999, ICOSA.

3. See "Report of the Special Bid Oversight Commission," 1 March 1999, ICOSA.

4. See "Second Report of the IOC Ad Hoc Commission to Investigate the Conduct of Certain IOC Members and to Consider Possible Changes in the Procedures for the Allocation of the Games of the Olympiad and Olympic Winter Games," 11 March 1999, ICOSA.

5. For a complete treatment of the IOC reforms within this context, see *IOC 2000 Reforms* (Supplement of the *Olympic Review*, December 1999/January 2000).

6. After Samaranch's prepared statement in English he then reverted to translated Castilian Spanish during question and answer discourse with congressional committee members. For a complete text of Samaranch's prepared opening statement, see "Capitol Hill Hearing Testimony," in Federal Document Clearing House, Inc. website (15 December 1999– [cited 1 March 2000]); available from Lexus-Nexus on the Internet (hereafter cited as Lex-Nex).

7. For Upton's remarks, see "In the Hot Seat: Samaranch Defends Olympic Reforms in House Grilling," *Salt Lake Tribune* website (16 December 1999– [cited 1 March 2000]), Lex-Nex.

8. See "Samaranch Unruffled by Charges in Congress," *Toronto Globe and Mail*, 16 December 1999.

9. For one of several newspaper accounts of Congressman Barton's remarks, see "Samaranch Also Speaks Stengelese," *New York Times* website (16 December 1999– [cited 1 March 2000]), Lex-Nex.

10. For Waxman's remarks, see "Lawmaker Suggests NBC Donation Was Bribe for Contract," *Salt Lake Tribune*, 16 December 1999. The reference to an "NBC Donation" refers to an original spontaneous $500,000 donation to the construction of the Olympic Museum made by Dick Ebersol of NBC on the occasion of a speech delivered on the evening of the long-term "Sunset" television contract signing. The $500,000 donation by NBC was later increased to $1,000,000. It might be noted that the U.S. home office of the FOX Television Network, a competitor of NBC, is located in Waxman's congressional district.

11. Congressman Waxman made this remark. See "IOC's Samaranch Weathers Storm on Capitol Hill," *Japan Economic Newswire* website (16 December 1999– [cited 1 March 2000]), Lex-Nex.

12. "In the Hot Seat: Samaranch Defends Olympic Reforms in House Grilling," *Salt Lake Tribune* website (16 December 1999– [cited 1 March 2000]), Lex-Nex.

13. See "Samaranch Sparkles in Washington," *Los Angeles Times* website (16 December 1999– [cited 1 March 2000]), Lex-Nex.

14. "IOC Head Testifies on Hill: Samaranch Is Asked about Reform Effort," *Washington Post* website (16 December 1999– [cited 1 March 2000]), Lex-Nex.

15. The sale of U.S. television rights for a Summer and Winter Olympic Games in one quadrennium amounts to approximately 60% of the total world sales of rights. Of the eleven TOP-IV corporate sponsors, nine have home offices in the United States.

16. Beginning in 2004 the USOC share of American television rights fee will increase to 12.75%.

17. For a composite sketch of Krimsky's contributions to and departure from the USOC, see "John Krimsky Leaves USOC, Hockey's Dave Ogrean Takes Marketing Helm," *Olympian* (July/August 1999): 42–43.

18. *USA Today*, 25 May 2000.

13. REFLECTIONS: COMMERCIAL REVENUE, THE SAMARANCH PRESIDENCY, AND CHALLENGES FOR JACQUES ROGGE

1. IOC, *Olympic Marketing Fact File* (Lausanne: IOC, 1998), p. 7.

2. E. M. Swift, "See Y'all in Sydney," *Sports Illustrated*, 12 August 1996. As cited by Alfred E. Senn, *Power, Politics, and the Olympic Games* (Champaign: Human Kinetics, 1999), p. 278.

3. IOC, *Olympic Marketing Fact File*, p. 7.

4. Stephen Wilson, "New IOC Chief Gets Down to Business," *Los Angeles Times*, 17 July 2001.   .

5. Ibid.

6. Senn, *Power, Politics, and the Olympic Games*, p. 281.

7. *Sydney Morning Herald*, 28 September 2000.

8. Michael R. Real, "Is TV Corrupting the Olympics? The (Post) Modern Olympics—Technology and the Commodification of the Olympic Movement," www.rohan.sdsu.edu/faculty/mreal/OlympicAtl.html, p. 7.

9. Richard W. Pound, "What Happens When It Goes Wrong? Notes on the IOC's Trials under Fire, 1998–1999," in Kevin B. Wamsley, Scott G. Martyn, Gordon H. MacDonald, and Robert K. Barney, eds., *Bridging Three Centuries: Intellectual Crossroads and the Modern Olympic Movement—Fifth International Symposium for Olympic Research* (London: International Centre for Olympic Studies, 2000), p. 1.

10. Zbigniew Brzezinski, "Moscow Choice Differs from Beijing," *London Free Press*, 18 July 2001. This article was prepared for the *New York Times*.

11. James Christie, "IOC Belittles Job by Pound," *Toronto Globe and Mail*, 16 July 2001.

12. Alan Abrahamson, "Passing the Torch," *Los Angeles Times*, 9 July 2001.

13. Christie, "IOC Belittles Job by Pound."

14. James Christie, "Canadian Takes a Pounding," *Toronto Globe and Mail*, 17 July 2001.

15. Quoted in Abrahamson, "Passing the Torch."

GLOSSARY OF SELECTED ACRONYMS

AAU	Amateur Athletic Union of the United States
ABC	American Broadcasting Company
ABC	Avery Brundage Collection
ABU	Asian Broadcasting Union
ACOG	Atlanta Olympic Games Organizing Committee
AENOC	Association of European National Olympic Committees
AIBA	International Amateur Boxing Federation
ANOC	Association of the National Olympic Committees
AOC	Australian Olympic Committee
ASA	Amateur Sports Act
ASBU	Arab States Broadcasting Union
ASOIF	Association of Summer Olympic Sports Federations
ATV	Asia Television Ltd.
BBC	British Broadcasting Corporation
BOA	British Olympic Association
CBC	Canadian Broadcasting Corporation
CBS	Columbia Broadcasting System
COA	Canadian Olympic Association
COJO	Montréal Olympic Games Organizing Committee
COOB'92	Barcelona Olympic Organizing Committee
CWL	César Walther Lüthi Telesport
EBU	European Broadcasting Union
FIFA	International Football (Soccer) Federation
FINA	International Amateur Aquatics Federation
FISA	International Rowing Federation
FSFI	Fédération Sportive Féminine Internationale
GAIF	General Assembly of International Sports Federations
GATT	General Agreement on Tariffs and Trade
IAAF	International Amateur Athletics Federation
ICOSA	International Centre for Olympic Studies Archives
IOC	International Olympic Committee
IOCA	International Olympic Committee Archives
ISF	International Sport Federation

ISL   International Sport & Leisure Marketing
LAOOC   Los Angeles Olympic Games Organizing Committee
LPOC   Lake Placid Olympic Games Organizing Committee
MM   Meridian Management
NASA   National Aeronautics and Space Agency
NBC   National Broadcasting Company
NHK   Nippon Hoso Kyokai (in Japan)
NOC   National Olympic Committee
OCO'88   Calgary Olympic Games Organizing Committee
OCOG   Olympic Games Organizing Committee
OIRT   Intervision (in Eastern Europe)
OTI   Organización de la Televisión Ibero-Americana
PCFRP   Personal Computer Files of Richard Pound
PFRP   Personal Files of Richard Pound
PGANOC   Permanent General Assembly of National Olympic Committees
RAI   Radio Audizoni Italia
SABC   South African Broadcasting Corporation
SATRA   Soviet American Trading Company
SLOOC   Seoul Olympic Games Organizing Committee
SOOC   Sarajevo Olympic Games Organizing Committee
TOP   The Olympic Partners (Programme)
TRIPS   Trade-Related Aspects of Intellectual Property Rights
TVB   Television Broadcast Ltd.
TVE   Televisión Española, Spain
TWI   TransWorld International
URTNA   Union des Radiodiffusions et Télévisions Nationales d'Afrique
USASA   United States Amateur Sports Act
USFSA   Union des Sociétés Françaises de Sports Athlétiques
USOA   United States Olympic Association
USOC   United States Olympic Committee
WADA   World Anti-Doping Agency
WIPO   World Intellectual Property Organization

ABOUT THE AUTHORS

ROBERT K. (BOB) BARNEY is Professor Emeritus of Kinesiology and Founding Director of the International Centre for Olympic Studies at the University of Western Ontario in London, Ontario, Canada. A native New Englander, he served four years in the U.S.A.F. during the Korean War, returning to college in 1955 to obtain his B.S. (1959), M.S. (1963) and Ph.D. (1968), all at the University of New Mexico, where he was an intercollegiate athlete in three sports as an undergraduate. Former president of the North American Society for Sport History (1990–1992), he has produced some 180 published works, almost 70 of which are on Olympic history. He was awarded the *Olympic Order* in 1997. He relaxes with classical music, crossword puzzles, and historical biography. He has recently marked the end of his sixth decade of "live and die" (mostly die) infatuation with the (mis)fortunes of the Boston Red Sox. He and his wife Ashleigh reside in London, Ontario, regularly spending autumns at the family homestead in the Lakes region of New Hampshire.

STEPHEN WENN is an associate professor of Kinesiology and Physical Education at Wilfrid Laurier University in Waterloo, Ontario, Canada. He obtained his B.A. and M.A. degrees in Physical Education at the University of Western Ontario in 1986 and 1988 respectively. Stephen received the North American Society for Sport History Graduate Essay Award in 1988. He concluded his Ph.D. studies at Penn State University in 1993 with the completion of his dissertation entitled, "A History of the International Olympic Committee and Television, 1936–1980." He enjoys tending to his backyard fish pond, jogging, recreational ice hockey, spending time with his family, and following the trials and tribulations of his favorite professional sport franchise, the Toronto Maple Leafs. Stephen, his wife Martha, and their two-year old son, Timothy, live in Waterloo, Ontario.

SCOTT MARTYN is an assistant professor in the Faculty of Human Kinetics at the University of Windsor in Windsor, Ontario, Canada. As a former

Social Sciences and Humanities Research Council of Canada Doctoral Fellow, Scott spends much of his time investigating the historical evolution of the Olympic Games and affiliated insignia as sport marketing properties. He concluded his Ph.D. studies at the University of Western Ontario in 2000 with the completion of his dissertation entitled, "The Struggle for Financial Autonomy: The IOC and the Historical Emergence of Corporate Sponsorship, 1896–2000." Scott has served on the executive councils of the International Centre for Olympic Studies, the North American Society for Sport History, and the International Society for Comparative Physical Education and Sport. His extensive knowledge in computer web-based design has enabled him to design and edit many national and international scholarly web sites. Scott and his wife Rebecca live in Windsor, Ontario.

INDEX